PetChiDog's GIANT Book of Chihuahua Care

PetChiDog

DEDICATION

We would like to thank the Chihuahua lovers who visit and are Members of the PetChiDog site for encouraging us to continually grow the website and produce this sort of book. Your loyalty means so much to us.

We also wish to thank Ruth of YankeeBelle Chihuahuas in Maine for her photo contributions; she is an outstanding Chihuahua breeder whose friendship and knowledge base is greatly appreciated. And, a heartfelt thank you to ChiChiBabies and MSD Chihuahuas for sharing some adorable and interesting photos for this book as well.

Finally, we send thanks to Faye Dunningham for allowing us to include her limited edition, re-worked training sections.

Table of Contents

Before You Begin.. ix

About the Chihuahua 1

A Brief Recap of History.. 1

The Breed Standard Explained 3

Applehead Versus Deerhead 7

Long Coat Chihuahuas 9

Long Coat Curly Haired Chihuahuas 10

The Molera 11

Where the Chihuahua Fits in With Other Breeds 12

The Chihuahua's Personality 14

Males Vs Females 16

PetChiDog's Chihuahua Survey 17

Size Variances 22

Chihuahua Colors... 23

Chihuahua Intelligence 27

Puppy Care.. 30

Supplies to Have 30

Puppy Proofing Your Home 36

Naming Your Puppy 38

Introducing your Puppy to Family & Home 40

The Importance of Early Socialization and Desensitization....................................... 43

Falling into a Schedule 44

How to React to Whining and Crying 45

Vaccinations.. 47

Top Puppy Questions 50

Growth Charts 52

Care Items – Chihuahuas of All Ages **54**

Leashes, Harnesses, Collars & ID Tags 54

Toys 57

Car Seats 62

All Other Supplies – Quick Summary 64

Housebreaking **65**

Overview 65

Tips Related to Age 65

Indoor vs. Outdoor 66

Preparing to Housebreak 67

How Often to Take a Puppy Out 70

Exact Instructions 71

How to Deal with Housebreaking Accidents 72

The Most Common Housebreaking Hiccups 73

Submissive Urination 76

Marking 77

Feeding and Nutrition **81**

Nutritional Needs 81

Calorie Requirements 82

All Meal Feeding Details 84

Main Meals 84

Main Meal Particulars 90

The Most Common Eating Issues 91

Snacks 96

Training Treats 97

Supplements 98

Water 100

Helping an Adult Chihuahua Lose Weight 102

Helping a Chihuahua Puppy Gain Weight 104

Teething & Chewing **106**

Two Issues, One Resolution 106

Teething Overview 106

Destructive Chewing Overview 107

Helping with Teething and Chewing Issues - Step by Step 107

Grooming **111**

Tasks and Timing 111

Specifics of Grooming Tasks 112

Shampoo and Coat Products 114

Baths 116

Nails & Dewclaws 118

Tear Stains 119

Dental Care **123**

Fur and Coat **126**

Normal Shedding 126

Serious Fur Loss 126

Alopecia X 127

Exercise & Activity **130**

Exercise Requirements & Restrictions 130

Dog Parks 132

Fun Things to Do 135

Dressing for the Weather 137

Heat Stroke 138

Training **140**

Teaching Proper Hierarchy 140

Heeling 141

Command Training 145

Behavioral Training **151**

Aggression 151

Barking 154

Jumping on People 160

Refusal to Walk While on Leash 162

Socialization & Desensitization Training 165

Behavioral Issues **178**

Begging 178

Clingy Behavior 180

Depression 182

Digging 184

Eating Feces 185

Eating Grass 189

Fear of Thunder and Lightning 192

Humping 193

Hyper Behavior 196

Licking and/or Chewing at the Paws 198

Nipping 202

Rolling in Feces 204

Running Away 206

Shaking or Trembling 207

Sleep 208

Situational Issues **211**

Afraid of Other Dogs 211

Having a Chihuahua and a Cat 213

Having More than One Dog 216

Rescued Dogs 219

Separation Anxiety 220

Your Chihuahua and Children 225

Your Chihuahua & Your Baby 227

Seasonal Care **229**

Summer Care 229

Winter Care 235

Health & Care – Body Part Specific **238**

Anal Glands 238

Ears 239

Eyes 244

Nose 248

Paws 253

Tail 255

Health- Stomach, Intestinal **257**

Vomiting 257

Diarrhea 262

Constipation 265

Health – Other **267**

Allergies 267

Arthritis 275

Bad Breath 278

Collapsed Trachea 280

Coughs and Other Noises - Quick Reference 282

Fleas 283

Heart Issues 286

Hernias 288

Hypoglycemia 290

Itching – Quick Reference 291

Lethargy 292

Luxating Patella 293

Mange...296

Reverse Sneezing 298

Skin Problems – Quick Reference 299

Smells & Odors 300

Spaying & Neutering..303

Worms 306

Female Issues **309**

Heat 309

Breeding 310

Pregnancy 312

Whelping...316

Eclampsia..318

Mastitis...318

Pyometra...319

Newborn Care...**320**

Weaning..320

Newborn Tips & Milestones 321

Age **323**

Senior Care 324

Life Expectancy of the Chihuahua 329

Safety and Happiness **332**

Traveling 332

First Aid...335

How to Prevent Your Dog from Being Attacked 342

The Importance of Veterinary Wellness Checks...345

Your Relationship with Your Canine Family Member..346

Lifelong Care Checklist..348

Before You Begin

If you see your Chihuahua as much more than 'just a dog', then surely you feel the weight and responsibility to care for and raise your Chi in the best way possible. We'd like to be there with you, for every step. That is our goal with this book, *PetChiDog's GIANT Book of Chihuahua Care* and our website, PetChiDog.com.

Both complement each other, with each format allowing for different methods of offering you information and resources, and each varies in the type of information. We encourage you to hold onto this book (there will be chapters that you find useful right now, and there will be some that will apply later) and visit the PetChiDog.com website often (which is continually growing and expanding).

Please note that while quite a few behavioral and health issues are covered in this book, this information is not intended to be a substitute for professional veterinary advice, diagnosis, or treatment. Always seek the advice of your veterinarian with any questions about your dog's health. Do not disregard professional veterinary advice or delay seeking advice or treatment because of something you have read here.

We realize that many of you reading this book are looking for specific recommendations for particular care items for your Chihuahua. It's important to note that this book is static; it is written and then out of our hands (and into yours). In fact, you could be reading this quite a few years after our last keystroke. However, canine care products are always evolving. New ones may come out that are improvements over present ones.

Therefore, it would be remiss for us to offer suggestions for certain items that may change by the time this book reaches you. For this reason, the Supplies page of our website contains our most current recommendations for many care elements and is updated as new options emerge. This book will direct you there, when appropriate.

Speaking of which (and not to be morbid), the website may not exist *forever*. Though, we certainly plan to keep the site going, even well-passed our retirement age. If you happen to have this book in your hands, say, in the year 2038 or later, we are just not sure if PetChiDog will still be there. If it is, come say hello. If it isn't, we believe that this book will still serve you well; it is a culmination of our entire knowledge base.

During the course of this book, certain brand names *are* mentioned. Proper trademarks for brand names are shown respect through the use of capitalization and/or italicized stylization.

Though you have lots of reading to do, please consider leaving a review for this book on Amazon once you feel that you have looked over enough of it to offer your thoughts. As independent publishers, your feedback is vital.

Now, let's start on the road to creating a wonderful, healthy, and happy life for your Chi!

Love, Hugs & Chihuahua Kisses,

The PetChiDog Team

About the Chihuahua

A Brief Recap of History

The Chihuahua is named for the Mexican state of Chihuahua in northwest Mexico. Chihuahua is one of 32 states of Mexico, its capital is Chihuahua City, it shares a border with the U.S. states of Texas and New Mexico, and it contains the

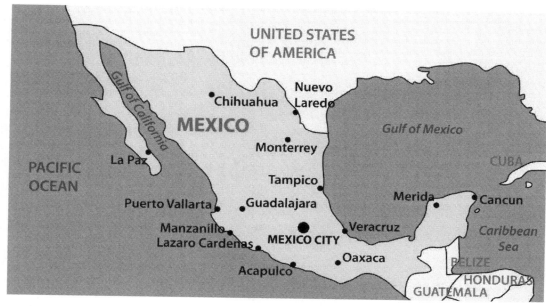

Chihuahuan Desert which extends into Texas, New Mexico, and Arizona.

Proven Mexican Ancestry: Though it has long been just theorized that the Chihuahua's ancestors were from Mexico, this has been confirmed by DNA analysis. In 2013, the KTH Royal Institute of Technology in Stockholm, Sweden released their findings regarding the ancestry of certain dog breeds[1]. They compared mitochondrial DNA from East Asian, European, and several American dog breeds to ancient archaeological samples.

Among the breeds that they tested was the Chihuahua, since its origins have long been debated. The Chihuahua *does* share a DNA type unique to ancient Mexican samples.

It All Starts With the Techichi Dog: The Chihuahua's ancestor, the Techichi dog, was a small desert canine. Sculptures and drawings created by the Mayans, dating to 500 BC, show this short-coated, roughly 10 to 20-pound breed.

The Toltecs civilization, which conquered the Mayans by 1100 AD, may have been the first people to fully domesticate the Techichi. After the Aztec people became the ruling class of Mexico, they brought the

1

Techichi into their own culture. The dog was a companion and was also used in religious ceremonies. This is documented via carvings found in Aztec temples and pyramids.

Interestingly, skeletal remains of the dog were found both in pyramids *and* at gravesites. For this reason, it is thought that the Aztec people believed that the dog would play a role as a guide into the afterlife. Though both affluent Aztec people and clergy considered the dog to be sacred, there is a theory that the poor, lower class did not agree. In fact, some say that the lower class may have used the dog as a food source.

When explorers arrived in the Americas, it is believed the Techichi was bred with dogs brought over and the end result is the Chihuahua that we have today. It is still up for debate as to which breed or breeds that was.

The European Link: Since it is theorized that a breed brought over by explorers from the Old World into the New World was crossbred to the evolving Techichi, the question becomes, 'Which breed of European descent was used?'

In general, it is thought that the Techichi was bred with small black and tan terrier-type dogs brought over by Spanish conquerors. One more detailed theory points to the island of Malta where a small breed existed that had a natural molera. The molera is the soft spot on the top of the skull where the three sections of the skull bone meet; it is very rare among dog breeds but was present with the breed found on Malta and is seen with today's Chihuahua.

Another possibility comes to us via a painting that exists in the Sistine Chapel in Vatican City, Italy. The painting, 'Scenes from the Life of Moses' by Sondro Botticelli, completed in 1482, portrays a dog that is similar to today's Chihuahua. Because the painting pre-dates 1518, the year Cortés set sail for Mexico, some theorize that this is the type of dog that was crossed with the Techichi.

[Photo attribution previous page: Sandro Botticelli, Scenes from the Life of Moses, via Wikimedia Commons. This image is in the public domain because its copyright has expired; copyright term is author's life plus 100 years or less; published before January 1, 1923.]

The Modern Chihuahua: When people in the United States first 'discovered' this tiny breed, they often referred to it as the 'Texas Dog' or 'Arizona Dog', named after the states that people traveled through when crossing the Mexican/United States border.

The Chihuahua was officially recognized by the AKC (American Kennel Club) in 1904, with a Chihuahua named Midget, being the very first to be registered. At that time, the club was only 20 years old (having been founded in 1884). And in 1904, only 52 breeds had been recognized thus far. Three other breeds joined the Chihuahua that year: the Boxer, the Schipperke, and the standard Schnauzer.

The Chihuahua's popularity took a while to form. This is because in the early 1900's most people that owned dogs preferred working dogs or guard dogs, not household pets. People living on farms used dogs to pull carts and herd livestock. Others owned dogs to chase away wild animals or possible intruders.

Things began to change in the 1960's when the mindset of 'dog ownership' transitioned more into 'pet ownership'. In 1964, the Chihuahua soared to popularity, becoming the 12th most AKC registered breed. In that year the number of recognized breeds had grown to 161. Since that time, the Chihuahua has held its place in the top 30. Ranking was #22 in 2013, #24 in 2014, #28 in 2015, and #30 in 2016. Though the ranking has dropped a bit, this is due, in part, to more breeds being recognized as the years go by. At the time of this writing, there are 190 AKC recognized breeds.

1. Pre-Columbian origins of Native American dog breeds, with only limited replacement by European dogs, confirmed by mtDNA analysis. Barbara van Asch, Ai-bing Zhang, Mattias C. R. Oskarsson, Cornelya F. C. Klütsch, António Amorim, Peter Savolainen Published 10 July 2013.DOI: 10.1098/rspb.2013.1142

The Breed Standard Explained

In order for a dog breed to be an official dog breed, a standard must be set. These are guidelines which state in detail what the particular dog breed looks like. This includes size, type of coat, facial structure, body structure, and so on. It may also include such things as expected personality or even type of gait.

The AKC follows breed standards that are set by the breed's parent club. For the Chihuahua, this is The Chihuahua Club of America. The CKC (Canadian Kennel Club), KC (The Kennel Club of the UK) and the FCI (Fédération Cynologique Internationale - which has over 80 member countries) all have very similar breed standards as the AKC. The wording may differ slightly; however, all agree on all major facets of exactly how the 'ideal' Chihuahua should look.

A breed standard has two purposes. It is a guideline for breeders in their attempt to produce dogs that best fit the standard and it is used by judges to assess dogs in conformation events at all levels from local up to national, on how closely they match the official standard guidelines.

Upon its inception into the AKC in 1904, both long and shorthaired Chihuahuas were categorized the same. In 1952, The Chihuahua Club of America, which writes the breed standard for the Chihuahua, voted to split the coat types into two varieties: long coat and smooth coat (short haired). Both varieties are included on one breed standard.

The AKC breed standard may be revised every 5 years; however, this does not mean that it will be. If revisions are made, most often the changes will be negligible. As of the time of this writing (2018), the standard has not changed since 2008.

The Chihuahua is in the Toy Group. The breed standard weight for well-recognized kennel clubs is as follows:

AKC: Not to exceed 6 lbs. (2.72 kg).

CKC (Canadian Kennel Club): Not to exceed 6 lb. (2.72 kg), 2-4 lb. (1-2 kg) preferable.

FCI: 1.5 to 3 kg (3.3 to 6.61 lbs.) preferred. A lesser weight of 500 grams (1.10 lbs.) and 1.5 kg (3.3 lbs.) is tolerated. Subjects weighing less than 500 grams (1.10 lbs.) and more than 3 kg (3.3 lbs.) shall be disqualified.

KC: 1.8 to 2.7 kg preferred (3.96 to 5.95 lbs.).

So, as you can see, there is a general agreement that a Chihuahua in the show ring will be under 6 pounds (2.72 kg) with the FCI allowing him to be a tad larger, 6.61 lbs. (3 kg), making the Chihuahua the smallest dog breed in the world. This said, many pet Chihuahuas are 7, 8, 9 or even 10+ pounds. You can read more details about this under 'About the Chihuahua: PetChiDog's Chihuahua Survey'.

Now, Let's Look at the Breed Standard: Since we are based in the US, we will look at the AKC standard. The standard is similar for FCI, KC and CKC. Per the AKC's most recent information at: www.akc.org/dog-breeds/chihuahua, based on The Chihuahua Club of America guidelines found at: www.chihuahuaclubofamerica.org, the following is the breed standard with our interpretations.

General Appearance - A graceful, alert, swift-moving compact little dog with saucy expression (appears fun-loving and bold), and with terrier-like qualities of temperament (attitude of self-importance, confidence, and self-reliance).

Size, Proportion, Substance | Weight - A well balanced (there is not one area of the body that severely over-powers the other, for example, long legs vs a short body) little dog not to exceed 6 pounds. **Proportion** - The body is off-square; hence, slightly longer when measured from point of shoulder to point of buttocks, than height at the withers (top of the shoulders). Somewhat shorter bodies are preferred in males. **Disqualification** - Any dog over 6 pounds in weight.

Head - A well rounded "apple dome" skull (apple dome VS deer head will be discussed ahead), with or without molera (the molera is a soft spot in the skull, covered with thick membrane). Item of interest: Back in 1933, a molera was *required*.

Expression – Saucy (repeated from earlier, meaning fun-loving and bold).

Eyes - Full, round, but not protruding (eyes are large but do not bulge out when viewed from the side), balanced (level with each other and same diameter), set well apart-luminous (shiny) dark (dark brown or black) or luminous ruby (eyes that appear dark red under certain lighting conditions, usually only found on white or very light colored Chi). Light eyes (light brown or hazel) in blond (light tan or fawn) or white-colored dogs permissible. Blue eyes or a difference in the color of the iris in the two eyes, or two different colors within one iris should be considered a serious fault.

Ears - Large, erect (standing up on their own) type ears, held more upright when alert, but flaring to the sides at a 45 degree angle when in repose (when resting or relaxed), giving breadth (width) between the ears. **Stop** (the area of angle change between the front skull and the nasal bone near the eyes) - Well defined. When viewed in profile, it forms a near 90 degree angle where muzzle joins skull. **Muzzle** - Moderately short, slightly pointed. Cheeks and jaws lean.

Nose - Self-colored in blond types or black **(tan or fawn coats *can* have light brown noses, but black is also acceptable. Most of the other coat colors have black noses).** In moles **(*see below)** , blues, and chocolates, they are self-colored **(the nose can be the color of the coat. Blue is a diluted black; skin pigmentation including the nose will be a steely navy blue, sometimes only discernable in bright sunlight. Chocolate Chihuahuas may have brown noses).** In blond types **(light tan or fawn coats),** pink noses permissible.

* Note: We believe 'moles' is a misprint and should be 'merles', making the sentence: *'In merles, blues, and chocolates, they are self-colored.'* Merle is a pattern of splashed color and may land on the nose, causing speckled nose pigmentation. Alternatively, on merles the nose color may match the darkest spots on the Chi.

For example, a merle with black spotting may have a black nose, if a merle's darkest color is red the nose may be a dark red, if the merle's darkest color is brown the nose may be brown). This part of the breed standard is quite different from that of the FCI's, CKC's, or KC's, because they do not allow for merles at all.

Bite - **(the incisor teeth meet exactly, surface to surface)** or scissors **(the incisor teeth in the upper jaw are in contact with but slightly overlap those in the bottom jaw).** Overshot **(the top jaw is physically longer than the lower jaw)** or undershot **(the upper jaw is perceptibly shorter than the lower jaw)** or any distortion of the bite or jaw, should be penalized as a serious fault. A missing tooth or two is permissible. **Items of interest:** In 1943, only a level bite was permissible. And, the FCI considers a missing tooth to be a fault.

Disqualifications - Broken down or cropped ears.

Neck, Topline, Body | **Neck** - Slightly arched, gracefully sloping into lean shoulders. **Topline (from the base of the neck to the base of the tail)** – Level **(when looking from the side, the line of the back is straight, there is no hump and it does not sink inward).** **Body** - Ribs rounded and well sprung **(rounded outward)** but not too much "barrel-shaped"**(like a Pug dog).**

Tail - Moderately long, carried sickle **(slight upward curve)** either up or out, or in a loop over the back with tip just touching the back. Never tucked between legs. **Disqualifications** - Docked tail, bobtail. **Item of interest:** Back in 1923, a bobtail was permissible.

Forequarters | **Shoulders** - Lean, sloping into a slightly broadening support above straight forelegs that set well under, giving free movement at the elbows. Shoulders should be well up **(not drooping down),** giving balance and soundness, sloping into a level back **(straight back without a curve or an arch).** This gives a well-developed chest and strength of forequarters.

Feet - A small, dainty foot with toes well split up but not spread **(toes are separated, not squished together, but also not too wide apart),** pads cushioned. Neither the hare **(elongated with the two center toes longer than the side toes)** nor the cat foot **(a foot with arched toes that are held close together).** **Dewclaws** may be removed. **Pasterns (front pasterns are the equivalent of a human's wrists and rear pasterns are the equivalent of a human's ankles)** Strong.

Photo: Grand Champion O'Reily, courtesy of YankeeBelle Chihuahuas in Maine. GCH St. James N Chinchars Luck Of The Irish "O'Reily" is sired by CH Dartan Non Stop Photo Op out of Dartan Peyton St. James. Not only is he an AKC Grand Champion but he placed first place in the open class at the 2011 CCA National Specialty & Best of Variety at the Tampa Bay Chihuahua Club Specialty in Feb 2012 along with multiple Best of Varieties at all breed shows.

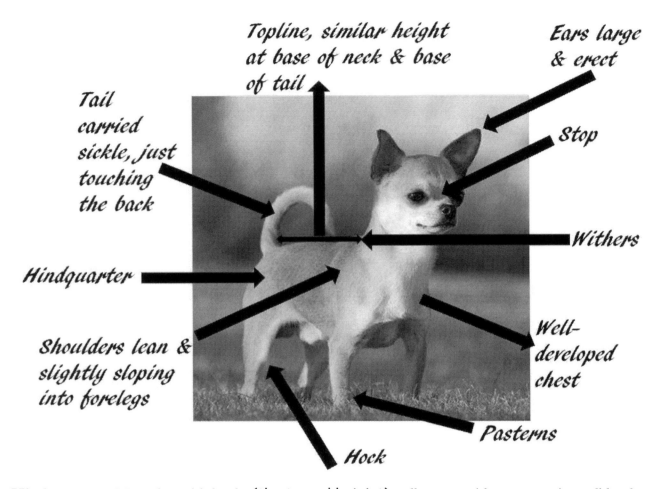

Hindquarters - Muscular, with hocks (the top ankle joint) well apart, neither out nor in, well let down, firm and sturdy. *Angulation* - Should equal that of forequarters. The feet are as in front. Dewclaws may be removed.

Coat | *In the Smooth Coats*, the coat should be of soft texture, close (tight) and glossy (shiny). Heavier coats with undercoats (2 different layers to the coat; inner and outer) permissible. Coat placed well over body with ruff (longer hairs on neck) on neck preferred, and more scanty (shorter) on head and ears. Hair on tail preferred furry.

In Long Coats, the coat should be of a soft texture, either flat or slightly wavy, with undercoat preferred (2 different layers to the coat; inner and outer). Ears - Fringed (hairs appear slightly feathered). Tail - Full and long as a plume. Feathering on feet and legs, pants (thick, long hair) on hind legs and large ruff on the neck (thick long hairs around the neck) desired and preferred. The Chihuahua should be groomed only to create a neat appearance (no unnecessary trimming should be done other than that which is needed to create a tidy appearance). **Disqualification** - In Long Coats, too thin coat that resembles bareness.

Color - Any color – Solid, marked (**secondary color**) or splashed (**merle**). **Note:** Only the AKC accepts merle coloring; the FCI, KC and CKC consider merle a disqualification.

Gait - The Chihuahua should move swiftly with a firm, sturdy action, with good reach in front equal to the drive (**front**) from the rear (**relatively speaking, long steps that are balanced**). From the rear, the hocks (**the top ankle joint**) remain parallel to each other, and the foot fall of the rear legs follows directly behind that of the forelegs.

The legs, both front and rear, will tend to converge slightly toward a central line of gravity (**come closer together**) as speed increases. The side view shows good, strong drive in the rear (**power comes from the rear legs**) and plenty of reach in the front, with head carried high (**holds head up high in a proud manner**). The topline should remain firm and the backline level (**back stays straight, with no hunching over**) as the dog moves.

Temperament - Alert, projecting the 'terrier-like' attitudes of self-importance, confidence, self-reliance. **Item of interest:** Back in 1943, neither gait nor temperament was included in the breed standard.

Disqualifications - Any dog over 6 pounds in weight. Broken down (**ears that never stand erect**) or cropped ears. Docked tail, bobtail (**abnormally short tail due to genetic fault**). In Long Coats, too thin coat that resembles bareness.

Item of interest: Per the breed standard of 1943, 1 to 6 pounds was allowed, with the preferred weight being 2 to 4 pounds; if there were two Chihuahuas being compared, the smaller one would be given preference.

Applehead Versus Deerhead

Only the applehead Chihuahua fits the breed standard of every major canine kennel club in the world; however, this does not mean that deerheads do not exist; they are quite prevalent.

The difference between an applehead and a deerhead Chihuahua:

The skull on an applehead is well-rounded, often compared to a cooking apple with the largest part of the dome between the ears. It is also rounded from the stop (the area of angle change between the front skull and the nasal bone near the eyes) to the back of the occiput (back of the topskull). The skull on a deerhead is sloped and more narrow.

The snout on an applehead is moderately short; the snout on a deerhead tends to be longer.

The body and legs on deerheads, may (but not always) be longer.

Applehead

Deerhead

What the breed standards say about this: Before we proceed, it's important to note that it's not uncommon for a certain dog breed to have a particular physical feature that is not mentioned in the breed standard or is even listed as a fault, but then appears quite often not only in households around the world but also in the show ring. Please keep this in mind as we dive deeper into appleheads versus deerheads.

According to the AKC and CKC (Canadian Kennel Club) guidelines, a Chihuahua should have:

Head: *A well rounded "apple dome" skull, with or without molera.* **Muzzle** – *Moderately short, slightly pointed.* **Cheeks and jaws** *lean.* **Stop** - *Well defined (the stop is the angle of change between the skull and the nasal bone near the eyes).*

The KC calls out for a very similar appearance:

Well rounded 'apple dome' skull, cheeks and jaws lean, muzzle moderately short, slightly pointed. Definite stop.

The FCI defines the face and skull shape in this way:

Skull : *Well rounded apple head (a characteristic of the breed)* **Stop**: *Well marked, deep and broad as the forehead is rounded above the set-on of muzzle.*

In addition, the FCI makes mention of 'deer type dogs' under their disqualifying faults section with: *Deer type dogs (dogs with an atypical or extremely stylized structure: refined head, long neck, slender body, long limbs).*

To summarize: It is the 'apple dome', i.e. applehead, that is expected and called out in all breed standards.

Why There are Two Different Head Shapes: Since the very first breed standard was written for the Chihuahua, the skull was expected to be a 'well rounded apple dome' shape. Yet, deerheads *have* appeared and most predominantly in the last two decades. All it takes is the pairing of two Chihuahuas with that head shape to start an entire bloodline of deerheads with many descendants.

As this physical trait became more and more apparent, the breed was *unofficially* categorized with one of the two head shapes. Though it is only the apple-domed skull that meets the AKC guidelines, both head types are popular and both are found in purebred Chihuahuas.

Though the pledge of AKC breeders is to breed for the 'betterment of the breed' and therefore to strive to produce Chihuahuas that match the standard with apple-domed skulls, some breeders instead choose to meet the high demand of potential owners who favor the deerhead shape. Those that purposefully produce deerheads may argue that all dog breeds over the centuries have been 'tweaked' and over time their size, coloring, and features have changed. Sometimes, the change is so great that after a certain point, if a particular look is widespread and consistent, it has broken off into its own variety. And in some cases, it has even branched out to become its own separate breed.

For example, the Akita Inu breed has two types: The American and the Japanese Akita Inu. They are different sizes and with very distinct and different coloring. Some countries now recognize them as one breed but two varieties and other countries see them as two distinct and separate breeds.

We don't see this happening anytime soon with the Chihuahua in regard to skull shape. This breed already has both long coat and short coat varieties. Separating the Chihuahua by apple and deer heads would lead to four varieties; something that would be unprecedented. In addition, with the 'apple dome' skull in the breed standard for over a century, one would be hard-pressed to make a case that both head shapes should be accepted and recognized.

This all said, please do not spend lots of time worrying about your Chihuahua's head shape. If you are not breeding your dog or entering your dog into the show ring, give no more thought to this. Your Chi is adorable whether he is an applehead, deerhead, or a combination of the two.

A note on behavior There are some who will say that the apple is calmer than the deer or vise-versa. It should be noted that any behavioral differences are due to the dog's individual personality and has nothing at all to do with head shape.

Long Coat Chihuahuas

As we have discussed, both the long coat and smooth (short) coat Chihuahua are different varieties of the same breed. The short coat appears more often than the long coat and is the more popular of the two; though both coat types are quite beautiful. Seen under 'About the Chihuahua: PetChiDog's Chihuahua Survey', out of 3,272 owners, 76% have a short coat Chihuahua and 24% have a long coat Chi.

The short coat appeared first. If you will remember what we discussed at the beginning of this book under 'A Brief Recap of History', the Chihuahua's ancestors, the Techichi, were a short-coated breed. It was only after breeders in the United States started perfecting the dog that other breeds with longer coats were brought in. The introduction of a longer coat was done deliberately to add variety and separately so as to not lose the short coat entirely. Breeds thought to be introduced to develop the longer coat include the Papillon, the Yorkshire Terrier, and the Pomeranian.

Breeding Facts: The long coat gene is recessive, meaning that it can 'hide'. A shorthaired Chihuahua may very well carry the longhaired gene, but not outwardly show it. Then, if mated to another shorthaired Chihuahua with the same recessive gene, the trait of a long coat may be passed down and appear in the litter, producing longhaired pups. In fact, one litter can contain both long and short coated puppies. It does not work the opposite way, however. Therefore, if you mate together two longhaired Chihuahuas, the only outcome will be longhaired Chihuahuas.

Special Characteristics: Longhaired Chihuahuas can take a little time to get their full coats, sometimes up to the age of 14 - 24 months. Once grown in, the texture of the coat is soft and can be either straight or slightly curly with or without an undercoat (although most do have two coats; inner and outer and this is preferred in show).

With good coat quality, the texture of the fur will feel silky and light. The outer layer is comprised of fine hairs and the undercoat is velvety. Unlike many longhaired breeds, longhaired Chihuahuas do not require any trimming since the coat tends to only grow out a few inches. Usually, males have a larger ruff around the neck and a thicker coat than the females do.

Ears on both genders should be feathery with fringes. For a very young pup, if the ears hold lots of hair, this can affect their ability to stand fully erect. In these cases, trimming or shaving the ears can help.

Since the coat does not grow overly long, there will not be much of a difference in regard to shedding. And, just as with appleheads and deerheads, there are no behavioral differences between long and short coats.

Long Coat Curly Haired Chihuahuas

The AKC breed standard tells us that the long coat Chihuahua should have a soft textured coat and it should be '...*either flat or slightly wavy, with undercoat preferred.*'

With longhaired Chihuahuas that do have the 'wave', it usually is slight. However, some Chihuahuas will have much more of a curl like the little guy here.

We have only seen a curl to this degree a handful of times, as it is exceedingly rare. It will occur if the curling gene is present and, at the same time, the coat grows a bit longer than typically seen with long coat Chihuahuas.

Photos (previous page and right): This curly haired long coat Chihuahua is Kahlua, photo courtesy of her owner Cayla Mendoza. Right, is Kahlua with a wet coat, after a bath.

The hair curl is caused by a mutation in the KRT71 gene. For some breeds, like the Poodle, that mutation in the KRT71 gene is fixed (always there). For other breeds, including the Boykin Spaniel, the Kuvasz, and the Chihuahua, among others, it is a variant (may be there).

DNA testing can look for this, by looking to the C allele. If it is dominant, it will be C/C (curly – and being dominant, the curl would be passed to litters). If it is C/c, the dog has both dominant and recessive alleles (if bred, either curly or straight may be passed on) and if it is c/c the dog is negative for the hair curl allele (and does not carry the gene at all, so if bred could not produce puppies with a curled coat).

The Molera

The molera is a soft spot in the skull

A molera, or fontanel, is a space between the bones in the skull where skeletal plates have not fused together. It is similar to the open fontanel that human babies are born with. It serves a purpose during the whelping process, making the skull more flexible as a pup travels through the narrow birth canal of the dam.

Though this is an area in which the skull bones essentially have an 'opening', it is comprised of tough membranes that protect underlying soft tissues and the brain.

Not all Chihuahuas are born with this; it tends to run in certain bloodlines and it's seen more often with appleheads. If present, it may or may not close as the pup matures. For Chi that are born with this, it will remain open for roughly 50% of them; yet, it *may* shrink in size as the skull partially fuses closer together. In cases when it fully closes, it can be a very gradual process, taking anywhere from 3 months to 3 years.

Looking back to 1933, it was a defining feature of the Chihuahua breed and was required in the show ring. That requirement has since been removed and dogs with or without a molera are seen equally. The wording in the AKC breed standard that covers this is *'A well rounded "apple dome" skull, with or without molera.'* The FCI, however, rules that *'Dogs with an open fontanel'* is a disqualifying fault.

If present, the molera will vary in size and shape, but in general will be the diameter of the tip of your pointer finger. Most of the time, this is only noticeable by touch. Despite what you may have heard or read, please note that the presence of a molera does *not* mean that a dog is prone to hydrocephalus (a condition in which there is an accumulation of fluid within the brain), seizures, or blindness. Numerous studies have shown no connections at all between a molera and any other health issue.

This said, there are a few precautions to keep in place. Normal touching of the area is fine. You may bathe, groom, play with your Chihuahua, and do everything else as you would otherwise. However, the area should never be intentionally pushed and this should be taught to everyone including young children that may be handling or playing with the Chi.

In addition, take extra care to try to prevent bumps or injury to the head. Food and water bowls are the biggest culprits. Use an appropriately sized and shallow bowl to prevent the head from bumping against the rim of the dishes. Do not allow rough play with other dogs, particularly larger dogs.

Where the Chihuahua Fits in With Other Breeds

There are several ways to classify a breed or make comparisons. Here's a fun look some interesting aspects.

AKC Grouping: As covered, the Chihuahua is in the AKC Toy Group. There are 21 breeds in this group: The Affenpinscher, Brussels Griffon, Cavalier King Charles Spaniel, Chihuahua, Chinese Crested, English Toy Spaniel, Havanese, Italian Greyhound, Japanese Chin, Maltese, Manchester Terrier, Miniature Pinscher, Papillon, Pekingese, Pomeranian, Poodle (toy), Pug, Shih Tzu, Silky Terrier, Toy Fox Terrier, and Yorkshire Terrier.

Pictured below: Pug, Maltese, Cavalier King Charles Spaniel, and Chihuahua

Country of Origin: The Chihuahua's country of origin is Mexico. There is only one other official breed with this distinction, the Xoloitzcuintli (also known as the Mexican Hairless Dog), and one in which Mexican origin is debated, the Chinese Crested Dog.

The Xoloitzcuintli, despite its alternate name, has two coat types: hairless and coated, with the latter having a very close and short coat. There are three size varieties of the Xoloitzcuintli: Toy (at least 10 and up to 14 inches [25.4 to 35.6 cm]), Miniature (starting at 14 and up to 18 inches [35.6 to 45.7 cm]) and Standard (starting at 18 and up to 23 inches [45.7 to 58.4 cm]). Note that for canines, height is from floor to withers (top of the shoulder blades). While height is not part of the breed standard for the Chihuahua, this can be compared to the breed's typical range of 6 to 9 inches (15.24 to 22.86 cm).

The Chinese Crested Dog ranges from 5.1 to 12 lbs. (2.3 to 5.4 kg) and has a height of 9 to 13 inches (22.86 to 33 cm). There are two coat types: the Hairless (hair just on the head, tail, and feet) and the Powderpuff (coat over the entire body). Despite the name, it is very unlikely that this breed originated in China and theories of an African origin are strongly debated; genetic evidence shows a link to the Xoloitzcuintli.

Pictured below: Xoloitzcuintli, Chinese Crested Dog, and Chihuahua

Size: Perhaps the most obvious aspect of the Chihuahua to touch on in regard to other breeds is size. With a breed standard weight of 6 lbs. (2.7 kg) or under, this is the smallest dog breed that exists. The Yorkshire Terrier comes close, with a breed standard weight of 7 lbs. (3.17 kg) or under and a typical height range of 7 to 8 inches (17.8 to 20.3 cm).

The Great Dane, which is one of the largest 'giant' breeds with a weight range of 99 to 200 lbs. (45 to 90 kg) and a height of 28 to 34 inches (71 to 86 cm), is often depicted as the complete opposite of the Chihuahua. A Great Dane named Zeus is in the Guinness World Records for being the world's tallest dog at 44 inches (standing 7' 4" [223.52 cm] on his hind legs). Though, the English Mastiff is another notable comparison with a weight range of 120 to 230 lbs. (54 to 100 kg) and a height range of 28 to 36 inches (70 to 71 cm).

Pictured below: Yorkshire Terrier, Chihuahua, Great Dane, and English Mastiff

The Chihuahua's Personality

A Contradiction to Say the Least

The Chihuahua's personality is, to say the least, contradictory at times. The AKC describes the Chihuahua as *'graceful, charming, and sassy'*, which is certainly a unique combination, yet one that most owners would agree with. As seen ahead in much more detail under 'PetChiDog's Chihuahua Survey', when asking owners to describe their Chihuahua in 3 words, both 'loving' and 'loyal' were very popular entries. Yet, there was also 'feisty', 'shy', 'hyper', and 'lazy'. The survey also showed that 9% of owners saw aggression as an issue, yet 'friendly' was another term entered quite often.

If it seems confusing that owners report both feisty and shy Chihuahuas, hyper and lazy ones, and aggressive and friendly dogs, there are a couple of things to keep in mind.

A notable aspect is that during this breed's entire journey over the centuries from desert dog to adored indoor companion, one thing was clear: most, if not all other animals - both those encountered and those kept under the same roof – were larger than the Chi. This set up defense mechanisms. In many situations, a dog as small as the Chihuahua will retreat (be cautious, shy, and/or nervous) or confront (bark up a storm or even be aggressive).

In addition, this breed is incredibly sensitive to his surroundings. How a Chihuahua is treated and trained will have a significant impact on behavior. This is applicable to both puppies and adults. Over 20% of Chihuahuas now living in loving homes were adopted; previous bad experiences before being rescued can affect behavior even after being saved and safe.

Much of Your Chihuahua's Personality Will Be Shaped By You

You will play a big role in your Chi's personality and this is particularly true if you have the opportunity to be there from the 8-week mark and on. However, behavior is shaped by owners to a certain degree no matter a dog's age. And, even if some behaviors or habits are ingrained, the right training techniques can bring about improvement, and in some cases, complete turnaround.

A vital component of shaping your Chihuahua's personality is to determine and clarify your goals. Though every household is unique, it's safe to say that you'd prefer a rather quiet dog that perhaps only barks when there is a valid reason (like a stranger lurking outside your door). And, that it'd be nice to have a friendly dog that did well around children and other animals, but not so brave that he runs over to unknown dogs ten times his size (that can be exceedingly dangerous).

Do you like to go for walks or explore outdoor markets on the weekends? If so, you'll want your Chihuahua to walk nicely beside you and have the confidence to handle crowds. Maybe you're a bit adventurous and would like your Chihuahua to accompany you on bicycle rides or even on a canoe. Envision the social skillset that you'd like for your Chihuahua to have, and embark on the journey there together as a team.

If there's one takeaway, it is that you should not leave your Chihuahua's personality up to chance or just see how it takes shape as the years go by. You are raising a dog, not just allowing one to live in your house. Your everyday actions and purposeful training methods will help cultivate your Chi's acceptance, tolerance, and ability to interact with you and the rest of the world in a positive way.

How to Help Shape Your Chihuahua's Personality

Keep in mind that no dog is perfect. It's an unattainable goal to expect your Chihuahua never to jump or beg, handle every encounter with others with polish, and refrain from ever doing anything wrong. Also, it's unlikely that a very shy dog will learn to leap into the arms of strangers or that a barker will be silent at all times. So, while you definitely should work on areas that need improvement, love your Chihuahua for the type of dog that he or she happens to be. Some are hyper, some are calm, some are shy, others are bold. Personality can be tweaked, but not completely reinvented.

But, do not just accept certain behaviors. Are there some tendencies such as barking or nervousness that are seen with a lot of Chihuahuas? Yes. But, this does not mean that you should sit back and not intervene. First, consider that you *may* be playing a role in your Chi's behavior, either from the absence of training and/or from household vibe. Then, remember that dogs *can* learn new habits and adjust their viewpoint when they are given proper guidance. If you avoid walks because your Chi barks or refuses to move, or you never take your Chi with you to stores because of bad experiences in the car, things will never improve.

Prepare in advance for certain behaviors that are commonly seen with Chihuahuas, and dogs in general, particularly if you have a puppy. It makes sense to initially read the sections in this book that pertain to what is happening with your Chi right now. However, if you have time, read through all of the topics to learn possible steps you can take to avoid certain behaviors in the first place.

Having the right foundation is key. Though you will be a lot of things to your Chihuahua… friend, parent, owner… the #1 role that you'll need to take is leader. Once your dog sees you as the unquestionable leader, you can set the tone and pace for every bit of socialization and training going forward. Remember that a leader can be a fair, forgiving, and loving figure. For this, be sure to read 'Training: Teaching Proper Hierarchy'.

Above all else, love. Whether it's just you and your Chihuahua or a house filled with both people and pets, the amount of unconditional love in your household will have the biggest effect on your Chihuahua's personality and overall happiness level. Your actions and words are always in play. Speak to your Chi with kindness (it can be a firm kindness when needed such as when training). Very few dogs can be happy when they are spoken to harshly. And, take the time to lovingly and routinely interact with your puppy or dog. Very few dogs are content when ignored and just expected to 'be there'.

Additionally, love does not just pertain to how you act toward your puppy or dog. Canines are incredibly astute at picking up vibes. If you're always arguing with your spouse or angry at your teenager, this will have an effect on your Chihuahua. And, if you're personally unhappy and stressed, it'll be difficult for your canine family member to be content and relaxed. Work to create peace both within yourself and your household.

Males Vs Females

Concerning personality: Maybe you've heard that females do better with children and males like to cuddle more. Or, perhaps that females are moodier, but males are worse at listening. The truth is that while any of that may be the case in individual situations, it's not true at all across the board. If you are thinking about getting a Chihuahua and are not sure if a boy or a girl is the right choice for you, consider the breed as a whole; it's much more important than gender. This all said, let's take a look at some aspects of males and females.

For *both* un-neutered males and un-spayed females, you may see the following behavioral issues: May be more territorial (reaction to visitors, barking out the window, etc.), may be harder to teach proper hierarchy (that the human is the leader), may mark more (territorial spraying of urine inside the house), may have stronger urges to run away, and humping (this is seen predominantly in males; however, females may do this as well).

Health: Allergies are the #1 reported health issue (based on our survey of 3,272 owners; see also 'About the Chihuahua: PetChiDog's Chihuahua Survey'), which is seen at similar rates among both genders. This breed is prone to certain conditions including luxating patella, collapsed trachea, hypoglycemia, inguinal hernia, mitral valve disease, and dental issues. All except luxating patella and inguinal hernia are seen evenly among genders (see 'Females', next).

Females — Female dogs have the risk of developing uterine infections or uterine cancer, breast tumors (which are seen - malignant or cancerous - in approximately 50% of un-spayed dogs), pyometra, and pseudopregnancy (false pregnancy). The risk for these issues can be significantly reduced or eliminated with spaying. Vaginitis is an issue seen with both spayed and un-spayed females. Some studies show that females are 1.5 times more likely to suffer from luxating patella than males. The Chihuahua breed is predisposed to inguinal hernias; while this can affect both genders, it is seen more often with females that have not been spayed, and may be more prone to develop when a female is in heat or is pregnant.

Males - Un-neutered male dogs have the risk for prostate problems including the very rare but serious benign prostatic hyperplasia (BPH), cryptorchidism (undescended testicles), and testicular cancer. The risk for tumors can be significantly reduced or eliminated with neutering. One health issue limited to males and seen in both neutered and un-neutered dogs is paraphimosis (the penis becomes stuck outside of its sheath).

Coat: Any correlation between coat and gender is anecdotal. Basic coat quality is linked to bloodlines. Later, elements that will affect coat texture and appearance include diet, health status, and your choice of grooming methods and products.

Care: Differences in care only come about if a female is not spayed. There will be the hygiene involved in keeping a female clean and tidy during the heat cycle.

Choosing a Gender for a Single-Dog Household: The matter of selecting a male or female puppy or dog is very personal. One way to help you decide is to think about what role you see your dog playing in your life. Will you see your puppy (and then mature dog) as a child of sorts? If so, would you prefer to think of your dog as your daughter or your son? Or do you find yourself thinking of a dog becoming your best friend? If so, do you envision that loyal companion as being a male or female?

In some cases, you will not know which puppy is right for you until you see a litter and one touches your heart just so. Keep in mind that some breeders may have ulterior motives for trying to push one gender over the other and that really is a shame since it is such a personal choice.

Same Gender vs. Opposite in a Multi-Dog Household: Which gender is best to introduce to an established dog? There is no wrong answer. However, transition and acceptance may be easier with opposite gender dogs. In either case of same or opposite gender, there will need to be a leader among the dogs; this is canine fact. Generally speaking, two of the same gender may struggle a bit harder to determine which of them is the 'top dog'.

Before you decide to bring in another canine family member, it can help to keep a close eye on your current dog to see how he/she interacts with other dogs and if he/she has a tendency to get along better with or be more tolerant towards either gender.

PetChiDog's Chihuahua Survey

At the start of 2018, we conducted an online survey revolving around Chihuahua appearance, behavior, health, and personality. PetChiDog.com site Members were asked several multiple-choice questions and allowed for comments, which helped us to gather more specifics regarding certain queries

The survey results were gathered after 7 days, with a total of 3,272 respondents. 68% of the participants were in the US, 11% in the UK, 11% in Canada, 3% in Australia, and the remaining 7% in various other countries. In regard to the gender of the Chihuahuas, there were 57% females to 43% males. The ages of the Chihuahuas were 3% young puppy (under 6-months-old), 14% puppy (6 to 12-months old), 45% young adult (1 to 3-years-old), 29% adult (4 to 8-years-old), and 9% senior (9+ years).

This sort of large pooling of owner information is a fantastic way for you to get a clear view of what to expect with a Chihuahua and to see how your puppy or dog fits in with thousands of others. You may find the results enlightening, let's take a look!

First, we asked: <u>How did you obtain your Chihuahua?</u>

A breeder, driving distance from me 23%
A shelter or a rescue 23%
A listing online, but not a breeder 13%
Other 12%

Someone I knew gave him/her to me 12%
Someone I knew had a litter 11%
A breeder, far away, had to travel 6%

It's interesting to see the diverse ways that Chihuahuas ended up in their homes, and that such a large number (23%, 752 Chi out of 3,272) were obtained through a shelter or rescue. This drives home a point that there are a lot of dogs waiting to be adopted. In looking over the comments left under 'Other' (12%), the most popular ways included pet stores (do be warned that many pet stores are stocked via puppy mills), literally finding the Chihuahua somewhere outside, taking over ownership from someone who could no longer care for the dog, and having offspring of their own dog.

Next, were some appearance questions. <u>How much does your Chihuahua weigh?</u>
Our survey branched off so that we were able to separate puppy weight from adult weight. For adults only, which were Chihuahuas 1-year and older (83%, a total of 2,715 Chi), the answers were as so:

More than 8.5 lb. (3.85 kg) 23%
5 lb. (2.26 kg) 11%
6.5 lb. (2.94 kg) 8%
5.5 lb. (2.49 kg) 7%
6 lb. (2.72 kg) 7%
7 lb. (3.17 kg) 7%
4 lb. (1.81 kg) 6%

7.5 lb. (3.40 kg) 6%
2.5 lb. (1.13 kg) 5%
8 lb. (3.63 kg) 5%
8.5 lb. (3.85 kg) 5%
4.5 lb. (2.04 kg) 4%
3 lb. (1.36 kg) 3%
3.5 lb. (1.58 kg) 3%

This falls in line with the expectation that while many Chihuahuas will fit the AKC standard of not exceeding 6 lbs., that weight is not realistic for all pet Chihuahuas. With 8% at 6.5 lbs., 7% at 7 lbs., 6% at 7.5 lbs., 5% at 8 lbs., 5% at 8.5 lbs., and 23% at over 8.5 lbs., this is a total of 54% of Chihuahuas (1,466 out of 2,715) that were larger than the breed standard's ideal. Those who chose 'More than 8.5 lbs. (3.85 kg)' were able to enter the weight. Many owners entered a weight in the 9 to 12 lb. range (4.08 to 5.44 kg) and a few were weights in the teens. Quite a few owners also left a comment that their larger-than-standard Chihuahua was muscular and/or healthy. And, there is no doubt regarding that; larger Chi are not necessarily overweight. This is discussed ahead, under 'About the Chihuahua: Size Variances'.

Then, we asked about coat: <u>Do you have a short coat or long coat Chihuahua?</u>

Short 76%   Long 24%

Ears are always a big topic when it comes to breeds that have erect ears. And, this breed does have interesting ears. Puppies are born with floppy ears; for most, they will stand erect as the pup matures. Though up when alert, they change positioning depending on how the dog is feeling; sometimes angled to the side and sometimes fully back. However, not all Chi have 'perfect' standing ears; the tip may flop over (also referred to a 'half-ear') or one or both ears may be floppy due to weak ear muscles, unable to stand. So, we asked **<u>Which describes your Chihuahua's ears?</u>**

Both standing erect 75%
Standing, but one/both can drop once in a while 12%
Floppy 6%
A bit floppy 5%
One is always standing, one is always down 2%

To read more about ear set and ear care, look to 'Health & Care– Body Part Specific: Ears'.

Next, we moved on to a behavioral question in an attempt to cover all the bases. We asked <u>What was the biggest challenge(s) you've had with your Chihuahua?</u>

We let owners know that health issues were not included in this (that's coming up next) and that they could choose as many issues that applied. There was an 'Other' option and a comment box.

Housebreaking 15%
Barking 14%
Separation anxiety 14%
Being scared or nervous 9%

Aggression (nipping, growling, etc.) 9%
Getting along with other dogs outside the house 8%
Tolerating cold weather 8%
Getting along with visitors 7%
Eating issues 6%
Refusing to listen to me 5%
Getting along with other pets 4%
Humping 3%
Refusing to go for walks/exercise 3%
Destructive chewing 3%
Disliking the car 3%
No challenges that I can think of! 2%
Other 1%

Some of the results were right on track with what to expect with a Chihuahua or any dog for that matter. Housebreaking, helping a dog cope when home alone, and barking are some of the most significant challenges that owners face. If this applies to you, this book offers effective advice for each of these. Look to 'Housebreaking', 'Situational Issues: Separation Anxiety', and 'Behavioral Training: Barking'.

Other results were in line with what can be seen with Chihuahuas more frequently than with some other breeds. This includes being nervous or scared, having aggression, getting along with other dogs, getting along with visitors, and tolerating the cold. In regard to having trouble with other dogs, if this is a matter of being afraid, there is helpful advice under 'Situational Issues: Afraid of Other Dogs', and if this is a matter of barking at them, see "Behavioral Training: Barking'.

For being scared or nervous, behaviors reported by 9% of owners, you may wish to refer to 'Behavioral Issues: Clingy Behavior' and 'Behavioral Training: Socialization & Desensitization'. For less-than-ideal interaction issues, see 'Behavioral Training: Aggression' which includes two follow-up questions regarding reported aggression, 'Behavioral Training: Jumping on People', and 'Behavioral Issues: Nipping'. And, be sure to read over 'About the Chihuahua: The Chihuahua's Personality'.

With toy breeds in general, and especially with the Chihuahua that is small with very little body fat, cold intolerance is common. So, it's not surprising that 8% of owners reported this issue. For help regarding this, refer to both 'Exercise & Activity: Dressing for the Weather' and 'Seasonal Care: Winter Care'.

Eating issues are reported by 6% of owners. If your puppy or dog is a picky eater or has some other quirks related to food, look to 'Feeding and Nutrition: The Most Common Eating Issues'. Refusing to listen, which 5% of owners reported, is directly related to hierarchy; for this, see 'Training: Teaching Proper Hierarchy'. Once that is established, you will have the right foundation to train for a host of issues, many of which are found in both the 'Behavioral Training' and 'Behavioral Issues' chapters.

Getting along with other pets was seen as an issue with 4% of Chihuahuas, and this can be very disruptive to the household. If your dog has trouble with another dog in the house, see 'Situational Issues: Having More Than One Dog', and if this is a matter of a cat, see 'Situational Issues: Having a Chihuahua and a Cat'. To finish out the other issues on the survey, see 'Behavioral Issues: Humping', 'Exercise & Activity: Requirements & Restrictions', 'Behavioral Training: Refusal to Walk While on Leash', the 'Teething & Chewing' chapter, and 'Safety and Happiness: Traveling'.

The next section of the survey centered around health issues. We asked <u>Has your Chihuahua had any of these health issues?</u>

Owners could check off as many as were applicable, there was an 'Other' option, and a comment box.

Allergies 18%
Joint related (patella/knee, hips, etc.) 11%
Other 11%
Issues related to breathing (collapsed trachea, etc.) 9%
Parasites (worms, fleas, mites) 8%
Eye problems 5%
Coat issues (Alopecia, thinning, etc.) 4%
Skin issues (not related to allergies) 3%
Organ related (liver, kidneys, etc.) 2%
Cancer 0%
Thyroid 0%
Diabetes 0%

For allergies (which typically affects 20% of all dogs), the occurrence rate with these 3,272 Chihuahuas is a bit lower, at 18%. If your Chihuahua has allergies, this book offers an excellent chapter for this that can help even if there have been struggles pinpointing the exact triggers or fully resolving symptoms. See 'Health – Other: Allergies'.

Joint-related issues were the second-most reported condition, at 11%, and we, unfortunately, did expect to see a relatively high number due to this breed being prone to patella luxation (knee). The Orthopedic Foundation for Animals (OFA), which keeps detailed records of how often certain issues occur with different breeds, ranks the Chihuahua at #22 out of 128 breeds (not a good place to be). For details regarding this condition, see 'Health – Other: Luxating Patella'.

We'll skip over 'Other' for a moment, which brings us to 'Issues related to breathing (collapsed trachea, etc.)'. With this, we expected to see at least a double-digit number but were pleased to see just 9% (though even 1% is too many). This may be linked to owner education regarding the use of a harness as opposed to a collar. To learn about prevention, see 'Care Items – Chihuahua of All Ages: Leashes, Harnesses, Collars, and ID Tags' and to read about this condition, see 'Health - Other: Collapsed Trachea'.

Parasites such as worms and fleas were reported by 8% of owners. Many worm infestations can be prevented; for this, look to 'Health - Other: Worms'. And for fleas, which are notorious for infecting dogs and tricky to resolve, look to 'Health - Other: Fleas'. Eye issues may involve a host of conditions including inflammation, dry eye, cherry eye, entropion (inverted eyelid), and eyelash issues such as distichiasis and ectopic cilia. For all of these, look to 'Health & Care: Body Part Specific: Eyes'.

Issues such as a thinning or balding coat were reported by 4% of owners, and this can be such a frustrating problem to contend with. There is a chapter devoted to this: 'Fur and Coat'. It was good to see that there were no cases of cancer, thyroid issues, or canine diabetes reported; though, both diabetes and cancer are seen most often among senior dogs, and just 9% of owners had Chihuahuas over the age of 9 (294 dogs out of 3,272).

In regard to the 11% 'Other' option, below are the most popular words from owners' comments.

plaque **stomach** sensitive lot **teeth** underweight
wobbly something unknown eye stool stone
term **yeast** hernia malnourish disease surgery food small issue fur **problem** today ear
cherry walking trachea unusual **gums** loose back get toy anal gland
leg **heart** cough bad

As you can see, 'teeth' and 'plaque' came up a lot, as did 'gums'. Unfortunately, dental problems are a major concern with toy breeds. Proper at-home dental care and professional veterinary cleanings, as needed, is vital to maintaining your dog's oral health. For this, look to the 'Dental Care' chapter.

'Stomach' and 'sensitive' are two more prominent words seen in the comments. If your Chihuahua is suffering from upset stomach issues, you will find very helpful guidelines under 'Health – Stomach, Intestinal'. And, in addition to this, if you believe that food allergies are to blame, look to 'Health – Other: Allergies'.

The words 'yeast' and 'ear' were entered quite a bit. Ear infections are very common with dogs, with yeast being just one of the culprits. For this, look to 'Health & Care – Body Part Specific: Ears'. And, 'cough' came up frequently; while this is a top sign of collapsed trachea, there are other possible causes. For this reason, the 'Coughs and Other Noises – Quick Reference' section in the 'Health – Other' chapter can help point you in the right direction. In regard to 'hernia', which appeared repeatedly, there are several types. The Chihuahua is prone to one of them, inguinal hernias, and umbilical hernias are the most common type for canines in general. For more information about these, see 'Health – Other: Hernias'.

Being so tiny to begin with, you don't want to see the words 'underweight' or 'malnourished', yet, this these are indeed issues seen with Chihuahuas, particularly puppies. If your Chi is having these sorts of issues, please refer to 'Feeding and Nutrition: Helping a Chihuahua Puppy Gain Weight'.

Several owners entered 'heart'. The Chihuahua is one of the breeds prone to mitral valve disease. For this and heart murmurs, you may wish to refer to 'Health – Other: Heart Issues'.

We wanted to wrap up the survey on a good note; so, we asked a few lighthearted questions. First, we wondered: <u>If your Chihuahua were a human, what age equivalent would you say he/she is?</u>

Young child (elementary school) 18%
Teenager 17%
Toddler 16%
Young adult 16%

Adult 15%
Pre-teen 12%
Senior citizen 6%

These answers are interesting when you compare them to the actual ages of the Chihuahuas in question, which were 3% young puppy (under 6-months-old), 14% puppy (6 to 12-months old), 45% young adult (1 to 3-years-old), 29% adult (4 to 8-years-old), 9% senior (9+ years).

On that same train of thought, we then asked <u>In which way do you see your Chihuahua?</u>

My family member 50%
My child 35%
My pet 7%

My friend 4%
Other 4%

These answers mostly fall in line with what we expected; however, we thought we covered all the bases and were very curious to see the comments left under 'Other'. Below are the most popular words.

best companion grand gift **everything** loyal member **baby** us **world**
little often god perfect serenity **joy** older bring girl **sweetheart**
service blessing family folk **loving** close

The final prompt of the survey requested, <u>Please summarize your Chihuahua's personality in 3 words</u>. These are the most popular words entered, and we are sure that you'll agree the results are pretty spot-on:

happy cuddly best caring **affectionate** bossy fun ever spoiled girl intelligent
little feisty boy active **brave** independent hilarious alert cute smart protective energetic goofy playful cheeky
shy loyal curious hyper baby friend kind adorable cautious **loving** lazy **clingy** funny spunky
stubborn **love** nervous friendly timid wonderful sweet dog crazy beautiful

Size Variances

The Chihuahua, known as the 'tiniest dog breed in the world', has a lot to live up to. With that as its tagline, the AKC standard stating that a Chihuahua is *not to exceed 6 lb.* (2.72 kg), and the AKC listing a weight range of 3 to 6 lbs. (1.36 to 2.72 kg; found at http://www.akc.org/dog-breeds/chihuahua), many owners undoubtedly expect to have a super-small puppy that grows up to be an exceptionally petite adult.

The truth of the matter is that a good number are in the 3 to 6 lb. range, a small number are less than this, and quite a few are larger (though still a very small dog). As shown in the previous section of 'PetChiDog's Chihuahua Survey', which complied the stats of 3,272 Chihuahuas, of the 2,715 adults (1 year and older), just 5% of Chihuahuas were under 3 lbs., at 2.5 lbs. (1.13 kg). Then, there were 41% in the 3 to 6 lb. range (1.36 to 2.72 kg). And, the largest percentage of Chihuahuas, 54%, were more than 6 lbs. (2.72 kg).

Teacup Chihuahuas: It is first important to note that 'teacup Chihuahua', 'toy Chihuahua' or any other such term is not an official variety of Chihuahua. There is only one Chihuahua breed, with only two varieties: long coat and smooth (short) coat.

Keeping in mind that the expected weight range (per the standard) is 3 to 6 lbs., 'teacup' is meant to imply that the dog is/will be much smaller than what is normally expected. So, in other words, smaller than 3 lbs. This is not only highly uncommon, it is also dangerous.

Adult Chihuahuas that are under 3 lbs. are going to be much more prone to hypoglycemia, cold intolerance, neck injuries including the condition of collapsed trachea, and a range of other injuries due to its small size including broken bones and other trauma. Note that trauma is the 2nd leading cause of death for puppies (all breeds) and the 2nd leading cause of death for adult Chihuahua dogs.

If you already have a very small 'teacup' adult Chihuahua (under 3 lbs.), there will be a greater need to ensure frequent small meals to keep blood sugar levels even (perhaps going so far as to 'free-feed' as opposed to scheduled meals), work to prevent the Chi from feeling cold (clothing, even inside may be needed), and give extra attention to safety both in and outside the house.

If you have a puppy that needs to gain some weight, look to 'Feeding and Nutrition: Helping a Chihuahua Puppy Gain Weight'.

If you are planning on purchasing a 'teacup' Chihuahua, please keep in mind that puppies advertised as such means one of two things: The puppy is indeed expected to be undersized (hence, prone to more health issues and injury) or 'teacup' is simply a marketing term used to lure in potential puppy buyers.

Larger Than Average Chihuahuas: As we covered, a large number of pet Chihuahuas are larger than what the breed standard calls out for. So, while Chi larger than 6 lbs. do not appear in the show ring, they are indeed in households around the world.

Part of the reason for so many Chi being larger than 6 lbs., is that some breeders strive toward the higher end of the weight scale to produce Chihuahuas of substance that will be less prone to health issues and injury. Inevitably, hovering close to the high end will result in some dogs that go over that. This said, AKC breeders do have an obligation to produce litters with 'betterment of the breed' in mind which means dogs that meet the standard.

With hobby breeders (that may not take bloodlines and pedigrees into consideration) and puppy mill breeders (that do not care about any of this at all) it's not uncommon to see larger than average Chihuahuas.

Another possibility, which is rare but something that has to be considered, is a Chihuahua being overweight. If you have a rather small Chi, this may seem like a silly notion to you; however, any breed can carry excess weight, even the Chihuahua.

If you have a larger-than-average Chihuahua, it'll be important to establish if this is due to body structure or excess weight. While looking at the rib cage (when wet, there is no outline of any ribs at all) can be a general indication of excess fat, it is best to have the veterinarian make this determination. If it turns out that your Chi is simply structurally larger than expected, there's nothing at all to be concerned about. In fact, your Chihuahua will be sturdier than his smaller counterparts and therefore less prone to certain health issues and injury. If the vet lets you know that there is a need to help your Chi lose a bit of weight, this can be done with very little stress by feeding lower calorie options and upping activity. There are more details about this under 'Feeding and Nutrition: Helping an Adult Chihuahua Lose Weight'.

Chihuahua Colors

Overview There are 28 AKC recognized colors (many are combinations) and 11 recognized markings that a Chihuahua may have. The difference between the AKC's and the FCI's accepted colors is that the AKC breed standard states *'Any color - solid, marked, or splashed'* (the 'splashed' referring to merle) and the FCI breed standard states *'All colours in all possible shades and combinations are admitted, except merle colour'*.

There are 9 colors that are part of an overall coat, which can be seen as solids:

As we move forward, please note that 'S' represents a standard color or marking and 'A' represent an alternate color or marking (though still accepted by the AKC).

Black (S 007) A solid black will not have any other color. If there is a small patch of another color, this will be black with a marking i.e. 'black with tan marking'. Nose, eye rims, lips, and paw pads will be black.

Chocolate (S 071) The when the 'B' allele color gene mutates to 'b', this creates chocolate which is expressed in skin pigmentation. The nose, eye rims, lips and paw pads will be brown. The coat will be a shade of brown, which can range from dark to light.

Cream (S 076) This is an off-white and it's not uncommon to have a cream with white markings, which makes it easier to see the difference between the two.

Fawn (S 082) This is a soft tan and a very common color with lots of different breeds.

Red (S 140) An intense and dark orange-brown. It's common for a red to be very dark red as a newborn and fade to a much lighter red just within the first few weeks. Some reds can fade so much that they appear to be a dark fawn or gold. The first Chihuahua ever registered with the AKC in 1904, Midget, was red.

Gold (A 091) This looks similar to fawn, yet is deeper and shinier.

Silver (A 176) Gray with a deep shine.

White (A 199) A completely solid white Chihuahua is very rare; most will be majorly white but with a secondary marking. For example, 'white with tan marking'

Blue Fawn (A 036) To understand Blue Fawn, we must understand blue. Blue is a diluted black and caused by a dilution gene. This will be expressed in skin pigmentation (nose, eye rims, lips and paw pads), which will range from a light silver to a deep navy that may, at first glance, appear to be black. When trying to determine black points from blue, this may be most noticeable when outside in bright sunlight. Blue fawn is a fawn that holds blue, as expressed in skin pigmentation.

Based off of those colors (with the exception of tan, which is not seen as a solid), there are some two-color combinations:

Blue & Tan (S 044) | Blue & White (A 045) | Fawn & White (S 086) | Chocolate & Tan (S 072) | Chocolate & White (A 271) | Gold & White (A 092) | Cream & White (A 077) | Black & Tan (S 018) | Black & Red (A 014) | Black & Silver (A 016) | Black & White (A 019) | Red & White (A 146) | Silver & White (A 182) Note that many two-color Chi have a third color, which is classified as a marking.

And, then there are some 'colors' which involve patterns:

First, are those with 'sable'. Sable refers to dark-tipped hairs. There is Black Sabled Fawn (A 354) which is sable (dark tipped hairs) over a fawn coat, Black Sabled Silver (A 353) which is sable (dark tipped hairs) over a silver coat, and Chocolate Sabled Fawn (A 358) which is dark chocolate tipped hairs over a fawn coat and the chocolate means that skin pigmentation (nose, eye rims, lips, and paw pads) will be brown.

Then, there are the 'brindles'. Brindle is a pattern of stripes. Colors may be in the brown range, with golds, tans, and browns striping through the coat. Or colors can be in the grey range, with white, grays, and black striping through the coat. The brindle (striping) may range from thin to thick (light to heavy). There is Blue Brindled Fawn (A 356) with blue being expressed in skin pigmentation, Chocolate Brindled Fawn (A 355) with chocolate being expressed in skin pigmentation, and Fawn Brindled Black (A 357).

There are 11 markings:

Black Brindling (S 073) The main coat will be a certain color (white or fawn, etc.) and there will be brindle (striped colors) over this. Brindle can appear in patches or essentially over the entire coat. Brindle may be heavy when a Chihuahua is young and then fade as the pup matures.

Black Mask (S 004) Black around the eyes, literally looking like a mask.

Black Sabling (S 072) The main coat will be a certain color (white or fawn, etc.) and there will be sabling (dark tipped hairs) over this. Sable can appear in patches or essentially over the entire coat. It may be heavy when a Chihuahua is young and then fade as the pup matures.

A silver Chihuahua with a black sabling could be registered as a Black Sabled Silver. This is up to the person who is registering the puppy. When it comes to sable markings vs. base color, often if it is just a small area of sabling, it will be checked off as a marking.

Merle Markings (S 035) The merle gene takes colors and causes a 'splattering' effect. There will be various spots and splashes of color that land randomly all over the coat and can also fall to the nose and other points of skin pigmentation.

As mentioned earlier, the FCI does not accept merle. While it is a beautiful color, it is also controversial because merle can lead to vision and hearing issues.

This is why: ***All dogs with merle*** have the Mm gene (one merle [M] allele and one non-merle [m] allele. ***All dogs without merle*** have the mm gene. ***If a merle (Mm) is bred to a non-merle (mm)***, this is fine; some of the resulting pups will be merle (Mm) and some will be non-merle (mm). ***However, if a merle (Mm) is bred to a merle (Mm),*** this will produce some merles (Mm), some non-merles (mm), and some double merles (MM). The double merle gene (MM) is linked to increased rates of deafness in one or both ears and microphthalmia which is a disorder of the eye in which one or both are abnormally small and that may cause blindness. **Image: Chihuahua on the left is a merle (splashed colors); note that the merle landed on the nose as well.**

Of course, the answer to this would be to never breed merle to merle. However, merle can be hidden (also known as cryptic). A dog can have the merle gene but not show this in the coat. Without a DNA test prior to breeding, a cryptic merle could be inadvertently paired to a known merle, thus producing puppies with the aforementioned issues.

Cream Markings (A 044) Cream colored spots on any other base color.

Fawn Markings (A 008) Light to medium tan markings on any other base color.

Red Markings (A 023) Red (intense, dark orange-brown) markings on any other base color.

Spotted on White (S 071) This marking refers to a base coat of white with spots of any other color. That secondary color will appear in patches ranging from small to large.

Image: 'Spotted on White' Chihuahua. Look at the middle marking, do you see the upside-down heart? Photo courtesy of MSD Chihuahuas

White Markings (S 014) This will be white markings on a base coat of any other color. A Black & White Chihuahua could, essentially, be labeled as a Black with White markings; however, most Black & Whites will be roughly 50/50 and a Black with White markings will be predominantly black with a minority of white.

Black Mask, White Markings (A 005) There is both a black mask and white markings.

Blue Mask (A 006) There is a mask; but, instead of black it is blue (diluted black). Blue will be expressed in skin pigmentation (nose, eye rims, lips and paw pads), which will range from a light silver to a deep navy that may, at first glance, appear to be black. The fur itself will range from a dark steeling navy to a light silver.

Names for Particular Markings: Markings may appear on any area of the body and there are terms used to describe the areas in which they appear:

Beauty mark. A small, distinct dot.
Blaze. A stripe running up the center of the face, running between the eyes and up over the forehead.
Flare. A blaze that widens as it approaches the topskull.
Collar. A secondary color running around the neck.
Kiss marks. Spots on the cheeks and above the eyes on the brow.
Saddle (Blanketback). A large patch of color across the back.

Color Changes: It is very rare for a young puppy to retain his exact coloring. As he matures, there will be transformations. Spotting may fade away or increase. Brindling or sabling may fade away. Base colors may lighted or darken. A breeder should never promise any certain color and owners should not expect to see their short coated Chi's final color until the 1 year mark. With longhaired Chihuahuas, you may not see the final color until the 14 to 24 month mark.

Eye Color: Just like humans, most puppies are born with dark blue eyes that transition as the pup matures. This is usually complete by the 8-week mark, but can take up to 6 months. The majority of Chihuahuas will have dark brown eyes. Blue eyes can be seen in this breed; however, it is considered a serious fault in the show ring. With Chihuahuas that have the merle gene, eyes may start off brown but change to blue or they may develop speckles since the merle gene can land in the eyes. Hazel and green eyes are also possible; with 'blond' (fawn or other light colors) and white Chihuahuas, light eyes (hazel, green, light brown) are permissible in show.

Ruby eyes are also permissible. The AKC refers to these as 'luminous ruby', meaning eyes that appear dark red under certain lighting conditions. This is rare and when it happens, it most often with white or very light colored Chihuahuas. This does not refer to eyes that appear bright red when a flash photo is taken. True ruby is detected in person and not via a photograph.

Chihuahua Intelligence

There are several factors that are looked at when theorizing just how smart canines, in general, are.

• **Word comprehension.** Dogs that live in households with plenty of interaction can understand an average of 165 words which is the equivalent of a two-year-old human. With work, this number can be greatly exceeded; Chaser, a Border Collie, was shown to under 1,022!

• **Memory skills.** This relates to remembering objects, people, places, commands, and so forth. Canines have both short and long-term memories, and all that is needed is repetition for something to move from short-term memory into long-term.

• **Awareness.** This includes the capacity to understand one's environment and make connections. For example, understanding that jumping in the car with toys means a trip to the dog park, but doing so without them may suggest a visit to the groomer.

• **Perception.** This is similar to awareness, yet it involves how a dog uses all of his senses to understand any particular event. He'll use a combination of vision, hearing, smell, touch, and sometimes taste to learn what something is.

You may be interested to know that using the earth's magnetic field, magnetoreception, is included in this as well. A study of magnetoreception with canines[1] proved that if a dog is off leash and without confining walls (able to make his own choices) and the Earth's magnetic field is calm (there are daily fluctuations as the earth rotates), they prefer to urinate and defecate with their bodies aligned on a north to south axis.

It is unclear why they prefer this, but they do. Over the course of two years, 70 dogs of 37 different breeds were studied. In total, they urinated 5,582 times and defecated 1,893 times. Without any impediments, they positioned themselves north-south instead of east-west.

• **Social cognition.** This involves a dog's ability to interpret subtle social cues. Studies have proven dogs can identify hidden toys simply based on their human's shrugs, nods, and even facial expressions. In this regard, canines were found to be more intelligent than chimpanzees and even human babies. It's a good point to keep in mind; your dog is picking up cues from you all of the time.

• **Problem Solving.** This involves how a dog can work out a problem, such as finding a hidden treat that is only released with a series of manipulation tasks. For example, a button is pressed by the paw, a lid needs to be lifted up, and a lever is moved aside. Many dogs can do this, with practice.

• **Emotions.** To gauge intelligence, many scientists take into account the range of emotions that an animal can feel. And, this is an interesting element as it also can help compare how smart a canine is compared to a human. As a human grows, his or her capability to feel and express certain emotions expands. For example, excitement is there from birth. Yet, contempt is not felt nor expressed until a child is about 5-years-old.

Numerous studies have shown that a canine has the same emotional intelligence of, at least, a 2 and 1/2-year-old human.

The emotions that are proven to exist in canines are excitement, distress, contentment, disgust, fear, anger, joy, suspicion, shyness, affection, and love. They develop in that order. With toy breeds, these emotions are fully intact by the 4-month mark (with larger breeds it can be up until 6-months).

Surprisingly, studies show a dog's development stops just short of feeling pride, shame, or guilt.
Dogs are certainly capable of walking proudly or looking guilty; so, how can this be? Well, pride develops at the 3-year mark in humans. Studies show that canines stop emotional development at *'about'* the 2.5-year mark equivalent, which is an estimate. Dogs are proven to feel shy (it is the 9th emotion to develop); if a dog is *not* feeling shy, one could say that he *is* feeling confident. Confidence and pride are very closely related.

In regard to shame and guilt, it's a controversial subject since so many dogs fully appear to show this emotion. Many studies have shown that dogs seem to look guilty regardless of whether or not they've done something bad (from eating treats to shredding paper), all based on an owner's speech and mannerisms when seeing their dog afterward.

Intelligence Ranking of the Chihuahua:
Stanley Coren, a professor of canine psychology at the University of British Columbia in Vancouver, authored The Intelligence of Dogs[2] in 1994 which lists the ranking of 130+ breeds in regard to how smart they are. The book was revised in 2006. Due in part to a lack of other sources, it's a popular method of comparing dog breeds. The ranking only shows one aspect of how intelligence is rated: working and obedience (ability to follow commands). Breeds were rated via survey forms sent out to 199 trial judges from the AKC and the Canadian Kennel Club, who based their opinions only on what they witnessed in the show ring. Later, owners were asked to rate their dog's abilities and some of the breeds fell into the same ranking order.

Only based on command elements, breeds were placed into 6 different groups of intelligence levels. Please note that many breeds were tied.

- 10 breeds are listed under the 'brightest dogs'.
- The next grouping holds 21 breeds ranked #11 through #26 and are labeled 'excellent working dogs'.
- The 3rd grouping holds the next 30 breeds, ranked #27 through #39 and are under the label of 'above average working dogs'.
- This is followed by 41 breeds at #40 through #54 which, according to these findings, have 'average working/obedience ability.
- The 5th grouping consists of dogs with 'fair working/obedience intelligence' which lists out the next 22 breeds, ranking in place #55 through #69. The Chihuahua placed here, at #67.
- The last set is the final 11 breeds, taking the ranks of #70 to #79, found to have the 'lowest degree of working/obedience intelligence'.

According to the judges involved, Chihuahuas did just 'fair' when learning new commands. They needed up to 25 repetitions just to begin understanding a command and between 40 and 80 repetitions to show reliability, but even then did rather poorly without reminders. ***However***, as discussed ahead in the 'Commands' chapter, dogs, in general, need about 40 repetitions of a command to have a good understanding and 60 to 70 repetitions to have a really good understanding. Then, upward of 1,000+ to be reliable in all situations. So, don't let this ranking fool you into thinking that your Chihuahua cannot learn commands or any other sort of training.

How to Help Your Dog Reach His Potential: A dog needs to be allowed to learn. For example, a neglected dog that lived in a crate would, sadly, have few skills. He would have the *capacity* to learn, but without being given opportunities, he would not assimilate any new information that furthered his intellect. The key for a dog reaching his potential is to be given plenty of chances to acquire information and hone skills. *There are things that you can do:*

1. Allow your dog to use his canine senses.

Bring your dog to a new environment or stay out with him in the yard to let him see, smell, hear, and explore. Hide a special treat in the house and encourage him to find it by smell alone. Now hide a treat and see if he can learn to find it by reading your cues of shakes or nods. Every chance to do these sorts of things allows the gears in a dog's mind to work.

2. Teach your dog word comprehension.

A dog can easily understand 165 words on average, as many as a two-year-old toddler. Your own dog is ready and able, and here is how you can do this: Choose 3 objects that are quite different from each other such as a cup, a ball, and a rope toy. Hold up each one, saying the corresponding word out loud. Do this over and over. Once you think your dog is ready, line up all 3 and give a command to grab one of them. Did he do it? Great! Give a treat reward and praise. Practice a lot, so that there's plenty of repetition. Next week, teach 3 more. Keep it going and try to use the words as much as you can so that your dog doesn't forget.

3. Teach your dog commands.

All dogs are ready to learn commands; it just takes enough repetition. It's a surefire way for a dog to gain self-confidence, it leads to better behavior, and it allows you to show off how smart your dog is.

1 Vlastimil Hart, Petra Nováková, Erich Pascal Malkemper†, Sabine Begall†, Vladimír Hanzal, Miloš Ježek, Tomáš Kušta, Veronika Němcová, Jana Adámková, Kateřina Benediktová, Jaroslav Červený and Hynek Burda. Dogs are sensitive to small variations of the Earth's magnetic field. Hart et all. Frontiers in Zoology 2013, 10:80. http://www.frontiersinzoology.com/content/10/1/80.

2 Coren, Stanley (1995). The Intelligence of Dogs: A Guide To The Thoughts, Emotions, And Inner Lives Of Our Canine Companions. New York: Bantam Books. ISBN 0-553-37452-4.

Puppy Care

Supplies to Have

Things will run much smoother if you plan ahead and have most, if not all, of the needed care items already set up before you bring your puppy home.

This list is also ideal for current owners of adult dogs that are facing certain issues such as accidents in the house, things being chewed, separation anxiety struggles, and more.

1 Defined Area.

You will want to have a method of having one defined area. Letting a puppy or dog roam the house is a surefire way to have puddles of pee everywhere, non-toy items chewed, increased feelings of isolation when home alone, and of course, it can be dangerous. Even as a puppy matures, the need for a defined space is there, which we will expand on in a moment.

Let's see options:

☹ **Crate. There are serious downsides to this:**
- Crates (also referred to as cages) are often too small; being in a confining, claustrophobic space can cause a dog to feel exceedingly stressed.
- In turn, stress can cause a pup to bark and/or whine much more than otherwise, or even become depressed.
- It does nothing at all to stop a puppy from going to the bathroom; puppies will urinate and eliminate when their bodies have to regardless of where they are.
- These do not allow enough room for a puppy to have all of his necessities to be as happy and comfortable as possible.

☺ **Gates. Gates to block off a room can work to some extent, at least to keep a puppy in one area; however, the downsides to gating off a room include:**
- Pee and poo able to be deposited over the entire room.
- Too large of an area to truly help with separation anxiety; toys and other aids will be too far spread out and may roll away or otherwise become inaccessible.
- Does not limit destructive chewing (unless the entire room is cleared out).
- Can be dangerous unless the whole room is puppy-proofed.
- Higher chances that a dog will not rest/sleep on his bed, which is needed for proper support.

✓ **Canine playpen.** The right canine playpen is beneficial in so many ways. Certain Iris playpens are recommended, which are 24" or 34" high (8 or 21 square feet, respectively) sturdy open-topped pens that are portable, and those with doors are often best. Note that extensions can be obtained if you decide to increase the footprint. Alternatively, portable 'pop-up' playpens can work as well (these have roofs). Benefits of a playpen include:

- Pee and poo are confined to pee pads. Within other areas of the pen, there will be a bed, toys, food and water, and any needed separation anxiety aids. The remaining area should be lined with pee pads. Since dogs rarely soil their own belongings, urine and stools will most often be deposited on the pads.
- Creates a 'den', which canines instinctively perceive as being secure and safe. This limits barking, whining, and stress.
- Keeps all of a dog's necessities in one spot; toys and other items cannot be moved or roll away to the point of being inaccessible.
- Higher chances a dog will rest/sleep in his bed.
- Offers a safe area for both when home alone and any time that you need your dog to be in one spot.
- Limits destructive chewing.

 Since playpens are always evolving, yet this book is static, current recommendations can be found on the Supplies page of the PetChiDog site, which is updated as we evaluate new options that may emerge. You can reach this by entering any page of PetChiDog.com; Look to the navigation which is in alphabetical order, and choose 'Supplies'.

2 Pee pads. Though your ultimate goal will be to potty train your pup to go to the bathroom in a designated bathroom area (preferably outside in most cases), pee pads will be needed until housebreaking is complete. And, even so, many fully-trained dogs still need these as back-up when home alone (see info regarding pee pads under the aforementioned 'canine playpen').

3 Perhaps a carrier crate (ask the vet). Sometimes veterinarians will ask that puppies be brought to the office in a carrier crate. This is done to help control the spread of infectious disease (such as kennel cough or bacterial lung infections) and to keep all of the animals under control.

Once you locate an excellent vet for your puppy, ask ahead of time what the protocol is for bringing your puppy to the office. Note that a puppy or dog should not be transported in this while in the car, as this offers no protection in the case of a car accident. See ahead for details on car seats.

4 Food. This includes both the 'old' kibble that the puppy has been eating and the 'new' kibble if you decide to change brands. Most puppies do not do well with quick changes in diet. For this reason, you'll want to have enough of both 'old' and 'new' food to make a gradual changeover. Many breeders offer samples of puppy food to new owners; however, the samples may only last a few days. Find out the exact brand and variety that the puppy has been eating and be sure that you have enough for two weeks, which is usually sufficient to make the switch.

Note that it does not matter how wonderful of a breeder it is that you obtained your puppy from, or how healthy your puppy appears to be, there's a good chance that you will indeed want to switch to a new food. Breeders have multiple dogs to take care of, and due to financial constraints, may opt for less-than-ideal kibble. Furthermore, a puppy may appear to be doing fine on a certain brand, but you must think about the long-term effects of an inferior diet.

You will also want to have dry snacks (which are fed in between meals), moist treats (which are given as a reward for housebreaking, command training, and more), and dental treats (one doled out each day).

Details about meals and snacks are ahead in the 'Feeding and Nutrition' chapter.

5 Honey. This is to treat hypoglycemia, which is a fast and sometimes dangerous drop in blood sugar levels. In severe cases without quick treatment, this can be fatal. Though it can happen to any breed at any age, it is much more common with toy breeds and young pups, and it is a condition that the Chihuahua is prone to.

Feeling the stress of a new home and/or not eating on a regular basis are two common triggers. At the first signs of hypoglycemia (trouble walking, confusion, weakness), a dollop of honey can be put on a fingertip for the puppy to lick off or gently rubbed on the gums or the roof of the puppy's mouth.

Some sources list Karo® syrup (corn syrup) as a quick remedy to level out blood sugar; however, it may have laxative properties. For this reason, honey is a good choice. Be sure to use pure honey and not a spread with additives. In severe instances of hypoglycemia, urgent vet care will be needed. There are more details about hypoglycemia under 'Health – Other: Hypoglycemia'.

6 Leash, harness, collar, and ID tags.

- Leashes. Two are recommended, a short 4 or 6-foot soft-handle leash and a retractable leash.
- Harness. This is not a breed that should be on leash and collar due to being prone to collapsed trachea, which can have life-altering consequences. A harness distributes pressure across the chest, shoulders, and back, as opposed to collars in which all pressure is placed on the neck.
- Collar (optional). While you should not connect a leash to a collar, you may still wish to opt for a lightweight collar that serves to hold your pup's ID tag.
- ID tag. Even microchipped dogs should wear an ID tag since microchips are useless unless someone has a scanner. The ID tag should list your cell phone number.

Since choosing the right accessories is vitally important for both puppies and adults, for full details please refer to 'Care Items – Chihuahuas of All Ages: Leash, Harness, Collar, & ID Tags'.

7 Grooming supplies. This should include quality shampoo, conditioner, leave-in coat spray, paw wax, nose balm, ear cleaning solution, brushes, a comb (just for long coat Chi), a canine toothbrush, canine toothpaste, grooming wipes, and eye wipes. For full details, please refer to the 'Grooming' chapter.

8 Food and water bowls. Food and water bowls should be stainless-steel or ceramic. Plastic bowls, even those labeled as BPA and/or PVC free, can cause issues including gradual discoloration of the nose. In addition, they scratch easily (it is within tiny nicks that bacteria can begin to grow) and are notorious for sliding around.

Be sure to use appropriately sized bowls; with over-sized dishes, it's easy for a puppy to bang his head against the rim when eating or drinking, and if your Chi has a molera (soft spot on the skull), you will especially want to avoid this. You may find that a bowl set, secured into a non-slip base, works great for keeping spills and messes to a minimum, as well as keeping the bowls in place. Since new puppies need to have food and water available at all times, you may wish to have two sets of food and water bowls. If not, be prepared to move them back and forth from the kitchen to the playpen, as needed.

9 A method of offering filtered water. While it is very common for pets to drink unfiltered tap water, this is possibly one of the biggest mistakes that owners can make, and one that can significantly impact a dog's health and lifespan.

The presence of toxins in tap water is well-known, and in fact, the EPA allows for 'acceptable' levels of many of them. The top 12 contaminants are fluoride (proven to be toxic to canines), chlorine, lead, mercury, PCB chemicals, arsenic, perchlorate, dioxins, DDT, HCB, dacthal, and MtBE. Most of these have been proven to cause serious issues including but not limited to thyroid imbalances, respiratory problems, cell damage, kidney damage, liver damage, nerve damage, seizures, and cancer.

In addition, Chromium-6, the carcinogen brought to light in the Erin Brockovich movie, is currently in the drinking water of over 200 million Americans.

Methods to offer clean, toxin-free water include giving bottled spring water, installing a filter to your kitchen tap, or using a filtering water pitcher. In regards to a pitcher, take note that some are great and some not so much. At the time of this writing, our top recommended water pitcher is made by Aquagear and is highly effective; it filters out Chromium-6, fluoride, lead, mercury, chlorine, arsenic, cadmium, chromium, copper, selenium, and more. Further details regarding unfiltered tap water are found under 'Feeding and Nutrition: Water'.

10 Dog bed. You may have planned to have your new puppy sleep in your bed, perhaps envisioning this as an enjoyable sleeping arrangement; however, there are many benefits to having a quality bed for your canine family member:

- Sleeping in an owner's bed can be dangerous (the pup can tumble off or be accidentally rolled over or smothered).
- Sleeping in an owner's bed can make it much harder for a puppy or dog to settle down in his own spot when home alone.
- Even if your dog does sleep in your bed, you'll want to offer a doggie bed for resting and taking naps, particularly when you are not home.
- Lying on the floor (even on a blanket or throw rug) long-term, can be detrimental to the body. All dogs should have a quality mattress that offers proper support and cushioning.
- A bed helps keep a dog warm; cold intolerance is common for the Chihuahua breed.
- Certain beds, like bolster beds, offer a feeling of security; this aspect is further enhanced if the bed is placed in a playpen (see previous Item #1).

For puppies, an appropriately sized bolstered bed is recommended, and a self-warming bolstered bed is an option. For dogs that love resting on the floor, a flat mattress can be a good choice. For those 8+ years, an orthopedic, memory foam mattress is recommended. And, during the summertime, you may wish to additionally offer a raised cot (with or without a shade umbrella); these are fantastic to help keep dogs cool both indoors and out.

11 Toys. You might be amazed at how helpful toys can be. When you have the right ones for your puppy or dog, they can resolve a host of issues including helping a puppy cope with teething, stopping destructive chewing, keeping a dog busy both when he's home alone and when you don't have time to offer attention at the moment, helping to resolve separation anxiety, boosting a dog's activity level, and as a means to create a strong owner-dog bond.

For new puppies, you'll want to have at least 3 to 4 teething toys. And, for all ages, other helpful toys include interactive toys, treat dispensing toys, chew toys, fetch toys, and for those that need it, a companion toy. For full details please refer to 'Care Items -Chihuahuas of all Ages: Toys'.

12 Car Seat. If you will be driving at all, even locally, with your dog in the car, not to use a canine car seat or car safety restraint is blatantly putting your canine family member at risk for injury and even death. In addition to this very vital reason, the right sort of car seat can help keep a dog comfortable and lessen motion sickness. For full details, please refer to 'Care Items – Chihuahuas of All Ages: Car Seats'.

13 Enzyme Cleanser. Urine contains certain enzymes that are not washed away with regular soap and water. If your pup pees inside the house (and most puppies will indeed have at least a few accidents) and the spot is not cleaned correctly, lingering odors will remain. Canines, with their amazing sense of smell, can pick up on those odors. It is akin to a blaring announcement that endlessly repeats '*This* is the bathroom area!', which greatly increases the odds that the pup will urinate there again.

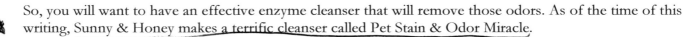

So, you will want to have an effective enzyme cleanser that will remove those odors. As of the time of this writing, Sunny & Honey makes a terrific cleanser called Pet Stain & Odor Miracle.

14 Poo bags. While your puppy may only be going to the bathroom outside in your yard for the first couple of months (a pup must have all puppy vaccinations before going to public places), you may still want to clean up the poo. If feces are left out in the yard this sets you and other family members up for stepping in it, it sets your dog up to try to nibble at it (coprophagia), and it can attract flies.

Once you start taking your puppy for walks, you'll definitely want to have these. Even if your neighborhood does not have posted rules regarding responsible pet ownership, leaving dog poop on sidewalks, along walking routes, or anywhere in the neighborhood is a surefire way to aggravate your neighbors. An easy method of bringing these along is to obtain a small 'poop bag dispenser' which clips to the leash.

15 Flea & Tick Protection. Puppies and dogs can easily catch fleas, even in the cleanest of homes. These tiny pests can jump 3 to 6 feet from dog to dog and can live embedded in carpeting inside and moist shady places outside. And, ticks are a concern in just about every state in the US; some more than others. While they are most active in the summer, they can awake from winter hibernation if there are several days without snow.

Fleas can cause tapeworm infection and plague (yes, this can still occur and is carried by fleas that pick this up from rodents), and a flea infestation can cause terrible itching for a dog, while the flea population spreads throughout the house. Ticks can cause disease including Lyme disease (spread through the blacklegged tick), ehrlichiosis (a bacterial disease spread by the Lone Star tick), and Rocky Mountain Spotted Fever (caused by several types of ticks).

While protection is important, the use of chemicals (pesticides) can cause terrible reactions. For this reason, you may want to opt for chemical-free products. Some natural elements that repel fleas and ticks include bergamot, cedarwood, citronella, eucalyptus, geranium, lavender, lemon, lemongrass, peppermint, rosemary, sage, and sweet orange.

Keep in mind that some heartworm protection products also protect against fleas and/or ticks. If so, there is no reason to 'double-up'. So, you'll want to check the labeling on what you are using to see what it covers. More details regarding ticks are found under, 'Summer Care: #7 Protect From Summertime Insects' and more information regarding fleas is found under 'Health – Other: Fleas'.

16 A good veterinarian. While not a 'supply' per se, we are listing this here, since it is so vitally important.

Most breeders, as stated in the sales contract, will ask that you bring your new puppy to a veterinarian within a certain amount of time from the day that you take your pup home. This is generally within 24 to 72 hours. This is to confirm that you received a healthy puppy.

But, no matter if you just obtained a new puppy from a breeder, adopted an older dog from a shelter, or brought home a dog of any age by any other means, a complete veterinary examination should be scheduled. New puppies need to stay on their vaccination and de-worming schedule. Older dogs may need booster shots. Dogs of all ages need to be seen to ensure that they are in good health. If there are any issues, you'll want them caught early.

The best veterinarian may not be the closest one to your home. You may wish to interview with two to three within reasonable driving distance. You can ask to set up an appointment specifically to meet the veterinarian and spend time getting to know about him/her and their practice. You may want to ask:

- How many Chihuahuas do you currently have as patients? Ideally, you will want a veterinarian who has experience with this breed.
- What is the protocol for issues that may occur on weekends/after-office hours? You will want to know that if something happens on a Saturday morning at 2 AM that someone will be able to help you.
- How long have you been in practice? While a new veterinarian may be wonderful, you may want to opt for a vet that has several years of experience.
- What are your rules for bringing in a sick puppy? You will want this answer to be that the ill puppy is crated and perhaps even brought in through a separate door; when you bring your pup there for a simple checkup, you will want your own dog protected from potentially very contagious diseases.

Optional Items - Aside from the aforementioned items, there are some other things that you may wish to have, depending on your exact circumstances and how your pup is doing. It can take a bit of time before you may know if any of the following items are needed::

Carrier method. A sling bag, carry-pack, or pet stroller can be very helpful to bring your puppy or dog out and about to a wide range of places (even those that may otherwise not allow pets) and/or if you will be taking very long walks that may be too much for your pup to handle.

Clothing. It's common for young pups to have trouble regulating body temperature, and this is especially true of toy breeds and particularly the Chihuahua. This breed can easily become quite chilled, even inside. A small, soft shirt can be just the thing to keep a pup cozy warm. Chi of all ages may appreciate a sweater or vest when it's brisk out, and a waterproof jacket or coat can be a great help during heavy rain and/or in the wintertime. More information is ahead under 'Exercise & Activity: Dressing for the Weather'.

Separation Anxiety Aids. Since puppies require less sleep and gain more awareness as each month goes by, things may seem to be just fine at first, but then as your pup matures, there may be separation anxiety issues that develop. For this, you will want to refer to 'Situational Issues: Separation Anxiety'.

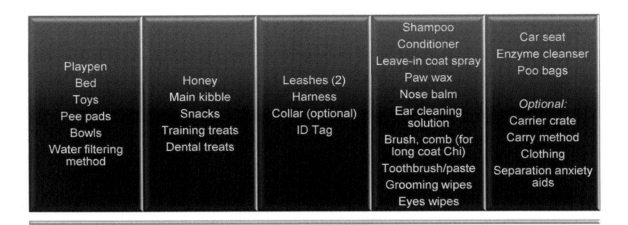

Summary of Items to Have for a New Puppy				
Playpen Bed Toys Pee pads Bowls Water filtering method	Honey Main kibble Snacks Training treats Dental treats	Leashes (2) Harness Collar (optional) ID Tag	Shampoo Conditioner Leave-in coat spray Paw wax Nose balm Ear cleaning solution Brush, comb (for long coat Chi) Toothbrush/paste Grooming wipes Eyes wipes	Car seat Enzyme cleanser Poo bags *Optional:* Carrier crate Carry method Clothing Separation anxiety aids

Puppy Proofing Your Home

Bringing a puppy or dog home requires preparation to make the house a safe one. It only takes one moment for you to lose track of where your pup is, for your little guy or gal to mouth and swallow something, be injured, or be poisoned. For this reason, puppy-proofing should be done beforehand, and on a regular basis going forward.

While this type of organizing of the home and yard is called 'puppy proofing' it is applicable to dogs of all ages, even seniors. Never assume 'Oh, my dog won't have any interest in that', because a dog will mouth something first and *then* decide if he has interest in it. Nothing is off limits.

Both Indoors & Out

- **Plants.** There are hundreds of indoor and outdoor plants and flowers that are poisonous. Outdoors, erect fencing or never fail in your supervision. Indoors, remove plants or place them up high and out of reach. Some of the most common plants in or around homes that are toxic include azalea, Boston ivy, carnation, daffodil, delphinium, Easter lily, gladiola, iris, ivy, marigold, mistletoe, peace lily, poinsettia, and tomato plants (entire plant except the ripe fruit).

Indoors

- **Medications.** Keep all medications, vitamins, and any dog supplements, in a safe area up high. Bottles can be pulled off of end tables or other low surfaces and a determined dog can quickly chew through a plastic container.
- **Trash.** Toy breeds can tip over small trash cans. Put these up high where your dog cannot get into them. Sanitary supplies and used razors are the most common trash dangers.
- **Toilets.** If you have a youngster in your home who uses a step to reach the toilet, your dog may find a way to use it also.
- **Cleaning supplies.** Lower cabinets that hold cleansing agents should be secured with childproof latches. Any time you use chemical cleansers, keep your puppy away from the area. With a curious puppy, fumes can enter the eyes and be inhaled; both of which can be harmful.
- **Electrical cords.** The shape and texture of these can be tempting to a teething puppy or a dog of any age that likes to chew. If the casing is chewed through, this can cause burns in the mouth and/or electrocution (which can be fatal). Tie up loose electrical cords with wrap ties and keep them out of sight. You can also run cords through cord concealers or even PVC pipe to keep them inaccessible. *[Photo: Dexter; Photo courtesy of YankeeBelle Chihuahuas]*

- **Hanging cords from window shades and curtains.** A puppy can get entangled and strangled by these. Tie them up, out of reach.
- **Small objects.** Keep small objects (coins, jewelry, pens, yarn, dental floss, rubber bands, paper clips, tiny children's toys, etc.) out of reach. These are all choking hazards, and some (coins, jewelry, etc.) can cause toxic poisoning.
- **Stairs.** If there is an open stairway that presents a possible fall hazard, block this off with a baby gate.
- **Cat litter boxes.** Many dogs will eat cat feces from the litter box if given a chance and this can be a dangerous health hazard since cat litter can cause intestinal obstruction. In addition, any intestinal worms the cat may have can be passed on to the dog (if the cat is in the process of being de-wormed, eggs and worms may be shedding into the feces). One solution is to place the litter box up high. Many owners choose the top of the dryer or washing machine.
- **Tobacco products.** Cigarettes, cigars, nicotine gum, and nicotine patches all contain substances that can be toxic or fatal to dogs.

Outdoors

- **Chemicals.** Cleaning supplies, gasoline, paint, lawn fertilizers, insecticides, and automobile supplies should be placed out of reach. Be especially cautious with rat/mice poison and antifreeze; these can taste fine to dogs but can be fatal if ingested.
- **Sharp objects.** Walk around your property and look for items that could be a hazard, such as upturned garden tools, exposed nails, or other sharp objects.
- **Poisonous mushrooms.** In North America, there are about 250 poisonous mushrooms. Unless you have extensively studied on this subject, it is near impossible to distinguish a toxic mushroom from a safe one, as they can look extremely similar. The green-spored parasol is the most frequently consumed poisonous mushroom in North America (it looks very much like the edible parasol mushroom) and grows prolifically on lawns. It is white with coarse brown scales; the gills (underneath) only turn greenish once the mushroom has fully matured.

Naming Your Puppy

Naming your puppy may involve a bit more than just choosing a name that sounds cute or has a nice ring to it. The right name can make training easier and can reduce confusion in the house if you have more than one pet.

Let's look at some factors that come into play:

Syllables. Both the number of syllables in the name and the beginning consonant sound will play a major factor. Dogs do learn to know their full names; however, they generally pay attention to just the first syllable of the word. That is why dog commands are very short. For example, 'Sit' instead of 'Sit down now'. When an owner does say, 'Sit down now', the dog is listening to and noticing the first syllable: 'Sit'. Therefore, if you name your pup 'Goliath', your pup will often respond to 'Gol'.

This does not mean that you need to choose a name with only one syllable. However, the name should have a strong sounding first syllable; as you will want your new pup to have an easy time learning his name.

Similar Names. If you have other pets in the home, it is best not to choose a name that begins with the same syllable as another pet. For example, 'Rocky' and 'Roxanne' or 'Andrea' and 'Andrew', as this can be very confusing for both of your pets. Names with strong second syllables that rhyme can cause mix-ups for pets as well, such as 'Boo' and 'Dew'. It will be best to choose a name that begins with a different sound than any other pets and any human family members for that matter too.

Unique or Popular? You may want to avoid choosing a very popular dog's name since this can be confusing if you have your little guy or gal at the dog park or another area that has lots of pets. This said, some of the most popular names are very endearing, so it *is* tempting.

Based on AKC registration of dogs in the US, let's look at the most common names:

Male dogs, top 10 in order: Max, Charlie, Buddy, Cooper, Jack, Rocky, Bear, Duke, Toby, and Tucker.

Female dogs, top 10 in order: Bella, Lucy, Daisy, Lola, Luna, Molly, Sadie, Sophie, Bailey, and Maggie.

And in looking at 5,086 submissions of PetChiDog site Members and visitors, the top 25 Chihuahua names are (in alphabetical order): Angel, Baby, Bella, Buddy, Chi Chi (or Chichi), Chica, Chico, Chloe, Coco (or Cocoa), Daisy, Gizmo, Honey, Lilly (or Lily), Lola, Luna, Max, Peanut, Penny, Poppy, Roxy (or Roxie), Sophie, Sugar, Teddy, Tinkerbell, and Zoey.

Though these each alone are not enough to have made the top 25, names that started with 'Little' were: Little Bear, Little Bit, Little Bits, Little Bit of Love, Little Brownie, Little Dane, Little Dude, Little Girl, Little Man, Little Blue, and Littles.

Teaching Your Puppy His/her Name: The sooner your puppy knows his/her name, the better. Calling out your pup's name can stop him right before he is about to have a housebreaking accident or is walking too far away from you.

Once you have chosen a name, you will want to use it as much as possible. Each time you wish to gain your pup's attention, say the name first before you say anything else. This should be said in a happy, yet confident tone. For example, 'Toby, dinner!', 'Toby, let's go for a walk', 'Toby, look at this toy!'.

If you have an opportunity to know in advance which puppy you will be purchasing, you can ask the breeder (or other person who has the puppy) to begin to say the chosen name to your pup, which will give him/her a great head start.

Giving Your Dog More Than One Name:
When you register your pup, he or she does not need to have just a first name. There is much more that you can do and there are several ways to do it.

You may want your dog to have a first name and a middle name or you maybe wish for him or her to have a regal sounding name consisting of three or even four words. The options are almost endless. Please note that the following applies at the time of this writing.

For AKC registration, you can give your puppy a name that is very long, up to 50 characters. However, the standard registration of a name is up to 36 characters; therefore, if you choose to go beyond that and up to the maximum of 50, it will cost $10 more to do so. Keep in mind that the space between each name does count as a character. For example Sir Charlie Cutie Pie has 18 letters; however, there are 3 spaces between the 4 words, giving you a total count of 21 characters which is under the 36 or 50 limit so you would be fine.

Option A: You can choose one name of 1 or 2+ words. Many owners will make sure that the common name that they call their dog is in there. For example, your puppy's registered name may be: Rowdy Rocking Cowboy; and then Cowboy would be the name that you commonly call your pup.

Option B: You may choose to have an 'also known as' in the official registered name. This is shown as 'AKA'. An example of this would be Living Life to the Limit AKA Cuddles.

Option C: You can have numbers in the name if you choose. These can be Arabic numbers such as 1, 2, or 3 or you can spell them out. The first option would look like this: *Smiling Each Day AKA Smiles 5*. The other option would look like this: *Smiling Each Day AKA Smiles Five*. When numbers are used, it is most often done by breeders who will choose similar if not exact names for each puppy, but then change the number that follows.

Words that are Not Permitted: Some words are not allowed to be part of a dog's name when registered with the AKC:

- 'Champion' anywhere in the name; this is reserved for dogs that have won at AKC show events.
- The name of the breed that they are, or any other official breed (a Chihuahua cannot be named 'Chihuahua, 'Beagle', etc.).
- Swear words.
- Male, Female, Bitch, Stud, Dam, or Sire.

- A registered Kennel name. Only breeders can do this, and they can only do so once they have proven to the AKC that they have had an established program for at least 5 years.

You can use the terms: Sir or Lady, and this is done a lot. For example, for a male one may choose something like Sir Winslow the Wonderful AKA Winds and for a female Lady Rose Petals AKA Flowers.

Introducing your Puppy to Family & Home

Please note that while the word 'puppy' is used quite a bit in this section, much of this will apply to an adult that is new to a home as well; after all, he is starting off somewhere different too!

No doubt you're excited and maybe even a bit nervous. This will be a time of change and transition for the new pup, you, and all members of the household. The key for things to go smoothly is to plan and prep.

The Overall Goal: A puppy needs a careful and organized introduction into your home. Without this, a new pup may become very stressed and overwhelmed. Stress on a dog of any age can cause not only emotional issues but also physical health problems, including hypoglycemia. It will be your job to show your new puppy his new world in a happy yet calm manner, orchestrate a smooth introduction to all the people and/or animals that will be his new family, and help him feel comfortable and welcomed.

Placement of Supplies: Have everything set up in advance. Things will be quite exciting, and you do not want the additional chaos of putting out the water bowl, setting up sleeping quarters, or running out to the store for forgotten items.

As we covered in 'Puppy Care: Supplies to Have', there are some items to have in advance. Let's talk about how to set these up and options for where to place them.

- **The playpen.** This will be your pup's special area, den, hideout, and little 'room' of safety. Your pup will rest here, sleep here, most likely go here voluntarily when he's exhausted and needs a break from interaction, and will stay here anytime that you are not home or cannot keep an eye on him.

  A pup should be safe within his playpen; but, certainly not isolated. The best spot for a playpen is in a well-lit, quiet corner of a room that is frequently used by the family. The living room, family room, or kitchen are often good choices. Do not place the pen near drafty doors or windows, in the path of glaring sunlight from windows, or too close to AC or heating vents.

  Also, take note of the type of flooring. With wall-to-wall carpeting, consider obtaining a sheet of linoleum that the pen can be placed over; this can be found at home improvement stores. This allows for easy cleanup, in the case of urine or stool deposits.

- **Toys.** Some toys can be left out in the main living area; keeping them in a toy box or container will help you keep track of them. Reserve a few toys for the playpen. Toys that will help your puppy when he's alone in the playpen include a 'stay busy' toy, teething toys, and if you opt to obtain one, a companion toy. These toys are discussed in detail under 'Care Items - Chihuahuas of All Ages: Toys'.

- **Bed.** The bed should be placed in the playpen, near or against one of the pen's walls.

- **Food and water bowls.** New puppies need to have access to food at all times until the age of 3 months, and water must be available at all times for dogs of all ages. Your two options are to have two sets of bowls (one for the kitchen and one for the playpen) or to move them back and forth as needed. If you opt for two sets of bowls, the bowls should be identical since puppies and dogs can become *very* attached to these.

  When your pup grows just a bit older (3 or 4 months old), there will be a third option; this is to have kibble in a treat-release toy for times in the playpen (it's a terrific method to help keep a dog busy and occupied) and to have water bowls in each area.

- **Pee pads.** These will be placed in the playpen on any area of the flooring that is not occupied by the bed, toys, or bowls. While your goal may be to house train your puppy to go to the bathroom outside (our recommended method), puppies have very little bladder and bowel control, so the pads will be for bathroom needs that occur when your pup is in his playpen. Even adults will need these if they are left home longer than they can hold their needs.

- **Leash and harness.** When you are home and supervising your pup, the leash should either be on your puppy as a tethering supervision method (as explained in 'Housebreaking') or very easily accessible. You may want to keep the harness on your puppy. This is because puppies may have to go to the bathroom as often as every 1 or 2 hours; you don't want to be taking the harness off and on that often, and doing so can interfere with the need to get your pup outside quickly. Do, however, take the harness off at night when your puppy is sleeping.

- **Training treats.** Take a small portion of these, place them in an air-tight zipped plastic sandwich bag, and have this near the exit door. You'll want to be able to grab these as you're taking your puppy out, as reward for housebreaking.

- **Kibble and snacks.** Keep these in a dark, cool area. Often, a lower kitchen cabinet is a good choice. Be sure to keep sealing the bag tightly. If you buy kibble in bulk and it tends to go stale, obtain an air-tight dog food storage container.

- **Bathing supplies.** Since most puppies do best with baths in the kitchen sink, you may want to store these in your kitchen.

- **Grooming supplies.** Brushes and other grooming tools should be in a basket or other container to keep them all together for easy access. Daily grooming wipes, if used to help control allergies, should be kept near the entrance door.

Note: Once you decide on where to place the water dish, playpen, toys, and more, do not change the locations if at all possible. Your puppy needs to know exactly where to go for what he is in need of.

Introduction to People: All of your friends and extended family may wish to be there for the arrival of your new puppy; however, it is best if he meets his immediate new family first and is introduced to friends, neighbors, and other family members at a later date. If meeting others occurs within the first couple of months, this should be done at home; you will not want to bring a puppy out to public places until he has had all of his puppy shots.

Introduction to Human Family Members: If you have other immediate family members, ask them to be sitting quietly in a room, for your arrival back with your puppy. A sudden barrage of loud voices, pets, and hugs from people that have rushed toward a small pup can be frightening, even though all intentions are good.

When you arrive home, an introduction should be made to each individual person, one at a time, so that the pup can gain a sense of their smell, voice, and touch. Children and adults alike should be asked to sit down to be at the puppy's level to say hello in a calm and pleasant tone. Each person should have a small treat; too many treats and your puppy's tummy may be full before he meets everyone. Expect the pup to sniff and be receptive to gentle petting; however, a pup's mind is bouncing around, with very limited focusing ability. No one should feel bad if the pup isn't all that interested in long cuddling sessions. That will come later.

Do not allow everyone to pick up the puppy and lift him into the air. Yes, it is tempting. But, suddenly being swept up before having a sense of who it is that is holding him can be very overwhelming on the first day.

Introduction to the Home: After spending 5 to 10 minutes with each person, the pup is ready for a tour of your home. He will need to get a solid sense of his surroundings. Show him where he can always depend on the water and food bowls to be, his playpen, his bed, and his toys. As you do, say the word of each item, 'water', 'toy', 'bed', etc. This should be done many times per day for the first week or two. You don't need the pup to interact with any given item; this is to help him learn where things are and to make a connection between the words and the objects.

Keep the tour inside for now. When your puppy is a bit older and has had all of his puppy shots, walk him around the perimeter of your yard. Training your puppy where his 'territory' ends may come into play in case your puppy gets loose.

While showing your puppy his new home is important, do not expect him to be overly aware right away. Young puppies have a hard time fully comprehending their surroundings. They can appear to be looking directly at a bright new toy but ignore it and saunter over to a table leg. They can scamper away when someone is petting them, plop down when called over, and otherwise be oblivious to what, exactly, is happening.

Introduction to Other Pets: If you have another dog or any other pets, this will be a crucial aspect of bringing your new puppy home. One cannot expect current pets to suddenly be socialized in the acceptance of a new dog and at the same time expect a new puppy to instantly know how to get along with other animals. It is unwise to assume that because a pet has a wonderful personality that they will become instant best friends with the new arrival. A sudden change of having a new puppy in the home can trigger quite a state of chaos if your pets are not ready.

Beforehand - Whether you have cats, dogs, or both, you should take time well *before* you bring your new puppy home to make sure that the cat(s) and/or dog(s) will get along well with a new dog. You can do this by having a friend, family member, neighbor, coworker, or other who has a dog come over for several visits. Ideally, it is best if you can find someone who has a Chihuahua. If not, the 2nd best option would be a helper who has a dog in the same class (toy breed).

When testing your current dog's behavior to a new dog, allow the animals to feel each other out. Keep a watchful eye for any trouble. If a dog stares at another, in almost a frozen state, this can be the posture displayed before biting. When testing your current cat's behavior to a new dog, the cat should have an 'escape route'; if she feels threatened, she may choose to use it instead of scratching. Allow the animals to feel each other out and keep a watchful eye for any intolerance. If your current cat does not tolerate a small dog, your new puppy could be very injured in a fight.

If you are *sure* that your current pet(s) is tolerable of another dog in the home, all that should be needed is a small period of adjustment.

The period of adjustment – There are a few things to keep in mind, to help everything run smoothly while both animals adjust to the new living arrangements:

- For the first 'meet and greet', allow the animals to sniff each other and do not force any interaction.
- If you have a cat, give the cat an escape route. If not, she may scratch at the puppy as a defense mechanism.
- Each pet should have their own personal areas for resting and sleeping. Food should be kept well apart; separate corners of the kitchen is best.
- If you have an older, established dog, keep careful watch when the new puppy is eating; an older dog may try to show dominance by taking his food.
- Your current pet(s) may feel jealousy if you lavish all of your attention on the new puppy. Be sure to give attention to established pets as well.
- It is not a bad sign if the animals ignore each other. This means that they do not see the other as a threat. In time, a dog or cat will get to know your new puppy and they can then become best friends.

We offer more details on resolving problems under 'Situational Issues: Having More Than One Dog'.

The Importance of Early Socialization and Desensitization

While puppies will become accustomed to many elements simply by being near them or experiencing them, it's important to ensure that your pup accepts all that surrounds him in his daily life. If not, fears can develop regarding certain aspects. Once a fear develops, it can be challenging to reverse it. Here are some tips:

Touch. It is imperative that a puppy learns right away that being touched will be a regular part of the day. It's beneficial to begin touch desensitization from day one; this way, by the time a pup's cognitive abilities are completely developed, he will already be accustomed to being groomed and handled. If not, you may find yourself with a dog that reacts badly when you try to brush him or refuses to let you take care of his teeth.

- Each day, take 5 to 10 minutes to brush the entire body. Don't forget all legs, armpit area, and even the tail.

- Run your finger over your puppy's gums and teeth; this prepares a pup to get ready for dental brushings.
- Wipe the eye area once per day. This will remove tiny debris that can irriate the eyes and can help prevent tear staining.
- Swipe down the coat with grooming wipes every few days. If there are urine splashes or small bits of feces stuck to the rear end, clean this area with a tushie wipe.
- Touch and handle each paw; this will prepare a pup for having the nails trimmed and having paw wax applied.
- While you may do this already if you are using the tethering method during house training, putting a pup's harness on and off and attaching the leash several time a day will help prepare a pup for being taken for walks.
- If there are other household members, have them participate in this as well. Down the line, you do not want your dog to be okay with you, but not others.

Sounds. While there should not be TVs blasting, machinery running non-stop, and other constant loud noises that will keep your puppy in a state of stressed alertness, do not walk on eggshells. You'll want your puppy to become used to normal household sounds.

This includes the microwave beeping, the doorbell ringing, the blender mixing, fans turning on, and so forth. The one exception that many dogs simply cannot tolerate is the vacuum cleaner. When you do need to vacuum, your pup may need to be placed in his playpen.

Events. Prepare to be anything but a homebody. While you will need to wait until your puppy has had all of his puppy shots before taking him out to public places (and we recommend waiting 2 weeks past this point), once your pup is old enough, it'll be time to get out there. Puppies that are socialized at a young age learn to behave well in a wide variety of settings and situations.

Walks around the neighborhood are great for daily exercise. But, heading out to parks, new walking routes, stores, dog-friendly restaurants, fairs, lakes, and so forth allow your puppy to gain confidence with new situations, sounds, people, and all of the elements out in the world. The topic of socialization is explored fully in 'Behavioral Training: Socialization and Desensitization'.

Falling into a Schedule

While you will want to have an organized, regular schedule for several aspects of care, the exact times that you do these routine tasks will vary depending on your work or school hours and your windows of opportunity.

Having a new canine family member is meant to be fun and an improvement in your life, not stressful. So, expect for there to be a period of adjustment while you get used to a new routine. In time, it will feel natural to brush your dog on certain days, wake up for early morning walks, apply paw wax or nose balm without giving it a second thought, and so on. Let's look at a guideline for common care tasks:

Daily

- Meals given 3 times per day (kibble left out at all times until age of 3 months), snacks given several times per day
- Water refreshed throughout the day
- Food and water bowls cleaned
- Brush the teeth
- Wipe the eye area
- Wipe the coat, if allergies and as needed if unclean
- Walks, at least 2 times per day, 20 minutes minimum each
- Command training (highly recommended)
- Fetch or other play activity, 15 to 20 minutes
- Take your pup out for housebreaking multiple times per day. Frequency will vary depending on the hours you are home.

Every 3 days

- Brush the coat, using a leave-in coat spray

Weekly

- Apply paw wax
- Apply nose balm, if puppy is prone to dry nose

Every 2 to 3 weeks

- Flea and tick repellent, if using an all-natural product

Every 3 weeks

- Give a bath

Monthly

- Heartworm protection (follow vet guidelines)

Every 6 Weeks

- Trim or file nails

How to React to Whining and Crying

Do be aware that it is normal for young puppies to cry when first in a new home. It is a big adjustment to go from the dam and littermates to a new environment. It's hard not to take it personally and wonder if you are doing something wrong. However - barring any health issues – there is nothing wrong, your puppy just needs a bit of time to adjust.

This phase will pass and usually only lasts a week or so. You can help by offering all of the comforts needed, which includes a warm place to sleep and toys to cuddle up to. If the breeder gave you an item with the scent of the puppy's littermates and/or dam, placing this with the pup will help as well.

It's normal to feel confused about when to go over to a crying puppy and when to ignore it. Human instinct tells us to rush over and offer comfort. However, in some instances, you will want the puppy to learn to self-soothe. If you go to a puppy each time he cries, he will determine that crying equals attention. Then, instead of outgrowing this phase, it can continue for quite some time.
How you react will depend on the puppy's age and whether it is daytime or nighttime.

Young pup, less than 3 months old, nighttime

Give attention at certain intervals so that the puppy receives a message that he is not truly alone, but does not think that each time he cries, someone will come running. During this first month, it will be a personal decision as to how often you check on him. Keep in mind that a pup may cry himself back to sleep within 10 to 15 minutes. So, a check every couple of hours, after that initial 15 minutes, can be done if you can handle the sleep interruptions.

 When you do check on him, assess the area for any drafts or over-heating, be sure that the pup is in his bed, offer a soft toy to cuddle up to, and give a few pets. If you suspect that the pup is thirsty, but confused about how to reach his water, assist him with this.

Young pup, less than 3 months old, daytime

If you are busy doing things in the house and you have your puppy in his playpen or other area, and he is whining, do not ignore your tasks, but do let him know that you hear and acknowledge his communication.

If possible, every 20 minutes or so, walk over to say hello (not in a soothing way, but in a matter-of-fact way) and offer a few pets and a smile. Then, if you are busy, move on to what you were doing. So again, not every time your puppy cries, but at intervals so that he learns that he has a loving family, but that crying does not equal instant attention.

3 months old & older, nighttime

At this age, you do not want to respond to crying at night unless you feel there is a legitimate bathroom need. If so, with lights as dim as possible and with making as little noise as possible, bring your puppy to his designated bathroom area. Only speak to say, 'Good, dog' and no more. This must be a serious time; any interaction, including speaking, can send the wrong message that whining to wake you up equals attention. Quietly bring him back to his area and leave it at that.

If you are rather sure that there is not a bathroom need, you will want to ignore any calls for attention. This is easier said than done and certainly goes against human instinct to rush to one's calls for 'help'. However, if you know that your puppy is safe and comfortable, you will want to offer the important lesson of self-soothing. This will allow your puppy to mature into a confident, emotionally strong dog.

Now, this is not to say that a pup should be on his own. You can give him tools to help. This includes a treat-release toy that holds kibble (great for pups that wake up too early in the morning), a 'stay busy' toy (though the noise of that may keep you awake!), and/or a companion toy. Details about these are under 'Care Items - Chihuahuas of All Ages: Toys'.

3 months old & older, daytime

Your pupppy is now at an age that being alone for certain periods during the day should be expected. This applies to when you are away, but also when home, but busy. Now is the time to set the foundation that you cannot dote over your pup every moment. If not, you'll find your household responsibilities slipping. When you are busy, ignore calls for attention, unless you suspect a bathroom need. When you are ready to offer ttention, do so during a quiet spell. You will not want your pup to think that whining equals you going over.

Vaccinations

Vaccinations are a crucial step in making sure a puppy will be protected against dangerous and often fatal canine diseases. Booster shots ensure that this protection carries on as a dog matures. There is no excuse not to have your puppy or dog vaccinated; having a clean home or not venturing outside often are not valid justifications.

Antibody Protection: A newborn puppy will have *some* antibody protection. Initially, this comes from the dam's bloodstream via the placenta.

The next level of immunity is from antibodies in the dam's milk. This milk (technically colostrum), only gives a puppy antibodies for a short period of time. Those antibodies will begin to lose effectiveness when the pup is between 6 to 20 weeks old.

It must be noted that a puppy will only receive antibodies against diseases for which the dam is up-to-date on vaccinations for (booster shots) or has been recently exposed to. For example, a dam that had not been vaccinated against or exposed to parvovirus, would not have any antibodies against parvovirus to pass along to her puppies. The puppies then would be susceptible to developing a parvovirus infection.

Why a Series of Vaccinations Must be Given: If a puppy was given just one vaccination, his body could block it. The age at which a puppy can effectively be immunized is linked to the number of antibodies in his system (what he received from the dam). If there are high levels of maternal antibodies that are present in a pup's bloodstream, these will prevent the vaccine from working. When the maternal antibodies drop to a low enough level in a puppy, immunization will be successful.

Because a puppy can be anywhere from 6 to 20 weeks old when this drop in maternal antibodies occurs, a series of shots are given to be sure one of them does its job. Therefore, if you have an older dog that received *some* of his vaccinations, but not the full round, he could be fully susceptible to all of the canine diseases that vaccinations are meant to protect him from.

The 'Window of Susceptibility': There is a period of time from 1 to 3 weeks in which the maternal antibodies in a puppy are too low to protect against disease, *but* are too high for a vaccine to work. This is called the 'window of susceptibility'. A puppy can still contract a disease even if he is right on schedule with vaccinations.

Therefore, any puppy that has not yet had his *full* round of puppy shots must be kept away from other animals and from any areas where there is even a *chance* that any animals passed through. Animals include pets and wildlife, with the exception of your own pets if you are 100% sure that they are up-to-date on vaccinations. As you will see on the schedule ahead, puppy shots are complete by the 12 to 16-week mark. We recommend waiting 2 weeks past that point, to be safe.

Vaccinations Before You Obtain Your Puppy: Depending on the age of your new puppy, a certain number of vaccinations will have already been given, usually between 2 and 3. At the time of this writing, 25 states in the US have laws that prohibit the sale of puppies under a certain age. For 23 of these states, the puppy must be at least 8 weeks old. For Virginia and Wisconsin, the age limit is 7 weeks old.

Even if your state does not currently have a law regarding this, it is unwise to take possession of a puppy under the age of 8 weeks old. They simply are not ready yet. Most reputable breeders will send puppies to new homes between the ages of 8 and 12 weeks. Before you bring home a new puppy, be sure to receive proof that vaccinations are up-to-date. If for some reason your puppy has not had any inoculations at all, your veterinarian will need to begin right away.

Typical Vaccination Schedule: While each veterinarian has their own exact vaccination schedule, vaccinations should always fall close to the schedule below.

5 weeks
- Parvovirus: For puppies at high risk of exposure to parvo

6 weeks
- Combination vaccine [1] without leptospirosis
- Coronavirus: where coronavirus is a concern

9 weeks
- Combination vaccine [1] without leptospirosis
- Coronavirus: where coronavirus is a concern

12 weeks or older (sometimes as old as 16 to 26 weeks)
- Rabies: Age at vaccination may vary according to your local laws

12 weeks
- Combination vaccine [1] [2]
- Leptospirosis: where leptospirosis is a concern, or if traveling to an area where it occurs
- Coronavirus: where coronavirus is a concern
- Lyme: where Lyme disease is a concern or if traveling to an area where it occurs

16 weeks
- Combination vaccine [2]
- Leptospirosis: where leptospirosis is a concern, or if traveling to an area where it occurs
- Coronavirus: where coronavirus is a concern
- Lyme: where Lyme disease is a concern or if traveling to an area where it occurs

Adult boosters [3]
- Combination vaccine
- Leptospirosis: where leptospirosis is a concern, or if traveling to an area where it occurs
- Coronavirus: where coronavirus is a concern
- Lyme: where Lyme disease is a concern or if traveling to an area where it occurs
- Rabies: Time interval between vaccinations may vary according to local law.

[1] *A combination vaccine,* often called a 5-way vaccine, usually includes adenovirus cough and hepatitis, distemper, parainfluenza, and parvovirus. Some combination vaccines may also include leptospirosis (6-way vaccine) and/or coronavirus (7-way vaccine).
[2] *Some puppies may need additional vaccinations against parvovirus after 15 weeks of age.* You will want to discuss this with your veterinarian.
[3] *According to the American Veterinary Medical Association, dogs at low risk of disease exposure may not need to be boostered yearly for most diseases.* You may want to speak to your vet about conducting routine titer tests. This is a method of measuring antibodies for certain diseases, via a blood

sample. If there are enough antibodies, your dog will not need a booster shot. If antibody levels are low, a booster will be recommended.

Do Small Dogs Receive Small Doses?

All dogs, regardless of breed or size, receive the same vaccine dose. When testing was done to ensure that vaccines could be considered safe, this was done using 'average' sized dogs. Over time, with millions of inoculations having been given, this has shown that the 'one size fits all' dose is generally considered safe.

Smaller dogs, however, do have adverse reactions more often than larger dogs. You may wonder if being given a 'half dose' is an option; there have not been enough studies yet to prove if this would be effective.

Reactions to Vaccinations: Immunizations stimulate the immune system in order to protect a dog against a specific infectious disease. While this is a vital step in keeping a dog healthy, this stimulation of the immune system may cause some symptoms that you should be prepared for.

Most are minor. In very rare cases, reactions can be more severe. Severe reactions are most commonly associated with vaccines for leptospirosis, rabies, and parvovirus. A comprehensive study of 1.2 million dogs by The American Veterinary Medical Association (https://www.avma.org) reports adverse reactions in 38.2 out of every 10,000 dogs.

Allergic reactions can range from mild to severe:

• **Mild.** Mild reactions include fever, sluggishness, and loss of appetite. These reactions usually resolve without any treatment needed.

• **Moderate.** There may be skin reactions (urticaria), which may show as hives or bumps. There can also be swelling that happens very quickly, redness on the dog's lips, around the eyes, and/or in the neck region. It is usually extremely itchy. Urticaria may progress to anaphylaxis, which is considered life-threatening. However, urticaria is the most common reaction in dogs if a reaction is to happen.

• **Severe.** The most severe reaction is anaphylaxis. This is a very sudden, life-threatening allergic reaction that causes breathing difficulties, collapse, and possible death. This is very rare. Symptoms usually include sudden vomiting, diarrhea, staggering, rapid drop in blood pressure, swelling of the larynx leading to airway obstruction (and inability to breathe), seizures, cardiovascular collapse, and in some cases, death. Both anaphylaxis (severe) and urticaria (moderate) are reactions that are triggered by antibodies that the immune system has made to some portion of the vaccine. If this is to happen, it usually occurs after the 2nd particular vaccine.

Diagnosis: There is no diagnostic test for urticaria or anaphylaxis; however, a quick physical exam will allow a veterinarian to recognize the signs immediately.

Treatment: Anaphylaxis (the severe reaction) usually occurs soon after vaccination, often while the dog is still in the veterinary clinic. Because anaphylaxis is an extreme emergency, the veterinarian will begin immediate emergency life support including establishing an open airway, oxygen administration, intravenous fluids to increase blood pressure, and medications such as epinephrine, diphenhydramine, and corticosteroids. Dogs that survive the first few minutes usually recover without lasting effects.

Urticaria (the moderate reaction) typically occurs soon after a vaccination; often while a dog is being driven home or shortly after a dog arrives back home. This requires you to return to the clinic for treatment immediately. Urticaria is usually treated successfully with injectable corticosteroids like dexamethasone or prednisone. Antihistamines such as diphenhydramine (Benadryl®) are only effective about 30% of the time for dogs with acute allergic reactions but may be given to help prevent recurrence of symptoms after corticosteroids wear off.

Mild reactions usually require no treatment. However, if symptoms persist for more than 8 hours, call your veterinarian.

Home Care and Prevention: Schedule vaccination appointments when you will be available to monitor your puppy for at least several hours after the vaccine is administered. Periodically check for any hives and/or swelling around the eyes.

Do not hesitate to call your veterinarian with any questions or concerns. While the veterinarian will record any adverse reactions to vaccines to possibly limit those vaccines from being given again, it is a good idea to keep a record for yourself.

A note about de-wormings: Parasites are a major concern for pets. We cover the details of this under 'Health – Other: Worms'. Just as with vaccinations, puppies need to be de-wormed on schedule. Some of the de-wormings will occur before you bring your new puppy home. The rest will be done when you bring your puppy to the vet. The typical schedule is at 2, 4, 6, and 8 weeks of age, then again at 3 months old and then 4 months old. After this, regular heartworm prevention will also cover these parasites.

Top Puppy Questions

While all of these aspects are covered throughout this book, sometimes it can help to have a summary all in one place.

Why is my new puppy acting sad?

It's hard not to take this personal. However, whining during the first week or so is normal. A pup just left the only home he ever knew and is in strange surroundings. Your puppy doesn't know you well enough yet to realize that you are a source of love and has not been in your home long enough to understand that he is in a place of safety. Keep offering the best care possible, and your pup will soon become accustomed to things.

Why is my new puppy shaking?

This can be low blood sugar (hypoglycemia) from not eating enough, feeling cold, and/or feeling afraid. For eating issues, encourage your new puppy to eat (some have to be reminded), but have realistic expectations (puppies do not eat a lot of food, but they do need frequent small amounts). For feeling cold, check for drafts and slip a shirt or sweater on the pup to see if that helps. And, for pups with anxiety, keep commotion to a minimum and create a safe environment with a playpen, bed, and toys to offer a sense of security.

At what age can I bring my puppy outside?

If you are 100% certain that other animals (pets and wildlife) cannot enter onto your property, you can take your puppy there starting at 8-weeks-old. In regard to these animals, this excludes any of your own pets, if you are 100% sure that they are up-to-date on their vaccinations. Once your pup has had all puppy shots (usually by the 12 to 16-week mark) heading out to public areas is okay. We, however, suggest waiting two weeks past that point, just to be extra safe. Check with your vet to confirm vaccinations are complete.

How big will my Chihuahua grow to be?

Despite the AKC breed standard of *'no more than 6 pounds'* (2.72 kg), a good number of Chihuahua are not in this range as adults. Our survey (see 'About the Chihuahua: PetChiDog's Chihuahua Survey') that complied the stats of 3,272 Chihuahua showed that with adults (2,715 Chi), just 5% were under 3 lbs. (1.36 kg), 41% of adult Chihuahuas were between 3 to 6 lbs. (1.36 to 2.72 kg), 31% were between 6.5 and 8.5 lbs. (2.9 and 3.85 kg), 23% were more than 8.5 lbs. (3.85 kg).

If you know the size of the parents, this will give you a good idea of how big your puppy will be as an adult; though, phsyical size can come from further generations backs. Ahead, the 'Growth Charts' section dives into this in more detail.

How often should I feed my new puppy?

Up until the 3-month mark, food should be available at all times. You may need to remind your pup where his food is, and encourage him to eat. Starting at 3 months, most pups can do okay with 3 meals per day, plus 3 to 4 snacks per day. You'll also be giving small training treats as part of housebreaking.

How much should I feed my puppy?

Exact feeding guidelines vary depending on the brand of kibble that you are offering, and your puppy's weight. Check the label on the kibble package; these are pretty spot-on. See more in the 'Feeding and Nutrition' chapter.

Why doesn't my puppy seem to want to play with me?

Puppies do not yet have full cognitive abilities and can get distracted very easily. You'll see a gradual increase in responsiveness as the weeks go by. No matter how oblivious your puppy seems to be, pick him up, gently handle him, perform grooming tasks including brushing, tempt him with toys, and speak to him a lot. All of these interactions will have a positive effect as your puppy becomes more aware.

When can I give my puppy his first bath?

While most puppies from breeders will come to you fresh from a bath, technically, you can give a bath right away. However, since this can be quite an experience for a new puppy, unless there is really a need, we recommend waiting a week or two for that first bath.

Do I have to bring my puppy to the vet?

Yes, you should. If you obtained your puppy from a breeder, you will need to have a veterinary checkup for the pup within a certain amount of time to validate the health guarantee. But, even if this aspect does not pertain to you, a checkup is vital. Vaccinations will need to be given, the vet will see if the pup is growing as he should be, and all possible health issues, including parasitic worms which are common to puppies, will be ruled out.

At what age will my puppy start teething?

This can vary quite a bit; however, it is generally in full swing by the 4 to 6-month mark. It will wind down a few months later, and be entirely complete by the 1-year mark.

How much should my puppy be sleeping?

If you add up both nighttime sleeping and naps, new 8-week-old puppies sleep quite a lot, 18 to 20 hours. Each week and month that goes by, a puppy will require a bit less sleep. Most adults sleep 12 to 14 hours, total.

Growth Charts

Weight Per Breed Standards: The AKC breed standard calls for a Chihuahua to be no more than 6 lbs. (2.72 kg).

How Much Adult Chihuahuas Really Weigh: To recap the results regarding weight of 3,272 adult Chihuahua (1+ years old) as seen in the results of our survey (see 'About the Chihuahua: PetChiDog's Chihuahua Survey'), weight was as follows:

2.5 lb. (1.13 kg) 5%
3 lb. (1.36 kg) 3%
3.5 lb. (1.58 kg) 3%
4 lb. (1.81 kg) 6%
4.5 lb. (2.04 kg) 4%
5 lb. (2.26 kg) 11%
5.5 lb. (2.49 kg) 7%
23%

6 lb. (2.72 kg) 7%
6.5 lb. (2.94 kg) 8%
7 lb. (3.17 kg) 7%
7.5 lb. (3.40 kg) 6%
8 lb. (3.63 kg) 5%
8.5 lb. (3.85 kg) 5%
More than 8.5 lb. (3.85 kg)

Is There a Way to Know How Big a Chihuahua Will Be?

It is not possible to have a guarantee by any means. However, if you obtain your Chi from a reputable breeder who has been breeding for quite some time, there is a better chance of knowing final adult size in advance, at least within a pound or so. While new dogs need to be introduced to breeding programs as time goes by, certain pairings will consistently produce a known weight range.

No matter how you obtain your puppy, looking at weight at a young age can be an *indicator* of final adult size. It's not a perfect science because a pup can have rapid growth, slower growth, or one with starts and stalls.

Our Prediction Rules:

Our prediction rule regarding 8- week-old weight for pups 1 lb. and under, is to take the weight, multiply it by 3 and then add .75 pounds. For Chi 1.25 to 1.75 pounds, to take the weight, multiply it by 3 and add 1.25 pounds. Finally, for larger Chi pups that are 2 pounds at 8 weeks, to take the weight, multiply it by 3 and add 2 pounds.

Our prediction rule regarding 4-month-old weight is to simply double the weight.

About Our Data: PetChiDog tracked a number of Chihuahua puppies to see how accurate the prediction rules were. There are two charts showing the results. The information was compiled over a period of 3 years, using weights from 87 to 102 Chihuahua puppies at any one given time, with data from 128 Chihuahuas in total.

Over the course of time, data collection stopped for some pups (owner stopped reporting, etc.). In those cases, contact was made with another owner as soon as possible and the data collection continued from that particular starting point with a new Chihuahua. For this reason, the pool of Chihuahuas fluctuated over the course of those 3 years.

Please keep in mind that this is for reference only. When looking at these charts, your Chihuahua may be having a growth spurt or a pause. In addition, these weights are not indicators of health.

8 Weeks old. The majority of Chihuahua pups were between 1 and 1.75 pounds at the 8-week mark. Adult weight was predicted using the 'multiply by 3, add .75, 1.25 or 2 pound,' rule. That led to accurate predictions (within .5 pounds) an average of 80% of the time.

Weight of Chihuahua at 8-Weeks (in lbs.)	.5 (8 oz)	.75 (12 oz)	1	1.25	1.5	1.75	2
Puppies That Were This Weight	5%	12%	15%	20%	25%	18%	5%
Predicted Adult Weight (in lbs.)	2.25	3	3.75	5	5.75	6.5	8
Predictions Correct (within .25 lbs.)	75%	80%	75%	90%	80%	75%	85%

4 months old. As we move into the 4-month mark and a pup is closer to his adult weight and growth is slowing down, predictions are even easier and slightly more accurate. The majority of pups were between 1.75 and 2.75 pounds. Here, predictions were correct an average of 90% of the time (within .5 pounds).

Weight of Chihuahua at 4-Months (in lbs.)	1.25	1.5	1.75	2	2.25	2.5	2.75	3	3.25	3.5	4
Puppies That Were This Weight	5%	7%	12%	12%	12%	17%	14%	8%	3%	5%	5%
Predicted Adult Weight (in lbs.)	2.5	3	3.5	4	4.5	5	5.5	6	6.5	7	8
Predictions Correct (within .25 lbs.)	85%	95%	90%	85%	90%	90%	80%	90%	90%	85%	85%

Care Items – Chihuahuas of All Ages

Leashes, Harnesses, Collars & ID Tags

The type of accessories that you choose are of the utmost importance; your puppy or dog's health and quality of life depends on it. First, this revolves around a vital health fact:

- **Like many toy breed dogs, the Chihuahua is prone to collapsed trachea.** This is a condition in which rings of cartilage surrounding the dog's windpipe collapse inward, often due to weakened cellular structure. While this can develop without further cause, pressure and stress on the neck can trigger this.

   What puts stress on the neck? A collar. We go into much greater detail ahead in our 'Health: Collapsed Trachea' section; however, suffice it to say, this is a very painful condition that causes terrible coughing fits and sometimes severe breathing problems. Dogs can never be fully cured.

Secondary to this, benefits of having the right accessories include:

- **Better control while on leash.** This relates to keeping your dog in proper heeling position while on walks (key in helping to establish proper hierarchy), and being able to position your dog should he be jumping or otherwise moving about in an undesired way.
- **Comfort.** The more comfortable a dog is while on leash, the less resistance there will be to take daily walks and accompany you where you need to take him.
- **Easier housebreaking.** As you'll see coming up, the right leash will play a role in house training your puppy.

Let's take a look at each type of accessory:

Leashes

Two different types of leashes are recommended.

Short, 4 or 6-foot lightweight, soft-handled leash. If you will be house training, this is needed as part of the 'tethering' method, which is when you are there to supervise your puppy and will be keeping him right next to you.

The short length ensures that your pup will always be close enough for you to quickly see any motions of starting to pee or poo. The lightweight aspect is always important, to keep unnecessary weight off of a pup or dog. And the soft handle is a vital element, as this allows you to slip it over your wrist or through your belt loop as part of the 'tethering'.

Adjustable leash. This is a leash that rolls in or extends out with the push of a button. This type of leash allows you to reel your pup in when you want him close or let it out to allow him more freedom such when playing fetch or doing other activities outside. Most adjustable leashes extend out 16 feet or so; but, there are some that allow for 24 feet, or even 40+ (though, these are typically used for professional training with larger dogs).

Harness

This is one of the most important care items to have, for both puppies and adults.

This is the apparatus that should be used any time that your Chihuahua is on leash. As opposed to a collar, the harness will distribute pressure, force, and tension across the shoulders, chest, and back, freeing the neck from these stresses that can potentially cause injury.

Choosing a Harness: Some owners shy away from harnesses due to a bad experience of their dog resisting or showing intolerance for it; however, in most cases, this is just a matter of the dog needing time to become accustomed to it and having one that is comfortable and designed for easy on and off.

There are two main types:

A strap, step-in harness can work well for adults, particularly those on the larger size. If choosing this type, nylon (and not leather) is best. Nylon is resistant to odors, weather resistant, washable, and sturdy.

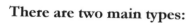

A wrap harnesses is the most popular type for toy breeds. There are several terrific ones that are designed for both safety and ease of use. This includes some made by Puppia and EcoBark. Reasons why these are recommended include:

- They are adjustable for a perfect fit.
- They are comfortable. Options include cotton or polyester air mesh (for breathability), which makes them durable but soft to the touch (won't chafe a dog's skin).
- These have sturdy o-rings (the round rings on the back between the shoulder blades, to which the leash is clipped).
- They are easy to put on and take off. Some have 'quick-snap' buckles on the sides. There are also several designs with Velcro closures, which are fantastic as well.
- They come in a wide range of colors so that a dog can make a fashion statement while safe on leash.

Not everyone places a collar on their dog; however, it is something to consider. Many owners keep their dog free of any accessory while in the house and then place the harness on when readying to go outside. And, this can certainly work out well for you.

Though, this not a good idea if your dog tends to try and dash out of the house when the door opens. Un-spayed and un-neutered dogs are more likely to try and escape than those that are fixed. However, even getting spooked or sensing another dog outside are reasons to try and run off. If your dog does take off, and in the unlikely event that he becomes lost, you may want him to be wearing an ID tag, even if he is microchipped.

Reasons to have your dog wear a collar with an ID tag include:

- If you clip the ID tag to the harness, *this only helps when the harness is on.* And, your puppy or dog will only be wearing the harness while on leash (i.e. for the most part, when you have hold of him and he can't run off to begin with).
- Even if a dog is microchipped, in the case of getting lost, this only helps if a dog ends up at a shelter that has a microchip scanning device.
- Some states have laws that require a dog to wear ID tags, this may be alongside proof of rabies shot.
- In some states, a loose dog without ID is considered 'abandoned property'.
- In some states a dog can be impounded for up to 48 hours if he is found without ID tags.
- Worse yet, in some states a dog can be euthanized as soon as 5 days after being found, if he has no ID.

You'll want to check with your town or city officials regarding the exact laws for your area.

Type: If you do opt for your dog to wear a collar, choose a lightweight one. Nylon can be a good fabric; as mentioned earlier, it is weather resistant, washable, resistant to odors, and sturdy.

Size: The general rule of safety and comfort is that once the collar is on, you can easily slip two fingers between it and your dog's neck. This allows it to be loose enough to avoid any constriction but be tight enough that it cannot slip off or be easily snagged onto something. Check for an adjustment need every 2 weeks for growing pups.

Some collars are designed with a built-in nameplate, and this can be a good choice if you don't like to hear the jingle of the tag whenever your dog takes a step. Alternatively, 'classic' dog ID tags hang from the collar. In either case, opt for quality stainless-steel, which is durable, weather resistant, and holds engravings rather well without fading.

In regard to what you'll want to have engraved on the tag, it should include the fastest and easiest method to contact you, and this will most likely be your cell phone number. If your dog is microchipped, you may want to have the microchip company's name and phone number on the tag as well.

Since canine accessories are always evolving, yet this book is static, current recommendations are on the Supplies page of the PetChiDog site, which is updated as new options emerge. You can reach this by entering any page of PetChiDog.com; look to the navigation which is in alphabetical order, and choose 'Supplies'.

Toys

Toys as Tools

Many owners find that they've stocked up on toys that do not hold their dog's interest for long or are subpar for their intended purpose. They may be stacked up in a corner of the house or spread out everywhere. One thing is for sure, they are not doing any good. In fact, if you have the wrong toys, you'd almost be better off buying nothing.

However, if you think of toys as being tools to meet the exact needs of your puppy or dog, having the right ones can have amazing benefits.

The 6 Types of Toys that Can Be Helpful

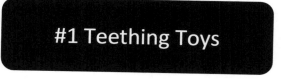

#1 Teething Toys

What's happening: The teething phase, which takes place as young as the 4-month mark and lasts up until the 6 to 9-month mark (and sometimes even up to 1 year) is a challenging one for both owner and pup.

As deciduous (milk) teeth are falling out, and primary adult teeth are cutting in, this causes discomfort and quite an intense itching. This, in turn, makes a pup desperate to soothe his woes. Without the right toys, a puppy may try to bite down on anything he can reach. Your puppy will be frustrated, and items in your house may be getting destroyed.

In addition, having excellent toys at this young age establishes a foundation for a lifetime of good chewing habits.

Qualities of the best teething toys: There are specific elements that you'll want to look for:

- **Properly sized.** When you have a toy breed like the Chihuahua, sizing is vital. If a young pup cannot fit the toy in his mouth, it will be useless.
- **Textures.** The needs of a teething puppy can change moment to moment. Sensations vary between pain and itching and can move to different areas of the mouth in the blink of an eye. Teething toys

should offer a variety of textures that can both 'scratch' and soothe. Small nubs and twisted rope are great for scratching, and toys with proper resistance help with discomfort.

- **Shapes.** One of the reasons why teething pups struggle so much and can go into a frenzy in their search for something to chew on, is that the 'itch' can be in a hard-to-reach spot. Effective teething toys will offer various shapes so that the toy can be worked into small crevices and certain pinpoint areas.
- **Enticement.** Some puppies need a bit of encouragement to mouth a toy, and for this, those with scents or flavors can work well.
- **Durability.** The last thing you want is a teething toy breaking apart within days. While no dog toy lasts forever, you'll want some sturdy ones that will stand up to near constant use.

Tips: 1. Puppy-proof the house, so that non-toy items are out of reach. When you cannot supervise, or for when you are not home, place your pup in his playpen to keep him surrounded by his toys. 2. Routinely check toys for wear and tear, and replace as needed. Wash toys once per week with warm water and soap.

#2 Chew Toys for All Ages

What's happening: Chewing urges do not always stop once a pup matures, many adults like to chew. It's a canine instinct to chomp on things, and some dogs chew as a stress reliever as they find it to be soothing. If a dog does not have toys that he feels are enjoyable, he'll look elsewhere to meet his chewing needs, and this often means non-toy items like your socks, shoes, pocketbook, etc.

In addition, chewing is beneficial for a dog to keep jaws strong and help keep gums and teeth healthy.

Qualities of the best chew toys: There are specific elements that you'll want to look for:

- **Properly sized.** As with many care items and supplies for Chihuahuas, sizing is important. If a dog struggles to fit a toy in his mouth or has trouble carrying it around, he may start to not even bother trying.
- **Consistency.** For this, a dog needs the right consistency to clamp down on. And, as he chews, it must be a pleasant and rewarding workout for the jaws.
- **Enticement.** Flavor is a key element for dogs that need to be reminded why chewing on toys is fun. And tasty chews will help keep a dog focused on his toy, staying busy until he's met his chewing quota.

Tip: More is not necessarily better. Five or six really great toys are far better than a dozen substandard ones. Once you've put together a

---

HOW TO REACT TO CHEWING ON A NON-TOY OBJECT

More is ahead under 'Teething & Chewing'; however, here's a quick summary of how to train your dog to chew on toys and not household objects:

1. Proof the house to remove as many temptations as possible.

2. Keep your dog within his playpen any time that you cannot closely supervise.

3. If you catch your dog chewing on a non-toy item, gain his attention. For some dogs, a loud hand clap works. Others will need something more effective like a behavioral training device that makes a harmless but attention-getting hissing noise.

4. As soon as your dog takes pause, offer one of his chew toys. If he tends to never take it from you, place a dab of peanut butter on it.

5. When your dog mouths the toy, give super-happy praise.

great collection, you can leave out half of them at any one time. The second set can be stored away, and these can be rotated out so that your dog always has 'new' toys. Do, however, keep any favorites; dogs can get very attached to certain toys and having them gone can be stressful.

#3 'Stay Busy' Toys

What's happening: While you probably wish that you could entertain your dog all day, it's just not possible. And dogs that are left with nothing to do, are often bored and frustrated. Chronic boredom can lead to sullen mood and even depression. And built up frustration can manifest as restlessness, disruptive behavior like excessive barking, or destructive behavior.

You'll want to have a few toys that are designed to draw a dog in and keep him focused, entertained, and busy. They'll provide fun and encourage independent play. This is relevant both when you are home but otherwise busy and when your puppy or dog is home alone.

Qualities of the best 'stay busy' toys: There are specific elements that you'll want to look for:

- **Properly sized.** This will always be a quality of any toy for a Chihuahua since an oversized toy will be hard to chew on, manipulate, or carry.
- **Interactive.** The toys will produce an effect when the dog interacts with it, for example nosing it, pawing at it, or chewing on it. In this way, the toy is essentially 'playing back' with the dog, which brings things to a whole new level, offering great incentive. Dogs will take action when doing so brings about favorable results. When they receive good feedback in return for seeking out and playing with a toy, they are more apt to seek it out again. With interactive toys, that feedback is automatic.
- **Entertaining.** Silly and/or unexpected noises are great for keeping a dog amused. Challenges that bring about reward also work well.

Tip: When your dog is home alone, and you want him to stay busy with his chosen toys, you won't want those toys to be rolling under sofas or otherwise becoming inaccessible. One of the best ways to keep a dog in one spot, with all needed necessities fully within reach, is to use a canine playpen. These are discussed in 'Puppy Care: Supplies to Have', though are applicable for all ages.

#4 Treat Dispensing Toys

What these do: Treat dispensing toys, also known as treat-release toys, hold kibble and release it slowly as a puppy or dog chews on it. These serve several useful purposes:

- It's a great way to keep a dog busy (both when home alone and if you need to tend to other things). If hungry, a dog may stay focused on a treat dispensing toy for 30 minutes, as opposed to the 3 minutes it may take him to eat his kibble from his bowl.

- On this same vein of thought, this is an effective method to slow down a dog that eats much too fast.
- This is also a good way to offer something interesting to a puppy or dog that wakes up too early in the morning. Prepared and placed down after a dog falls asleep, these can provide some distraction when a dog first wakes up.

Qualities of the best treat dispensing toys: There are specific elements that you'll want to look for:

- **Properly sized.** An oversized toy will make it much harder to work any food out of it.
- **Adjustable.** You may want to opt for an adjustable one; this way you can decrease or increase the difficulty level, depending on your dog's abilities.
- **Durable.** Since these will take a lot of bites, you'll want one that can stand up to the test of time.

Tips: 1. These types of toys can hold your puppy or dog's regular dry kibble or mini dry treats.

2. If your dog seems to need more incentive to use the toy, you can mix dry kibble with a bit of 100% all-natural smooth peanut butter, and then place it in the toy.

3. Do be sure to clean these on a regular basis.

#5 Bonding Toys

What's happening: Most toys serve the purpose of having a puppy or dog play by themselves; but, taking time to play with your canine family member is important as well. You may not realize just how much your dog craves having special time with you until you start to set aside 20 minutes or so each day to do so.

Puzzle games are great for this type of one-on-one time. These have levers, buttons, and other such challenges that need to be manipulated by a dog to receive a treat hidden within. It'll be your job to help show your dog what to do. This is an excellent confidence booster and a wonderful bonding experience.

In addition, toys that address the issue of inactivity, which is a big problem with dogs, and particularly with toy dogs that are kept inside for safety reasons, are fantastic. Staying physically active helps a dog release pent-up energy that is often misdirected elsewhere, including excessive barking and destructive chewing. Some dogs can even become withdrawn or depressed when they do not receive enough exercise.

While at a minimum of two walks per day is recommended, you'll find that a classic game of fetch is an excellent way to give your dog a burst of cardio exercise, while having a fun time together. Play outside to enjoy some fresh air, or inside a long hallway on rainy days!

Qualities of the best bonding toys: There are specific elements that you'll want to look for:

- **Properly sized.** As with all toys for Chihuahuas, it must fit the dog. Playing fetch with a ball that's too large will bring an end to the game pretty quickly. And, for puzzle-type games, your dog must be able to manipulate the various levels and lids.
- **Correct skill level.** For puzzle toys, you'll want these to be at the right level, with levers and buttons that your dog can maneuver.

Tips: 1. Try to schedule playtime instead of hoping to find the time. If it's not planned, it's easy for a slew of other tasks to take precedence and before you know it, the day is coming to a close. All you need is 15 to 20-minutes set aside for this.

2. Your level of enthusiasm will go a long way in how well your dog responds. Halfheartedly tossing a ball or checking your phone while playing will hardly make for a rousing, exciting time. But, if you jump up, speak in a happy voice, shake the ball, dance around a bit, and then toss it while saying, "Goooo get it!', your dog will match your vibe and be rearing to go.

#6 Companion Toys

What's happening: It's more common than not for dogs to have to stay home alone, at least for a portion of the day, as owners need to work, go to school, or be away for other responsibilities. And, with this comes the issue of separation anxiety. Dogs can be overwhelmed with feelings of isolation and loneliness.

There are quite a few things that you can do to help fix separation anxiety issues; one of them is to offer companion toy. These are intended to mimic a living creature (often a puppy). This is achieved via accurate sizing, and two elements that make a toy 'alive': a heartbeat and body warmth. It will be as *close* to another dog that you can get without actually bringing home a new puppy.

Qualities of the best companion toys:

- **Realistic heartbeat and appropriate warmth.** Take care that the 2 features that make this toy what it is, need to function realistically. The pulse should be rhythmic. Warmth should radiate evenly and only felt when a dog snuggles close.
- **Proper sizing.** For this, you don't want to go too little. The idea is for a dog to have a 'friend' to cuddle up to, not to plop down on top of, unable to see or use it.
- **Replaceable parts.** Since the mechanism that provides the heartbeat will have internal moving parts, you'll want this to be replaceable, should it ever wear out. This way, you are purchasing the toy once and can keep it working essentially forever.
- **Reasonably priced warming packs.** With these toys, a warming pack (which is typically optional) is inserted into the belly of the 'puppy'. These run out of warmth after a certain amount of time. If you find that your dog finds comfort in this element, you'll want to know that obtaining these will be friendly to your wallet.

Tip: These are great for when a dog is home alone, but are also fantastic for those mourning the loss of a friend, trying to adjust to a new home, or for generalized anxiety.

Since dog toy options are always evolving, yet this book is static, current recommendations for teething, chew, 'stay busy', treat-release, bonding, and companion toys are on the Supplies page of the PetChiDog site, which is updated as new toys emerge. You can reach this by entering any page of PetChiDog.com; look to the navigation which is in alphabetical order, and choose 'Supplies'.

Car Seats

You'll be making a lot of choices regarding your Chihuahua's care, and all of them will have consequences. Yet, perhaps the one decision that has the greatest influence connected to possible injury or death is to use or not use a car seat.

Car accident injury can be life-altering, and death can be violent.

• **If an accident occurs and a dog is not restrained, he will be thrown with a certain amount of force.** This is known as 'crash force', and while there are several factors at play, an easy way of estimating this is weight x speed. Here are some examples:

➤ If a car is traveling 35 MPH, a 4-lb. puppy will be thrown as if he is a 140-lb. object.
➤ If a car is traveling at 55 MPH, that same pup will be thrown as if he is a 220-lb. object.
➤ Going 55 MPH, an adult Chihuahua of 6 lbs. will be thrown as if he is a 330-lb. object.

This of course, is enough to injure a dog horribly, if not fatally. In addition, the force of a 100+ lb. object being thrown is a risk to both the driver and other passengers.

For those who may assume that they are cautious drivers and that an accident is highly unlikely, here are some facts to know:

- The average person will have 3 accidents in their lifetime.
- Most accidents happen near home; approximately 70% occur within 15 miles of home.
- Having a dog loose in the car is the *cause* of some accidents:
  ➤ Statistically speaking, this falls under the category of distracted driving, which kills almost 3,500 people per year in the U.S.
  ➤ Per a combined AAA/Kurgo survey (https://www.kurgo.com/dog-travel-statistics), 65% of owners admitted to being distracted by their pets while driving. This includes holding their dog when they brake, reaching over to restrict their dog's movements, and petting their dog.
  ➤ But, taking your eyes off the road for just 2 seconds doubles your chances of being in an accident.
  ➤ In fact, if you're going 55 MPH and take your eyes off the road for 1.5 seconds, you will have traveled one-third the length of a football field.
- Some of the top causes of car accidents are out of your control. Of the 5,000,000+ car accidents that happen each year, 22% are weather-related.

In addition to this, the right type of car seat can significantly decrease motion

sickness, which is common for both puppies and adult dogs. It is particularly bad for toy breeds that are too small to sufficiently see out of the window/receive fresh air from the window.

Symptoms of motion sickness include: • Nausea • Vomiting •Dizziness • Excessive drool • Excessive panting • Restlessness • Panic • Consequently, fear of being driven in the car

Motion sickness is caused by:

- A disconnect between what the body is feeling and the eyes are seeing. The inner ear (which contains sensory organs for hearing and balance) and the body (which is swaying with each turn, deceleration, and acceleration) is telling a dog that they are moving. But, the eyes are not properly seeing the road.
- Many unrestrained toy breeds are not even tall enough to feel air coming in through the window, another cue that would help resolve the disconnect.

The right car seat can help by:

- Keeping a dog raised high enough to see out of the windows.
- Keeping a dog raised high enough to feel fresh air currents.
- Keeping a dog's body stable to decrease the amount of swaying that occurs with stops, deceleration, and acceleration.

The best type of car seat for a toy breed is a raised booster seat that is designed for small dogs. This will ensure proper height, as well as defined space to keep the body secure. Here are a few tips to keep in mind:

- Canine car seats typically attach to your car's seat via the car's seat belt.
- Inside the canine car seat is a buckle. This is meant to be connected to a dog's harness, NOT his collar. Attaching this to a collar could cause severe neck injuries. So, even if the packaging on the box shows a dog wearing a collar, ignore that and place a harness on. See also, 'Care Items - Chihuahuas of All Ages: Leashes, Harnesses, Collars, and ID Tags'.
- The safest spot for your dog is in the middle of the back seat, due to front passenger airbags that typically deploy within 1/20th of a second when there is an accident equivalent of a 14 MPH barrier collision. The airbag will explode out at 200 MPH which can be fatal to a dog.
- If you *do* place your dog's car seat in the front seat, be sure to disable the passenger airbag, and slide the car's seat as far back as it can go.

Extra tips to help reduce motion sickness:

1) Right after a meal is not the best time for a drive; if possible, wait at least 1 hour.
2) But, 15 or 20 minutes before leaving, offer a small, dry snack.
3) In addition, a bit of sugar can help calm a queasy stomach; often 1 small jelly bean given 15 minutes before getting in the car does the trick.
4) Even when in a proper car seat, many dogs cannot put up with extended rides. There may be a tipping point at which confinement and motion are getting to be too much. The best thing to do is to give your dog a break *before* he reaches this point. For long rides, you may want to take a break every 30 minutes. Pull over into a safe area, have your dog on leash, allow him to stretch his legs, go to the bathroom if needed, and have a drink and/or a small snack.
5) Avoid having the car be too hot; it's best to have it slightly cool even if this means placing a shirt on

your dog.

6) Keep a window open just a bit; not too much as to be overwhelming, but just a tad so that your puppy or dog can feel the movement of fresh air.

 Since canine car seats are always evolving, yet this book is static, current recommendations for car seats are on the Supplies page of the PetChiDog site, which is updated as we evaluate new designs and options that may emerge. You can reach this by entering any page of PetChiDog.com; look to the navigation which is in alphabetical order, and choose 'Supplies'.

All Other Supplies – Quick Summary

Below is a full list of supplies for all ages; most are discussed throughout this book.

- Accessories; Leash, harness, collar (optional), ID tag (optional, but recommended)
- Allergy aids, if needed
- Bed
- Bowls
- Brushes (and a comb, if longcoat Chi)
- Car seat
- Carrier method (optional)
- Cooling mat (optional, summertime)
- Cotton balls (for baths)
- Clothing (optional, but recommended depending on the weather)
- Dental treats, canine toothbrush & toothpaste
- Ear cleanser
- Enzyme cleanser (for housebreaking)
- Flea and tick protection
- Food (main kibble, snacks, training treats)
- Grooming wipes
- Nose balm
- Paw wax
- Playpen (optional, but highly recommended)
- Poo bags
- Separation anxiety aids (if needed)
- Shampoo (plus conditioner and leave-in spray)
- Skincare items (if needed)
- Supplements (if needed)
- Tear stain remover (if needed)
- Toys; (teething, chewing, 'stay busy', owner/dog bonding, treat dispensing, companion)
- Water filtering method

Housebreaking

Overview

When it comes to house training, this will be a combined effort and a partnership in learning. You'll take the important role of teacher, and your canine family member will be an excellent student, as long as you follow all of the necessary guidelines.

The actual fundamentals of housebreaking are not overly complicated and will work if you follow all of the rules, all of the time.

First, we will first detail all basic steps to abide by. Once you have that down pat, we'll dive into some of the most common hiccups that can occur and exactly how to deal with them. Never label a dog as 'untrainable'; there is always an answer!

How Long It Takes to Housebreak a Puppy

Of course, this is not something that happens overnight and not even something that happens within a few weeks. It is a gradual process. The exact time that it takes for a puppy to be 100% fully housebroken will depend on a few factors.

Two of the most critical elements will be how strictly you stick with the training and how many learning opportunities your puppy has. Therefore, a lot of this depends on you. It will be essential for you, and anyone else in the house that is responsible for your pup, to follow the housebreaking guidelines to a tee and to take advantage of every chance to teach these important lessons.

In busy households in which a puppy does not have guidance for most of the day, housebreaking can still be done, but will often take longer than in a house where an owner is at home most days. All said, it typically takes 2 to 4 months for house training lessons to be fully understood.

Tips Related to Age

With puppies: A puppy as young as 8-weeks-old is ready to start learning all about going potty in his designated area. One thing to keep in mind, however, is that puppies should not be brought outside to any areas that other dogs or wildlife could have had access to until they have had all of their puppy shots. We suggest waiting two weeks past that point.

This will typically be by the 12 to 16-week mark; but, do check with your veterinarian. Animal access does not include any other pets that you may have, as long as you are 100% positive that they are fully up-to-date on vaccinations. So, do keep this in mind when you choose a spot as the designated area for your pup to potty in.

With older dogs: It's not uncommon for an adult to find his way to a new home; whether this is through a shelter, a rescue, or a re-homing of another sort. Even if you have been told that your dog is housebroken, you will still want to follow through with all of the training steps. This is because you will want to be sure that your dog understands your rules and where his bathroom area is within your property.

Owners of adult dogs can be thrown off when reading housebreaking advice, due to the word 'puppy' being used so much. They wonder, 'Okay, but what should I do for my adult dog?' The truth of the matter is, if you have a healthy adult or senior, there are no deviations and there are no additional steps. Every single rule and guideline that works for puppies works for adults.

However, keep in mind that adults and seniors have a higher incident rate of urinary tract infection, bladder infection/stones, and kidney infections/stones, all of which can cause problems with bladder control. So, you will want to pay particular attention to a sudden occurrence of accidents. This is always a reason to have possible health issues ruled out.

Indoor vs. Outdoor

The outdoor training method is recommended. However, it is possible to teach a puppy to use indoor pee pads, a grass mat, or another indoor potty area, particularly if you are persistent and you have a puppy that is cooperative. Do know that a puppy may resist or have a hard time with this. Canines have a natural instinct to want to 'choose just the right spot' to urinate or eliminate, and a small indoor area does not allow for this.

The indoor method is best if you live in a home in which the outside yard area is not easily accessible (having to go down a flight of steps is typically not a valid excuse), or there are extenuating circumstances that prevent you from taking your dog outdoors.

Also, the number of hours that your dog will be without supervision comes into play. If your dog will be home alone for 9, 10, or 11 hours most days, and you are essentially never there to train him, there is little choice other than indoor training.

Tips for Indoor Training:

- Do **not** disregard any of the housebreaking rules and guidelines. With a chosen designated area indoors, you **should** still use a containment method, supervise, have your pup on leash to bring him to that area, offer reward and praise, and follow all other aspects of training.

- Consider if you want to use pee pads, pee pads within a holder, an artificial grass mat, or another type of indoor training method. What works best for you will depend on the layout of your home and your personal preferences. For the sake of simplicity, we will refer to the indoor area as having 'pee pads' for the next tips.

- If you work outside the house or are normally gone for any amount of time during the day, the indoor designated area should be in the area that your pup will be when home alone, such as a canine playpen (details ahead). You may be thinking that you'd prefer to have your pup use pee pads near the exit door, in a mudroom, or another area. However, how will the pup reach that area when home alone? Will he be freely roaming the house? If that is the plan, re-think this. It's dangerous and a surefire way to end up with non-toy items chewed and a pup that is stressed by being alone in a large (at least relatively speaking) house.

Technically, you can have two designated areas. The playpen (when your pup is home alone) and another area like the mudroom (for when you are home). However, this can cause a lot of confusion. It's recommended to have just the playpen with a door. When you are home, the door stays open; your dog can enter to go to the bathroom. When you are not home, your dog is in the playpen and the pee pads are used (at first, because there is no other option, and later due to training).

- If your puppy misses the pad when having a bowel movement, move the feces onto the pad for a small amount of time, to transfer the scent to the pad.

- If your puppy misses the pad when urinating, before you use your enzyme cleaner (details ahead), wipe up the urine with paper towels and place those onto the pad for just a bit of time to allow the scent to transfer.

- If you only need to use the indoor method for a short amount of time (for example, during an extreme cold spell in the winter), choosing an area like the garage or mud room can help. This way, your dog is being led away from his normal living area to a designated bathroom spot. This can maintain consistency and keep the concept of housebreaking on track for when the situation changes back (the weather improves, etc.).

Going forward, we will refer to your chosen spot as the 'designated bathroom area', and this will be the term used whether you are training indoors or outdoors.

Preparing to Housebreak

You may wonder what you have to prepare for. Shouldn't you just get to it right now? While you can and should bring your puppy outside to avoid accidents in the house, there are 6 things that you'll want to have in place. Taking time to be fully prepared will ensure that you will do a great job as a trainer and that your pup will be able to be a good trainee. If not, you may find yourself facing certain housebreaking struggles.

#1 Choose a Designated Area

Never just allow your pup to go in the yard 'somewhere'. One specific area should be chosen as the designated bathroom area and your pup should be brought to that same area each time that you take him out.

In addition, never just let your dog outside by himself. Of course, doing so will not allow you to enforce the designated area; but, in addition to that, urinating or having a bowel movement in an area due to coincidence is not the same as learning. When you accompany your dog, this allows you to bring him to the one specific area and importantly, be there to give praise and reward as soon as the deed is done to teach essential housebreaking lessons.

Not to mention that being outside alone, even in a fenced-in yard, can be quite dangerous. A puppy can try to dig under a fence, find a small hole to crawl through, or another animal may find their way into your yard. And, there is always the risk of swallowing pebbles or eating toxic plants or weeds.

Here are some tips on choosing the area:

- Ideally, it will be an area of at least an 8 to 10-foot diameter.
- Consider all of the seasons. What may be easily accessible in the spring may be hard to get to in the winter. If you live somewhere that receives snow or bad weather, choose a spot that you can easily reach no matter what.
- Do not have this be close to a busy outdoor family area. If you have an outside spot that is frequently used for barbecuing or for kids to play, you'll want to pick a place that is at least 10 feet away.

#2 Choose a Containment Method

Not having this is the downfall of a huge number of housebreaking failures. ***This is for any time that you are not closely and directly supervising your pup.***

A dog that is not fully housebroken should never be allowed free reign in either a room or the house if he is not being supervised. If you permit this, there will inevitably be puddles of pee and little piles of poo all over your home.

And, every single time that a dog urinates or defecates inside the house is a step in the wrong direction.

In addition, if your dog slept in the bed with you and there were issues of peeing on the bed, having your dog in his own area will eliminate that problem as well. While it's always pleasant to cuddle up with your best friend, untrained puppies and dogs should not be allowed in the bed; to do so is just asking for trouble.

Another plus to creating a contained area is that it is an integral part of setting up the right environment for when your dog is home alone. When a dog has a defined space that contains his supplies, it speaks to his canine instinct to have a 'den', which brings about a sense of security.

One of the best methods for house training containment is to have an indoor canine playpen. Note that this is not a crate. Crates are terribly confining, lend zero aid towards housebreaking, usually lead to a dog stepping in his own feces and urine, and can cause both physical and emotional stress.

Within the playpen will be a bed, food & water bowls, toys, and pee pads. Since dogs will rarely soil their own belongings, chances are high that pee and poo will be deposited onto the pads.

So, you will find that an indoor canine playpen is a valuable tool for training, as well as where you will want your dog to be when you are away from home (at least until he is fully housebroken and/or he does not have separation anxiety).

Iris makes some great playpens, and if you'd like to see our most up-to-date recommendations, look the Supplies page of the PetChiDog site. You can reach the Supplies page by entering any page of PetChiDog.com. The navigation is in alphabetical order, choose 'Supplies'.

#3 Have a Supervision Method

This is for all times that you are home and will be supervising the pup.

It's far too common that an owner will be 'watching' their pup, but then he scampers away behind the sofa or around the corner. The owner may be right on the trail, but when they jog over to grab the pup, there's already a puddle of pee.

An effective method to ensure that you are closely supervising is to literally make it impossible for the aforementioned scenario to happen. And that can be accomplished by safely tethering your puppy to you via a harness and a 4 or 6-foot leash.

About the harness: When tethered, the last thing you want is for any tension to be on the neck, as neck injury including collapsed trachea, is a top concern. For this reason, use a harness, not a collar. A harness doesn't press against the windpipe; it displaces pressure over the chest, back, and shoulders. We like some of the Puppia and EcoBark harnesses, and if you'd like to see our current up-to-date recommendations, you may find these on the Supplies page of the PetChiDog.com website.

About the leash: You will want the leash to be lightweight and soft-handled. The soft handle will allow you to slip the handle around your wrist, or slip it through a belt loop on your slacks.

#4 Have the Right Training Treats

REWARD AND PRAISE

Any time that a puppy or dog is trying to learn something, he is going to be more motivated to focus, be better able to soak in the knowledge, understand that he did something right, and look forward to the next lesson if he is properly rewarded. This goes hand-in-hand with praise (details ahead).

Eventually, you will not need to offer a reward for each successful bathroom trip. Once your pup is trained, your words alone will suffice; however, it is recommended to occasionally give treat rewards to reinforce lessons and show that you appreciate that rules are being followed.

Tips:

1) When choosing the training treat, you will want to carefully opt for one that is:

- 100% all-natural and wholesome; meaning that it does not contain any chemical preservatives, artificial flavoring or colors, fillers such as corn or soy, by-products, or generic meats or oils.
- Considered to be extra tasty.
- Moist (these work better than dry for reward)
- Small enough that it can be doled out multiple times per day without causing your dog to feel full and potentially getting in the way of meals.
- Is not one that is given out at any rate. It should be a special treat reserved only for reward.

You may also wish to refer to 'Feeding and Nutrition: Training Treats'.

2) Keep a small plastic zippered sandwich bag of your chosen training treat right by the exit door. There will be times when you are hurrying out with your pup for immediate bathroom needs, and you do not want to waste time in getting them. Be sure to keep the sandwich bag closed so that your pup does not smell them beforehand.

#5 Choose the Cue Words

CUE WORDS! GO TOILET

Dogs learn best when they can make a connection between words and actions. So, it will be important to decide on a phrase that will be spoken each time you take your pup out to the bathroom area. You'll want this to be a short phrase (since dogs pay little attention to anything past a few syllables), and you'll want everyone in the house that may take your pup out to be on the same page about which phrase will be used.

Some common cue words to use include 'Go potty', 'Potty time', 'Pitty-potty', 'Let's go bathroom', and 'Get busy'.

[handwritten: FIRST WATER THEN ENZYME CLEANER]

#6 Have a Quality Enzyme Cleanser

Cleaning soiled areas the right way is very important. Urine contains certain enzymes. These are not washed away with soap and water. While the area may smell clean to you, your dog (with his amazing canine sense of smell) will be able to pick up on those lingering odors.

Those odors send a powerful message to a dog that essentially advertises, 'This is the bathroom area!', and a dog rarely ignores that. He will then want to go to the bathroom in that spot again as opposed to signaling that he needs to go outside.

So, you will want to first clean the area with soap and water, as you normally would, but then follow this with an enzyme cleanser specifically designed to eliminate lingering urine odors. Sunny & Honey makes a very effective one.

To Summarize Your Prep: You will be ready housebreak your puppy in an effective manner once you:

1) Have chosen a good location for your dog's designated bathroom area that will be relatively easy to reach all year round.

2) Have set up a playpen or other effective containment method for your dog to be any time that you cannot keep a very close eye on him, including to sleep at night.

3) Have a harness and lightweight short leash for proper supervision when you are home with your dog and can have him near your side.

4) Have special training treats in a zipped plastic bag right by the exit door.

5) Have decided on the housebreaking cue words.

6) Have a quality enzyme cleanser to properly clean any accidents in the house.

[handwritten: POOING ON WALKS = NOT GOOD FOR HOUSE TRAINING!]

How Often to Take a Puppy Out

The more you take your puppy outside, the more chances you will have to teach a housebreaking lesson. If your pup does not pee or poo, you've lost nothing except a small window of time.

Even if there is no indication of having a bathroom need, still bring your puppy out:

1. Immediately upon your pup waking up (both in the morning and after naps).

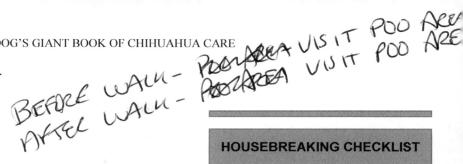

(handwritten note) BEFORE WALK - POO AREA VISIT POO AREA
AFTER WALK - POO AREA VISIT POO ARE

2. Right when taken out of the playpen.

3. 20 minutes after eating a meal.

4. 20 - 30 minutes before bedtime.

5. Before and after every walk. A massive mistake that owners make is allowing their dog to pee or poo when out on walks. If you do this, you miss a huge opportunity to house train. Therefore, visit the designated area before you bring your pup for a walk. Also, once the walk has ended, do not go right inside. Bring him back to his bathroom area to see if he needs to go.

Ideally, your dog will never pee or poo when out on short daily walks; he will always do so in his designated area.

(handwritten note in left margin) TAKE HIM TO THE POO AREA

6. Every 2 hours for a 2-month-old, every 3 hours for a 3-month-old, etc. It is important to try and extend the time like this so that bladder and bowel muscles are given the opportunity to grow stronger. If a puppy is never given a chance to hold his needs, it can take much longer for those muscles to reach their peak strength.

7. Any time that your pup makes a motion to go to the bathroom and you are close enough to stop it (i.e. your pup is tethered to you or you see this while he is in his playpen). Clap your hands and give a firm 'Oh!' (not a 'No'), then either immediately bring your pup out or carry him outside.

Exact Instructions

(handwritten note) NEVER SAY 'NO' ONLY 'OH' (CLAP)

Once you are sure that you are fully prepped, everyone that takes care of your pup is on the same page, and you have an idea about how often to take your puppy out, it will be time to get serious about housebreaking.

Here is exactly what to do and say. Some of this will be slightly repeated from earlier, since this covers all steps, in order.

1. **Keep your puppy with you, by your side as often as possible.**
If there is a motion to pee or poo, clap your hands loudly and give a loud, firm 'Oh!' to cause him to pause. It does not help to yell out 'No!' if a pup has only started to squat or lift a leg. Because, after all, a puppy cannot be 'wrong' for having the urge to urinate or eliminate.

2. **Your prep (as detailed earlier) should allow you to exit quickly with your pup on leash and harness, but carry him if you must.** You will be grabbing the small plastic zipped bag of treats on your way out.

(handwritten note) WORDS AND ACTION ASSOCIATION

3. **As you head to the area and as your puppy is doing the deed, repeat the cue words,** so that your pup can make an association between those words and his actions.

HOUSEBREAKING CHECKLIST

✓ Pup never roams the house; he is in his playpen or closely supervised by you

✓ Have ONE designated area

✓ Puppy is taken out on schedule & whenever he makes a motion to pee/poo

✓ Pup is always taken out on leash and supervised

✓ Be patient; sit in a chair, if it helps

✓ Great praise and a training treat is given when the pup pees/poos

✓ Remain calm and do not scold for accidents

✓ Accidents are cleaned with an enzyme cleanser

✓ Try to avoid any pee/poo'ing during walks. Visit the designated bathroom area BEFORE & AFTER walks

✓ Handle nighttime bathroom needs to show it is a serious time

✓ The last meal of the day is about 2 hours before sleepy time, but can be slightly adjusted

4. Stay in the designated area *only*; do not allow your pup to roam. He should be on the short 4 or 6-foot leash, or retractable leash set to 6 feet or so. Now is not the time to run around or play.

5. Allow your puppy a good 15 minutes to find the perfect spot within the designated area, and for his bowel and bladder muscles to relax. As a pup matures, he will be able to release his needs much faster, but puppies can take a while.

If you do not allow for this time, and you go back into the house too early, your pup may very well be ready to pee or poo soon after he's back inside. So, set out a chair, bring your phone, and/or grab a book; be ready to patiently wait while your pup sniffs around.

6. If your puppy pee or poos and seems to be done, offer the reward treat right away. Give praise at the same time as you give the treat. Praise will be the word 'good' along with your chosen word for bathroom trips. So, for example, 'Good pitty-potty', said in an *extremely* enthusiastic voice.

7. If you are not sure if your pup is done, offer the reward and allow him the rest of the time window to see if he also needs to pee/poo. *WATCH FOR SNIFFING - CUE MORE ON THE WAY*

8. If your pup has pee'd or poo'd, and seems to be sniffing around to do the other, hold off on the treat so that he is not interrupted. But then give it to him as soon as the session is complete.

How to Deal with Housebreaking Accidents

How you respond to accidents will have a huge impact on housebreaking success. Here are important tips:

1. Don't inadvertently set your dog up for an accident. Dogs can only hold their needs for a certain amount of time; at a point, the bladder and bowels will release. If you follow all of the rules as mentioned earlier, there will rarely be any accidents. This includes:

• Any time that you cannot keep a very close eye on your puppy, have him in his playpen with pee pads.

• When you are supervising him, take this job seriously. Limit his movement by closing doors that lead out of rooms, and if needed, use the tethering method as described earlier.

2. If you catch your pup in the act of urinating or eliminating in the house, do something to interrupt him such as clapping loudly (don't scare him). Immediately take him to his bathroom spot, give lots of praise and a treat if he finishes there.

3. Don't punish your dog for accidents. Rubbing your dog's nose in it, taking him to the spot and scolding, or any other type of punishment may only make your dog afraid of you or afraid to eliminate in your presence.

4. As mentioned under 'Preparing to HouseBreak: #6 Have a Quality Enzyme Cleanser', any soiled area must be properly cleaned to remove lingering urine odors. If not, a dog will be more prone to use that area again.

5. If your dog is having a lot of training accidents, this can point to certain health issues, such as a bladder infection, UTI, or kidney issues. Therefore, if your dog is urinating or defecating in the house despite proper training, the veterinarian should rule out any issues that can cause loss of bladder or bowel control.

The Most Common Housebreaking Hiccups

My puppy pees when I pick him up.

Some puppies urinate when excited. It can happen simply from being overwhelmed with attention or with the expectation of attention. This is also known as excitement urination behavior. If your puppy appears to be doing this, you may find a few things to be helpful:

1. Try to play with your puppy outside.
2. Bring your puppy to the designated bathroom area to urinate before playtime.
3. For pups that easily become over-excited, it is best to approach from the side and slowly introduce playtime.
4. Puppies that display this behavior should not be directly picked up. It is best to kneel beside your puppy, pat him a bit, and then gently roll him onto your lap. This eliminates the sudden excitement of being swept up.

My dog pees or poops as soon as I bring him back inside.

It is important to make sure that your dog is focusing on the task and to allow enough time.

In regard to focusing, make sure that your pup is not multitasking:

- There should be **no** playing or roaming around the yard.
- Keep your dog on a 6-foot leash or retractable leash let out about 6 feet.
- Stand in the middle of the designated area, and allow him to circle within that spot. While he may sniff and look around, do not engage in any play or talk that may disturb him.

In regard to time, it would be very helpful if dogs went on cue. But, some need up to 15 to 20 minutes for bowel movements (bowel muscles need to relax first). With urination, a dog may release half the bladder and need a bit more time to release the rest. Set up an outdoor chair, bring your phone, or flip through a book, but give him enough time.

If this is truly a matter of peeing immediately after coming back in, a good trick is to come in and then hold your dog on your lap. A dog will not pee on his owner when held this way. The only exceptions are if there is a health issue that is causing a weak bladder, *high* levels of stress, or a legitimate need to go to the bathroom in which the dog struggles to hold on, but the bladder lets go. Therefore, keep him on your lap for about 10 minutes and then carry him right back to the designated bathroom area. Most likely, he will pee at that time.

My dog can't hold his needs for more than an hour.

Sudden loss of bladder or bowel control can be a red flag warning of a health issue. So, this should be ruled out first. With a full and complete checkup to ensure that there are no issues, an owner can then look to other reasons.

Barring any health issues, this is frequently a matter of a dog needing to strengthen bladder and/or bowel muscles. Here's how it works: Young puppies have very little control over holding their needs. As pups grow, bladder and bowel muscles grow stronger; but, the degree to which they strengthen depends, in part, on your actions.

If you took an 8-week-old pup outside every 2 hours and stayed doing that once he turned 3, and then 4-months-old, his body would remain accustomed to going every 2 hours. The key will be to gradually let there be longer intervals between visits to the designated bathroom area.

It will be a careful balance between closely supervising him *and* bringing him out a bit later than normal. Always use the confinement or supervision methods, as discussed earlier. Aim for 15 minutes longer than usual and slowly work out from there. A dog that is used to going every 3 hours cannot suddenly learn to hold on for 8 hours; however, if this is done in 15-minute intervals over the course of days and weeks, he can certainly work his way there.

My dog pees or poops at night when I'm sleeping! He didn't even wake me up.

There are a few things you can do; Please note that this refers to middle-of-the-night bathroom needs, early morning issues are next.

1. Bring your dog outside both 1 hour before bed, and then 20 minutes before bed, allotting the 15 to 20 minutes we touched on earlier.
2. Try to have your dog's last bite of the day be 2 hours before bed.
3. Do not, however, limit water.
4. Have your dog in a defined area, so that messes are not deposited around the house. The playpen set-up that we discussed works well for this. If you are not alerted to a bathroom need, there is a good chance that the pads will be used.
5. Make sure that your dog gets enough exercise and activity during the day, which can help provide a good night's sleep. This includes 2 to 3 walks per day (20-minute minimum each) plus a 15 to 20-minute session of cardio (fetch or similar game).

My dog pees or poos very early in the morning.

There are several things you can do:

1. Experiment with changing your dog's last meal of the day to be 1 or even 2 hours earlier. By doing this, there is a better chance that he will pee and poo when taken outside in the evening for his last bathroom trip before bed. If you do this, offer a small dry snack at the time that your dog usually had dinner.

2. Alternatively, the opposite may work. If you feed your dog 2 hours later than usual, he may not need to eliminate until 2 hours later than normal the next morning. If you do this, offer a small dry snack at the time that your dog usually had dinner.

3. Exercise your dog more in the evening. While you don't want to offer exercise too close to bedtime, taking a longer walk than normal or playing an energetic game of fetch about 2 hours before bed can help tire a dog out so that he sleeps longer in the morning.

4. In certain instances, some type of noise may be waking a dog. This may be birds chirping, a neighbor closing his car door, etc. Moving your dog's sleeping area to one that is more insulated from outside noises may help. Another option is to use a white noise machine to block out sounds that may be disturbing your dog's sleep.

5. Sometimes, a dog will wake up and bark because he is bored; an owner may mistake this for a bathroom need. The owner takes the dog out, and since he's outside, he does let out some urine. But, if the dog was able to keep himself occupied when he woke, he may have stayed busy before barking to gain an owner's attention. For these cases, it can help to sneak a treat-release toy into a dog's sleeping area once he is down for the night. When he wakes, he'll discover it and may remain happily quiet, at least for a little bit.

[handwritten margin note: BARKING EARLY CAN BE CAUSED THROU BOREDO AND NOT BAT ROO NEE]

My dog goes to the bathroom everywhere in the house!

If this is a full emptying of the bladder and the problem started suddenly, this can point to a health issue such as bladder infection or urinary tract infection. This warrants a veterinarian visit.

If this is a light spraying of urine, often in repeated areas, this may be a matter of territorial marking. Look to the upcoming 'Marking' section for details on this.

If this is a matter of a dog not understanding housebreaking rules, you will want to start over from scratch. Even if you put months into training your dog, if there are urine and feces all over the house, clearly something went wrong. Often, it is due to a skipped step. With housebreaking, skipping over steps to save time usually just wastes time. Read back through this chapter, with a commitment to follow each rule.

My dog rips apart/moves his pee pads.

A pee pad holder can work in these cases. At the time of this writing, a good one is the Dogit Training Pad Holder. It has a raised edge to contain puddles, and it holds a pad firmly in place. There are also some cat litter boxes that can serve as good pee pads holders for dogs.

In addition, be sure that your dog has the right chew toys to satisfy chewing urges, the right 'stay busy' toys to keep him occupied, and 2 to 3 walks per day and a 15 to 20-minute session of cardio to release pent-up energy that may be manifesting as restless behavior.

My dog keeps missing the pee pad. *Play pen*

This can happen if a dog's area is too large, such as half of a room sectioned off with gates. Opposite to this, we do not suggest leaving a dog in too small of an area, since this can cause claustrophobic-type feelings, which can be both physically and emotionally stressful. However, the area should be only big enough for a bed, food & water, a toy area, and pee pads. Dogs rarely soil their own belongings, so having a defined, smaller space often means that the pads are indeed used.

A 24" high (8 square foot) playpen is often a good size for puppies. Extensions can be obtained for adults.

Submissive Urination

This refers to a dog urinating upon seeing or interacting with his owner, other people, or other dogs. It can be confusing to see this because it often appears as if the dog has lost bladder control due to being scared, and this can be particularly troubling if it's done to an owner who never gave the dog a reason to feel that way.

Signs of submissive urination:

• Dribbling urine or emptying of the bladder, as if control has been lost.
• Submissive body stance (cowering down, possibly shaking), looking up to a person with a look of fear or hanging the head down in 'shame' with refusal for eye contact.
• A 'submissive grin'; this can be mistaken for a 'mean' growl since teeth are showing, but is actually the pulling back of the corners of the mouth, which is a type of canine appeasement. A dog may lick his lips, squint his eyes, and/or wiggle the body while making this 'grin'.

Reasons for submissive urination:

Despite the term, this may be done for reasons other than fear. Possible triggers also include:

• Excitement
• Nervousness
• Confusion
• Sensory overload

Issues often mistaken for submissive urination:

• Health issues, including but not limited to urinary tract infection (UTI), bladder infection, kidney issues. If you suspect any of these, bring your dog to the veterinarian.
• Housebreaking issues. If so, a dog will urinate inside at other times as well, not just upon seeing you or someone else.
• Marking. If so, a dog will spray urine in the house; it will not be a full and quick release of the bladder.

Tips to resolve this:

In reaction to other dogs:

1. Do not rush or force your dog to interact with other dogs.
2. Start working on socialization and desensitization training, to allow your dog the opportunity to gradually become accustomed to other dogs. Details can be found under 'Behavioral Training: Socialization & Desensitization Training' and 'Situational Issues: Afraid of Other Dogs'.

In reaction to you:

1. Bring your dog outside to the designated bathroom area quite frequently. If you feel that you are already doing this, still add 2 to 3 more trips each day.

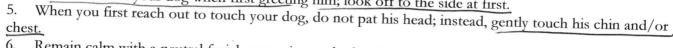

2.   Do not have immediate, direct contact. For example, if your dog always pees when you enter the house and greet him, do not greet him right away, get a glass of water, thumb through the mail, and then say hello.

3.   Do not stand and hover over your dog; kneel down to say hello.

4.   Do not stare at your dog when first greeting him; look off to the side at first.

5.   When you first reach out to touch your dog, do not pat his head; instead, gently touch his chin and/or chest.

6.   Remain calm with a neutral facial expression and relaxed body stance in response to any submissive urination. Simply gather your cleaning products, and clean up the puddle.

As time goes by, the behavior should improve; if not, it will be time to reassess if there are any health issues that could be affecting the bladder.

In reaction to other people outside of the household:

1.   If this happens when guests arrive:

   o   If your dog likes guests and urines due to excitement, have him first greet them outdoors.
   o   If your dog is fearful of guests, have him secure within his playpen, with his bed and toys so that he feels safe.

2. If it happens with people that you know, and you feel comfortable in recruiting them, have them follow all of the same guidelines as mentioned earlier under 'In reaction to you'.

3. In all cases: Start working on command training, or reintroduce this. This is a surefire way to help boost a dog's self-confidence.

Marking

If your dog is marking, no doubt you are feeling a bit frustrated. However, this can be resolved. You'll want to read through this section carefully since strict adherence to the guidelines is needed for success.

What is Marking? When a dog has a legitimate need to urinate, he or she will empty their bladder. Opposite to that, with marking:

-   Small amounts of urine will be sprayed out; the dog will not release his entire bladder.
-   The dog is house trained and does not eliminate feces in the home, but only urinates inside.
-   The dog marks vertical objects (such as table legs) and/or marks entrance points to the house. In some cases, the owner's bed is marked and/or the entrance to the owner's bedroom.

Some Facts to Know:

-   Both genders are capable of marking; however, males do this more than females.
-   Even if a dog is fixed he/she may mark; however, neutered males and spayed females mark far less often than dogs that are intact.
-   Technically, this is not a housebreaking issue. Even if there is a complete understanding of house training rules, a dog may still develop marking behavior.

Other Things That Can Be Mistaken for Marking: Even if your dog meets the criteria as listed, there is still a chance that something else is going on. And since identifying the real problem is the only road to actually resolving it, it is important to assess if your dog has other issues that need to be addressed:

Not being 100% fully housebroken. This is quite common as an issue misidentified as marking. Your dog may very well pee and poo when you bring him outside. But, this in and of itself does not mean that your dog is trained.

If you are timing it just right, your dog may be urinating and eliminating where he stands, which just happens to be in the designated bathroom area. If so, this is a matter of convenience, timing, and coincidence, not of your dog truly understanding that he is following guidelines; in reality, he only followed his owner out the door and to a spot in the yard.

If you believe that your dog has a housebreaking issue, and not a marking issue, refer back to the 'Housebreaking' chapter to make sure that every rule is followed.

Health issues. There are a number of issues that can cause a dog to lose control of his bladder. This includes but is not limited to urinary tract infection (UTI), bladder infection, bladder stones, kidney infection, kidney stones, and diabetes.

Reasons why a Dog Marks: If all health issues have been ruled out and if you are sure that your dog fully understands the housebreaking rules, it is then time to look at reasons that may be prompting marking behavior.

✓ **Improper understanding of hierarchy.** This is the most common reason that dogs mark. The hierarchy is the balance of leadership in the house. In a dog's mind, there is no such thing as everyone being equal; there is always a leader (Alpha) of the family (pack) in the house (den), and anyone under the leader is a follower (Beta), as they follow the leader's rule. This is the canine way.

If a dog feels that he is the leader (Alpha), he may mark to hold onto his perceived title. And if he even thinks that the position is up for grabs, he may mark to try and gain it.

While an owner may feel that it is blatantly obvious that they are the leader based on all that they do for their dog, that dog may have much different ideas. And with toy dogs, we must remember that essentially, size does not matter here. A dog will not automatically assume that his human is his leader because the owner is 10 times his size.

If a dog feels that he is superior to his humans, he may mark his territory (and he *is* following canine rules by doing this). Alternatively, some dogs that believe they are in charge, will feel that as leader, one of their roles is to protect the household. When a dog protects, he does this by claiming territory; it is a dog's way of saying to potential trespassers: 'I am here, this area is mine, I will protect everyone who resides here, keep away!'

Urine is then sprayed over areas that the dog considers to be important. This typically includes areas near entrance doors, though it may be vertical objects as well.

In addition, a dog may mark his owner's bed, near the bed, or at the entrance to the bedroom. This is a very interesting aspect since many owners feel personally insulted if a dog is peeing on their bed. This is often mistaken for the dog 'getting back' at their human or doing this out of spite. But in reality, it is typically a case of a dog marking his owner's bed to protect his human from outsiders. In a funny way, this is actually a compliment!

In some cases, a dog will urinate on his owner's leg when the owner is standing or on the foot when the owner is sitting; this is often a clear sign of *severe* improper understanding of hierarchy.

Note that if a dog pees on his human when cuddling on the lap, this may be due to a health issue (that is causing a weak bladder), high level of stress, or in rare cases, a legitimate need to go to the bathroom.

✓ **Competition with other pets/animals.** In a house with proper hierarchy, the humans are the leaders (Alphas) and the dog is the Beta. However, in multiple-dog homes, within the 'animal pack' of Betas, there is also a leader. In other words, there is always an 'Alpha Dog' in the literal sense. If it is not clear (in the dog's mind) who the 'head dog' is, there may be a 'battle for dominance' and marking is one way that dogs do this.

✓ **Stating sexual availability.** This is one reason why territorial marking is so much more prevalent with unfixed dogs. With an un-neutered male, there are strong urges to mate. They can sense un-spayed females from up to 3 miles away. So, your neighbor's dog, the dog down the street, or even one completely out of view may be triggering your unfixed male to announce that he is there.

With un-spayed females, as the heat cycle comes around, hormones are climbing and so is the urge to mate. While females cannot sense potential mates as their male counterparts can, what they do like to do is announce their presence so that males can find them.

MARKING CHECKLIST
✓ Urine is cleaned with an enzyme cleanser
✓ Block visuals to other dogs, if possible
✓ If the dog marks one specific area, turn that spot into a play area
✓ Keep a close eye on your dog & use distraction if he starts to mark
✓ If you can't keep a close eye on your dog, have him behind a gate or in a canine playpen
✓ Reassess if proper hierarchy is in place
✓ Consider neutering/spaying all pets

Trying to figure out the reason for marking: While there are always exceptions, some general guidelines that may help you know which reason is the cause of marking is as follows:

- Marking on your bed and/or at the entrances to the house (fixed or intact dogs) – Improper hierarchy
- Intact dog marking all over the house – Mating urges and/or improper hierarchy
- Marking on objects belonging to visitors - Improper hierarchy
- Peeing on someone's foot or leg - Improper hierarchy
- Peeing on someone's lap – Health issue, stress, and/or legitimate need to urinate
- Peeing inside only when home alone – Legitimate need to urinate
- Marking if there is more than one pet in the house – Battle for dominance within the 'animal pack', may be concurrent with other reasons

How to Stop Marking Behavior: Please note that these should be done after all possible health issues are ruled out.

1) If your dog is not neutered or spayed, you may wish to consider having this done. See also: 'Health – Other: Spaying and Neutering'.

2) Properly clean any marked areas with an enzyme cleanser. If you wash the area with water and soap, it won't be effective. The scent of soap can trigger a dog to mark in order to cover that scent up AND regular soap does not remove lingering urine odors that signal dogs to mark the spot repeatedly. You'll want to use a quality enzyme killing formula that breaks down the tiny particles found in urine, leaving no traces behind.

3) Try to block your dog from seeing other dogs walking near the home. Depending on the layout of your home, curtains can be closed, etc.

4) Try to make the area in which your dog is marking into a play area. Give him toys there, use the spot to interact, etc.

5) Do not allow your dog to have free reign in the house. Give him one room (via gates) or have him in a playpen when you cannot supervise.

6) When home with your dog, maintain close supervision. As soon as you see your dog get into position to urinate, make a loud noise to distract him (loud hand clap, shake of a can with coins in it, or a behavioral device that lets out a short hissing noise like The Company of Animals Pet Corrector) and then immediately bring him to his bathroom area. Give enthusiastic praise and reward if he urinates there.

7) Work to establish proper hierarchy. This includes never giving meals or snacks until a 'Sit' is obeyed, humans enter and exit the house first, and always having a dog obey a heel while walking. As to not repeat text, full details are under 'Training: Teaching Proper Hierarchy'.

Marking Behavior with More Than 1 Dog:
Since a dog may mark to battle for ranking among the animals and will often stop once a leader is chosen, you can help by establishing which dog is the Alpha Dog.

If two dogs are the same gender, it's usually the older dog. If it's a male and female relatively close in age, it'll be the male. However, you can take notice when the dogs are playing. Is one of them more outgoing? Is one dog pushier when it comes to choosing toys? Which dog runs to the kitchen first for dinner? Noticing this will help you know who is trying harder to be the Alpha Dog.

Once you know, you can then help both dogs. Essentially, you will do everything for the Alpha Dog first. When it is time to feed your dogs dinner, give the Alpha Dog his food first. When handing out treats, the Alpha Dog gets his first. When it is time to take the dogs outside for a walk, put the harness and leash on the Alpha Dog first. These small gestures help the dogs feel secure that you- the main leader- are showing them that you understand the order of the 'pack'.

Remember that the dog that is not the Alpha Dog is just as important and loved as the other. Not being the Alpha Dog is not a negative thing. Both dogs will be less stressed by knowing where they fit in. In addition, follow all of the general rules of stopping marking behavior.

Feeding and Nutrition

Nutritional Needs

Canines require a wide range of certain nutrients to keep their body functioning at optimal levels:

Protein (and amino acids). Protein is a vital building block for the entire body: bones, muscles, cartilage, skin, and blood. Dietary protein contains 10 amino acids that a dog cannot make on his own, which all play important roles, including providing the carbon chains needed to make glucose, which is a primary energy source. The 10 essential amino acids found in meat protein are arginine, histadine, isoleucine, leucine, lysine, methionine, phenylalanine, threonine, tryptophan, and valine. Studies show that dogs can sense when their dog food lacks a single amino acid and may even avoid eating it.

Carbohydrates. Dogs need a certain amount of energy to fuel normal day-to-day activities. Growth, pregnancy, lactation, and exercise all increase these energy requirements. This energy comes from carbohydrates, as well as protein and fats.

Healthy Fats. Dietary fat is the most concentrated source of energy for a dog. It also provides essential fatty acids (important for skin and coat health) and aids in how nutrients are transported and used by the body. Fat is involved in cell integrity and aids in regulating the metabolism.

Vitamins & Minerals. This includes:

- Vitamin A - For vision, organ function, and the immune system.
- Vitamin B1 (thiamine) - For energy metabolism; important to nerve function.
- Vitamin B2 (riboflavin)- For energy metabolism; important for vision and skin health.
- Vitamin B3 (niacin) - For energy metabolism; important for the nervous system, digestive system, and skin health.
- Vitamin B6 (pyridoxine)- For protein metabolism; helps make red blood cells.
- Vitamin B12 (cobalamin) - For making new cells; important to nerve function.
- Vitamin C (ascorbic acid) - An antioxidant, is part of an enzyme needed for protein metabolism, important for immune system health, aids in iron absorption.
- Vitamin D - Helps the body absorb calcium.
- Vitamin E – Is an antioxidant.
- Vitamin K - Activates bone proteins.
- Beta-carotene - Important for eye health and a strong immune system. Keeps skin healthy. About 3% of this gets converted in Vitamin A.
- Biotin - Needed for energy metabolism.

- Calcium - For strong bones and teeth. Helps blood clot and helps nerves send messages. Also aids in muscle contraction.
- Folic acid - Helps with protein synthesis.
- Phosphorous - Works with calcium to keep bones and teeth healthy.
- Omega-3, 6, and 9 - Plays a role in cell structure and function, helps keep skin and coat healthy.
- Magnesium - Helps the body absorb other vitamins, is needed for proper bone growth and is used in the production of protein.

Calorie Requirements

It's understandable that you may wish to know how many calories your puppy or dog requires. And this sort of question can be answered; however, it is much more important to focus on feeding the best food possible than it is to count every calorie. This info is, for the most part, just to satisfy curiosity.

The number of calories that a puppy needs to fuel his growing body or an adult needs to maintain weight depends on a few different factors:

Activity level. This is one of the most significant factors. There are surprisingly very few studies that have been done regarding how many calories canines burn when walking or doing other activities. However, it is generally accepted that a typical canine will burn 65 calories during a 1-hour walk. A Chihuahua, we estimate, due to his diminutive size, would burn 1/3 to 1/4 of this, which is around 20 calories or so.

This may not seem like a lot since humans can burn anywhere between 200 and 400 calories per hour when walking, depending on their pace, weight, and so forth. Nevertheless, since a tiny dog requires much fewer calories per day than his human family members, those 20 or so calories are going to count against a much smaller daily number.

Age is another important aspect to factor in. Puppies have a higher metabolism than adult dogs. The 1st year is one of rapid growth, which requires nutrients and calories to fuel a growing body. This evens out around the age of 10 to 12 months. Then, as a dog matures into a senior, the metabolism slows down even more. Seniors 8 years and older may burn anywhere from 50 to 100 fewer calories per day. On top of this, activity for a senior dog often decreases as there may be issues with arthritis or other age-related conditions that affect mobility.

Health Issues. Some health conditions may affect a dog's metabolism and therefore his calorie needs. This includes but is not limited to hypothyroidism and heart problems. In addition, some medications may cause weight gain even if a dog is not eating more food; this is usually due to water retention, and others can cause increased appetite, resulting in a dog consuming more food and calories.

Spayed/ Neutered Dogs. Despite many assumptions about this, in most cases, a spayed or neutered dog does not need fewer calories than those that are intact. For the small percentage of dogs that *do* gain weight after being fixed, it is theorized that this may have to do with the fact that the dog is calmer; he is not pacing all day rearing to find a mate or acting hyper due to hormones. While pacing and other such actions do not count as 'exercise', this *does* fall under the category of NEAT (Non-Exercise Activity Thermogenesis), which is the energy (calories) expended for random movements (for humans, this is tapping one's fingers, sorting through the mail, etc. For canines this is moving the tail, chewing on a toy, etc.)

So, a calmer dog equals a dog that is burning fewer calories and therefore that dog does not require as many.

The figures involved here are *very* tiny; however, over the course of a year or two, this can add up.

Calories in the Food You Feed Your Dog: Some owners opt for home cooking. While you will have many choices of ingredients, here are the counts for some of the most popular food items:

White breast chicken (no skin) = 124 calories for 4 ounces, sugar snap peas = 10 calories per 1/4 cup, sweet potato = 62 calories per 1/4 cup, white rice = 66 calories per 1/4 cup, carrots = 14 calories in 1/4 cup (chopped), blueberries = 21 calories per 1/4 cup, raspberries = 17 calories per 1/4 cup.

Concerning commercial dog food, calorie count alone does little to tell you if a kibble is excellent, terrible or something in between. But, on the whole, better brands have a higher calorie count per cup, since inferior brands pack the food with fillers, which contain very few calories (or nutrients).

How Many Calories a Puppy Needs: This is for the age of 2-months to 1-year and therefore with such an age range, these numbers are a general guideline only.

Puppies need more calories per pound of body weight than adults do; roughly 55 calories per pound of body weight, compared to an adult dog that requires approximately 40 calories per pound of body weight.

Due to growth spurts and stops, these numbers are very general and should not be strictly adhered to. Following feeding guidelines on your chosen kibble, seeing a healthy gradual weight gain, and adhering to the veterinarian's recommendations will tell you are feeding your puppy enough. Variations in metabolic rates can alter these numbers by as much as 20%.

Weight 1 lb. (0.45 kg) = approx. 55 calories | Weight 3 lbs. (1.36 kg) = approx. 165 calories
Weight 2 lbs. (0.90 kg) = approx. 110 calories | Weight 4 lbs. (1.81 kg) = approx. 220 calories

At the 1-year mark, you can then refer to the guidelines below for the calorie needs of an adult dog.

How Many Calories an Adult Needs to Maintain Weight: The following is a general guideline only, as each dog is unique. Figures are for adult dogs that are done growing and have reached their full width and height. Variations in metabolic rates can alter these numbers by as much as 20%.

Note: The first calorie amount is an estimate for an adult that exercises 1 time per day (35 calories per pound of body weight), the second amount is an estimate for an adult that exercises 2 to 3 times per day (40 calories per pound of body weight).

Weight 2.5 lbs. (1.14 kg) = approx. 88 calories | approx. 100 calories
Weight 3 lbs. (1.36 kg) = approx. 105 calories | approx. 120 calories
Weight 3.5 lbs. (1.59 kg) = approx. 123 calories | approx. 140 calories
Weight 4 lbs. (1.81 kg) = approx. 140 calories | approx. 160 calories
Weight 4.5 lbs. (2.04 kg) = approx. 158 calories | approx. 180 calories
Weight 5 lbs. (2.26 kg) = approx. 175 calories | approx. 200 calories
Weight 5.5 lbs. (2.50 kg) = approx. 193 calories | approx. 220 calories
Weight 6 lbs. (2.72 kg) = approx. 210 calories | approx. 240 calories
Weight 6.5 lbs. (2.95 kg) = approx. 228 calories | approx. 260 calories
Weight 7 lbs. (3.17 kg) = approx. 245 calories | approx. 280 calories
Weight 7.5 lbs. (3.40 kg) = approx. 263 calories | approx. 300 calories
Weight 8 lbs. (3.62 kg) = approx. 280 calories | approx. 320 calories
Weight 9 lbs. (4.08 kg) = approx. 315 calories | approx. 360 calories
Weight 10 lbs. (4.54 kg) = approx. 350 calories | approx. 400 calories

Senior Calorie Needs: Seniors may need fewer calories than their active, adult counterparts. The number of calories required per day will vary greatly from dog to dog (because health and activity levels vary so much), yet may be in the 33 calories per pound of body weight range.

Malnourishment at this stage in life can affect lifespan and exacerbate any health issues, so you'll want to make sure that your senior is eating a bit less due to decreased activity causing decreased appeitite, and not because of another reason. A senior dog may have trouble eating due to tooth infection or loss, health conditions, or side effects of medication, all of which require veterinary care.

While the following can be used as a general reference point, it is highly recommended to discuss calorie and nutritional needs with your dog's veterinarian, if you have any concerns. These figures are for dogs 8+ years that are fairly inactive (if your senior still runs around and goes for daily walks at a good pace, calorie requirements may not decrease). Variations in metabolic rates can alter these numbers by as much as 20%.

Weight 3 lbs. (1.36 kg) = approx. 100 calories | Weight 7 lbs. (3.17 kg) = approx. 231 calories
Weight 4 lbs. (1.81 kg) = approx. 132 calories | Weight 8 lbs. (3.62 kg) = approx. 264 calories
Weight 5 lbs. (2.26 kg) = approx. 165 calories | Weight 9 lbs. (4.08 kg) = approx. 297 calories
Weight 6 lbs. (2.72 kg) = approx. 198 calories | Weight 10 lbs. (4.54 kg) = approx. 330 calories

Remember, always use common sense over calorie counts, and in most situations calorie counting is not needed when a dog is healthy, eating quality meals, and receiving regular exercise.

All Meal Feeding Details

What you choose for main meals, snacks, and training treats, and the aspect of filtered vs. non-filtered water, has a direct significant impact on your dog's health; both now and in the future.

Main Meals

There are over 2,000 different dog food brands and recipes. And a huge percentage of them are severely lacking in a number of ways. Many of the ones that you see stacked up high in supermarkets or pet supply stores are the biggest culprits. Inferior dog food can cause a host of troubling issues including immediate allergic reactions and long-term health effects. It is vital to understand what can be in dog food and how this can affect your canine family member.

What to avoid:

Many of these are not rare ingredients that only pop up in random, unknown dog food brands once in a while. These are very common elements in a LOT of commercial dog foods.

☠ **Synthetic preservatives.** Butylated hydroxyanisole (BHA), butylated hydroxytoluene (BHT), and tert-butyl hydroquinone (TBHQ) are known carcinogens. Ethoxyquin and propylene glycol (PG) are toxins. ***And, these do not necessarily need to be labeled.*** Chemical preservatives added to protect 'protein meals' - in low enough quantities - counts as an 'incidental additive' and you will not see it on the label.

These artificial preservatives can make a dog sick, cause terrible allergic reactions, and cause future health issues including cancer.

☠ **Artificial coloring dyes.** Blue 2, Red 40, Yellow 5, Yellow 6 can cause allergic reactions.

☠ **Artificial flavoring.** MSG (monosodium glutamate). Numerous animal studies have proven this to be toxic to the liver, brain, thymus, and kidney. This can cause severe allergic reactions including itching and rash, but also heart palpitations and moodiness. Look out for soy extracts and soy concentrate; these contain MSG.

☹ **By-products.** This will be labeled as 'chicken by-product', 'beef by-product', etc. These are animal parts that are deemed unfit for human consumption and may include lungs, brain, bone, intestines, stomach, spleen, liver, kidneys, and undeveloped eggs. Many brands put this in dog food since it is much cheaper than human-grade meat.

☹ **Generic meat.** Shocking but true, and completely legal, is the process of adding in meat and body parts from roadkill and zoo animals that have died. Generic meats also include cats, dogs, and other animals that have been euthanized.

Some states have laws dictating that only livestock and fish can eat rendered meat from dead pets; however, it is commonplace for some companies to bypass this law by selling out-of-state. Also included with this are expired meat from butcher shops, restaurants, and grocery stores.

How common is this? Every month, approximately 200 tons of dead pets are shipped out of Los Angeles and into rendering plants. And there are an estimated 165+ rendering plants all across the country that churn out this 'food' for livestock, fish, and pets. You'll see this listed as 'meat', 'animal', or 'animal meal'. And look out for 'animal fat' or 'animal oil'.

☹ **High corn and grain count (may exclude rice).** These are cheap fillers added to bulk up food. Many dogs are sensitive to or allergic to corn (includes corn germ meal, corn gluten meal, and corn bran) and grains (includes wheat, oats, barley, and other cereal grains which may be listed as hominy feed).

Words to Look Out For

- butylated hydroxyanisole (BHA)
- butylated hydroxytoluene (BHT)
- tert-butyl hydroquinone (TBHQ)
- ethoxyquin
- propylene glycol (PG)
- Blue 2, Red 40, Yellow 5, Yellow 6
- MSG
- soy, soy meal, soybean, soy extract, & soy concentrate
- by-product
- meat
- animal
- meal (only in some cases)
- corn, corn meal, corn germ meal, corn gluten meal, corn bran
- grain, oat, barley, hominy feed, wheat middlings
- peanut hulls
- menadione

Rice can be an exception; with rice, the hull, bran layer, and cereal germ is removed and for this reason, rice is often tolerated very well.

☹ **Soy.** Soy can cause allergic reactions; this can be listed as soy, soybeans, and soy meal.

☹ **Other fillers and additives.** There is almost an endless list; however, some to avoid include wheat mill run (may be listed as wheat middlings) which is what's swept off the floor of wheat factories, peanut hulls which is a cheap filler, and menadione which is linked to liver toxicity, the abnormal break-down of red blood cells, and allergies.

◇ **Meal (depends).** Be careful here. Technically, 'meal' refers to a meat that is cooked prior to being added in; this *can* be a way to offer a dense source of protein. But, it can also be from animals that were diseased or were dying on route to facilities; these meats are pulverized and heated to very high temperatures.

Consequences of these ingredients:

- **Allergies.** There is a long list of possible signs of food ingredient allergies; however, keep in mind that your dog may have just ONE of these, which warrants a reason to switch foods. Symptoms include:

  o Itching (may manifest as chewing and/or licking at the paws, or scratching)
  o Rash
  o Hot spots
  o Irritated skin
  o Scabs
  o Poor coat texture
  o Wheezing
  o Irritated eyes
  o Runny eyes
  o Reoccurring ear infections
  o Digestive issues (flatulence, diarrhea, nausea, vomiting)

  Much more information regarding allergies is covered under 'Health - Other: Allergies'.

- **Malnutrition.** The body will be lacking core nutrients. Short-term this can cause poor energy levels, poor muscle tone, and behaviors may manifest such as consumption of grass and/or feces. Long-term, it leads to health issues.

- **Health issues.** This ranges from weak immune system to organ damage to cancer.

Less than ideal brands?

A considerable number of dog food brands are less than ideal. Some are downright dangerous. There are far too many to list; however, Dog Food Advisor (https://www.dogfoodadvisor.com), which has been rating dog food since 2008, gives just a 1 or 2-star rating to some or all of the recipes of the following brands (as of the time of this writing): Alpo, Atta Boy! , Ben's Best, Beneful, Cesar, Country Acres, Defender, Everpet, Good Sense, Gravy Train, Iams, Kibbles 'n Bits, Pedigree, Purina, Royal Canin (some recipes are 3-star, see below), Simply Right, Solid Gold, SportMix, Total Canine, Trader Joe's Kibble, Tuffy's, and V-Dog.

And many are rated as only 3-stars; this includes, but certainly is not limited to Artemis, Back to Basics, Bil-Jac, Blue Buffalo, Caliber, Canidae Life Stages, Diamond, Eukanuba, Halo Vigor, Natural Balance, Nutro, Royal Canin, and Triumph.

What to look for:

Now that we know what to avoid and the consequences of those ingredients, let's see what you will want your puppy or dog's food to have:

✓ Naturally preserved. Kibble will be preserved using vitamin E (may be listed as mixed tocopherols), and/or vitamin C (may be listed as ascorbic acid and/or ascorbyl palmitate), as well as some plant extracts including rosemary, sage, and/or clove.

✓ Natural flavoring and no coloring.

✓ Protein will come from wholesome animal sources including chicken, turkey, lamb, fish, and beef. There will be no by-products or generic meats.

✓ Grain-free or wheat-free. No corn, wheat, or soy. For many dogs, rice is just fine. Though, some of our top recommended brands are completely grain-free.

✓ No other fillers or controversial additives.

✓ Helpful extras such as:
- o Glucosamine and chondroitin, which is beneficial for joint health
- o Omega-3 and/or 6, from fish oil and secondarily from flaxseed, for healthy skin and coat
- o Probiotics for immune health
- o Antioxidants to help prevent disease

✓ Balanced levels of protein, carbs, healthy fats, and fiber. This can vary; however, a good guideline is:
- o Protein in the mid to high 30's (34 to 36%)
- o Carbs, which are a primary source of energy, between 30 and 40%
- o Healthy fats around 15%
- o Fiber 4 to 7%

✓ Healthy blend of natural vitamins and minerals (not synthetic) from real, wholesome fruits such as apples and blueberries.

✓ Made in the US or North America (some of the best wild fish are caught off of the Canadian coast).

✓ Appropriately sized for toy or small breed dogs. Most kibble designed with medium or large dogs in mind will be too large Chihuahuas to comfortably eat and will not be designed for a small dog's digestive system.

 Since dog food brands are always evolving, yet this book is static, our current recommendations for superior kibbles are on the Supplies page of the PetChiDog site, which is updated as new recipes emerge. You can reach this by entering any page PetChiDog.com; look to the navigation which is in alphabetical order, and choose 'Supplies'.

Home cooking: Home cooking can be a good option if you enjoy preparing food. In some cases, it can be cost-effective, particularly if you buy in bulk. Some additional supplements are needed, however. This includes:

- A canine vitamin and mineral daily supplement. It's near impossible for any recipe to contain all necessary vitamins and minerals; Manufactured brands add vitamins & minerals to their mix, and you will need to as well.

- Omega-3 fish oil. Since it is difficult to offer proper omega-3 levels (unless you are feeding your dog lots of fish), you may want to consider adding in a daily serving of liquid fish oil, which can be mixed into a meal.
- Glucosamine and chondroitin. As mentioned earlier, these are beneficial for joint health.

Also see: 'Feeding and Nutrition: Supplements'.

Ingredients to choose from include:

40% meat/fish: This includes white chicken meat or turkey (de-boned, no skin, baked or broiled), lean beef, fish (mackerel, whitefish, salmon, herring, walleye, flounder), lamb, bison, and/or pork (should not be the main protein source, but can be blended into meals). Other sources include beans such as lima beans, kidney beans, and butter beans (must be cooked).

25 % vegetables: This includes peas, carrots, spinach, zucchini, green beans, and butternut squash. You can also offer kale, cauliflower and broccoli (in moderation since these foods can cause gas,). Pumpkin in moderation is fine but typically reserved to help ease upset stomach issues. Canines can eat tomatoes; however, this is typically used as an ingredient in mixed meals, to add flavor.

25% carbs: This can include oatmeal (plain), white or brown rice (if no intolerance), potato, and/or sweet potato.

10% fruit: This includes blueberries, raspberries (both are low calorie, high in antioxidants, and water-packed), strawberries, banana, mango, pear, and apple (no core, no seeds). Dogs can also have watermelon and oranges in moderation.

Added extras: This can include cottage cheese, plain whole white yogurt, and/or eggs (most dogs do best with scrambled eggs vs. boiled eggs).

All food should be mixed very well and served warm. When you refrigerate extras, be sure to put the food in air-tight containers.

Recipes:

Meatloaf

Ingredients:
- 2 small eggs, slightly beaten
- 1/4 cup baby peas
- 1/2 cup shredded carrots
- 1 pound of mixed ground lean hamburg and ground chicken
- 1 cup plain oatmeal
- 8 ounces of tomato paste
  - ➤ You will need a steamer, a strainer, a large bowl, a baking sheet, aluminum foil, and non-stick cooking spray.

Directions:

1) Preheat the oven to 450°F (232°C).
2) Steam shredded carrots and peas for 4 minutes. Then drain and allow to cool.

3) Place all ingredients in a large bowl (egg, peas, carrots, meat, oatmeal, and tomato paste) and mix very well to combine them.

4) You can shape this into a bone or a heart shape (just for fun) or a loaf shape. Place this on a foil-lined baking sheet with a touch of non-stick spray on it.

5) Bake for 30 minutes or until an internal temperature of 160°F (71°C).

6) Remove from oven when done, dice into cubes, and allow to cool for 10 minutes before serving.

7) Offer a handful of blueberries and raspberries for a healthy, antioxidant-packed dessert.

Foods a Dog Can Eat

Protein	Vegetables	Carbs/starch	Fruits	Extras
• chicken • turkey • lean beef • fish • lamb • bison • pork • kidney beans • lima beans • butter beans	• peas • carrots • spinach • zucchini • grean beans • butternut squash • kale • cauliflower • broccoli • pumpkin (reserved for upset stomach issues) • tomato (reserved for mixed meals)	• oatmeal (plain) • rice (white or brown, if no intolerance to rice) • potato • sweet potato	• blueberries • raspberries • strawberries • banana • mango • pear • apple (no core, no seeds) • watermelon (don't overdo it) • oranges (don't overdo it)	• cottage cheese • yogurt (plain, white) • eggs (scrambled is often best)

Meat & Veggies Mix

This is a grain-free recipe.

Ingredients:
- 1 pound of ground turkey or ground chicken
- 2 medium sweet potatoes
- 1/4 cup of sweet peas (canned)
- 1/4 cup of carrots diced into bite-sized pieces (cooked, canned)
- 1/2 cup of spinach (can be frozen spinach)
- Teaspoon of extra-virgin olive oil
  - ➢ You will need a frying pan, a microwave, a fork, a knife, a stirring spoon, and containers to hold extras.

Directions:
1) Add the olive oil to the frying pan and turn the heat to medium.
2) Crumble the ground turkey or ground chicken into the pan. Stir as it cooks (about 10 minutes) and break up any large pieces.
3) While the meat is cooking, use a fork to poke a few holes in the sweet potatoes and microwave them (about 8 to 10 minutes or until soft in the middle).
4) If you are using frozen spinach, cook as directed (can be done in the microwave as well).
5) Once the meat is just about done, lower the heat and add in the peas, carrots, and spinach. Stir until the vegetables are warmed. Remove the pan from the heat and set to the side.
6) Once the potaotes have cooled, dice into bite-size pieces.
7) Blend the diced potatoes into the rest of the ingredients that are in the pan.
8) Serve this warm. Refrigerate the rest for future meals for up to 1 week.

Main Meal Particulars

Dry vs. Wet: Both have their pros and cons. Dry kibble is excellent for the teeth, and some of the highest quality manufactured foods are dry foods. Wet food (both canned and homemade food) is often more appealing to a finicky eater. However, dry food often leads to good bowel movements, and wet food can cause runny stools. When all is said and done, if you are offering a manufactured brand, dry food is the much better option.

In the case of a finicky eater, you may wish to add a bit of wet dog food to the dry mix; if you do, it is best to stick with the same brand. Another option is to add a serving of liquid fish oil (excellent for skin and coat issues), which dogs find highly appealing in regards to both scent and flavor. A little goes a long way; the typical serving size for a small dog like the Chihuahua is 1/2 pump of fish oil per day.

Free-Feeding vs. Scheduled: Free-feeding is the method of leaving out food all day long and allowing a dog to eat whenever he wishes. Scheduled feeding is the method of choosing certain times throughout the day to offer full meals.

When a puppy is under 3 months old, it is recommended to free-feed. Most Chi can then transition to 3 meals per day, plus snacks. However, if your Chi is undersized or is struggling to gain weight as expected, free-feeding may need to continue and/or a high-calorie supplement may need to be added (see also: 'Helping a Chihuahua Puppy Gain Weight', further ahead in this chapter). The reasons that scheduled meals are recommended are:

- It offers a structured environment.
- It will allow you instill proper hierarchy by having your dog first obey the 'Sit' command before the bowl is placed down. For more, refer to 'Training: Teaching Proper Hierarchy'.
- It often correlates with a heartier appetite.

When you do scheduled feedings, it is important to choose times and then stick with this. A dog's body tends to fall into a rhythm which it's best not to throw off, and consistent food helps keep glucose levels even. If you are rushed and inclined to forget, it may help to set a timer to remind you.

How Often to Feed Your Chihuahua: Before 3-months-old, puppies should be free-fed. After 3-months-old, many Chi can do well with 3 meals a day, plus 3 to 4 dry snacks in between meals. In addition to this will be training treats; however, these rarely affect appetite.

When to Feed Your Chihuahua: The exact times that you choose for breakfast, lunch, and dinner are entirely up to you, as long as they are spaced apart. You'll want to decide on meal times that fit in well with your particular schedule, while not causing your puppy or dog to go with an empty stomach or have meals so close together, that appetite is not there.

- ***For breakfast***, do not wait too long after your dog wakes up since an empty stomach can lead to issues of throwing up bile. Typically, after a dog's morning bathroom needs are done, it's time to eat.

- *Lunch is tricky if you are not going to be home*. While you can leave some fresh food in your dog's bowl that may be paid attention to later in the day, be sure that this is placed within the playpen or is otherwise readily accessible and easily noticed. Another option is to place kibble (or kibble mixed with 100% all-natural smooth peanut butter) into a treat-dispensing toy.
- *Dinner* is generally at the time that you probably eat, between 5 and 7 PM. You'll want at least a 2-hour window between dinner and bedtime; but, this can be adjusted as needed.

Meals and any moderate exercise should be spaced one hour apart. This is to help prevent bloat, which is caused, in part, by exercising right before or after eating.

How Much to Feed Your Chihuahua: How much you feed your Chi will vary depending on the exact food that you are offering. If you have chosen a high-quality manufactured brand, *trust the feeding instructions*. If you find that your dog eats far under the expected amount, reevaluate how many snacks you are giving and if your dog is receiving enough exercise (which burns calories and ups the appetite).

The Chihuahua, being so small, requires a very small amount of food, at least in comparison to us humans. And this element is at the root of many owners believing that their puppy or dogs does not eat enough.

Note that the label on your chosen kibble will most likely show **amount per day, not per meal**. For example, for Wellness Complete Small Breed Puppy, a 6 to 11-week old pup that is between 2 and 4 pounds only needs 2/3 cup PER DAY. With their adult formula, a 5 to 8-pound adult only needs 1/2 to 3/4 cup PER DAY.

If you are feeding homecooked food, the amount per day can vary from 2/3 cup for puppies to 1 cup for adults and will depend on the exact ingredients and your dog's age, activity level, and individual metabolism. Typically, what a dog eats in 15-20 minutes is enough for that meal.

Switching Foods: A sudden change in diet can cause upset stomach and other issues. If you wish to change over to a different brand of dog food or to homemade food at any time in your dog's life, slowly make a change as not to disrupt the digestive tract.

This is the method that usually works well:

- **Week 1:** 3/4 'old' mixed well into 1/4 'new'
- **Week 2:** 1/2 'old' mixed well into 1/2 'new'
- **Week 3:** 1/4 'old' mixed into 3/4 'new'
- **Week 4:** Fully eating new food

The Most Common Eating Issues

It's important to note that most issues are surprisingly easy to resolve; however, this involves taking your place as leader, making some executive decisions, and sticking to your guns. So, let's take a look at some common problems and how to deal with them.

My puppy or dog doesn't eat enough. While it may seem that your little guy or gal never eats enough, if your puppy is growing (with no concerns from the vet) or your adult is maintaining, this means that the right about of food is being eaten.

This is not to say the food itself is offering the right amount of protein and other nutrients, so be sure to offer a superior brand. However, in regard to pure intake volume, puppy growth or adult maintenance is your cue that it's on track.

Remember, what may seem like a minimal amount of food to you is often appropriate for a toy breed dog. Young puppies typically need about 2/3 cups PER DAY (plus snacks). If you are offering 3 meals a day, this is less than 1/4 cup PER MEAL. Adults typically only require 1/2 to 3/4 cups PER DAY (plus snacks).

Keeping this in mind, it can help to:

1) Know exactly how much your dog weighs. Many owners estimate; however, to feed the proper amount, you'll want to know your puppy or dog's exact weight. If you have an accurate scale at home, you can do this by weighing yourself first, then weighing yourself while holding your dog. If you have a young pup, a kitchen scale may be sufficient. If you do not trust your scale to this degree or do not have an accurate scale, all it takes is a quick trip to the vet to find out. Most vets will not charge a steep fee for a fast weight check.

2) Once you know what your puppy or dog weighs, read the labeling on the kibble. These are not arbitrary numbers; most are pretty spot-on. Do, however, note that if a puppy or dog is not as active as he should be, calorie requirements may not be as high.

3) Keep your dog active. This breed should have at least two walks per day, plus a 20-minute session of cardio, such as a game of fetch. Not only does regular exercise help fend off a host of health issues, but it also keeps the appetite healthy.

4) Measure your dog's food as you are filling the bowl and be sure to do so using a dry measuring cup, not a liquid measuring cup or a scoop. Liquid measuring cups have a pour spout (photo, left cup); Dry measuring cups have a flat top and are meant to be leveled off (photo, right cups).

5) Be sure that your dog's bowl is in correct proportion to his body. Sometimes if the bowl is too deep, a dog can bump his forehead on the edge of the bowl or have a hard time reaching the food. And, a big bowl can make it difficult for a dog to find a comfortable eating position.

6) If it turns out that the amount eaten is not close to the suggested amount, yet your puppy is growing as expected, or your adult is maintaining, reassess how many snacks you give out. Generally, a Chihuahua does well with 3 or 4 small snacks in between meals. If too many are given, you may need to cut back on these so that appetite is stronger when meal times come around.

7) If you suspect that your puppy is not growing or if your adult is losing weight, there may be a serious health issue at play. Many health conditions cause decreased appetite; have your Chihuahua checked by the veterinarian ASAP.

My dog is a terribly picky eater.

This is one of the most commonly reported issues. And may involve:

- A dog seeming to only like a food for a short amount of time before deciding that he doesn't like it.

- Having to supervise or offer encouragement for a dog to eat enough.
- Eating just one single food item (i.e. chicken with no other ingredients), which is dangerously unhealthy.
- Outright refusal to eat certain foods.

It is important to note that dogs have taste buds and can appreciate good flavors and turn their noses up at bad ones. So, to a certain degree, your dog has a right to make it clear what he does and does not like. Some dogs love a fish recipe, others prefer lamb, and still others enjoy a classic chicken flavor.

In addition, this refers to a dog's stubbornness, and not a health issue such as vomiting or otherwise getting sick from food. For that, you'll want to refer to 'Health – Other: Allergies', which covers food allergies and what to do.

This said, a dog will be as picky as you allow him to be. There may be a chance you feel your dog is an exception to this rule. Not so. Dogs will be picky to the degree that owners allow. **And with *that* said**, as long as you give in, this issue will not, and cannot, be resolved. If you do not want your dog to be picky any longer, you must summon the willpower to stand firm. But, since the Chihuahua can develop hypoglycemia from not eating, you'll need to carefully monitor things while you work to not give in to stubborn behavior.

Therefore, first be sure that you are offering a high-quality, superior kibble and that your dog is not allergic to any of the ingredients. *Also*, be sure that you have realistic expectations; see the previous 'My puppy or dog doesn't eat enough'.

Then, choose 1 or more of these methods to make the food of *your* choice more appealing:

- Add a dash of liquid fish oil, preferably wild-caught salmon oil. Mix this in very well.
- Drizzle a bit of low-sodium chicken or beef broth over the food. Mix this in very well.
- Warm the food in the microwave; be sure not to overheat.

And, finally, place the food in the bowl and walk away. Do not stand over your dog to see what he does; you must give the appearance that the food that was offered is not up for debate.

Some time may pass in which your dog does not believe that you are being serious. Surely, if he holds out long enough, you will cave in and offer a different food, hand-feed him, or take other such actions. But, to a canine, eating is primal survival; it's one of the strongest instincts a dog has. If you stand firm, your Chi should eventually eat.

If your Chi still has not taken a bite for one hour, remove the bowl for 20 minutes. Then, place it back down. If needed, as each hour passes, repeat this.

The longest that you'll want to go is to the point of the next meal. Stubborn dogs may very well hold out that long; but, they typically make up for it at the next meal time. Monitor your Chi during this time for any signs of hypoglycemia (wobbly walk, confusion, lethargy), and if needed rub some honey on the gums (see also 'Health – Other: Hypoglycemia').

Note that if your dog does not eat whatsoever and continues refusing food at the next planned mealtime, this points to an issue that warrants an immediate vet visit. In some cases, you may be instructed to offer a nutritional gel (see also 'Feeding and Nutrition: Helping a Chihuahua Puppy Gain Weight' and/or 'Supplements') or medication to help stimulate the appetite.

My dog only eats if I hand-feed him. This can become a trap for many owners. You hand-fed your dog just a few times, and now it is expected all of the time, with a refusal to eat any other way.

First, rule out any health issues. Collapsed trachea or conditions in which neck movement causes pain can be a possible explanation. If you suspect this, bring your dog to the veterinarian ASAP.

Then, reassess your dog's bowl to make sure that it is sized correctly and not too deep. Many dogs that love being hand-fed do better with raised bowls. If the bowl *is* raised, your dog may prefer a floor-level dish or a flat plate.

Finally, stand firm. Place your dog's food into his bowl and do not hand-feed. As we covered earlier, there will be a period of time in which your dog stands firm as well. Your goal is to outlast this. You can find other ways to baby and spoil your dog; this book covers a lot of them!

My dog refuses to use a bowl and only eats off of the floor. This is generally due to a personality quirk, and not worth 'fighting' over. Do, however, place the food on a small, flat plate for sanitary reasons.

My dog hides his food/brings it to a different spot. The most common reasons for this center around a dog's need to protect his food, and includes:

1) If the dog was the runt of the litter (the smallest puppy), this could have reinforced this type of behavior. The smallest pups are commonly pushed aside by littermates and have to 'fight' for their food.

2) Rescue dogs are also known for this behavior, as many have gotten used to always being hungry and when given food, they feel that they need to protect it.

3) Dogs that do not feel secure that their food is safe may move it to another room where they believe it is protected. This can happen if:
- The kitchen is a very noisy room.
- If there are other dogs in the home and a particular dog feels a need to compete for food.
- Or if people sit or walk too close to where the dog dish is.

You can resolve this by:

- If you typically hand out snacks in other areas of the house, this will need to stop. Treats should only be given in the designated eating area.

- Ensure that your dog has a quiet, undisturbed area to eat, with no one walking by, no loud noises, and with no one talking to your dog or trying to play with him during meal times. If you have multiple pets, give each one their own separate corners to eat in.

- When your dog takes any food out of the dish, immediately take the food and put it back. Get ready to be tested; your dog may try to move it ten times before giving in to your request. It will be worth it. While this can seem like a game, it is not. Keeping a very close eye on things and not allowing any eating outside of the designated area will show your dog that if he wants his tummy full, he must eat where you ask him to.

My dog eats too fast. Some dogs gobble down their food too quickly and this is not good for the stomach or the digestive system. In fact, it can lead to bloat (gastric dilatation volvulus), which is a life-threatening condition. While this is not common with the Chihuahua breed, it can happen to *any* dog breed.

This can be resolved by using a slow-feed dog bowl (be sure to choose stainless-steel) or by placing a slow-feed stainless-steel porcelain ball into the dish that you already have. Both work to displace food so that it takes longer for a dog to eat his meal.

Another option is a treat dispensing toy, and this is a particularly good choice if you'll be leaving a meal for when your dog is home alone.

My dog won't eat often and this leads to vomiting up bile. Bile issues can usually be resolved with 3 small meals per day plus 3 to 4 dry snacks.

For refusal to eat 3 meals: If a dog eats a very large meal (relatively speaking) he'll be too full to eat others. If this is the case, cut back on meal size, which will lead to acceptance of 3 meals per day.

If this is a matter of eating 3 meals per day, but refusing snacks, cut back on meal size for all 3 meals, which will lead to the acceptance of snacks. See also: 'Snacks', which is coming up next.

My dog guards/protects his food.

Some dogs can be very protective of their food. They may growl at, snap at, or even lunge at people or other animals that are nearby. There are a few steps to help resolve this:

1. Assess if there is an aggression issue aside from this food issue. This may include your dog growling when you try to groom him, snapping at you when you take away a toy, etc. If so, training will be in order. For this, please refer to both 'Training: Teaching Proper Hierarchy' which is needed to show your dog that *you* are the leader and 'Behavioral Training: Aggression'.

2. Assess if you are feeding your dog enough. If your dog is right on the borderline of receiving enough food, he may very well be maintaining his weight but is ravenously hungry at each meal time. This alone can cause a dog to feel over-protective of his food. If needed, add in a few extra snacks per day and/or increase serving sizes of each meal.

3. Offer a stress-free eating environment. Have the dish set up in a quiet corner where there is no foot traffic, people chatting away or watching TV close by, pets running around, etc. Dogs deserve to eat in peace without being bothered.

4. Desensitize your dog to having you near the bowl. This can be done by tossing special treats (see also: 'Feeding and Nutrition: Training Treats') into the bowl as your dog eats. In this way, you are teaching him that you coming nearby during mealtime can be a good thing. After you've done this at least one meal per day (and up to 3) for about a week, things should resolve. However, every now and then, repeat this so that lessons are not forgotten.

Snacks

Note that for clarity, snacks refer to dry treats given in between meals. Training treats, which are typically moist, are important as well, and are covered in the next section. You will want to give your Chihuahua snacks for a few reasons:

- Toy breeds tend to burn off energy sources quickly, so snacks given in between meals help offer consistent fuel for the body.
- Dogs can vomit up bile if their stomach is too empty. Giving dry snacks can help resolve this.
- For dogs with a hearty appetite, snacks keep them content while waiting for meal times.

Just as much thought should go into what you give your dog for snacks as it does in regard to main meals. Every detrimental ingredient that can be found in some dog foods can be found in some dog snacks. This includes chemical preservatives, artificial coloring, artificial flavoring, by-products, generic meats, 'meals', corn, grains, soy, and other fillers. To review the details of these ingredients and what harm they can cause, look back to 'Main Meals'.

In addition, you'll want to be very wary of dog snacks/treats/chews made overseas. As of December 31, 2015, the FDA received 5,200 reports of issues seen with treats imported from China, including those made with chicken, duck, and sweet potato. These reports consist of over 6,200 dogs that have gotten ill, leading to 1,140+ deaths.

Finally, some dog chews are hard to digest or are made of ingredients that the body cannot digest at all, and this can lead to dangerous internal blockage.

Snacks to avoid:

☠ Any with the aforementioned additives and/or ingredients
☠ Any made outside of the US and Canada
☹ Rawhides ☹ Pig ears ☹ Bones

Qualities to look for in snacks include:

✓ 100% all-natural and wholesome, with no chemical preservatives, artificial coloring or flavoring, by-products, generic meats, corn, wheat, soy, fillers, controversial additives.

✓ Made in the US or North America (some excellent snacks are made in Canada, and some of the best wild fish are caught off of the Canadian coast).

✓ Dry. Dry crackers or biscuits are for in between meals. Moist and chewy treats are for reward (next section).

✓ Appropriately sized for toy or small breed dogs. Snacks designed with medium or large dogs in mind are typically too large for a Chihuahua to comfortably eat.

 Since dog food snacks are always evolving, yet this book is static, we have placed all of our current recommended snacks on the Supplies page of the PetChiDog site, which is updated as new options emerge. You can reach this by entering any page of PetChiDog.com; look to the navigation which is in alphabetical order, and choose 'Supplies'.

'Real Food' snacks:

You may want to give your puppy or dog some wholesome foods like veggies and/or fruits for snacks, and this can be a good idea for several reasons:

1) Studies show that diets rich in both fruits and vegetables reduce the risks of many types of cancer.
2) They are packed with essential vitamins, minerals, and fiber.
3) The fiber in fruit causes a slow rate of absorption of fructose (natural sugar); so, giving moderate amounts of fruit will not create a 'sugar rush'.
4) They offer a good amount of nutrients in a small package; which is perfect for this toy breed.

Fruits - You'll want to stay away from the cores of fruit, and there are some fruits such as grapes which must be avoided. However, the following are safe and healthy without super-high levels of fructose: pear slices, banana, blueberries, raspberries, strawberries, and mango. Fruits that can be eaten, but should be given in moderation (due to higher levels of fructose) include watermelon and oranges.

Do NOT give: Grapes, raisins, current berries (or current jam), or cherries. These are toxic.

Vegetables – Some dogs like munching on veggies for snacks, or these can be added to meals. Good choices include peas, carrots (baby carrots can be given raw), spinach, zucchini, green beans, and butternut squash. In small to moderate quantities, kale, cauliflower, and broccoli. And pumpkin, which is typically reserved for intestinal issues.

Training Treats

Training treats are a surefire way to find success when training for housebreaking, barking issues, commands, heeling, and just about any lesson that you are trying to instill.

Every detrimental ingredient that can be found in some dog foods can be found in some dog training treats. So, it bears repeating to be on the watch for chemical preservatives, artificial coloring, artificial flavoring, by-products, generic meats, 'meals', corn, grains, soy, and other fillers. To review the details of these ingredients and what harm they can cause, look back to 'Main Meals'.

In addition, just as with snacks, you'll want to be very wary of dog treats made overseas. Again, worth repeating, is that as of December 31, 2015, the FDA received 5,200 reports of issues seen with treats imported from China, including those made with chicken, duck, and sweet potato. These reports consist of over 6,200 dogs that have gotten ill, leading to 1,140+ deaths.

There are some other important elements to keep in mind:

- Training treats should be reserved to reward good behavior, and not given as a regular snack. When dogs are learning (be this housebreaking, commands, or other), they need reasons to want to keep trying. Special treats only given out during lessons can be one of those reasons.
- Training treats should be moist; these work better for reward than dry ones.
- Training treats are meant to be tiny. These may be handed out in succession; so, you do not want something that will make your dog feel full or otherwise spoil his appetite for dinner.
- They should offer a quick burst of strong flavor; cheese, bacon, rabbit, peanut butter, lamb, and salmon are all flavors that canines seem to especially love.

Note: 1. When training for anything, keep a small zipped sandwich bag nearby that holds a day's worth of training treats. Keep these in your pocket when doing close-contact training such as commands or heeling, and near the exit door when housebreaking, so that you can grab them on the way out.

2. Praise should be given at the same time the training treat is palmed for a dog to take it. In most cases, this is 'Good', followed by the cue word such as 'Sit', 'Bathroom', etc.

 Since canine training treats are always evolving, yet this book is static, current recommended treats are on the Supplies page of the PetChiDog site, which is updated as we evaluate new offerings and flavors that may emerge. You can reach this by entering any page of PetChiDog.com; look to the navigation which is in alphabetical order, and choose 'Supplies'.

Supplements

Generally speaking, a dog does not need a dietary supplement if there are no health issues, he is eating a superior dog food, and is not a senior or approaching the senior years. Let's take a look at some supplements and ways that these can be beneficial.

Daily Vitamins and Minerals ⮌ For dogs on a home cooked diet

A good daily vitamin and mineral supplement for canines will have (in alphabetical order: calcium, copper, folic acid, iodine, iron, phosphorus, potassium, magnesium, niacin, vitamin A, vitamin C (ascorbic acid), vitamin D3, vitamin E, vitamin B1 (thiamine), vitamin B2 (riboflavin), vitamin B5 (pantothenic acid), vitamin B6 (pyridoxine), vitamin B12, and zinc.

Glucosamine, Chondroitin ⮌ For joint health

Most people refer to canine joint health supplements as just glucosamine, but this is typically combined with chondroitin, and can also include MSM and Coenzyme Q10 (CoQ10).

The function of these revolve around a dog's joints and cartilage:

- *Glucosamine* produces glycosaminoglycan, which repairs body tissue and cartilage (from normal wear and tear or issues stemming from injury or age).

- *Chondroitin* works along with glucosamine by maintaining proper fluid levels in the tissue around the joints for good shock absorption and lubrication and also supplies nutrients to the cartilage.
- *CoQ10* is a naturally occurring enzyme found in cells throughout a dog's body. It plays many roles, but mainly supports the immune system, proper function of blood vessels, and works as an antioxidant.
- *MSM* is not naturally occurring in the body. This is an organic compound supplement that works to increase flexibility and reduce pain and inflammation.

Dogs that can benefit from glucosamine and chondroitin supplements include:

- *Those 8+ years.* As a dog ages, the body produces less glucosamine and chondroitin. This leads to joint pain and stiffness, and eventual wear and tear bad enough that osteoarthritis can develop. Note that this is often referred to as just 'arthritis', but technically arthritis refers to inflammation of the joints and osteoarthritis is the degenerative disease caused by deterioration of joint cartilage.

  This can be quite painful and affect a dog's mobility. There can be difficulty walking, trouble rising, problems sleeping at night, and other mobility issues, and behavioral changes.

  It is wise to be proactive about this, and not wait until osteoarthritis sets in to give this supplement to your dog. While it cannot entirely prevent the disease, it can slow it down. Note that dogs without osteoarthritis do not necessarily need additional CoQ10 or MSM.

- *A senior diagnosed with osteoarthritis.* As we covered, it's best to preemptively give a dog glucosamine and chondroitin as he is nearing his senior years. This said, if a dog is diagnosed with osteoarthritis, the veterinarian will almost always suggest this supplement. And many times, it will be the 4-ingredient formula with glucosamine, chondroitin, MSM, and CoQ10.

- *Dogs that have had luxating patella or other joint-related injuries or conditions.* Any damage to joints can cause lasting mobility issues and also increases a dog's chances of developing osteoarthritis in that area. Therefore, this supplement can help a dog recover and help slow down the development of issues in the future.

Omega-3 Fish Oil ⮑ For some allergies symptoms, common skin & coat issues, arthritis

Omega fatty acids are vital for good skin (quality, proper moisture, and elasticity) and coat health (optimal texture, health, and ability to grow). It can help with issues related to allergies (dry skin, itchy skin, skin sores), it can help with seborrhea, and in some cases, it can help prompt the coat to re-grow (often in conjunction with other remedies). See also 'Fur and Coat: Serious Fur Loss'. This is also a good supplement to help reduce pain and inflammation in dogs with arthritis or joint conditions such as patella luxation.

If you are offering a superior dog food, it has added omega-3 and/or 6 in it; however, to help treat the aforementioned issues, an additional supplement is often needed.

Several types of oils contain omegas including flaxseed, canola, walnut, and soybean. These only provide omega-3 ALA (alpha-linolenic acid). Some algae provide omega-3 DHA (docosahexaenoic acid). However, you will want to offer omega-3 EPA (eicosapentaenoic acid) and DHA, which are the most effective types for skin and coat health. Omega-3 EPA and DHA is derived from fish. Preferably, you'll want this to be from wild fish, and a liquid formula is one of the easiest to offer as it can be mixed into meals. Most dogs find the scent and flavor exceptionally appealing.

Probiotics ➲ For certain stomach issues

Within the digestive tract of canines (and humans), there is both 'good' and 'bad' bacteria. When the balance of these is thrown off, with more 'bad' than 'good', it can cause diarrhea, runny stools, constipation, or other related issues. Sometimes, this balance can be disturbed for unknown reasons; though, certain health conditions can be to blame.

Probiotics ('good' bacteria) helps restore gastrointestinal health (barring any underlying health conditions) and additionally aids in boosting the immune system. It's important to note that there are many different strains of 'good' bacteria. There is bacillus laterosporus, lactobacillus casei, and 20+ more with equally long, hard-to-pronounce names. For this reason, it may be best to offer one that has multiple strains.

High-calorie Nutritional Supplement ➲ For weight gain

These are meant to deliver nutrition and calories to puppies that are struggling to gain weight or adults struggling to maintain weight and are only recommended once all possible underlying health issues have been ruled out and/or treated.

The important aspect is that these are designed to deliver nutrition and calories in a small serving. And the reason why it's vital to get a lot in a tiny amount is that puppies and dogs that have trouble eating enough need a simple, palatable method of getting nutritional boosts even if they are not receptive to food. A gel makes that happen. One of the most reputable ones is Tomlyn's High Calorie Nutritional Gel (Nutri-gel)®.

This is a pleasant tasting gel that delivers protein, healthy fats, and a wide range of vitamins and minerals. There are 28 calories per teaspoon. Puppies need about 55 calories per day for each pound of body weight. So, for example, a 2-pound pup needs about 110 calories per day and one teaspoon of this delivers 25% of those needed calories.

See also: 'Feeding and Nutrition: Helping a Chihuahua Puppy Gain Weight'.

Water

When we think about our dogs having a balanced diet, we don't always think about the fact that what they drink plays a huge role in this. Just as for humans, water has many purposes.

It helps with the absorption of nutrients. It aids in the digestion of food. Adequate amounts will allow the intestines to work as they should to produce healthy stools. It lubricates everything from joints to the spinal cord to internal tissues. And, it also serves to help regulate a dog's body temperature. Essentially, water is the life force of all living mammals and a dog can only last 2 to 3 days without it. The amount that a dog drinks, along with the quality of that water, will have a huge effect on his health.

How Much Water a Dog Needs: This varies depending on several factors including activity level, age, and the weather (both temperature and humidity). Most dogs need a *minimum* of 1-oz of water per each 1-lb. of body weight, per day. Therefore, a 4-lb. Chihuahua (1.81 kg) needs at least 4 oz. (1/2 cup) per day, a

6-lb. Chihuahua (2.72 kg) needs at least 6 oz. (3/4 cup) per day, and an 8-lb. Chihuahua (3.62 kg) needs at least 8 oz. (1 cup) per day. Note, it's always better to aim a bit higher.

Health Issues that Cause Increased Thirst: If a dog seems desperate for more water or makes attempts to drink from other sources such as puddles in the yard, etc. this can point to a health condition, including, but not limited to:

• *Diabetes.* Increased thirst is often the very first symptom. Others signs include change in appetite, weight loss, fruity smelling breath, weakness, a thinning or dullness of the coat, and/or vomiting. Left untreated there may be UTI's, skin infections, eye problems including cataracts, and blindness. This disease strikes 1 in 500 dogs. This is not just a concern for adults or seniors; puppies can develop this as well.

• *Liver disease.* Increased thirst is among the leading signs of liver disease. Other symptoms include loss of appetite, confusion, vomiting, diarrhea, dizziness, a yellowing of the eyes, weakness, and/or blood in the urine. Left untreated there may be fluid buildup in the abdomen (ascites) and/or seizures.

• *Kidney disease.* Increased thirst is one of the first signs of problems with the kidneys. Other signs include change in urination, urination at night, uncontrolled dribbling of urine, blood in the urine, decreased appetite, dulled coat, weakness, diarrhea, and/or vomiting. Left untreated, it can lead to kidney failure at which time there may be a buildup of waste products in the body that manifests as uremia (a distinct ammonia smell), mouth ulcers, severe weight loss, loss of muscle mass, anemia (presenting as pale skin and weakness), dangerously high blood pressure, difficulty breathing, and/or seizures.

• *Cushing's disease.* The most prominent sign of this with dogs is drinking excessively which leads to excessive urination and sometimes incontinence issues. Other signs include increased appetite, lethargy, and poor coat health. Over time, approximately 90% of all dogs with Cushing's will develop a potbellied appearance, due to hormone fluctuations, increased body fat, a weakening of abdominal muscles. Left untreated, there may be coat loss, a darkening of the skin, and/or skin infections.

• *Cancer.* Many types of cancer can lead to increased thirst, including adrenal and pancreatic cancer.

• *Stomach/Intestinal ailment.* Any time that a dog is eating less than normal due to illness, the body may try to make up for this by drinking more. In addition, stomach ailments involving vomiting and/or diarrhea can cause a dog to become dehydrated quickly.

Why Unfiltered Tap Water is Terrible for Dogs: The sheer number of toxins in most tap water is shocking and it's amazing that it's legal. The federal law regarding tap water in the States is outrageous. Only 91 contaminants are regulated (at the time of this writing) and are allowed to be in tap water in 'acceptable' amounts.

Unfiltered tap water can contain:

• **Chromium-6**. This is the carcinogen brought to light in the Erin Brockovich movie, and as of 2018, is in the drinking water of over 200 million Americans.

• **Fluoride**. This is exceedingly toxic to dogs (and also proven to be unsafe for humans). This chemical was originally used to kill rats; it causes tooth disease, bone loss and deformities, and can lead to kidney disease, hormone problems, and even cognitive damage. Additionally, it is proven to cause osteosarcoma, which is the #1 cause of bone tumors in canines, developing in 8,000+ dogs each year in the US.

- **Barium.** This is a metal that comes from the erosion of natural deposits in the earth and is also a run-off from metal refineries. This is shown to cause unsafe elevations in blood pressure.

- **Beryllium.** This comes from many sources including metal and coal factories and aerospace, defense, and electrical companies. Long-term consumption is linked to intestinal lesions.

- **Chlorite.** This is a by-product of water disinfectant. Possible long-term health effects are anemia and central nervous problems.

- **Chloramines.** This chemical is purposely added to tap water to control microbes. It can cause eye and nose irritations, stomach problems, and anemia.

- **Antimony.** This comes from the discharge of petroleum refineries, fire retardants, and electronics that cannot be fully filtered out. It can affect blood glucose levels.

- **Trichloroethane (1, 1,2).** This is a waste product from the discharge of industrial chemical factories. Long-term ingestion can lead to liver, kidney, or immune system problems.

What to do: There are 3 good choices that will ensure that the water your dog drinks will be safe and only serve to be a part of a healthy diet.

1) Have a filtering device connected to your kitchen tap. Once in place, you'll only need to replace the filters every other month or so.

2) Use a filtering water pitcher that removes toxins as water is dispersed. Aquagear® makes a very effective one.

3) Offer bottled spring water. An adult Chihuahua needs about 1 cup per day. One gallon (16 cups) will last about 8 days.

A note about distilled water: Never mistake distilled water for spring water. Distilled water is made by boiling water to extreme temperatures and capturing the steam, which is then bottled. During this process, all trace minerals, even the ones that canines (and humans) need such as magnesium and electrolytes are removed. In addition, this type of water draws minerals from the body, which exit via urination. Consumption of distilled water is linked to heartbeat irregularities, blood pressure abnormalities, osteoarthritis, hypothyroidism, coronary artery disease, and other issues.

Helping an Adult Chihuahua Lose Weight

It's not uncommon for Chihuahua owners to be a bit confused about adult weight gain; after all, how can the smallest breed that exists have a weight problem? But, canine obesity is a real and serious issue that is not just limited to medium and large breeds. Carrying excess weight is all relative; a Chihuahua can indeed become overweight, particularly those that are naturally on the large size (above 6 lbs.), given enough time of eating too much (especially if it's a low-quality food) and exercising too little.

Common problems with being overweight include:

- **Stress on joints and bones.** In particular, this relates to hips and knees.
- **Possible breathing problems**, which can interfere with exercise.
- **Decreased mobility.** It is a vicious circle that overweight dogs cannot move around well, but moving around could help them lose weight. Being overweight can cause a dog to have trouble with everything from rising from a down position to navigating steps.
- **Strain and stress on the heart.** Excess weight puts a strain on the heart and the entire circulatory system.
- **Increased risk of disease.** Such conditions as canine diabetes and even cancer are seen at higher rates in overweight dogs.

But, before you jump on a plan to help your dog lose weight, first have health issues ruled out: Conditions that can cause weight gain include Cushing's disease (other signs include increased appetite, increased thirst, lethargy, coat loss, and poor skin health) and hypothyroidism (other signs include lethargy, mental dullness, dry or oily skin and/or coat, and/or coat loss).

And, consider the difference between being oversized and overweight: Though the breed standard calls out for a dog that does not exceed 6 lbs. (2.72 kg), it's not uncommon for pet Chihuahuas to be between 7 and 10 lbs., and in some cases, even more. So, just because your dog may be bigger than others that you see, does not necessarily mean he is overweight.

Your vet can help you determine if your dog is carrying excess weight. And, a general guideline that you can do at home is to look at the rib cage area when your dog is wet after a bath. If you cannot see any outline whatsoever of the rib bones, this is a sign that your adult dog may be carrying too much fat.

Then, if you know what your dog needs is a bit of a boost in the right direction, there are ways to do this in a healthy manner that will not cause a dog to be miserable:

Decreased calories and increased activity: Your goal will be to decrease calories without decreasing the amount of food that you offer and increase your dog's activity level.

#1 Change the diet to both a quality food (if applicable) and a low-calorie formula. If your dog has been eating a less-than-ideal dog food, it will be time to make a switch to a better one. If he is already on a 4 or 5-star food, that brand should offer a healthy-weight variety.

If you are making a change in brands, do this over the course of 3 weeks to avoid an upset stomach. Week one: 3/4 old to 1/4 new, week two: 1/2 and 1/2, and week three: 1/4 old to 3/4 new. By week four, your dog will be fully transitioned over.

#2 Only offer low-calorie options for snacks and rewards. Anywhere from 10 to 30% of a dog's daily intake can come from snacks. And, it is not recommended to stop giving these.

Snacks are an important part of a dog's diet to keep him satiated between meals, and treats should be given to reward good behavior (reinforcing housebreaking, command training, heeling, etc.). And no dog wants to stop receiving goodies from his humans. So, the key is to offer something that will be well-received but has fewer calories than regular dog treats.

You can offer some wholesome foods such as raw baby carrots. And low-calorie options like peas, cucumbers, and even some fruits like blueberries and raspberries can be added to meals. Berries can be frozen and given as snacks as well. There are also a few top-quality manufactured treats that meet all the requirements of what you want in a treat, but with fewer calories; as of the time of this writing, Fruitables Skinny Minis is highly recommended.

#3 Gradual increase in activity. While making changes to meals will play a big role in helping your dog lose a few pounds, gradually increasing daily exercise will bring about faster success. It is important to note that dogs carrying excess pounds may already have trouble taking long walks or keeping up a good pace. So, the goal will be to incorporate small changes that will have a big impact over time. If there are any doubts about your dog's ability to go for walks, discuss this with the veterinarian beforehand.

Here are some tips:

1) Aim for two 20-minute walks per day, adding on 5 minutes each week until you reach a max of 30 to 35 minutes per walk. If your dog has been completely sedentary, start at 10 minutes and work up from there.

2) Aim to go at a pace that is brisk for your dog, increasing intensity only as he works up his endurance. You won't need to (and it's not recommended to) build up to a full-out run; but, a dog should be trotting along with an active gait. Be sure to reach this goal gradually.

3) Don't let the bad weather stand in your way. Unless there is heavy rain, a snow storm, or below freezing temperatures, have the goal be to get outside with your dog every day. The key is for both of you to be dressed warm enough, and for your dog to be properly protected. If you feel cold, even if your dog is fine, you may want to get back into the house too soon. If your dog tends to get chilly, and this is common for this toy breed, a lined or padded vest can be extremely helpful.

4) Work around the summer heat. When it's hot out, head out for walks both early in the morning and then later in the evening when the sun is readying to set. Stay in the shade, if possible. And bring along plenty of water so that you can take breaks and allow your dog to re-hydrate.

How Much Weight Loss to Expect: This should be slow and steady. Do not rush this. A good rule of thumb is to aim for 1/4 to 1/2 pound per week. This is a marathon, not a sprint. And changes that you make in regard to both your dog's food and activity level should be life-long changes with the goal of increased health and mobility.

Helping a Chihuahua Puppy Gain Weight

Puppy Weight Gain: Unlike larger dogs, Chihuahuas do not have a long way to go to reach their adult size. In the case of a 1-pound Chihuahua that is going to be a 6-pound adult, a gain of just 8 pounds will happen over the course of 9 months or so. For this reason, there will be lots of days and maybe even some weeks here and there with very little weight gain.

Aside from the newborn phase when gains are seen each day, weight gain can be sporadic. A Chihuahua that is genetically predetermined to be 4 lbs. and another that is destined to be 8 lbs. will both start off relatively the same size, but arrive there on very different paths. And, even two Chihuahuas that both land at 6 pounds as adults may take dissimilar routes. Some will make gains with seemingly smooth progression, but things will slow down in the final 2 to 3 months of growth, and some will have lots of rapid gains, slow gains, and even some stalls.

If you feel that your Chihuahua puppy is not gaining weight as needed, do not let this be just an assumption. Gains of just ounces cannot be determined by eye. Of course, each time you bring your pup to the vet for vaccinations and examinations, this will involve checking the weight. At home, the easiest method is to use an accurate digital kitchen scale. If you do not have this type of scale or do not trust the one you have, all it takes is a quick trip to the vet to find out your pup's weight. Most vets will not charge a steep fee for a fast weight check.

Reasons Why a Puppy May Need Help Gaining Weight: Keeping in mind that most puppies are going to be plodding along on their own individual course and intervention won't be needed, several scenarios warrant action:

- **Appetite can't keep up with growth:** Normally, a growing body in need of fuel triggers the appetite, and puppies eat enough to supply the body with what it needs. However, some puppies are not able to muster a large enough appetite. A pup's stomach is very tiny, and unless he has the inner drive to eat multiple times per day, and enough to fill his stomach, he may need some extra help.

- **Poor nutritional intake:** If a puppy is fed a kibble that is heavy in fillers, he may indeed be eating, but not taking in enough nutrients. Fillers are worthless ingredients added to food to bulk it up. They contain no nutritional value. You'll want to be sure to feed your puppy a superior food. Read more about this under 'Feeding and Nutrition: All Meal Feeding Details'.

- **Health issues:** There are health conditions and diseases that can prevent a puppy from gaining weight as he normally should. This includes parasites (roundworms and tapeworms, in particular) and gastrointestinal upset. Less common but possible is tumors, kidney disease, and liver disease. For this reason, you will want to be sure that the veterinarian performs a complete examination if the pup shows any signs of illness or any are suspected.

To Summarize: Do not judge this by eye. For puppies that *are* struggling to gain weight, keep in mind this may be a normal stall or phase of slower growth. All health issues should be ruled out and food should re-reevaluated.

How to Help a Puppy Gain Weight: With health issues ruled out, a pup on a superior puppy food, and a determination that there is a need to help the pup gain weight, one of the most effective and easiest methods to prompt weight gain is to offer a high-calorie nutritional gel supplement ***in addition to regular meals.*** This is because one of the main problems is that a little puppy cannot be expected to eat a large amount of food; a gel allows nutrient and calorie delivery, without the need to chew and without filling the tummy.

One like Tomlyn's High Calorie Nutritional Gel (Nutri-gel) offers 28 calories per serving (one teaspoon). Small puppies only need about 55 calories per pound of body weight. So, in looking at a 2-lb. pup, he would need about 110 calories per day. A boost of 28 calories is about 25% of calories required for the day. Double the dose, giving a teaspoon twice per day, and he's receiving half of what he needs for the day.

If there are still issues, the veterinarian may prescribe medication to help stimulate the appetite.

Teething & Chewing

Two Issues, One Resolution

Teething is the phase when a young pup is losing his deciduous teeth (also known as puppy teeth or milk teeth) as adult teeth are pushing through; it typically causes intense itching and discomfort that results in strong chewing urges. **Destructive chewing**, which refers to an older dog chewing on non-toy items, involves intense and often out-of-control chewing urges. Both of these issues can be handled efficiently with the same set of steps, with just a few variations. For this reason, both will be discussed and then merged in the 'How to Help' section, for the sake of simplicity.

Teething Overview

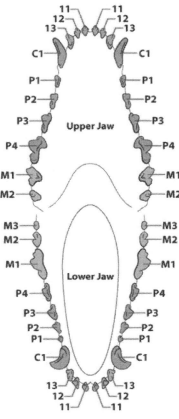

Age of Teething: Puppies begin to lose their deciduous teeth around the 4-month mark. It ends around the 9-month mark. However, pups can begin as young as 3-months, and it can last up to the 1-year mark.

Typically, it happens in this order:

• 4-months-old: the incisors begin to grow in
• 5-months-old: the canine teeth begin to grow in
• 6-months-old: the molars begin to grow in
• 9-months old: all teeth have ascended and teething is complete.

Issues Seen During Teething:

Where do the deciduous teeth go? In many cases, a pup will swallow a tooth if it falls out when eating. Other times, it may simply fall out and onto the ground, often overlooked due to its very small size.

An adult tooth is erupting through, but the milk tooth has not fallen out. This is not that uncommon, but must be handled by the vet. A retained milk tooth will cause an adult tooth to erupt in an abnormal position, creating a 'double row' of teeth. If this is not addressed, this can cause severe misalignment of permanent teeth. It is usually quite easy for a veterinarian to remove a milk tooth without anesthesia due to very tiny, shallow roots. If caught early enough, most often the adult tooth will gradually slide over into its normal and expected place. If milk teeth are very stubborn and/or if there are lots of retained milk teeth, in which removal will require anestheisa, *and* a pup is due to be spayed/neutered, the veterinarian may recommend having those teeth pulled during the procedure to limit anestheisa to just once.

The ears flop down. With breeds that have naturally erect ears, the muscles at the ear base can temporarily weaken during the teething phase. This can cause the ears to become floppy during this time. One ear or both may be affected, an ear(s) may drop down randomly, or just the tip may flop over (known as a half ear). As the pup transitions out of the teething phase, the ears should stand back up. See also: 'Health & Care – Body Part Specific: Ears'.

Behavioral Issues Seen During Teething: When a puppy is teething, there is moderate to severe itching and discomfort. It comes and wanes; however, each day there will be periods of time that it is quite intense.

The only thing on the mind of a teething puppy is to make the unpleasant sensations go away. The habit of seeking out toys is not very strong yet. Therefore, nothing is off limits. Just about anything that a puppy can mouth, he will. Each item may be chewed on to find out if it relieves the teething pain and itching, regardless of whether or not it is a toy.

In addition, a pup might nibble or chew on his owner's fingers or side of her hand. While the nips can be gentle at first, this can develop into more intense type chewing that is just about the equivalent of a bite.

Destructive Chewing Overview

There are 4 main causes of adult chewing problems that occur with dogs over the age of 1-year-old:

1. In some cases, this develops because proper methods were not in place during the teething phase. The dog never learned right from wrong. Therefore, chewing on non-toy objects has become the norm.
2. Stress or boredom can cause a dog to display excessive chewing tendencies. This is most often seen with dogs that spend time home alone.
3. Restlessness can build up; a dog that does not have a way to release excess energy can only hold this in for so long. After a certain amount of time, building frustration can manifest as destructive chewing.
4. Lack of proper chew toys. If a dog is not equipped with the right chew toys, and he has the primal canine urge to chew, what else is he to do but look for alternatives.

Helping with Teething and Chewing Issues - Step by Step

With chewing and teething issues, there are no magic words. It will be up to you to put some work into setting things up correctly and obtaining the correct aids. If you are committed to this, issues can indeed be resolved. Please note that these steps are numbered for a good reason; if you skip any of these steps, you may not have very much success.

#1 Help Your Dog Meet Exercise Requirements

Bring your dog for at least two walks per day and have a daily session of fetch or other activity that allows your dog to run around. If you are already doing this, add on an extra walk or 10 minutes or so to the activity session. This will help release excess energy and allow a dog to feel calmer when back inside the house.

#2 Proof the House

Despite the term, 'puppy proofing' is not just for puppies; it is applicable to dogs of all ages. Go through the house, room by room, and remove as many non-toy items as possible. Be sure to follow each proofing suggestion, even if your particular do has not had an issue with it yet. This will be to not only stop issues now but prevent them in the future.

- All shoes, gym bags, pocketbooks, remotes, books, magazine holders, small throw rugs, keys, and *anything* that may be on the floor or within reach of your dog should be moved to new areas out of reach. Just this step alone completely resolves the issue of chewing shoes and other such objects.
- Comb the floors to pick up any dropped items including coins, hair pins, and other small things that can be inadvertently ingested.
- Wrap any electrical cords or cable wires with cord concealer. This step completely eliminates any issues of a dog being electrocuted from chewing on such things.
- If you have an older dog that is even suspected of being able paw open lower cabinets, place child-proof locks on them.

#3 Have a Designated Area for Your Dog

Teething puppies and older dogs with chewing problems should never be allowed to have free reign in the house when home alone, when an owner cannot keep a very close eye on them, or when sleeping.

One of the best ways to create a designated area is with a quality indoor canine playpen. These are also highly recommended as an important step for helping with separation anxiety issues, and as a vital part of properly housebreaking a puppy. The pen will be your dogs 'den' and he should be there anytime that you are not able to be right by his side.

Some owners resist the playpen method, wanting their canine family member to be 'free'. However, free and able to chew anything and everything in a house is not the proper place for a teething puppy or dog with a chewing habit. And, a playpen is not a jail; it is a good-sized (24" or 34" high; 8 or 21 square feet, respectively, and some are expandable) designated area that holds all of a dog's essential items and keeps a dog safe. Set up properly, it can be a happy and comfortable place.

Within the playpen, there should be 4 main areas: Eating and drinking area (food and water bowls), resting and sleeping area (a quality bed), play area (toys) and bathroom area (pee pads - applicable for untrained pup and dogs of all ages that may need this 'just in case').

When choosing a pen, options are heavy-duty molded plastic pens with or without a doggie door or pop-up pens. Iris makes a few excellent playpens, and if you'd like to see our most current recommendations, look to the Supplies page of the PetChiDog site, which is updated as new products emerge. You can reach the Supplies page by going to any page of PetChiDog.com; look to the navigation which is in alphabetical order and choose 'Supplies'.

The best place for the pen is a quiet corner of a room frequently used by the family, such as a living room or kitchen.

#4 Arm Your Dog with the Right Tools

If a puppy or dog does not have the right teething or chew toys, he is being set up for failure. Without a means to satisfy chewing urges, he is being offered no other alternative than to chew on non-toy objects. You may be thinking, 'I have tons of toys for my dog, it's not helping.' But the idea is not to have a huge heap of them. In fact, this can be counterproductive if the good ones are hidden at the bottom of the pile and rarely discovered. The goal is only to have ones that effectively meet a pup or dog's chewing needs and quell his urges. Therefore, a huge part of this will be to ensure that you carefully select a few good teething toys and dog chews that do their job.

Recommended Teething Toys: It can be a bit tricky to find excellent toys for toy breeds because many are sized for medium and large breed dogs (who, at the puppy stage, are often bigger than a full-grown Chihuahua). So, look for those designed for toy breeds or those that have extra-small or small size options. Those with nubs make excellent 'scratchers' for itchy gums. Twisted rope toys can be fantastic as well. A helpful tip is to wet the rope toy, place it in the freezer for about an hour, and offer it to your puppy once it's chilled. The cold will help reduce teething pain.

Recommended Chew Toys for Older Pups and Adults: As with teething toys, comes the issue that many chew toys are sized for larger dogs. And, if you do find one that is small, will it still work effectively? Look for chew toys that are 'puppy' toys for other breeds, or that are designed just for smaller dogs. They should be durable and textured to please a chewing machine. Additionally, and exceedingly important to the entire method of helping with chewing issues, is that the toy must be designed to promote engagement and hold a dog's interest.

Those that release treats can be super-helpful and conquer two issues at one time; chewing and boredom. Durable 'low stuffed' squeaker toys are also great. And, to resolve problems with a dog that really needs encouragement to play, have at least one talking toy.

To summarize thus far: To prevent issues of having pent-up energy, you are making sure that your dog meets daily exercise requirements by offering plenty of walks and supervised sessions of cardio.

You have proofed the house and removed as many temptations as possible. Also, you have a playpen for your dog to be in any and all times that you cannot closely supervise. It holds a quality comfortable bed, food and water, and a nice supply of 3 or 4 quality teething toys and/or chew toys. This immediately will resolve all issues such as a dog ripping apart the under-rim of a sofa, chewing on shoes, digging and gnawing at carpeting, mouthing electrical cords, turning into a woodchuck to eat away at the legs on your kitchen table, and other such behaviors.

Now, we will discuss how to react and what to do if your dog is right by you, but is trying to chew non-toy items.

#5 Teach Your Dog to Stop Chewing on Non-Toy Items

Once you are set up with the previous elements, it will be time to start implementing some rules. It is important that everyone in the household is on board so that rules are followed at all times. As long as you have the patience to stay with things, and can outlast your dog, new healthier chewing habits can take the place of older ones.

The basics of this are: Interrupt, Redirect Focus, Reward. This is a fundamental training technique that works very well for many behaviors aside from chewing, such as barking, jumping up, and other such things.

#1 Interrupt. Anytime that your dog is about to chew on something that is not one of his teething or chew toys, immediately stop his action and gain his attention. For some dogs, but certainly not all, a firm 'No!' or clapping your hands loudly will be enough. Do not be discouraged if this fails, since many pups and dogs are used to hearing 'no' to the point that it holds little meaning and clapping is not always loud enough.

If needed, you may want to incorporate a canine training tool that releases a short hiss of compressed air. These are designed to produce a particular sound that usually works very well to cause a dog to stop and take pause. One such device is The Company of Animals Pet Corrector.

#2 Redirect Focus.
The *moment* that your dog has taken pause, redirect his focus to something that he will find to be pleasing, and perhaps even more enjoyable than what he was just chewing on. For this, attention should be directed to a tempting teething or chew toy, using one that meets the elements discussed under '#4 Arm Your Dog with the Right Tools'.

You may find that one of two things work best: You can have this be one of your dog's favorite toys; in other words, one that you are confident he will be happy to be reminded of. Or, have this be a 'secret' toy that you have stashed away, but keep close at hand, to offer just for these circumstances.

For dogs that really need encouragement to mouth the offered toy, dabbing it with a touch of peanut butter beforehand often does the trick. And, do not forget that your level of enthusiasm matters.

#3 Reward.
This is not needed in all circumstances because you don't want to interrupt a dog if he's happily chewing or playing with an approved toy. But, if your pup looks up at you, or takes pause, it is a good idea to say, 'Good, boy/girl!' in a happy tone and/or give a small pat. Dogs are highly aware of their human's vibe, even if nothing is said. Once your dog is displaying great behavior, stress is lifted from the room. And your canine family member will be well aware of that.

Chewing on Large, Immovable Objects:
You've proofed the house so that no small objects can be picked up and chewed, but what about the big ones? Table legs are a favorite for many dogs, as well the bottom of sofas and other furniture. **Let's tackle this:**

#1. Do not allow access to those objects when you can't watch your dog. If your dog is ripping apart carpeting or has just about chewed off the leg on your dining table, he's been allowed to do it. When you cannot watch your dog, follow the procedures under '#3 Have a Designated Area for Your Dog'.

#2. Use the Interrupt, Redirect Focus, and Reward training, as mentioned earlier, if your dog goes towards something that you do not approve of.

#3. Use a deterrent spray. While following the aforementioned guidelines will nullify the issue, if for some reason you cannot put those rules into place, you may wish to try a deterrent spray. These contain particular flavoring agents, most often a bitter taste, that in theory, deter a dog from wanting to mouth or chew on things. Some are more effective than others, and none work for all dogs. Oddly enough, some dogs do not mind the bitter taste. That said Grannick's Apple Bitter Spray is one of the well-rated ones.

Chewing on you:
While it can seem cute at first when a young pup softly nibbles on your fingers or the side of your hand, it is not a good idea to allow this to happen. It can very easily develop into a habit, and then you'll be in trouble when sharp teeth start to grow in. There are several methods to use, depending on if this behavior spirals:

1. Pull back your hand as if you are offended, let out a sharp 'Ouch!' and move away. This mimics what young pups are used to with littermate playtime. One nips at the other, the victim lets out a yelp and removes himself from play.
2. If this continues, use the training mentioned earlier of sharply getting your dog's attention and offering an approved chew toy.
3. If this does not work, and your dog is getting aggressive, you will want to place him in his playpen for a timeout. This mimics what serious offenders receive in the canine world, which is temporary banishment from the 'pack'. More detailed steps can be found under 'Behavioral Issues: Nipping'.

Grooming

Tasks and Timing

There are several grooming tasks that you'll want to do on a regular basis. Let's take a look at what is needed, how often, why, and what can happen if you fall behind.

Task	Timing	Why	Consequences if not done
Wipe the eye area	Daily	To remove any discharge or debris & prevent tear stains	Possible irritated eyes, possible tear stains
Brush the teeth	Daily	To remove plaque	Dental issues including tartar buildup, and possible gingivitis, periodontal disease, tooth decay, infection, and/or eventual tooth loss
Wipe down the coat (if allergies), touch-up wiping	If allergies, any time that the dog enters back into the house. Spot-cleaning as needed	To remove pollen and other outside allergens. To touch up the coat if dirt, feces, or urine	Continued allergy reactions, feces and/or urine stains and odors
Rinse off the paws (if allergies)	Daily, any time that the dog enters back into the house	To remove pollen and other outside allergens that can cling to the paws	Continued allergy reactions
Brush the coat, using a leave-in spritz	Every 3 days for a short coat, every 2 to 3 days for a long coat.	To distribute body oils, stimulate hair follicles, remove debris, protect the coat. Specific for long coats: To separate hairs to prevent mats	Body oils will accumulate, coat vulnerable to damage. Specific for long coats: hairs may start to tangle
Apply paw wax	Once a week	To protect paws. Summer: hot walking surfaces. Winter: frozen walking surfaces, 'snowballing', & traction. Year-round for healthy paw skin	Possible summertime burns, winter slipping, 'snowballing', and/or discomfort from cold, year-round dryness, peeling & cracking
Apply nose balm (only as needed)	Once a week	To prevent chapping and/or drying for those that have sensitive noses	Nose may start to dry and peel, can lead to cracking
Give a bath	Once every 3 weeks	To cleanse away accumulated body oils and debris. To improve skin & coat health	Body oil odor, blocked skin pores, dry skin, coat becoming greasy
Trim/file nails (by you or a groomer)	Approximately once every 6 weeks	To keep nails at the proper length	Possible chipped or broken nails, ingrown nails

Specifics of Grooming Tasks

Wiping the eye area. If the eye area is only cleaned during baths, there may be some problems. Discharge and buildup (rheum, also known as 'sleep' in the eye) can cause irritation (and worse in some cases). This, and small bits of food and other debris should be wiped off before they can enter the eyes. In addition, if the eye area is not kept clean, tear stains can develop. Ahead in this chapter are all the details you need to know to remove stains; however, if you are not in need of this yet, work to prevent ever reaching that point.

Use a quality eye wipe or basic canine body wipe that is formulated to pick up debris while being gentle. Since you'll be using this on the face and around the eyes, it's recommended to use a hypo-allergenic, non-fragranced wipe. You can save fragranced wipes for the body, for as-needed touch-ups.

At least once per day, gently wipe around the eyes, using one clean wipe per eye. Start at the inner corner and swipe up and around to the outer corner. Then start at the inner corner and swipe down and around to the outer corner.

Brushing the teeth. Dental issues are such a common occurrence with toy breeds, there is an entire chapter dedicated to dental care. However, as a summary, you will want to brush your dog's teeth on a regular basis. Daily is recommended.

Do not assume that a dog does not need the teeth brushed or that it can be done 'every-so-often'; plaque is continuously produced round-the-clock. While a daily dental treat will remove some plaque, it may not remove all of it. And, if this task is ignored, you will almost certainly regret it, as you watch your dog struggle with dental issues (and your wallet will not like it either).

An alternative to brushing is a dental spray; this can work relatively well; but, should be reserved for dogs that truly do not tolerate having their teeth brushed. More details can be found under 'Dental Care' (next chapter).

Wiping the body/coat. There are a few reasons to routinely wipe down the coat with grooming wipes:

- To remove allergens. If your dog is suffering from seasonal (airborne) allergies, part of the steps to resolve this is to reduce or remove as many allergens as possible. Wiping down the coat each time a dog comes back in from being outside is an important part of this.
- To remove general dirt and debris that can cling to a dog during normal playtime outside.
- To remove tiny bits of feces that commonly cling to fine hairs around the anus and/or urine that splashes up onto the body (for both males and females).

So, you'll want to spot-clean, as needed. You can use your basic grooming wipes for all of this, or grooming wipes along with special 'tushie wipes'.

Rinsing off the paws. This task is applicable if your dog has allergies, done for the same reason as wiping down the coat: to remove allergens; though, of course, if the paws are muddy or dirty from walking outside, a quick rinse will keep your house clean. Even if you are using a paw wax, as recommended (see next paragraph), that creates a safe barrier between the paws and elements on the ground, allergens will adhere to this 'shield', and you will not want them tracked back into your home. It's generally easiest to pick up your Chihuahua and wash the paws off in the kitchen sink.

Applying paw wax. The aspect of paws having the thickest and strongest skin on the body should not be confused with them being invincible. In fact, paws are very vulnerable to all sorts of weather-related injuries and issues. Applying paw wax weekly can help:

- Offer a layer of protection from hot walking surfaces in the summer.
- Offer a layer of protection from frozen walking surfaces and any ice-melt chemicals in the winter, as well as help provide good traction on slippery surfaces, and prevent 'snowballing'. Snowballing refers to when a dog steps on snow, the snow melts between his paw pads and toes, and it refreezes into ice; this stretches out the sensitive skin on those areas, which can be very painful, as well as lead to cracked skin.
- Repel allergens that may otherwise cling to the paws (still rinse the paws off after coming in, if your dog has allergies, so that allergens are not tracked into the house).
- Keep paw skin healthy and moisturized.

Paw wax gradually wears off; so, for indoor dogs that spend an average amount of time outside, this usually needs to be applied once per week. Use a good wax that absorbs quickly and still allows the paws to 'breathe' while protecting. And, if the paws are dry, peeling, or cracked, a quality paw wax applied 2 to 3 times per day can help heal those issues.

Applying nose balm. This is not needed for every puppy or dog; it is only applicable to those with sensitive noses that become overly dry, chapped or otherwise damaged. If your dog does tend to have a dry nose, you'll want to look into possible causes such as not drinking enough water or too low of a humidity level in the house. For chapping, this commonly happens in the winter; a dog will lick his nose, cold wind will chap it a bit, he'll lick it again in response, and it becomes even more chapped.

In these circumstances, a quality nose balm can offer protection from outside elements and help a nose heal. For maintenance, apply a dab once per week. For treating nose issues, apply liberally 1 to 3 times per day.

Brushing the coat. The coat should be brushed on a regular basis for several reasons:

1) To distribute body oils. Natural body oils are continually produced and they can accumulate rather quickly. Brushing helps distribute the oil down through the hairs, which can help keep the coat nice and shiny.

2) To remove debris and dead hairs. Coats can be a magnet for all sorts of tiny debris, from carpet lint to specks of dirt. Additionally, when hairs shed back into the coat, they can mix with body oils (which can then cause an odor) and/or block natural air flow to the skin.

3) To keep skin and coat healthy, via massage. The act of brushing stimulates hair follicles, which leads to better skin and coat health.

4) Applicable to longhaired Chi, to prevent tangles (also referred to as mats or knots). Tangles are twists of hairs that get knotted together. If a tangle is not removed, it can keep growing, pulling in more and more hairs, twisting tight and pulling on the skin. Each time you brush your longhaired Chi, you'll be separating hairs and using a daily leave-in conditioner, which has many benefits including tangle prevention.

Types of recommended brushes:

For long coats: A double-sided pin and bristle brush with coated tips. Use the pin side to do an initial sweep to separate the hairs, the bristle side for full body sweeps, and the pin side again to 'finish' off the coat.

For short coats: A soft bristle brush with sturdy bristles long enough to penetrate the coat but not so sharp as to scratch the skin or cause discomfort.

For both coat types, for shedding: A small short slicker brush with coated tips.

Brushing tips:

Brush using a leave-in spray. Brushing a dry coat can cause hair breakage via split ends. And, importantly, using a light mist of a leave-in conditioner spray offers the benefits of protecting the coat from contact friction and sun exposure, helping to repel outdoor allergens, helping to prevent tangles, locking in moisture to prevent dry fur, and has the added plus of making a dog smell nice and clean. More details regarding leave-in's are under 'Shampoo and Coat Products' (the next section in this chapter).

If your long coat Chihuahua has a tangle, address this right away. A tangle should never be left alone; these usually grow larger by the day. There are 2 choices: You can try to work it out with your hands to see if you can untangle the knot or you can clip it off with a proper de-matting tool.

To attempt to work out a tangle by hand, cover both of your hands – liberally – with your dog's leave-in spray or bathing conditioner. Just as you would try to work out a shoelace knot, with your hands super-slippery, patiently try to untangle the mat, pulling tiny sections of hair out from it. If you decide it has to be snipped off, use a mat-remover tool. These are designed to remove a mat without damaging the rest of the coat. At the time of this writing, the Safari Mat Remover is recommended.

How often to brush: Aim to brush your smooth coat Chi every 3 days and your longhaired Chi every 2 to 3 days.

Shampoo and Coat Products

Everything you use on the coat will either be detrimental or beneficial to both skin and fur. So, it's important to take your time to choose wisely.

The shampoo

Inferior shampoos will be formulas copied from low-cost human hair products; it is much cheaper for companies to do this than to design them based on a dog's needs. These often have:

X **Soaping agents** that are harsh on a dog's skin such as sodium laureth sulfate (SLES), sodium lauryl sulfate (SLS), and ammonium lauryl sulfate (ALS), which can cause dry, irritated skin.

X Incorrect pH, typically between 4.5 to 5.5 (that can strip off the protective cuticles from hair shafts and leave the coat exposed). An exposed coat is vulnerable to the sun, the wind, dry air, cold air, static, and contact friction, which can all lead to poor coat health.

☠ **Parabens and phthalates**, which are chemicals used in some pet products; the EPA has found that parabens may be linked to adverse effects to the endocrine system (produces hormones that regulate metabolism, growth, tissue function, reproduction, sleep, and mood). And phthalate has been linked to birth defects.

☠ **Other harmful ingredients** including methylchloroisothiazolinone (a carcinogen), cocomide DEA (toxic to organs), and a host of fragrances and/or coloring that can cause allergic reactions.

X Will have nothing at all to improve skin and coat, such as moisturizing or restorative ingredients or anti-itch properties for dogs with allergies.

Superior products, on the other hand, will be designed with the needs of canines in mind. These will have:

✔ **Coconut-based or other plant-based cleansers,** which can be very gentle yet effective as opposed to harsh soaps.

✔ **Correct pH** of between 6.5 and 7.5, for healthy skin and strong healthy fur.

✔ **No parabens, phthalates, sulfates, or other harmful additives.**

✔ **Will contain moisturizing, healing, and restorative all-natural organic ingredients that are beneficial for skin and coat.** If the shampoo has the right combination of quality ingredients, it can help resolve any current issues and leave skin and coat healthy and strong to better withstand elements that can cause damage. Such ingredients as almond, vanilla, shea butter, aloe vera, coconut oil, tea tree oil, and eucalyptus oil are fantastic. Orange or mango can help if dog tends to hold odors.

The conditioner

No matter which shampoo you use, you will want to follow this up with a quality rinse-out conditioner.

- The bathing process causes hair cuticles to open; if they stay open, the coat is vulnerable and exposed. A good conditioner will smooth these cuticles down.
- Inferior conditioners can be oily which makes them hard to rinse out properly. This can leave a coating on the skin that blocks skin pores and prevents proper air circulation. An effective, superior conditioner does its job and is rinsed out, leaving behind only its benefits.

A leave-in coat spritz or spray

Shampoo and conditioner can offer wonderful benefits during baths and even a bit beyond that; however, what about in between? As we touched on under 'Brushing tips', a good leave-in has many benefits, including:

✔ Protecting the coat from contact friction; when a dog brushes up against any surface (floor, furniture, bed, etc.) the friction that occurs can be damaging.

✔ Protecting the coat from sun exposure; summer sun can have a drying effect.

✔ Helping to repel outdoor allergens; most allergens are too small for the eyes to see; but, these microbes (pollen, etc.) often cling to the coat.

✔ Locking in moisture to prevent dry fur; gives the coat a nice texture.

✔ Has the added plus of making a dog smell nice and clean. Always a plus!

✔ For long coats, helping to prevent tangles.

Note: Do not soak the coat with a leave-in spray; it is meant to be lightly spritzed, preferably while brushing.

Since body-care products, shampoo, and other coat care products are always evolving, yet this book is static, current recommendations for grooming wipes, dental care items, paw wax, nose balm, shampoo, conditioner, leave-in coat spray, and more can be found on the Supplies page of the PetChiDog site, which is updated as new products and tools may emerge. You can reach this by entering any page of PetChiDog.com; look to the navigation which is in alphabetical order, and choose 'Supplies'.

Baths

The Timing of Baths: A bath should be given every 3 weeks and any time that your dog has gotten very dirty. For example, running through a muddy puddle.

This is not an arbitrary time frame. Body oil is constantly being produced; it aids in keeping the skin moisturized, so it's a good thing. However, it does not evaporate, it accumulates. At just about the 3-week mark, there is enough accumulation that it needs to be cleaned off. There will be a collection of tiny debris caught in this oil, the amount of oil is significant enough to block skin pores, and a bad odor can develop.

The reason why you do not want to give baths much more often than the 3-week mark, is because a bath (given the correct way and with the right products) completely removes old, accumulated oil, allowing you to start with a 'clean slate'. But, if oils keep being washed away too frequently, it can be hard for the body to keep up. And this can lead to dry skin, which can roll into a host of other issues.

Sink or Tub? Young puppies often do best in the kitchen sink. It is not so overwhelming and if a puppy can have good bathing experiences when young, he will be more prone to accept baths. If a puppy has a bad and frightening experience, this can lead to a dog that is fearful of water and this makes giving baths exceedingly difficult. For these reasons, it is suggested to begin by giving baths in a clean kitchen sink. If you wish to transition to the bathtub (and you do not have to), this can happen as your dog grows and becomes accustomed to the water, the bubbles, the scrubbing, and all that is involved.

Steps for Giving Baths:

1) Have all your needed items right by your side so that you don't need to leave your puppy or dog alone. This will include a comb & brush, 2 washcloths, cotton balls, shampoo, conditioner, and a quality towel.

2) Give the coat a good brushing. The goal is to remove any dead hairs. And, for long coats, to have the hairs separated in preparation for the bathing process.

3) Place a bath mat or towel in the base of the sink/tub to prevent your dog from slipping.

4) Have the tub/sink filled with water before you place your dog in, as running water can be startling. Take care that the water is warm; not too cool or too hot. Test it with your inner wrist. Cool water will give your dog the chills and hot water not only can scald the skin but also triggers the hair cuticles to close, which means that your quality products cannot work as effectively.

5) Gently place cotton in the ears to prevent water from entering the ear canal. You can tear away pieces from a cotton ball to do this. Do not place the cotton deep.

6) Wet the entire body by using a nozzle. If you do not have a nozzle, a small container to scoop can work. At first, water may roll off the coat and body oils may prevent water from getting through the coat, so make sure that the coat is thoroughly soaked before adding any shampoo.

7) Do not be shy when using the shampoo. Use enough so that every area of the body is cleansed in the same way.

8) Scrub well and down to the skin. During the 3 weeks or so that you last gave a bath, body oils have been slowly accumulating; these need to be scrubbed away so that you can 'start fresh'. Go over every area of the body including armpit area and paws. For the underbelly, genital area, and around the face, use your soft washcloth.

9) Rinsing is very important. Even with a terrific shampoo, soap residue left behind can cake on the skin. If so, it can mix with body oils and begin to clump. Using a nozzle works well to reach down through the coat to make sure all the shampoo is properly rinsed out.

10) Now it's time for the conditioner. Use a generous amount to cover all areas. Massage this in for 2 to 5 minutes and then rinse well.

11) Remove your dog and wrap him in a quality, absorbent towel.

12) Remove the cotton from the ears. Using a thin, clean washcloth, dry the outer ears and the inner ears (as far in as you can comfortably go).

13) To dry a long coat, do not rub; always pat and dab. For both coat types, once you're done with the towel drying, you can spritz the coat lightly with a leave-in conditioner and then allow your Chi to air-dry. Blow-drying is not necessary unless you gave a bath and then suddenly had to bring your dog outside on a cool to cold day. If you do decide you have to use the blow-drying, keep the setting on low and stop as soon as the coat is dry.

Nails & Dewclaws

Nails

How often nails need to be trimmed: A dog's nails need to be trimmed every 4 to 8 weeks, and this depends on how fast they grow and to what extent there is some natural filing down as the dog walks on various surfaces. Typically, there is a characteristic 'click-clack' sound when a dog walks over hard surfaces that will alert you to the need.

If left to grow, they can become ingrown (which can be very painful), may become uneven which can throw off a dog's natural gait, or can split or crack.

Groomer vs. at home: You may choose to take care of this grooming task at home or have a groomer do this. It's common for owners to feel nervous doing this themselves. Each nail has a vein that runs down the center of it, called the 'quick', and if a nail is clipped too short, this vein will be nicked and can bleed quite profusely. There are styptic powders that can help stop the bleeding. If you do choose to do this yourself at home, we recommend having one of these styptic powder products.

Methods: There are two basic methods to trim nails back: A clipper (similar in concept to what you use on your own nails, but designed for canine nails) or an electronic filer/grinder. Many owners find grinders much easier to use than clipping tools; they quickly grind the nail down without having to cut it at all. The pros are that this is less invasive and very fast. The con is that it can be noisy and some dogs do not like the sound.

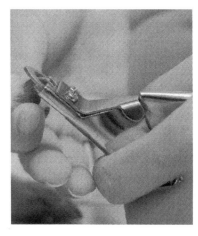

Desensitization: If your dog runs when it is time to trim the nails, you can begin by just training him to get into the *position* of trimming, without actually doing so. This can be done by laying your dog on his side and leaning over his body. Gently hold his paw and touch the nails. If he lies still, give lots of praise. As time goes by, and your dog seems comfortable with lying down and allowing you to touch his nails, you can then carefully trim them.

If you find that your dog just won't sit still or that you dread filing or clipping the nails, it's best to allow a groomer to complete this task.

Directions: Cut/file right to the 'nail hook' (the area where the nail begins to curve slightly). Only cut/file tiny bits at a time, 2 millimeters or so. Note that if you are using an electronic filer, this can file away the nail VERY fast. Each time you trim a piece or file a bit, stop to take a look. As you slowly cut/file away small pieces, you will eventually see a gray or pinkish oval of color in the nail. This is your sign to stop.

Recommended grinder: If you think that you may want to try a grinder instead of clipping, as of the time of this writing, we recommend the Dremel 7300-PT 4.8-Volt Pet Grooming Kit. It is sized nicely for toy breeds and it has 2 rotation speeds so that you can file in stages. However, for dogs under 6 pounds, you may find it best to additionally obtain the small 100 to 120 grit sanding band.

Dewclaws

What these are: Dewclaws are the extra nails that are located very high on the side of a dog's paw. They are so high, that you could describe them as being located on the dog's ankle. With young puppies, these are merely tiny, soft nails. As a pup grows older, these slowly evolve into an appendage.

Removal when young: Some breeders have a pup's dewclaws removed to help prevent issues that they can cause. Because of where they are located, a dog can easily catch the dewclaw on fabric, the sofa, carpeting, etc. This can cause a lot of pain and it takes a long time for the claw to heal if it is ripped in this way. If dewclaws are not removed, in time they may begin to grow jagged and crooked, which can also cause discomfort.

When removed at a very young age, the process is rather simple. It is often done by the veterinarian when a pup is just 3 or 4-days-old, when it can be easily slipped out.

Removal when older: When an older pup or an adult has their dewclaws removed, they are not soft, pliable nails any longer. What can be described as an extra 'toe' grows in the area of the dewclaw that is made of flesh, muscles, ligaments, and tissue just like any other body part. Therefore, removal is considered an amputation. The dog is put under anesthesia to have this done. Since dogs can be very sensitive to anesthesia, it is best to avoid having this done unless the benefits of surgery outweigh the discomfort a dog is having with a dewclaw.

AKC show preference: For AKC show, there is no preference in regard to front or rear dewclaws.

Trimming: When you are trimming the nails, do not forget about the dewclaw, it will need to be cut just like the other nails. If left alone, it can grow long and back into the dog's leg, which can be very painful.

Brushing tip: If your dog has dewclaws, be careful when brushing the coat. Sometimes it is easy to forget that a dewclaw is there and it can be caught in the brush. Always take care to go around this.

Tear Stains

What these are: Tear stains are discolored fur under and/or around a dog's eyes. The fur develops a pink, red, rust, or brown tinge. Often, the texture will feel dry and a bit 'crunchy', similar to straw.

There are several causes of tear stains; though, all circle back to some element being deposited under and/or around the eyes via a dog's tears, hence the term. Sometimes, but not always, you can know the root cause by the color of the stains. Those that are pink or red are often indicative of yeast infection, also referred to as 'red yeast infection' (caused by hairs frequently being moist).

Age of onset: Since it can take several months for tear stains to develop, you rarely see this with very young pups. Also, since certain causes may be inadvertently introduced to a dog at any time, these can develop at any age.

How to Prevent and Remove Tear Stains: To fix the problem of tear stains, one must take a 3-step approach. If not, there may be little success or just temporary results.

Step #1 Eliminate the Top Causes

There are several common reasons why dogs develop tear stains. If you can address all of these, you are well on your way to never seeing them again.

#1 Inferior food. This includes artificial additives (coloring, flavoring, and/or preservatives). Or, it can be linked to corn or wheat ingredients. These can cause an allergic reaction that results in excessive tearing (see #4), and then staining. You'll want to be sure to feed your dog a top-rated brand that contains zero additives and either no corn and wheat (but has rice, which is usually well-tolerated) or none at all (grain-free formula).

#2 Tap water. A high mineral count in tap water can lead to tear staining. And in addition to this, and of a much more serious nature, there are hundreds of chemicals, toxins, and carcinogens in tap water all throughout the US. We recommend using a filtering device for your kitchen tap, a filtering water pitcher, or offering bottle spring water. For more details on this, please refer to 'Feeding and Nutrition: Water'.

#3 Wet hairs (water). Any time that hairs remain damp, this sets up the perfect foundation for yeast growth. This may happen in the genital area, ears (yeast ear infection), or on the face which causes a red yeast infection, a leading cause of stubborn tear stains.

Every time that a dog drinks his water, tiny drops splatter up to his face. And if a dog is on a wet food diet, this can bring moisture up to the face as well. To prevent this cause, dry your dog's face if it has become wet or wipe the face with hypoallergenic, fragrance-free grooming wipes at least once per day (see #5).

#4 Excessive tearing. Both tears and saliva contain some level of iron. If a dog's eyes are runny (even slightly), as the area under or around the eyes become damp with tears, the iron can cause discoloration. Additionally, this brings about damp, wet hairs (see #3), compounding the problem. While many dogs will naturally have some eye discharge, moderate to excessive discharge can be caused by allergies (more common) or eye disorders (less common, but possible). So, these issues should be assessed.

#5 Lack of daily facial upkeep. Unattended damp hairs can develop into stains. You can prevent this by wiping the eye area at least once per day with quality hypoallergenic, fragrance-free grooming wipes or facial wipes.

#6 Plastic bowls. Even those that are BPA free can trigger contact reactions that cause discoloration to facial hairs, as well as nose discoloration (over a period of months or years) and/or dry nose. Use stainless-steel or ceramic bowls for both food and water.

#7 Health issues. Excessive tearing leads to wet hairs around the eyes which in turn leads to staining. So, if you notice that your dog has runny eyes, this will be a top concern. Many conditions can be at the root of tearing including allergies, inverted eyelashes, a tear to the cornea, blocked tear duct, eye infection, and more. For this reason, the veterinarian should diagnose the cause of excessive runny eyes. Once any health issues are resolved, you can then concentrate on removing the staining. You may also wish to refer to 'Health – Other: Allergies' and/or 'Health & Care – Body Part Specific: Eyes'.

Step #2 Daily Maintenance

Though this was briefly covered as one of the *causes* of tear stains, it is *also* an essential part of fixing the issue. If you are working only to prevent tear stains, you can opt for a 'basic' quality canine hypoallergenic fragrance-free eye wipe or grooming wipe. Be sure to choose a good brand that is gentle to this sensitive area.

However, if despite ruling out all possible causes, your dog is prone to developing staining and you find yourself in an uphill battle, you'll want to take this up a notch by using canine eye wipes specifically formulated to prevent and remove stains as your basic maintenance wipe.

Please note that no matter how wipes are marketed, using these as your only remedy to fully fix set-in existing stains can be a very slow method. However, quality ones can be fantastic as a daily maintenance wipe and as a good foundation for the use of more powerful products, if needed.

There are some great all-natural wipes formulated with plant-based ingredients including coconut oil and juniper berry that are very effective. Boric acid (though terribly dangerous as a liquid in large amounts) can be an effective ingredient as well when formulated to be on cotton pads in very diluted small amounts. Do not attempt to create your own boric acid mixture at home.

Step #3 Remover

No doubt, you have already thought of this. In fact, in your quest to remove tear stains, you may have already tried one or most of them. Yet, the stains may have only faded a bit, or they may have not nudged at all. There are a couple of things to keep in mind:

1) If you do not resolve all of the possible causes, even an excellent tear stain remover can only do so much. It is akin to using paint remover on your living room walls while another person is simultaneously brushing paint on. So, if your dog is eating a dog food with additives, drinking unfiltered tap water, has plastic bowls, does not have his face wiped daily, and/or has runny eyes that have not been resolved at home or treated by the vet, do not expect tear stains to vanish or at least to not come back after you treat them.

2) What works for one dog may not work for another. Every dog is unique and each type of stain (triggered by one or more possible reasons) responds differently to different remover products. You can even have two dogs of your own and need a separate remover for each of them. So, if you've tried one and had less-than-stellar results, it may be time to give another great brand a try.

Good and Bad Removers: While researching tear stains in dogs, you may have come across many home remedies. Some of them are very dangerous and some just do not work.

At-Home Treatments to AVOID:

☠ **Bleach. DO NOT USE THIS.** Severe risk of blindness.

☠ **Boric acid mixed with corn starch. DO NOT USE THIS.** Homemade concoctions of this can be dangerous to use around the eye area. Boric acid *can* be effective *but only* when formulated to be on proper wipes in small amounts.

☠ **Cornstarch powder. DO NOT USE THIS.** This can irritate the eyes.

☠ **Milk of Magnesia, corn starch, and peroxide. DO NOT USE THIS.** This can cause irritation or damage to a dog's eyes.

☠ **Lemon. DO NOT USE THIS.** This can irritate the eyes.

☺ **Tums.** Tums (calcium carbonate) does not work and dogs on good diets do not need extra calcium.

☺ **Adding vinegar to drinking water**. Most puppies and dogs do not like the taste and will be reluctant to drink their water. And, there is little proof this works.

☺ **Buttermilk.** In powder form, this is a supposed treatment touted by some sources. The dosing is 1/4 of a teaspoon per day. There is no proof that this work.

Recommended Removers: The remover should be a topical solution that is easy to apply, gentle yet effective, and be safe for dogs of all ages.

We hesitated to place the names of recommended removers for the same reason that we are not listing other specific brands. This book is static, yet products are always evolving. Newer, better products may become available at any time. An exception is being made in this case; these are well-established removers and it's hard to envision others developing something that will top them. So, keeping in mind that this is at the time of this writing, Eye Envy, Betta Bridges, and TropiClean are recommended.

Prescribed Medications: In some severe cases, a veterinarian may prescribe antibiotics or anti-fungal medications. Note that the antibiotic tetracycline should not be given to puppies that have not yet cut all of their adult teeth, as this may cause permanent stains on teeth that have not erupted.

Dental Care

Dental care is so important, it deserves its own chapter. In fact, out of all the care tasks related to the body, it is the one that has the most significant impact on your dog's health and wellbeing.

What happens: At-home dental care and professional care (as needed), is vital for all dogs; however, this is particularly true for toy breeds, as they are very prone to dental decay.

Every second, around-the-clock, plaque is being produced. It is a clear, sticky substance that clings to teeth. It is not fully removed from chewing on toys or treats. Within 3 days, it starts to harden into tartar (also referred to as calculus), which is much more difficult to remove.

As these substances grip a dog's teeth, they eat away at the enamel. Tartar can also travel *under* the gum line where it eats away at teeth, unseen. This often leads to tooth decay, gingivitis (gum disease), periodontal disease, and eventual tooth loss. There can also be tooth infection(s), infection that travels up into the sinuses, and the risk of full-body sepsis which can be fatal. As you can imagine, halitosis (bad breath) is common as well.

What to do: If you have a puppy or if your older dog has just had a checkup and you were told that there are no dental issues, immediately start an at-home program of proper dental hygiene to avoid any future issues. Note that even puppies can benefit from at-home dental care; decay on the deciduous (milk) teeth can travel to adult teeth that have not yet erupted. Another reason to start young is to have a pup become accustomed to having his teeth touched; this makes it a lot easier to do brushings once that pup matures into an adult.

If you are not sure if your dog's teeth are without issues, schedule a veterinary exam. The teeth will be examined and any current issues will be resolved. Note that this may involve a 'full dental', which requires sedation (more info ahead on this). Then, you can implement an at-home program of proper dental hygiene to help prevent future issues.

Details of an at-home program of proper dental hygiene: There are several steps to take to ensure that your puppy or dog's teeth stay clean and healthy.

Brush Your Dog's Teeth Each Day

Brushing is the most effective method to remove plaque. **Here are some tips:**

- Use an appropriately sized canine toothbrush. Those with 2 or 3 sides can be helpful, as these cover more surfaces than a flat 1-sided toothbrush.

[handwritten: nge ✱ brush of excellent quality.]

- A finger-brush can work as well. This is a small, rubber-tipped doodad that slips over your pointer finger.
- Use a quality canine toothpaste. Never use human toothpaste. Human toothpaste contains fluoride which is toxic to canines, possibly contains xylitol which is toxic to canines, and has foaming agents which can make a dog choke.
- Opt for a quality canine paste that is flavored to encourage tolerance to brushings; vanilla or chicken are good choices. And of course, a reputable brand will be non-foaming and non-toxic, since dogs are meant to swallow the paste.
- Brush for a good 2 to 3 minutes, once per day. If you want to do it twice, that's all the better!
- While it is perfectly safe for a dog to swallow quality canine paste, you may wish to wipe excess paste away with a clean piece of gauze.

A slow introduction to having teeth brushed: For puppies that are not used to this, you may wish to start slow and gradually ease into things. For the first week, set aside 10 minutes per day to have your pup sit down with you. Rub your finger all along his teeth. As you do this, use a cue phrase, such as 'tooth time', so that a connection can be made between the words and the actions. Give praise and reward when the session is complete. After that first week, graduate up to a finger-brush or small canine toothbrush.

[handwritten mark] For older dogs that may not tolerate having all of their teeth touched in this way, start off with a finger-brush; if possible, graduate up to a regular canine toothbrush after a period of adjustment.

Or Use a Dental Spray or Dental Wipe

Though not our method of choice, if your dog struggles with having his teeth brushed, you may wish to opt for a quality dental spray that is designed to loosen and remove plaque or a quality dental wipe that is meant to help remove plaque. Note that while these do have their place for dogs that have no tolerance for a canine toothbrush, these are typically marketed as being able to 'remove all plaque and tartar' and this may be a bit of a stretch. You will still want to adhere to the following dental care tips.

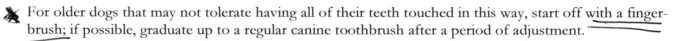

Offer a Daily Dental Treat

These are specially designed edible treats that can remove a good amount of plaque. Be sure to offer ones that are appropriately sized for your puppy or dog. Also, since these are very hard treats (they have to be, to remove any plaque or tartar), you will want to supervise your dog when giving this. Do not offer this sort of treat if you will be stepping away or leaving the house.

Use a Dental Supplement, if Needed

If your dog has a history of dental issues, you may want to step things up a notch by also offering a supplement that is added to the water. As with dental sprays, these may be marketed as 'removing all plaque and tartar', but should be used in conjunction with other cleaning methods (brushing or sprays and dental treats), not in place of them. These typically have an anti-microbial formula that works to kill germs and bacteria in the mouth (and the bowl). Some are also very effective in helping resolve bad breath.

Professional Cleanings, as Needed

Even with stringent at-home cleanings and care, many dogs need professional cleanings every so often. And, for those that had a lack of dental care in the past, this is a 'must'. If you have adopted a rescue or otherwise taken in an older dog, never assume that adequate dental care was done up until that point.

When a complete examination and cleaning is performed by the veterinarian, this is typically referred to as a 'full dental'. This is usually done with a dog lightly sedated. If this is something that is being considered, your dog should be pre-screened to make sure that he is healthy enough for anesthesia.

The following is usually performed:

- X-rays are taken to assess teeth and bones of the mouth.
- A flush is given to kill bacteria in the mouth.
- A dental probe is used to measure any pockets found between the teeth and gums.
- Teeth are cleaned, typically with ultrasonic scalers. Tartar is removed from both above and below the gum line.
- A special solution is applied to highlight any areas of remaining tartar, which are then removed.
- Teeth are polished.
- Though the x-rays will be quite telling, once all teeth are cleaned, they are each visually inspected for any signs of disease.
- A flush is given a second time.
- A plaque-guard agent may be applied.

 Since canine dental care products are always evolving, yet this book is static, our current recommendations for toothbrushes, canine toothpaste, dental chews, sprays, and other at-home dental care products are on the Supplies page of the PetChiDog site is updated as we evaluate new products. You can reach this by entering any page of PetChiDog.com; look to the navigation which is in alphabetical order, and choose 'Supplies'.

Fur and Coat

Normal Shedding

The Chihuahua is considered to be a light to moderate shedder. Times of seasonal shedding can vary depending on the climate of where you live and your dog's environment.

The shedding process in dogs is triggered, in part, by changes in light. This happens twice per year. When days start to become shorter in autumn this triggers the body to shed some fur as a thicker winter coat grows in. When days start to become longer in the springtime, this again sends a trigger to the body to shed the slightly thicker winter coat that previously grew in. This type of shedding lasts for approximately 2 months, for each of the time periods. It is more noticeable for those that also experience a marked change in temperature as well.

Whether your dog has an obvious seasonal shed or not, there will always be some level of year-round shedding. This is because a dog's fur is quite like a human's in the aspect that it has a growth cycle. It grows, pauses, and falls out on a continual basis. It is for this reason that you should be prepared to brush the coat to pull out dead hairs on a routine basis, regardless of the time of year, season, or weather.

Serious Fur Loss

Please note that this section is a general overview regarding health issues that can cause coat loss. Alopecia X is covered in the next section.

Typical issues associated with a thinning coat are:

• **Irritated skin.** If the coat thins down enough to have a closer look, you may see that the skin underneath the thinning area is pink, swollen, and/or has a rash. This is not always the case; however, in most instances, coat loss and skin problems go hand in hand.
• **Itchy skin.** In some cases, when a dog scratches and/or chews at himself, it will cause hairs to fall out. Opposite to this, thinning or bald areas may cause the skin to itch, which in turn prompts a dog to scratch.
• **Odd patterns of fur loss.** There may be circular patterns of thinning fur or other unusual shapes where the coat is becoming bald.

The 8 Top Reasons for Coat Loss: There are many reasons why a dog's coat may thin and become bald in some spots; however, these are the most common causes:

1) Parasites. One parasite that causes coat loss is demodectic mange, typically with fur loss around the eye area, trunk, and/or legs. In some cases, the balding areas will show skin lesions that look irritated or are crusted over. For more regarding demodectic mange, refer to 'Health – Other: Mange'. Ringworm is also a possibility. The telltale signs are circular bald spots that appear on the head, paws, ears, or limbs. There may be a red spot in the middle and the area may or may not crust over. For ringworm, refer to 'Health – Other:

Worms'.

2) Thyroid Issues. Both a low level of hormones (hypothyroidism) or high levels (hyperthyroidism) can cause coat loss. With these issues, problems are often seen over larger areas of a dog's coat and are not concentrated in one area. If this is the cause, the fur is often dry and brittle.

Other signs of hypothyroidism include: lethargy, trouble concentrating, intolerance to the cold, unexplained weight loss, thinning coat, poor coat texture, skin scaling, and/or skin infection.

Other signs of hyperthyroidism include: hyperactivity, rapid breathing, heart murmur, enlarged thyroid glands in the neck, difficulty breathing, increased appetite (but a dog may have weight loss, despite this), increased thirst, increased urination, vomiting, and/or diarrhea.

3) Stress. When a dog is highly stressed, a condition called telogen effluvium may develop, in which a large number of coat follicles are forced into a lengthy resting phase. One to two months afterward, those hairs may then shed off, especially after a thorough brushing or a bath. Since this is a delayed reaction, coat loss often occurs when the triggering event is over and things have already resolved. Typically, the coat will grow back without any intervention.

Events that may be perceived as overly stressful include but are not limited to loss of a family member (human or pet), moving to a new home, and severe levels of separation anxiety. If you suspect severe stress due to separation anxiety, you may wish to refer to 'Situational Issues: Separation Anxiety'.

4) Allergies. Either seasonal, contact, or food allergies may affect both skin and coat. Many allergens cause itchiness, and in turn, a dog may scratch to the point of fur loss. Allergies can also cause such poor coat quality that dry fur breaks off. You may wish to refer to 'Health – Other: Allergies'.

5) Diabetes. Seen in both adolescent and adult dogs, most owners first notice the symptoms of increased thirst, weakness, and weight changes. A thinning or dulled coat is also a sign.

6) Cushing's disease. This is a disease in which the adrenal glands over-produce too much cortisol hormone. This most typically affects dogs over the age of 6, but can be seen in younger dogs as well. Other signs of this include bruising, increased thirst, increased urination, and weakness.

7) Folliculitis. This is an infection of the hair follicles that may be accompanied by blisters with a pus-type discharge and/or crusting on the skin where the coat is thinning. In some cases, spots may become bald and weeks *later* the sores and blisters of pus will appear. This is typically treated with a round of antibiotics.

8) Alopecia X. This is a broad term applied to coat loss with unknown causes, though in some cases there may be a link to hormones. Alopecia X is covered in full in the next section.

Alopecia X

Alopecia X refers unknown hair loss, with the 'X' standing for 'unknown', though it is thought to be linked to hormones in some cases. This can strike any dog breed and it can happen at any age.

There is a particular type of Alopecia X, called Color Dilution Alopecia, that is seen with dogs that carry the blue color gene; therefore, this can be seen with the Chihuahua breed. Color Dilution Alopecia often develops between the ages of 6 months to 3 years. It may affect the whole coat or just the areas of the coat in which the blue is expressed (typically dulled black or silver hairs). All other symptoms are the same and treatment is the same.

Symptoms: Fur becomes very dry, hair shafts break, and patches of baldness appear which may be in circular patterns. For many dogs, there will be a major thinning over the body or complete loss of coat (though the face is not often affected). There can be scabs and scaling as well.

Diagnosis: All other causes of coat loss need to be ruled out. Typical testing should include a blood panel, a urinalysis, thyroid testing, adrenal hormone testing, and a skin biopsy.

Treatment:

Spay/neuter. For intact dogs, veterinarians often recommend spaying or neutering, as it is thought that Alopecia X may be related to an imbalance of estrogen or testosterone. This said, while doing so may trigger regrowth, it is sometimes just temporary. Do, however, keep in mind that there are health benefits to sterilization regardless of whether or not there is a coat loss issue.

Cortisol; take caution. In some cases, a veterinarian may recommend medications that suppress adrenal gland function; however, these can have quite serious and severe side effects, so continuous monitoring must be done, and these do not work for every dog. Cortisol can weaken the immune system, leading to vulnerability to diseases and infections.

Side effects include dizziness, drowsiness, depressed mood, skin rash, nausea, diarrhea, vomiting, and/or loss of appetite. Very dangerous side effects include bloody diarrhea, collapse, severe electrolyte imbalance, and rapid destruction of the adrenal gland which may result in death. Furthermore, overdose can lead to Addison's disease.

At-home treatment options. Once ALL possible health issues have been ruled out, your veterinarian has diagnosed your dog with Alopecia X, and you have followed the vet's advice in the treatment of this and any other secondary health issues, a 3-step approach *may* restore the coat:

Step #1 Melatonin

Melatonin is produced by the body at night and works to regulate sleep patterns. It has been found to help some dogs regrow coats. Please note that in many cases, it is a combination of melatonin and other at-home treatments that will offer the best results.

This can cause some drowsiness; in fact, it is sometimes given to dogs to help with anxiety. And, it can sometimes interfere with medications, so you'll want your vet to give you the 'okay' for this.

Dosing for dogs under 10 pounds is 1 mg per day, best given at night. It may take up to 3 months to see if it is helping. If coat growth occurs, continue the melatonin until it seems to have plateaued. After maximum regrowth has been achieved, the dose is gradually tapered down over the course of several months to a weekly dose. Some dogs can ultimately discontinue this; however, if it is discontinued and the fur falls out again, the condition may not be responsive to melatonin a second time.

There is typically no difference between melatonin packaged for humans and those packaged for pets, though there can be a huge difference in quality. Be sure to obtain just melatonin and not one that has Valerian root or any other additions. Nature's Bounty is a reliable brand and offers 1 mg tablets.

Step #2 Omega-3 fish oil

As covered in 'Feeding and Nutrition: Supplements', omega-3 EPA and DHA are the most effective types of omega for skin and coat health. We recommend a liquid omega-3 fish oil derived from wild fish. This is given once per day, with the allotted amount (usually 1/4 to 1/2 pump, depending on weight) added to one meal. Be sure to mix this in well; if not, a dog may pick and choose just the kibble with the fish oil, as both the scent and taste can be very appealing to canines.

Step #3 Specialty skin lotion, shampoo, and conditioner

Specialty lotion: Just the act of massaging in a lotion each day can help tremendously; this stimulates blood circulation to the hair follicles, which in and of itself can prompt coat growth. However, doing so with rich, restorative ingredients can be just the thing to grow the coat after a severe thinning or balding episode. Use a soothing lotion that heals and regenerates with ingredients such as aloe vera, coconut oil, hemp seed oil, shea butter, honey, and tea tree oil.

It is recommended to apply this as follows:

1. Massage a quality lotion into the skin (wherever the coat is thinning) **2 times each day for 7 straight days**, for at least **5** minutes.
2. After this first week is complete, massage it into the skin (wherever the coat is thinning) **1 time each day**.
3. If you reach a point where the coat is growing back in, continue to use every other day for a few weeks. Once the coat is fully restored, you may wish to use this once per week as maintenance.

Note: You will want to make sure that once applied and massaged onto the skin, the lotion does not rub off. Slipping a cotton shirt on your dog can help with this. You may want to go one size up from what your puppy or dog normally wears so that the fabric covers more of the lower back and/or rear legs if these are affected areas.

Specialty shampoo: You'll want to use a shampoo that really revs up the healing and prompts regeneration. A combination of peppermint and tea tree oil can be a very effective blend for this. Other additional ingredients that can help include lavender, chamomile, rosehip seed oils, aloe vera, and oat proteins. When you are trying to help the coat regrow *and* you are using superior products, you can shampoo your puppy or dog much more often than normal, up to once a week. Once you have gently lathered up your dog, allow the product to soak in for a good 10 minutes. Rinse well and be sure to pat the coat dry, do not rub!

Conditioner: Typically, shampoos meant to restore skin and coat health are exceedingly luxurious; however, the bathing process causes hair cuticles to open, so you'll still want to use a conditioner to smooth them down.

 Since products are always evolving, yet this book is static, current recommendations for omega-3 fish oil, and restorative lotions, shampoos, and conditioners are on the Supplies page of the PetChiDog site, which is updated as needed. You can reach this by entering any page of PetChiDog.com; look to the navigation which is in alphabetical order, and choose 'Supplies'.

Tip: Be sure that your dog rests and sleeps on a supportive mattress or bed. Resting or sleeping on hard floors is not only bad for joints but also bad for the coat.

Exercise & Activity

Exercise Requirements & Restrictions

Exercise is all relative; toy breeds need to exercise just as larger breeds do, and will receive just as many benefits from it, which are numerous.

Avoiding excessive exercise when under 10 months old: While of course you never want to push a dog of any age to his limits, you'll want to pay particular attention to not allow young puppies to overextend themselves during the age of 8-weeks to 10-months. This time is one of rapid growth, and very excessive exercise can affect growth plates. Growth plates are somewhat soft areas at the end of bones; the cells there are continually dividing, which allows those bones to properly grow as the pup matures into his adult size. Once growth is complete, the plates close.

If a puppy is put under too much physical stress, there can be damage to those plates which can lead to malformed or shortened limb(s). ***Do note, however***, that normal walking and play is ***not*** considered excessive. You *will* want to avoid lengthy full-out runs or forcing activity when the pup has reached his limit.

Age to start taking walks: A puppy should have all of his puppy shots before going for walks or out to any public areas. Until this time, a puppy is not fully protected from certain diseases that can be contracted in areas where there were or are other dogs or wildlife. Puppy vaccinations are typically complete by the 12 to 16-week mark; however, you will want to confirm this with your veterinarian. Additionally, you may wish to wait two weeks past that point, just to be safe.

Benefits of exercise: There are many reasons to offer regular daily exercise:

1) It helps a dog maintain muscle tone, which in turn helps a dog maintain good posture and allows the muscles surrounding the hips and knees to be strong and supportive.
2) It is good for the heart and reduces the risk of heart disease.
3) It helps keep the metabolism functioning properly.
4) It helps stimulate the appetite.
5) It allows a release of any pent-up energy, which in turn gives you a more well-behaved dog. Dogs that receive regular outdoor exercise display less destructive behaviors at home.
6) It allows a dog to engage his canine senses (hearing, scenting, sight), which often leads to a more emotionally satisfied dog.
7) It will enable a dog to be exposed to stimuli, which eventually leads to less reaction (i.e. barking at other dogs).

How much exercise is needed:

Walks: Two daily walks, each for a minimum of 20 minutes, is recommended. If this is not feasible, the next alternative would be one 30-minute walk. The pace should be considered brisk for your puppy or dog. If there is a lot of restlessness, barking, chewing issues, and/or trouble sleeping at night, consider increasing this to three 20-minute walks.

Free cardio: It is also ideal to incorporate a 20-minute session of cardio each day.

Walking tips:

Going for walks is the most traditional method of offering daily exercise for a dog. There is always a Point A and a Point B, which helps ensure proper duration. And, unlike free-running, speed can be adjusted by you, as you see fit. Here are some tips to keep walks safe and fun:

1) Stick to a schedule. When walks are scheduled, owners are more prone to follow through. And dogs, with their incredible inner time clocks, quickly learn to look forward to this time.

2) Work on heeling skills, if needed. Once proper heeling is mastered, it makes walking more enjoyable for both owner and dog. Walking in tandem, without a dog pulling on the leash or stopping every few moments, makes this moderate exercise something to look forward to. If your puppy or dog refuses to walk alongside you or keeps stopping every other moment, look to 'Behavioral Training: Refusal to Walk While on Leash'. And, for exact heeling methods, see 'Training: Heeling'.

3) In the summer, head out before 10 AM and/or after 5 PM, avoiding the hottest times of the day. If you couldn't get out early enough to beat the heat for the morning walk, and if the temperature is over 90°F (32.2°C), it is best to skip that session as overheating may be a problem. Instead, opt for an indoor exercise activity (suggestions are ahead in this section) or plan to go later when the sun is lower in the sky.

Be sure that your dog's paws are protected from hot walking surfaces. A good paw wax can help quite a bit (see: 'Grooming: Specifics of Grooming Tasks'). Even with paw wax, some walking surfaces may be exceedingly hot; blacktop pavement typically heats up the fastest and most severe, followed by red brick, and then cement. You can test the ground with the back of your hand to see if you can comfortably hold it there for a slow count of 10. If you cannot, stick to the grass or shaded areas. Dog shoes are another option; but, not all dogs like to wear them.

4) In the winter, be sure to still go for daily walks unless it is below freezing or there is dangerous precipitation. After all, if we kept our dogs inside all winter long, this could be very detrimental to their health. Dress both yourself and your dog in appropriate outerwear. For your puppy or dog, this may be a lined vest or waterproof coat. More is ahead in this chapter under 'Dressing for the Weather'.

You'll also want to protect your dog's paws from ice-melt chemicals and/or sand (even if you do not use these products, these can be tracked in and spread around by vehicles), snowballing (when snow melts between the toes and/or paw pads, refreezes into ice, and then splits the skin), and slippery surfaces. This can all be accomplished with a quality paw wax.

5) Visit the designated bathroom area before the walk. It should never be your plan to allow your dog to poo or pee along the walking route. This can disrupt a dog's understanding of his house-breaking rules. Always take him to his designated bathroom area both before a walk and after returning.

Free cardio tips:

The quintessential game fetch is always a great choice for this. Dogs catch on to this quickly, it can be played right in your own yard (or down a long hallway on rainy days), and it is a terrific owner-dog bonding experience. Here are some tips to keep these sessions safe and fun:

1) Unless you can do this in a secure fenced-in yard, have your dog on leash. There are adjustable leashes that extend out 26' or so, which is typically plenty of length for chasing after balls.

2) Use a properly-sized fetch toy. Grab a pack of colorful mini tennis ball to make it easy for your dog to see the ball and mouth it. More details on these can be found in 'Care Items - Chihuahuas of All Ages: Toys'.

3) Bring along your enthusiasm. Your level of enthusiasm will generally dictate how engaged your puppy or dog is.

Dog Parks

It'd be nice if all parks specifically for pets would be a safe place where our dogs could romp around and maybe even make friends with other dogs. However, there are some real concerns about the safety of dog parks.

Not every dog park is set up the same, so it's a good idea to investigate if your local park could have one of the following hazards:

1) Being attacked by another dog. This is a sad topic since the main reason owners bring their dog to dog parks is to allow their pet a pleasant environment to meet and greet other dogs. In theory, this is a great idea because once a dog is exposed to any trigger - including other dogs - over a period of time, he is much more likely to act calm during future encounters.

But the startling fact is that dog parks have been the scene of terrible and even deadly attacks:

At a dog park in South Euclid, Ohio, in which dogs of all sizes played in the same area, a Siberian Husky fatally mauled a Chihuahua named Rizzo. After this incident, city officials are trying to raise money to build a separate small-dog enclosure at the park.

At a dog park in Ashland, Oregon, a Chihuahua was killed by a German Shepherd. In this park, there was a separate small enclosed area that many owners were mistaking for one reserved for toy dogs, but in fact was just another spot for dogs of all sizes.

At the Hollenback Dog Park in Wilkes-Barre, Pennsylvania, a 1-year-old Chihuahua named Bentley was fatally mauled by three Husky-mixes that entered the small dog area of the park after allegedly being left unattended. Bentley's owner suffered 17 bite wounds to her right hand trying to save him but was unable to stop the attack.

At the Bear Creek Dog Park in Medford, Oregon, a Chihuahua named Bailey was mauled by a German Shepherd. He did not die right away; poor Bailey suffered broken ribs, a punctured gallbladder, and a punctured, collapsed lung. Emergency vet intervention could not save his overwhelming respiratory problems and he died 4 days later.

At the Tanglewood Park dog park in North Carolina, a Chihuahua had to be euthanized after being attacked by a large, female Newfoundland dog. The owner tried to pull her Chi out of the dog's mouth and was bitten in the hand.

In Austin, Minnesota, a Chihuahua was killed by a pit bull that somehow got into a dog park's section for small dogs… And the list goes on.

How to keep your dog safe: Attacks like those almost always happen in dog parks that do not have separate areas for small and large dogs. So, look for a dog park that has these separate enclosed areas for dogs based on size. Many parks are adopting this method to avoid tragedies.

Even if your dog is running around only with other toy breeds, you'll still want to keep an eye on things since a small dog may be aggressive as well. Though this is less likely to result in a fatal attack, it can cause an emotional scar. Warning signs are that the other dog will have a frozen stance, raised hackles, and may bare his teeth.

By no means should you let this scare you from going to a dog park; the benefits of playing with other dogs and the socialization skills that come from that far outweigh any small chance of issues, just play it safe.

Another option is to go to a park that is not necessarily labeled a 'dog park' but rather is a park that does allow dogs if on leash. There will be far fewer dogs. This is also a good idea for dogs that do not do well with large groups of other canines.

2) Catching parasites.
There are several ways that a dog can catch fleas or worms from other dogs. With fleas, these can jump up to six feet from one animal to another. And in regard to worms, a puppy or dog can become infested with parasites by eating the feces of other animals or grass that is contaminated via feces.

How to keep your dog safe: Using year-round flea protection is the best way for you to keep your dog safe from fleas, not only when at parks but any time your dog is in the same area as other animals. Ensuring that your dog is protected from worms is a 'must' as well. Many heartworm protection meds also protect against some worms; so, be sure to read the labeling. At any rate, you'll want to prevent your dog from ingesting feces or grass. At parks, keep a close eye on things to intervene if needed. See also 'Health – Other: Worms', 'Behavioral Issues: Eating Feces', and 'Behavioral Issues: Eating Grass'.

3) Communal drinking water hazards.
Some parks have public fountains for dogs to drink from; these are not necessarily safe. There are a couple of diseases that can be transmitted via shared water including the papilloma virus (which causes painful warts to grow in a dog's mouth) and respiratory diseases.

How to keep your dog safe: It can help to make sure your dog is fully hydrated before you leave for the park and bring along your own supply of water in a travel jug. Every 30 minutes or so, before thirst sets in, have your dog take a break with you to rest and drink the water that you brought.

Another good reason to bring along your own fresh water is that a park's water supply may be shut down for maintenance at any time or during colder months so that pipes do not freeze in the winter weather.

Things to Bring to the Dog Park

1- Poo bags. Since you expect other owners to pick up their dog's poop, you won't want to forget to bring bags so that you can do the same. It's also a good idea to bring some extras in case someone else wasn't as prepared as you are and asks to borrow one.

2- Water with a collapsible bowl or travel container. You may opt for a bottle of spring water and a collapsible travel bowl or a canine travel water container in which the lid doubles as the bowl. Either way, it's a good idea to bring about twice the amount that you think you'll need. Anything can happen, from the water being tipped to your dog overheating and if it does, you'll be happy that you brought extra.

3- Canine grooming wipes. Several things can stick to a dog's paws including lawn care chemicals, pollen, and other allergy triggers, or bits of feces your dog may have stepped in. So, you may wish to wipe your dog's paws before you put him back into your car. Use one wipe for each paw.

4- Hand sanitizer. Due to the #3 suggestion above, you'll want to be able to sanitize your hands once you've cleaned off your dog.

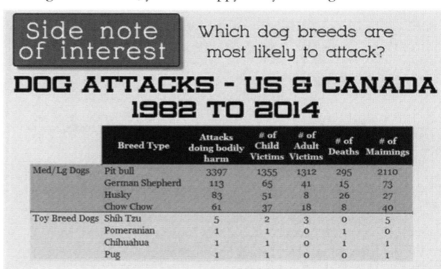

Side note of interest — Which dog breeds are most likely to attack?

DOG ATTACKS - US & CANADA 1982 TO 2014

	Breed Type	Attacks doing bodily harm	# of Child Victims	# of Adult Victims	# of Deaths	# of Maimings
Med/Lg Dogs	Pit bull	3397	1355	1312	295	2110
	German Shepherd	113	65	41	15	73
	Husky	83	51	8	26	27
	Chow Chow	61	37	18	8	40
Toy Breed Dogs	Shih Tzu	5	2	3	0	5
	Pomeranian	1	1	0	1	0
	Chihuahua	1	1	0	1	1
	Pug	1	1	0	0	1

When to Avoid Going to the Dog Park

1. If your un-spayed female is in heat. Every single un-neutered male dog that can reach her will try to mount her. This is unsafe for both your female and for you as you try to break them up. The tricky thing is that a female may be entering heat before owners notice the signs. For this reason, if your dog is not fixed, keep her on leash and watch how she reacts to other dogs. If she raises her tail and tries to present herself, that's your clue to pick her up and head back home.

2. If your dog is overly shy. Though you may want to work on training your dog to be better socialized, it is never a good idea to move from zero to one hundred. Dogs that have trouble being in social settings will need gradual, incremental exposure and suddenly being put into such an overwhelming situation is never helpful.

Fun Things to Do— Blowing bubbles

Things you can do at home:

1. Play an indoor game. An easy one to set up is 'Find the Treat'. You'll need a small treat and 3 cups (that are not transparent). Set the cups in a row and hide the treat under one. Shuffle them. Encourage your puppy or dog to find the right one by sniffing or pawing the cups over.

A game for rainy days is Hide 'n Seek; you hide and your dog has to find you. Order a 'Sit' while you hide, have a helper hold your dog, or place a gate or other similar object 95% of the way closed to give you time to run to a chosen spot.

Always plan your hiding spot so that your dog doesn't catch you standing in a room, have treats in your pocket so that you can give reward as soon as you've been found, and increase the difficult level. The first time you hide, choose an easy spot in the next room over such as behind a sofa, by the 5th or 6th game, you can be in the bathtub with the curtain drawn, in various closets with the doors open only enough for your dog to fit through, or underneath blankets. A session of about 10 'finds' is usually ideal so that the game ends when your dog hasn't yet become tired of it. This leads to wanting to play again the next day.

2. Set up a sprinkler (summertime fun). Most dogs are enthralled at water being whipped out, just about any sprinkler (other than high-powered ones) can be used, and it's a great way to help a dog stay cool.

3. Teach a new command. All dogs should know the basic commands, so if this isn't the case, now is the time to start working on 'Sit', 'Stay', 'Come' and 'Down'. If those are down pat, how about 'Shake Hands'? This sort of training is well worth the time; it instills proper hierarchy, is a fun way to bond, and can give a dog a boost of self-confidence. See also 'Training: Command Training'.

4. Blow bubbles for your dog to chase. It's a great way to offer a bout of exercise and it's just as fun for owners as it is for their canine companions.

Things to do that involve leaving the house:

1. Choose a completely new walking route. Choose a destination and see if you can arrive there by different roads than you'd normally take (just be sure that there are safe sidewalks). Or, visit a neighborhood that you've always wanted to live in and walk there as if you've already moved in!

2. Visit a dog-friendly store. This is a particularly good idea during cold months when you and your dog may both be experiencing cabin fever. While you'll want to call ahead to make sure, there are many chain stores that generally allow dogs including Macy's (a huge pet supporter), just about every pet supply store including Petco, Bass Pro Shop (even if you're not into hunting and fishing gear, it can be fun to walk around), Barnes and Noble bookstores, Bloomingdales, Anthropologie, Bebe, Foot Locker, the Gap, and Bed Bath and Beyond.

3. Go for a picnic. Pack up a lunch and a blanket and you are both ready to enjoy some outdoor time and a new experience.

4. Visit a dog-friendly beach. Beaches are not just for the summer months. Offseason can be a great time to bring a dog to the shoreline. There are fewer people, and it's easier to have fun near the water without distractions.

Even winter can be a good time to go since in many areas it will snow inland but not near the water. Just check to see what the temperature will be along with the wind chill, which is often stronger right on the coast. If it calls for it, bundle your dog up in a warm parka and let him see how much fun it is to explore the area.

5. Treat both you and your dog to a spa day. Spas meant for both owner and dog to enjoy together are starting to pop up. There are some that offer fun things like Jacuzzi tubs for owners to pamper their pets (or the facility will wash your dog while you relax). There are also some owner & pet spas that offer aromatherapy, massaging baths, and nail treatments. To see what is available in your area, do a web search for 'owner and dog spas' plus the name of your city or town.

6. Go for a hike. Search the web for 'easy' hike trails in your area; you may be surprised what is in your town or close by. While a toy breed's pace will be a lot slower than yours, going for hikes can be exhilarating for both of you. It offers a bit of a fun challenge and beautiful views (and scents for your dog) that are not found in your neighborhood. Follow the same rules as for regular walks, keeping your dog on leash and harness, and taking breaks for rest and water. If the trail will be sandy or contain small pebbles, protect the paws with a paw wax. For very rough terrain, consider doggie shoes (though not all dogs will tolerate these).

7. Visit a farm or orchard. Depending on the season, it can be a great time to go strawberry picking, apple picking, or even explore a pumpkin patch. Often, apple orchards also have peach trees and other fruit trees to fill in between apple season. It can be a great way to do something new with your dog and afterward (or during), you can sample the fruit. Strawberries are one of the fruits safe for dogs to eat. Peach and apple can be given to dogs if you cut out pieces (only the core, seeds, and pits are toxic).

8. Treat both you and your dog to a meal at a dog-friendly restaurant. You might be surprised how many restaurants there are that allow dogs, and if you can find one that has an outdoor eating patio, all the better! Some have menu items for dogs. Starbucks has a 'secret' menu item called a Puppuccino; It's an espresso shot sized paper cup full of whip cream (most dogs can tolerate dairy when given in moderate amounts).

In n' Out has a burger specifically for dogs called the 'pup patty' that even comes in its own doggy bag. At Tim Horton's, you can order a sugar-free doggy version of their 'Timbits', which are bite sized doughnuts. There's even a restaurant chain called the Shake Shack located along the east coast that offers the 'Pooch-ini', which is ShackBurger dog biscuits, peanut butter sauce, and vanilla custard, or the Bag O' Bones which is a bag of five ShackBurger dog treats. At the Laughing Dog Brewing Co. in Idaho, your dog can't drink beer such as the Alpha Dog, but he will be welcome inside.

9. Visit a pet-friendly museum, historical site, or tourist site. Just a sampling of places that allow dogs includes the Pioneer Museum of Alabama, The Old Sacramento Historic Area in Sacramento, The Museum of America and the Sea in Mystic CT, the Railway Museum in Union IL, the Historic Deerfield Village in Deerfield MA, the Museum of the Prairie Pioneer in Grand Island NE, and the Zilker Botanical Gardens in Austin TX.

Things to do that require a bit of planning:

1. Bring your dog bike riding with you. Of course, you'll need a bicycle (you can rent, borrow, or buy) and a canine bike basket. There are both front and back carriers. Some bicycle baskets for pets have tops to keep a dog shaded, or rain covers should the weather take a turn. Some also come with pockets that hold dog toys, water, and other needed on-the-go items.

2. Go to a doga class. Doga is a yoga class that owners do with their dogs. These are just beginning to pop up, with doga now in New York, Seattle, San Francisco, Jacksonville, Fla., some cities in Canada, and even overseas in Japan. These are sometimes run by yoga studios; however, others are organized by canine rescue groups and shelters. During the class, owners help their dogs facilitate different poses and some places also include doggy massage.

3. Join a canine freestyling dance group with your dog. Freestyling dance is a dog sport that is a mixture of obedience training, tricks, and dance. There are places that offer beginner classes where you and everyone else is new to this sort of activity, allowing you to have fun and learn if this is something you and your dog would enjoy.

4. Or plan to attend a freestyle competition. The Canine Freestyle Federation lists out both places where you can take classes and events where you can watch.

5. Sign your dog up for agility classes. This offers an exciting yet challenging environment in which you will learn to guide your dog over, around, and through all sorts of obstacles. Your local SPCA may offer these classes and all sorts of canine training gyms and facilities offer these as well. Dogs of every breed, size, and age can do this and you'll never know how much fun it can be unless you try.

6. Visit a national park. There are 58 national parks in the US; chances are that one near you allows dogs at least in some areas of it. An example is the Catalina State Park in Tucson, Arizona. Many trails are not suitable for dogs or allow them, but the Canyon Loop Trail which is 2.3 miles does allow pets. It offers a rolling trail through spectacular views in an area home to 170 species of birds and even ends with a 'doggie swimming hole'. At Nelder Grove in Oakhurst, California, dogs are welcome to join owners to take walks among giant sequoia trees. The Shadow of the Giants Trail here is about 1 mile long, which is a perfect length for a toy breed to walk. At the Dead Horse Point State Park in Moab, Utah, though many trails are a bit too long for a toy breed to maneuver, there is a 1/2 path on the western side that leads to an overlook of Shafer Canyon where you can see where the car went off the cliff in the movie Thelma and Louise. See what's in your area or within reasonable driving distance, and make a day of it!

Dressing for the Weather

Due to very little body fat, this breed has a low tolerance for the cold. And, if there is precipitation, this makes it all that much harder for a Chihuahua to feel comfortable.

A puppy or dog may shiver when outside and even once back inside as the body takes time to warm up. Bad experiences like this can lead to a dog being reluctant to venture out with you for daily exercise. As previously covered, daily exercise is important, not just for good physical health, but also for emotional wellbeing.

So, while you will want to avoid taking your Chi outside for walks in the winter when it is well below freezing or there is dangerous precipitation or during the summer when it is exceedingly hot, do not let normal weather conditions stand in your way of enjoying walks or even playing some fetch. For both comfort and to stick with a schedule of activity, you may find that your Chihuahua does much better when having an extra layer of warmth on the core body.

As a side note, it's not all that uncommon for Chi puppies and even older dogs to feel chilly indoors, even if owners feel comfortable. For this reason, if your Chihuahua tends to shake and shiver inside the home, a shirt or sweater can be helpful (see also: 'Behavioral Issues: Shaking').

Here are guidelines that may help:

Temperature: 32°F (0°C) or colder, taking into account wind chill factor: Protection to the core body (sweater, vest, or coat).

Precipitation, snow: Paw wax or dog booties. If snow is actively falling, a waterproof vest or coat.

Precipitation, rain: Allowing a dog to become wet from the rain, if the temperature is warm, is not a bad thing. It is part of desensitization to events and to different elements. After all, you don't want your dog to cower every time it sprinkles. Dogs do just fine in light rain, if the time is limited to normal walk times (20 to 30 minutes) and it is above 60°F (15.5°C). However, if the temperature is 60 degrees or colder, consider protecting your dog from the rain with a raincoat, as a soaked coat in lower temperatures can lead to a bad chill. There are also some pet umbrellas that cover a dog as he is walking on leash.

Dogs that are intolerant even with tepid weather: While hypothyroidism or other health conditions can cause cold intolerance, most often this is a just a matter of toy breeds like the Chihuahua easily becoming chilled. If placing clothing on your puppy or dog does not help, you'll want the veterinarian to rule out possible health issues.

Heat Stroke

Overview: Exercising in hot weather or exercising for too long poses the risk of heat exhaustion (stress or stroke). Risk of heat exhaustion should not prevent you from exercising your dog, but it is something to be mindful of. It is a good idea to know the signs, should this occur, so that you can quickly react.

What happens: Heat exhaustion occurs when a dog's body cannot keep its internal temperature in a safe range. Dogs do not have efficient cooling systems (like humans who sweat) and therefore can easily overheat.

- *A dog's normal body temperature* is between 101 and 102.5°F (38.3 to 39.2°C).
- *Heat stress* is when a dog's body temperature rises to 103°F (39.4°C). You'll need to provide intervention to help your dog cool down.
- *Heat stroke* is the next phase (which can happen very quickly after heat stress), in which a dog's body temperature reaches 106°F (41.1°C) or higher. This is considered life-threatening.

Signs of Heat Stress and Heat stroke: This includes or more of the following signs:

- Rapid panting   • Bright red tongue   • Red or pale gums   • Thick, sticky saliva   •Depression
- Weakness   • Dizziness   • Vomiting (sometimes with blood)   •Diarrhea

• Slow capillary refill time (CRT); in many cases, testing the response time of blood flow to the gums can let you know if your dog is in distress. Press a finger onto your dog's gums. When you release it, the pink color should return within 2 seconds. If it takes longer than this, this is red flag sign of heat stress.

 If not treated, it can lead to shock, coma, and eventual death.

What You Should Do: Because transporting a dog in this state, without stabilizing them first, can be fatal, many vets recommend the following steps:

1. **Immediately upon noticing any of signs**, bring your dog into an air-conditioned house. If you are away from home and cannot seek shelter inside, bring your dog into the shade.
2. **If you are not sure about signs,** take your dog's temperature (also refer to 'Safety and Happiness: First Aid'). A temperature of 103°F (39.4°C) means to take steps right away, 106°F (41.1°C) is a life-threatening emergency.
3. **Call the vet and report your dog's condition.** Based on your dog's temperature and/or clinical signs, the vet may recommend immediate transport *or* for you to stabilize your dog first.
4. **Work to cool down your dog's body.** Do not use ice. Soak hand-towels in cool water, and place these over your dog, focusing on the core body, paws, groin area, and forelegs. It can help to run a fan near your dog to displace the air. If outside and unable to reach shelter, soak any extra clothing with water (a good reason to always bring along extra water) and place these on your dog.
5. **Offer cool water to drink**, but control this to avoid rapid ingestion all at one time.
6. **Monitor your dog's temperature.** Most veterinarians recommend working to bring body temp down to 103°F (39.4°C) before transporting a dog.
7. **Seek vet care afterward, regardless.** Even if you are able to stabilize your dog and he seems okay, enduring this type of event puts tremendous stress on the body.

What the Veterinarian Will Do: The veterinarian's goal is to lower body temperature to a safe range (if this has not been done already) while working to prevent dangerous complications. Treatment may include IV fluids and oxygen and monitoring for shock, respiratory distress, kidney failure, heart abnormalities, and blood clotting issues. Blood samples may be taken before and during the treatment.

Aftercare: Dogs with moderate heatstroke often recover without complications. In severe cases, there can be permanent organ damage; treatment for this will vary, depending on the exact issue. Prevention will play a more important role than ever; once a dog suffers from heat stroke, the risk of it happening again increases.

Prevention: Following these guidelines can help prevent serious problems.

• Extra monitoring during exercise for dogs with heart disease, obesity, older age, or breathing problems should be implemented. Discuss with the vet how much exercise your dog can handle.
• Provide access to water at all times.
• Do not leave your dog in a hot parked car even if you're in the shade or will only be gone a couple of minutes. The temperature inside a parked car can quickly reach up to 140°F+.
• On soaring hot days, restrict exercise and don't take your dog out with you.
• On hot days, avoid places like the beach and especially concrete or asphalt areas where heat is reflected and there is no access to shade.
• Wetting down your dog with cool water or having your dog rest on a canine cooling mat can help him maintain a normal body temperature.

Training

Teaching Proper Hierarchy* *Key is Consistency*

Teaching proper hierarchy can help with house training, barking, jumping up, and just about every behavioral issue a dog displays, in which listening to his owner is required for resolution. It is also essential to have in place before any sort of command training.

What is Hierarchy? Hierarchy is the status and ranking order of every member of the household, both humans and pets. Dogs see hierarchy, even if you do not give it much thought. To dogs, the order of hierarchy is very clear: Within the den (house) lives the pack (all humans and animals), and that pack has a leader (the Alpha). Everyone under the leader is a follower (Beta) since they follow the leader's commands. In some groups or settings, there is an Omega, which is considered a 'weak link'; this is often seen in wild packs of dogs or wolves. This is the canine way of seeing things, and there are no exceptions.

Who is the Leader? Are you sure it is you? Do not make the mistake of assuming that such a small breed will know that you are the leader. In some cases, a dog may have no idea that their human even considers themselves to be in charge. For these dogs, unless it is made exceptionally clear, they will either struggle to understand who the leader is, attempt to take on the role themselves (most dogs will step up if no one does), or mistakenly believe that they are indeed the leader.

Male and female differences: Both males and females can have a misunderstanding of hierarchy. However, it tends to vary a bit by gender. Males are more apt to believe that they themselves are Alphas, while females tend to be confused about hierarchy, often believing that no one is currently in charge, which creates a sort of 'mental chaos' while this important canine order is up in the air.

Behaviors seen: If a dog believes he is the leader, or at the very least feels there is not a clear leader, behavior will be quite different than if he were a Beta. He will protect the house; this is often done by barking at visitors and marking territory by spraying urine in key areas. The dog will also have no reason to listen to anyone that is not an Alpha, so he will sit where he wants, walk when he wants, be brushed when he feels like it, and generally make all decisions for himself. If someone tries to insist that he do things he doesn't wish to do, he may make his opinion known by growling or nipping.

The burdens of being Alpha: When a dog is challenging their human for the role of Alpha, this can be very stressful. And, if a dog believes that he has this role already, it's a heavy responsibility to carry. While there may be some initial struggles and resistance, once a dog is taught proper hierarchy, this usually releases stress. The burden of that role can be left to someone else, and the dog can enjoy life as a protected and cared for Beta.

How to teach proper hierarchy: Teaching a dog that you are the leader (Alpha) is not all that difficult. The problem is that many owners do not do this consistently. You, and every other human in the house, must follow the rules every day. If you stop, a dog may begin to believe that his leader is weakening. And in the canine world, a weak leader is not a good one; a dog may then step forward to take on the leadership role.

So, again, these steps are not complicated, but it will be up to you to follow them exactly and at all times.

#1 Make it clear that you provide the food. If your dog arrives to his dish and finds food there, he will not know that you are responsible for it being there. For this reason, before any meal is placed down or any snack is given, your dog must obey a 'Sit' (you may wish to refer to 'Training: Command Training'). Then, wait for a count of 5, and offer the food.

#2 The leader eats first. Normally, there is at least one time per day that both you and your dog eat at the same time (or at least begin eating at the same time!). During these occasions, you must make it clear that you are allowed to begin eating first because as the leader, that is your privilege.

First, prepare his meal and leave it on the counter. Then, prepare your meal and place it on your table. Next, sit down and make sure that your dog sees that you take several bites. He may jump, bark, whine, and/or circle; however, ignore this. There is no need to correct the behavior since it only lasts a few moments.

During a quiet moment (when your dog takes a breath in between barks or is landing down from a jump), rise and take his bowl into your hand. It is now that you refer to item #1, having your dog obey the 'Sit' command before placing down his meal.

#3 The leader enters and exits the 'den' first. Any time you and your dog are both leaving the house or coming back inside, you will enter/exit over the threshold first, followed by your dog. You will need to practice this, getting down the technique of stretching out your arm to keep him right inside/outside of the doorway.

Giving new toys - 'sit' command.

#4 Some things must be earned. While you do not need to do this for every little thing, when giving a new toy or an item that your dog may consider to be something of value, he'll need to obey the 'Sit' command before receiving it.

#5 When on leash, do not allow your dog to walk ahead of you. When you allow a dog to lead the way, he often takes this literally. You'll want your dog in a heeling position, which means to your immediate left; not ahead and not behind. Instructions to train your dog to heel are in the next chapter.

Note: If there are others in the house, *everyone* (excluding young children) should take follow these rules. For food-related aspects, take turns. If not, you may find that your dog listens to you, but not others. And, this is the last thing that you'll want.

Heeling

> Faye Dunningham, a popular canine trainer who has several well-regarded books on Amazon, has contributed this expanded, re-worked, special-edition training section regarding heeling.

Before we commence, please note that this type of training can be used for a dog of any age. In addition, there is no dog breed that is exempt from being able to learn any training of any sort.

Moving in Tandem

Canine instinct does not tell a dog to walk beside a human, taking the owner's cues for speed and direction. This must be taught. When first brought out on a leash, a dog will do as he wishes. He will chase a butterfly, stop to smell flowers, and try to run ahead and explore. It is the owner who must show the dog what is expected.

This is done with heeling, which is almost like an art form. It is the rhythm of dog and human walking in unison. When heeling, a dog is very aware that the human is in charge. The dog's human controls pace, direction, and decides when to stop or reverse course. When your dog is fully trained to heel, he will properly follow along whether you are walking, jogging, or suddenly stop. A dog that heels always walks beside you and does not run ahead, lag behind, or stop for any reason other than if you stop.

There will be plenty of times that you will not mind when your dog takes his time to explore the world. However, heeling or not heeling can affect every day of your life; walking can be fun or it can be frustrating.

Some owners skip over this training because they believe that it will be too difficult. It is a shame since just one month of training can be the foundation for a lifetime of enjoyed walks.

Before Heading Out

There are a few things to keep in mind before you begin:

1) Your dog should know the 'sit' command. This is customarily the first command that is taught, and for good reason; many other commands are built off of it, including 'Heel'.

2) You will want to put a harness on your dog. With a collar, if your dog lunges forward or if you pull too hard on the leash, this can place too much stress on the neck. Also, you will find that with a harness, you have more control over your pup when training him to heel. Allow a little while for your pup to get used to the harness. It can take a week or so for full acceptance.

3) You will want to have a short leash. With heeling, there is no reason for your dog to ever be in front or behind you; so, a short 4-foot or 6-foot leash is all that is needed. A retractable leash, set short, can work as well.

4) When exiting the home, you should exit first. And after the walk is complete, you should enter back into the home first. This is part of training your dog to understand that you are the leader; and this goes a long way in regard to any sort of training, including heeling.

5) Teaching a dog to heel works best if walks are done at a certain time each day. Canines have impressive internal clocks, able to sense when things "should" happen. Dogs of all ages do best when they know what to expect. While the chosen time should fit in well with your schedule, also think about your dog's needs as well. It's hard for a dog to learn when he's tired and in need of a nap.

6) Lastly, choose a special treat that you will give to your dog upon completion of the walk. The treat should be one that is not given normally as a snack. It should be special enough that your dog learns it is only given if a session of listening to you, such as this, occurs. Keep the treat hidden in a pocket so that your dog does not see it or smell it, which would potentially cause him to pester you for the treat and not focus on the heeling lesson.

Understanding the Heeling Position

Heeling is when your dog walks on your left with his head no further ahead than the extension of

your left foot. It is done this way because the majority of people are right-handed. While this is the customary positioning, if you are left-handed, feel free to train your dog to heel to your right if that is what feels best for you.

With left-heeling, you will hold the handle of the leash in your right hand, allow the leash to cross past your body, and then grip it near your left hip. This will allow you complete control to keep your dog in proper position. And, the harness, as discussed, will allow you to move your dog along, even if he resists walking.

Time Tables to Keep in Mind

These training sessions should be done each day, with each session lasting approximately twenty minutes.

It usually takes about two weeks for a dog to have a good understanding of how to heel. Even when it seems that he is well-trained, keep offering words of praise and the confirmation word of "Heel" as you walk along. Eventually, whenever you give the command "Heel", your dog will immediately go over to your left side and stay beside you.

Training Your Dog to Heel

Once you have chosen a good time for walks that works well for both you and your dog, you have him on a harness and short leash, you have a treat in your pocket, and you have exited the home first with him following you, you will now begin. Have your dog on your left side, leash handle in your right hand, leash crossed over the front of your body, and the leash gripped with your left hand, near your left hip.

1) Command a 'Sit'. **This is the starting position.**

2) Slap your left hip two quick times, give a firm 'Heel' and start walking.

3) Abide by the following guidelines:

◆ ***Any time that your dog tries to walk ahead of you***, stand in place and do not move. Using a harness, this will not injure or hurt your dog. Your dog may try several times to keep walking. Do not pull on the leash. Simply remain standing and do not move. While you are remaining in one spot, essentially glued into place, any time that your dog comes very close to you, talk to him and give a gentle pat. This shows that staying near you means that the leash will not frustrate him.

As soon as your dog stops trying to walk ahead by himself and is remaining near you, give the leash a quick, light tug and continue walking.

◆ ***Any time that your dog walks beside you***, keep repeating the command word of "Heel" in a happy yet firm tone of voice so that he connects his actions with a command word. Furthermore, offer words of praise as you go along, first in the form of "Good Heel" to reinforce his actions and then with "Good Boy" or "Good Girl". This said, do not stop to pet your dog; just keep going.

As you walk, change your pace; take turns walking slower and then faster. Also, do not just walk in a straight line; most dogs stay more focused if the walk is a fun challenge. You can help make this entertaining by winding around telephone poles, taking turns, and more. The first time that you take a turn and your dog does not, he will quickly realize that he must heel to you. You will make that turn and your dog (on harness and short leash) will have no choice but to follow along.

Of course, be very careful, as accidentally stepping on your dog can cause injuries. But, walk confidently and show your dog that you are in control. If he tries to go another way, walk as if you do not notice that he is not exactly following along. The harness will not injure the neck and he will catch up to you as long as you do not increase speed.

4) As you are nearing your front door at the end of the walk, stop walking and command a 'sit'. **This is the finishing position.** Give praise and a training treat. Finally, give an "Okay" and let your dog free of the strict heeling positioning to signal that he does not need to obey the heel any longer.

Resistance to Walking

Walking surfaces: Some dogs are very resistant to walking, and in some cases, this can be contributed to the surface that they are being asked to walk upon. When a person is wearing shoes, it is very easy to forget that street surfaces can be extremely hot if the weather is warm and sunny. While a dog's paws are sturdy, they are made of skin, albeit thick skin. They have nerves that feel burning sensations, pain and/or injury.

Some dogs are very sensitive to ground texture, and sand can be a big factor. It is so much fun to walk along the shore of the ocean, a lake, or another body of water that has a sandy shoreline. But, sand particles can cause a dog to feel discomfort.

For both of these issues, a good paw wax can help as it will be a barrier between your dog's paws and the ground.

Weather: Some dogs do not do well in the heat, and struggling to catch their breath can make focusing on other tasks, like heeling, very difficult. Not to mention that exercising in hot weather can bring about heat exhaustion. In the winter, if a dog feels cold, likewise he may not be able to focus. Therefore, limit walking in hot weather, and place appropriate gear on your dog if needed in the wintertime, such as a vest or jacket.

Mood: Just as some humans like to exercise in the morning, others like to take walks at lunchtime, and yet others prefer evening workouts, so may your dog. Try to learn what time of the day your dog wishes to have exercise. Working together, you should be able to pinpoint the time of the day that your dog most wishes to stretch his legs and accompany you on a journey around the neighborhood. Once he has learned to heel, you can then adjust the time of the daily walk to better fit your needs and schedule, if this is desired.

Owner enthusiasm: Some dogs need a bit of encouragement to join their owner for a walk. The tone of your voice will send a message as to whether your dog should perceive a walk as a fun activity or a dreaded undertaking.

Dogs pick up on not just the words that we say, but also in the way that we say them. <u>When getting ready to leave for a walk, it will be helpful to sound very excited. Talk as if you are about to leave on an amazing adventure. Act enthusiastic.</u> And do use a very <u>loving but firm voice.</u> It may take a couple of days of speaking like this to send the message, but it should lead to a dog thinking the equivalent of, "If my human is excited about walking, maybe I should be also!"

Outright refusal to walk: If a dog truly shows a strong dislike for walking and basically plants his paws down, ready to hold his ground, refusing to move, treats may be needed to use as motivation.

If this is the case, when you are out, any time that your dog is walking nicely with you, randomly *Crispy Bacon* give him treats. It is suggested to offer truly exceptional treats if a dog needs a lot of incentive.

One treat that works very well in this situation is crisp bacon. Bacon is actually not an unhealthy food if it is given in moderation and prepared properly. It is suggested to fry it or microwave it to a very crisp texture. Doing so releases much of the fat. Then, place the pieces between paper towels and squeeze it all together, so that the paper towels soak up most of the remaining grease.

As the last step, crumble the bacon up so that you have small little pieces. You can transfer them into a plastic sandwich bag and have that bag in your pocket. As you are walking, now and then repeat the word "Heel", walk for a few more seconds, say in a happy tone "Good Heel!" and then without pausing much at all, reach into your pocket, grab a pinch of the crumbled up crisp bacon, and put it right in front of your dog's mouth so that he can quickly eat it.

Command Training

Before you Begin: A dog of any age, from a young puppy to senior, can learn basic commands. If you take the time to train for this, you'll find that there are several benefits:

1. It makes life easier when you can successfully communicate with your dog; you say something, your dog responds with an appropriate action.
2. It can come in quite handy to stop your dog from doing something he should not, as a command can interrupt his actions.
3. Training sessions are a great way for you and your dog to bond together, as you'll be working as a team.

4. And finally, dogs get a huge boost of self-confidence when they learn commands. Dogs are smart, and allowing a dog to use his brain and perform well for you enhances his self-esteem and gives you an overall happier dog.

The actual steps for command training are rather easy! These steps have been essentially the same for decades. What makes a huge difference is how you prepare yourself for this training (this first section) and how closely you adhere to the training steps.

Realistic Expectations *Encouraging learned behavior.*

Fully understanding commands is a gradual process. As noted back in 'About the Chihuahua: Chihuahua Intelligence', this breed was ranked at #67 under the grouping of 'fair working/obedience intelligence', said to need up to 25 repetitions just to begin understanding a command and between 40 and 80 repetitions to show reliability, but even then did rather poorly without reminders.

Putting that one polling aside, most dogs generally need 60 to 70 repetitions for 'good' understanding. Yet, that is just the beginning. Once the command is learned, it should be taught in a variety of settings, with different pacing, with distractions, sometimes with a treat reward, sometimes without, etc., so that a dog obeys it under all circumstances. Some trainers estimate that this brings the number up to 1,000 needed repetitions. Some say it takes 10,000.

So, with this in mind, a reasonable expectation is that it will take 100 repetitions for your dog to have a decent understanding of a command, and then a *minimum* of 1,000 times of using it afterward to truly have a strong understanding. This may seem like a lot. Yet, you'll be happy to know that 1,000 repetitions is achieved with a command practiced 5 days per week, twice per day, consisting of 25 repetitions each session, for a total of 4 weeks.

Once you reach that point, it becomes an automated, learned behavior. This means that your dog will not even think about what to do or what is expected. Right when you say the command, your dog will perform the action. And, because it is automated, a reward for doing so will not be expected.

The time and effort you put into command training is definitely worth it. As long as you naturally give commands (a 'Sit' before a meal is given, a 'Down' when company comes over, etc.) lessons will not be forgotten and your dog will be trained for life!

Preparing to Train *Keep treats very close by.*

Train before eating treat.

You'll want to have some things in mind, and some things set up, for the fastest route to success:

#1 The need for confidence. Any speaking during the training should be in a firm yet friendly manner and praise should be spoken in an exceedingly happy voice.

#2 The right training treats. As we discussed in 'Feeding and Nutrition: Training Treats', reward treats should be extra delicious, moist, small, and something that is reserved just for training.

#3 Timing of treats. Your puppy or dog will need to understand exactly what he did that earned him the reward. Therefore, you'll want to have your chosen training treats in a shirt pocket (or another easily accessible area), and a few cupped in your hand so that you can give a treat at the *exact* moment that your dog does what you asked, or at least makes a good attempt. Give the treat by allowing your dog to take it from your open palm.

#4 Maintain your dog's interest. If a dog knows that he's not doing what is expected, he can start to get discouraged, and disinterest soon follows that. So, if your dog is struggling with a certain part of a command, backup to an easier level. Let him earn rewards for doing great, and *then* try to move up a level.

#5 Your mood matters. Canines are remarkable at picking up on their human's vibe. Hiding inner feelings is difficult. So, if you are having a super busy day and/or are feeling stressed, this can affect how the training goes. While you want to be very consistent and not miss too many days in a row, if you're really not in the mood, wait until the next day.

#6 Train when your dog is hungry. Training treats are not all that appreciated right after dinner! While your dog should not be so hungry that he cannot concentrate on commands, do be sure that there's a desire for rewards.

#7 Physical prompts may be required. While it's better for a dog to listen to your words instead of you physically moving him, in some cases you may need to give gentle physical prompts. This helps a dog get a general idea of what is expected.

#8 End in a good place. The *worst time* to end a command training session is when a dog is struggling with a step and the owner says, 'Okay, that's it for the day!' with mild frustration. End while your dog is still having fun and has not yet tired of it.

Certain Training Words

Certain words should be used for two reasons: For consistency and because they are short (canines pay the most attention to the first syllable). Let's take a look at some words that you'll be saying a lot:

 "Uh-Oh" – This is said if a dog makes an incorrect action. Your instinct may be to say "No"; however, it's best never to say that word and instead say "Uh-oh" in a fun, amused tone of voice.

 "Okay" – This is the word used to release your dog from his position. For example, if you are training him to sit, he needs to know when he can stop doing it.

"Good [insert command word]" – "Good, *Sit*", "Good, *Come*", "Good, *Down*", etc. Instead of saying "Good, boy!" or "good" plus your dog's name, it is best to say "good" and then the command word/action. This reinforces the training.

Teaching the Sit Command

The goal will be to have your dog sit squarely on his rump and remain there until released.

This is often the first command that is taught and one that a puppy or dog will learn the quickest.

1. Stand or kneel right in front of your dog, holding a treat in your hand a little higher than your dog's head, allowing him to see it.

2. Slowly move the treat straight back over your dog's head. This should cause his nose to point up and his rear to drop. If his rear does not drop, keep moving the treat straight backward toward his tail. The *instant* his rear touches the floor, palm the treat and mark the action by saying "Good Sit!" in a happy voice.

3. If your dog is not moving as expected to the food lure, have him on leash and harness. Gently push down on his rump and pull up on the leash at the same time to guide him into a sit. Even though you assisted, the *instant* his rear touches the floor, palm the treat and mark the action by saying "Good Sit!" in a happy voice.

4. Once your dog sits down on command, work on keeping him in a sit until you release him. When his rear is down, wait to give the reward while saying "Siiiiit…. Siiiiit", then palm the treat and mark the action by saying "Good Sit!" in a happy voice. Take a quick step back and give an "Okay!" Most dogs move out of position at this point.

Troubleshooting: If your dog sits, but then gets up right away, in a gentle but firm manner, keep placing your dog back into a sit.

Teaching the Down Command

The goal will be for your dog to rest on both his chest and belly or chest and hip.

1. With your dog sitting facing you, hold a treat to his nose and lower it slowly to the floor.

2. Your dog *may* follow the treat with his nose and lie down, at which time you can palm the treat and mark the action by saying "Good Down!" If your dog semi-lies down, slide the treat slowly on the floor, either away from or toward him; his body may adjust as you move it around. Be patient; if you can keep him interested, he should ultimately lie down.

3. If your dog is not responding to the treat being slid, put gentle pressure on his shoulder blades, pushing down and to the side. Give praise, "Good Down!", and a treat when he drops to the floor.

4. Once your dog is consistently lying down, wait for 3 to 10 seconds before giving the treat. With your dog lying down, say "Wait…wait" and then finally an excited "Good Down!" while palming the treat. Varying the time before actually giving the treat will help your dog focus.

Troubleshooting: If your dog does not stay down, don't give reward; instead, command another 'Down'. If he will not stay in position, have him on leash and harness, and then hold the leash to the floor with your foot to keep him down until you give the release word of "Okay". You will not step so close as to force his body down; your foot on the leash will simply keep him in place. With a proper harness, this should not cause injury.

Teaching the Stay Command

The goal will be for your dog stay where he is, as long as he is within hearing distance, and only come to you once you release him with an "Okay"

This is one of the most difficult commands for a dog to learn; it goes against a dog's instinct to run to his owner.

1. Have your dog on leash and harness. Start with him sitting or lying down, as he is less likely to move from those positions. Stand directly in front of him and in a serious tone, say "Stay", holding your palm flat, almost touching his nose.

2. Move a short distance away, keeping eye contact, and then return to him. As long as he stayed sitting or lying down, praise him with "Good Stay!" and palm a treat. Follow with "Okay", as he may very well rise up at that point. This way, he'll make the association that his action of rising coincided with your release word of "Okay".

3.   If your dog moved from his stay before you said "Okay", gently but firmly put him back in the spot where he was originally told to stay. Wait for a count of 5, then give an "Okay".

4.   Gradually increase the time you ask your dog to stay, as well as the distance that you move away from him.

5.   Any time that your dog starts to have trouble, move closer to make it easier. Then, as he gets the hang of it, move further way for more of a challenge.

 Troubleshooting: If your dog keeps breaking his 'Stay' before you say "Okay", hide the treat well; he may be too focused on receiving it.

Teaching the Come Command

The goal will be that on your command, your dog immediately comes to you.

❶ Once this is learned, it should be reinforced often so that lessons are not forgotten.

❷ Never use the command for something that your dog truly dislikes.

❸ For this command, you will need to reel your dog to you in order for him to understand the command; so to prevent injury, ONLY do this with your dog wearing a harness and NOT a collar.

1.   With your dog on a 6-foot leash and a harness, and sitting those 6 feet away from you, command him to "Come" just one time. If he comes over, praise with "Good Come!" and palm a treat. If he does not come over, quickly reel him to you and immediately praise with "Good Come!" and palm a treat.

2.   Repeat this over and over, keeping your dog on leash even if you do not need to reel it in all that much.

3.   As your dog is grasping the idea of the command, use a retractable leash so that you can do this at 10 feet, then 15 feet, and so on.

4.   When you are ready to practice off-leash, do so in a safe fenced-in area. Have the leash attached to his harness, but keep the handle on the ground close to you. If your dog does not obey your command of "Come" one time, but instead walks in a different direction, say "Uh-oh", pick him up and carry him to the spot from where you originally called him from.

If you give the command "Come" one time, and your dog stays in place, repeat as before, by picking up the leash and reeling him over to you. Immediately reward him with the praise of "Good, Come!" and a treat.

Troubleshooting: If things are not going well while out in the yard, go back to the beginning steps of training on-leash and keep the distance between you and your dog short. Once he does well 10 times, try off-leash once again.

Shake Paw, Left and Right

The goal is to have your dog raise his paw to his chest height, to shake 'hands'. When the command "Shake" is given, the dog shakes with his right paw. When the command "Paw" is given, the dog shakes with his left paw.

"Shake" or "Paw" is not a necessary command; but, it is a nice additional element for having a well-behaved, well-trained dog. Since the majority of people of owners are right-handed, you may wish to work on the right paw first:

1.   With your dog sitting right in front of you, hide a treat in your left hand, and hold it low to the ground.

2.   Encourage your dog to paw at it by saying "Get it" and "Shake". The moment the paw comes off the ground at all, immediately praise with "Good Shake!" and palm a treat.

3.   Repeat this over and over. Gradually raise the height of your hand, until he is lifting his paw to chest height.

4.   Repeat these steps on the opposite side to teach 'Paw', using the words of "Good, Paw" when he follows along.

Troubleshooting: If your dog tends to 'nose' your hand instead of pawing at it, quickly withdraw your hand and start over. If he does not lift his paw whatsoever, you can gently lift it for him and then reward, gradually using support to move him as he learns to lift it on his own.

Behavioral Training

Aggression

❶ *It is important to note that an owner can resolve some aggression issues; but, some cases require calling in a professional canine trainer. You should not try any of these training methods if you believe that your dog may bite or cause injury to yourself or any other person or has proven to be a biter (clamping the jaws onto the skin and penetrating the skin with teeth); that type of severe aggression will require oversight and intervention by a professional canine trainer.*

❷ *If your dog has suddenly become aggressive, this warrants an immediate veterinary examination. Even if the last appointment was very recent, something may have happened from then to now. Please do not try any of the following training methods until you are 100% sure that your dog is without injury or illness.*

How Common is Aggression Among Chihuahuas?

Our survey of 3,272 owners that had Chihuahuas comprised of 45% young adults (1 to 3-years-old), 29% adults (4 to 8-years-old), 14% puppies (6 to 12-months-old), 9% seniors (9+ years), and 3% young puppies (under 6-months-old), with a gender ratio of 57% females to 43% males, showed that 9% of Chihuahuas had or have some type of aggression issues (see 'About the Chihuahua: PetChiDog's Chihuahua Survey').

To get a better understanding of aggression seen with Chihuahuas, there were two follow-up questions in the survey. Let's look at the results. **First, we asked: <u>In what way is this aggression showing?</u>**

My Chi growls 27%
My Chi tries to nip 24%
My Chi barks in a threatening way 20%
My Chi actually bites 15%
My Chi chases after people or animals 8%

Then, we asked: <u>Who is this directed toward?</u>

Just strangers 18%
Just visitors 17%
Everyone! 9%
Me and others in my home 7%
Others in my home, but not me 7%
Just other dogs 7%
Other animals 6%
Just me 5%

To summarize, most Chihuahuas that showed aggression did so by growling or nipping (51%). This was mainly directed at people outside the household; though, being aggressive toward household members and the owners themselves was reported as well.

Training for Aggression Toward Visitors

Before you train: As discussed in this book, all dogs (regardless of breed or size) see their world as one of hierarchy. Within the den (house) lives the pack (all humans and animals), and that pack has a leader (the Alpha). Everyone under the leader is a follower (Beta) since they follow the leader's commands.

If a dog does not accept his human as the leader and/or tries to take the position of leader himself, this can lead to aggression, particularly with a dog that is very territorial due to hormones. Therefore, with aggression, two things can help, even without training:

- Have your dog spayed or neutered. Intact dogs are far more territorial and therefore aggressive than their fixed counterparts.
- Be sure that your dog sees you as the clear leader. Refer to 'Training: Teaching Proper Hierarchy'. If your dog is so aggressive toward you that you cannot train him to understand proper hierarchy, this is a huge red flag that a professional canine trainer is required for the aggression issues.

Preparing to train: There are a few things you will need to have in place for this training:

#1 Have your dog trained to obey a 'Sit'. See also 'Training: Command Training'. If your dog is so aggressive toward you that you cannot train him to follow the sit command, this is a huge red flag that a professional canine trainer is required for the aggression issues.

#2 Helpers that consist of friends, extended family, and/or neighbors that your dog has growled at or showed some aggression toward.

#3 Training treats. These should be extra delicious, moist, small, and something that is reserved just for training. You may wish to refer to 'Feeding and Nutrition: Training Treats'.

#4 Defined 'time out' area. Part of this training involves temporary social isolation. Since you established yourself as the leader (see 'Before You Train'), you will use the standing to temporarily 'banish' your dog from the 'pack' via complete and utter ignoring, aka social isolation. You can use a dog's playpen; however, you do not want your dog to associate the playpen with a negative element. For this reason, you may wish to obtain baby gates and block off a section of a room just for this purpose.

#5 Have your dog on a harness and a short leash. You will want to have full physical control of your dog without accidentally harming him.

Training:

1. The goal of this training is to have your dog see the trigger (your helper) while rewarding for any good behavior and socially isolating your dog for bad behavior.

2. Supply your helper with a few training treats. You can give this to them beforehand, or leave a zipped sandwich bag of these outside your front door for them to grab when they arrive.

3. Have your dog by your side, on leash and harness. When you know that your helper is about to arrive, command a 'Sit'.

4. When your helper knocks on the door, call out in a friendly voice for him/her to enter.

5. It is now you will take action for every good (calm) or bad (aggressive) behavior. Every full minute of good behavior is met with praise ("Good dog") and a training treat reward. Every sign of aggression results in your dog being *immediately* moved into his 'time-out' area for a full 10 minutes. The reason that this time-out is relatively short, is because when there is a visitor in the house, a dog is on full-alert. He will not focus elsewhere, which could lead to not noticing the 'banishment'.

- o During the time-out, it is vital that your dog be 100% **completely and utterly** ignored. He must be ignored to the point that he questions if his leader (you) is so disappointed by his behavior that he is being 'banished' from his pack.
- o This means NO eye contact. NO speaking to your dog. No reacting to barking. Nothing. Just continue speaking with your helper as if your dog has disappeared into thin air.

6. After the 10-minute time-out is complete, allow your dog the opportunity to 're-enter the pack'. As before, every behavior, good or bad, is reacted to (praise and treat or time-out).

Tips:

1. Have the 1st visit last for about 15 minutes. Increase the visits by 5 minutes per day until a maximum time of 30 minutes.
2. Have different helpers come to visit on different days.
3. If this training is not successful after a two-week period of near daily training, it will be time to seek the aid of a professional canine trainer.

Training for Aggression Toward You and/or Family Members

Before you train: The same 'pre-training' aspects previously discussed apply with this as well. Any possible health issues should be ruled out, you may want to consider having your dog spayed or neutered, and you'll want to be sure that your dog sees you and any other human family members as the rightful leader(s). And again, if your dog is so aggressive toward you that you cannot train him to understand proper hierarchy, this is a huge red flag that a professional canine trainer is required to help correct the aggressive behavior.

Preparing to train: Some of the same pretraining prep is needed as previously discussed; you will want a defined 'time out' area and appropriate training treats.

Training, Step #1: More Stringent Hierarchy Rules

Aside from the typical rules in place to ensure proper hierarchy (food is not given until the dog obeys a 'Sit', you enter and exit the house before your dog, a heel is needed for walking, etc.), dogs with aggression issues will need some stronger, clearer rules that not only leave no doubt that you (and other humans in the house) are the leader, but that there is no way that you're ever stepping down from your title.

This will include:

#1 The dog does not sleep in any human's bed. Even if your dog is aggressive towards one person and not another, he must not sleep on ANY human's bed, and should instead have his own quality canine bed (as we recommend at any rate).

#2 The dog is always kept at a lower physical level than the owners. Do not sit on the floor with your dog and do not allow your dog to sit up on the sofa with you.

Training, Step #2: Reaction to Aggression

You will follow the same principles as discussed in 'Training for Aggression Toward Visitors', which is praise and treats for good behavior, and time-outs for aggressive behavior. These are the exact steps:

1. As soon as your dog displays aggression, he is placed in his time-out area. Follow the same rules of 100% completely and utterly ignoring him.

2. The time-out will last 5 minutes past the point that your dog notices that he is being 'banished'. Depending on how focused or distracted your dog is, it can take anywhere from 5 to 15 minutes to notice the 'banishment' and be bothered by it. Pacing or whining is a good indication that a dog has indeed noticed. Wait 5 minutes past this point. Of course, if your dog growls when you go to release him, leave him there. An additional 5 to 15 minutes may need to be added on.

3. At the moment of release, interaction is limited. He is not spoken to very much; just a short "Okay, let's try again" is sufficient. He is also not petted.

4. Place your dog in the very same position that he was in when the aggression occurred. For example, if he was relaxing near the fireplace and growled while you walked by, move him back there and walk by again.

5. Behaving is NOT rewarded with a treat (yet), but with more interaction. You can now speak freely and pet him. Any aggressive behavior results in another time-out, in the same manner.

6. If your dog continues behaving, after 10 minutes, offer praise, ("Good dog") and a training treat.

Note: Do not let down your guard; steps to instill proper hierarchy should be followed indefinitely. If this training does not work, it is highly suggested to seek the help of a professional canine trainer who can work with your dog one-on-one, in your home.

Barking

There are two main elements to a dog's bark: Understanding what your dog is trying to communicate to you and controlling unnecessary barking.

<u>Canine Vocalizations</u>

A dog can have a range of vocalizations; not all need to be corrected:

Barking with a high tone. This is an attention-seeking bark. A dog wants something (to go outside, to be played with, etc.). It essentially means, "Hey, over here!"

Barking in a low tone. This is typically a sign that a dog perceives a possible danger (a group of people standing close to the house) or he senses a change which interrupts his normal environment (a flock of birds overhead, a wind chime). If you are with your dog, it essentially means, "Look at that!" If a dog is home alone, it is akin to saying, "I'm on alert!"

Growling. This is a warning. It typically happens after barking in a low tone ("I'm on alert!"). The bark may turn into a growl if a person, animal, or object (such as a car) comes too close to a dog and will be akin to saying, "Don't you dare touch me!" If the trigger approaches what a dog considers to be his property, it is akin to saying, "Get away!"

If a dog's body is lowered into a pre-striking position, the growl is then saying, "I may bite if you don't leave or if you try to hurt me!" A dog that is growling sometimes combines this with 'tooth snapping' noises. Tooth snapping is a dog's way of saying, "I have teeth and I will use them if I have to!"

Howling. Some breeds (like Alaskan Malamutes, Beagles, and Foxhounds) howl to call out to other dogs, to say "Hey guys, let's rally around!", or to call out in case there are other dogs in the vicinity but not seen or sensed, as a way to ask, "Is anybody there?"

Whining. Also referred to as whimpering, this is a sign of being in emotional distress (when home alone, etc.), when feeling physical frustration (when confined but want to be running free, etc.), or when in physical distress (injured or ill). It is a dog's way of crying.

Yelping. This is quick, high pitched noise that is a clear and immediate indication that a dog has been injured. A yelp will be a much shorter duration and higher tone than a high pitched, attention-seeking bark. A yelp from a dog is let out the instant he feels pain. It is comparable to a human yelling 'Ouch!" For this reason, always investigate the trigger for any yelp.

Moaning. While a human may moan if they have an injury, a dog may let out a low-tone moan when he's feeling happy (having the tummy rubbed, etc.).

Pick Your Battles

The #1 thing to keep in mind is that no amount of training is going to completely stop barking. Humans speak. Dogs bark. A dog is going to be vocal. It is a good idea to choose your battles because you simply can't train a dog to be silent all of the time. Let certain barking slide, if it is short-lived.

What you do want to train for is unnecessary, nuisance barking that's driving you up a wall. So, look at the war field, choose your battles, and ignore the rest. With that in mind, let's dive into the most common barking scenarios, and exactly how to respond in a way that will train your dog to quiet down.

When a Puppy Barks at Night

Overview: Having a puppy bark all night long or start barking early in the morning before you're ready to wake up is certainly one of the most frustrating issues that new owners face. And one thing is for sure; it can leave you worn out and sleep deprived. You may not know if your puppy is lonely, has to go to the bathroom, is uncomfortable, or if it's something else entirely.

Fortunately, when you have the right set-up for your puppy and a firm plan in place, it's much easier to cope with this. And, when you react in the right way, this sort of barking can be resolved rather quickly.

What to do:

1. Create a safe, secure, and comforting environment that offers the chance to self-soothe.

• You'll want your puppy to be in a secure, defined area that holds food, water, and certain toys. In this way, your pup will have the ability to eat, drink, and stay busy without you rushing over.

• Using a small canine playpen is a good method to do this. These are also great for keeping a pup confined to limit housebreaking accidents and/or destructive chewing, and to serve as a dog's area when you're away from home.

• Within the pen, there should also be a quality bed. Since young pups can get easily chilled and because most like to feel snuggled, a small bolster bed often works well.

• There should be a water bowl; make sure that this is filled with fresh (preferably filtered) water.

• You'll also want to have some food within reach. Young puppies under 3 months old should have food available at all times, including nighttime. So, for puppies this age, have some kibble in a small bowl. Additionally, have some in a small treat dispensing toy, that can be placed in the pen after the pup falls asleep so that it's found in the morning. For puppies over 3 months, just the treat dispensing toy can be used.

• A companion toy can be helpful. These are designed to provide comfort to dogs that are home alone and are meant to mimic living creatures (typically dogs), via being a good size, with a rhythmic heartbeat and realistic warmth. This type of toy is discussed in more detail under 'Care Items - Chihuahuas of All Ages: Toys' and all of our current recommended toys can be seen on the Supplies page of the PetChiDog.com website.

2. Now that your puppy has the right setup, know when and how to respond to barking.

• **Many owners assume that a puppy may be barking due to having to go to the bathroom.** However, until house training has been underway for some time and there is a strong sense of what is expected, a young puppy will not be barking to be brought outside. This is not to say that the pup won't go to the bathroom if you take him out; most likely he will once he's there. The bladder often 'wakes up' once the pup does.

So, there are two approaches to this. If you highly suspect a housebreaking need, you can bring the pup out. However, if you have pee pads within the pen, there's a good chance that a puppy will pee on them, and fall back asleep (see next point).

You may wonder how it is that the pup will know to use the pads. He won't. It'll be by default. When in a defined space that holds a bed, food and water bowls, and toys, you will line the only other available areas with pee pads. Since dogs rarely soil their own belongings, pee and poo are deposited on the pads as the only option.

If you do bring your puppy out, this should be done with minimal lighting and very limited speaking to show that it is a serious time. If you give pets, play, or even speak much, this can prompt a puppy to bark at night, knowing that attention will be received after doing so.

• **If your puppy has just gone to the bathroom and you know that is not the cause, or you have decided to have him use the pads, it'll be time to teach self-soothing lessons.** This is always easier said than done. After all, it is human instinct to want to go to a puppy in need. And, it's awfully difficult to ignore constant barking. However, every time that you respond to barking, you are teaching the pup a lesson that barking means you'll come over. What reason would he have to stop?

And, it's even worse if you wait but then eventually give in to the barking, because then you are teaching the lesson that if the pup barks long enough, it will result in you going over. Now, there's motivation to bark even longer and harder. This can have lasting effects, in which barking continues for many more months that it would otherwise.

It's hard for a new puppy to get accustomed to his new home, and there should certainly be empathy. However, you also want your pup to learn to be secure with himself and to be independent enough that you do not need to be right by his side for everything to be okay.

When you know that your puppy is safe within a playpen, is warm, and has food, water, and toys (to stay busy and for comfort), if you ignore barking until the pup wears out and falls back asleep, this will lead to nighttime barking lasting only a matter of weeks.

Barking Like Mad at Home

Maybe your dog sits on the sofa, looking out the window, and barks like a maniac. Or maybe, while you're trying to relax, your dog starts barking at you and just won't stop. You might shush him, keep saying 'no' but are being ignored, or are listened to momentarily before the barking kicks in again. No doubt, this sort of incessant barking can be exceedingly frustrating, and it may seem as if you have no control over your dog.

There are 3 steps to resolving this:

1. Ensure that all essential needs are being met.
2. Establish yourself as the leader, so that your commands are listened to.
3. Interrupt and refocus.

So, let's dive into these:

1. Ensure that all needs are being met.

• **Be sure that your dog is receiving enough daily exercise.** This is vital for good health, but also has the very important benefit of allowing a dog to release pent-up energy.

The very minimum requirement is two 20-minute walks per day. But, some need more than this. If your dog seems overly hyper, try adding on 10 minutes to each walk. Also, be sure to have cardio sessions; fetch is the easiest and more effective way to give a dog a good workout. Stock up on some mini tennis balls, and have a 15 to 20-minute session each day. If you can schedule this happen at the times that your dog typically gets antsy, all the better.

• **Provide enough mental stimulation.** This includes things that you can do with your dog, such as puzzle games, playing hide n' seek, heading out to explore new places, and command training.

This also involves things a dog can do by himself, and a good collection of toys including chew toys and interactive 'stay busy' toys will give a dog options to pass the time. It can help to rotate toys; keep half out and half tucked away (aside from the most-loved favorites). Every week or so, swap them, so there will always be some 'new' ones.

• **A low-key environment will help**. It's common for dogs to pick up on the household vibe and mimic it. So, if there is loud music, blaring TVs, children screaming, other pets running around, lots of foot traffic, or an otherwise chaotic scene, it's near impossible for a dog to remain calm. He's going to bark at all this sort of stimuli.

2. Establish yourself as the leader.

Before you can train your dog to stop barking, you need to be sure that you've established the fact that you should be listened to. You may assume that your dog sees you as the leader, but this is not always the case.

One of the easiest and fastest ways to make this clear is to expect a 'Sit' before any food is given; this includes both meals and snacks. You'll want to command a 'Sit', wait for a count of 5 once it is followed, and then place the bowl down or offer the treat. Additional methods include always keeping your dog in a heeling position when walking (to your immediate left side), and having the dog enter and exit the through the doorway to the house after the human does so. You can read more about this under 'Training: Teaching Proper Hierarchy'.

3. Interrupt and refocus.

For this, you will need a way to interrupt th barking. Sometimes, a loud hand clap and a quick firm 'Hey' or 'No' works. However, if you find that it doe not, you may want to incorporate a training tool.

The Company of Animals Pet Corrector is a safe yet effective method to gain a dog's attention. It is used by canine trainers and works by releasing a short hiss of compressed air. This particular sound usually works very well to cause a dog to stop and take pause.

Once the barking has stopped, and you have your dog's attention for a moment, you'll want to redirect his focus elsewhere. You can work on a few commands, play a game together, or direct your dog to an intriguing toy. If using a toy, typically one that makes an interesting noise or one that speaks will do the trick. No matter what you choose as your dog's new focus, if the barking as stopped, reward for this with praise and a training treat after 1 to 2 minutes of being quiet.

Barking at Visitors

Note that aggression, and not just barking, toward visitors is a separate issue and is covered under 'Behavioral Training: Aggression'.

Handling this type of barking is a bit different because when a dog barks in response to visitors to the home, this is a valid reason. Barking is canine instinct to alert others that someone is approaching or entering the territory. So, trying to completely stop this will be in vain. However, a good goal to have is to teach your dog that just a few barks are all that is needed. In fact, you can teach your dog that letting out a few barks is actually appreciated. Your dog will learn that his job as 'watchdog' is going well, and you'll have quiet once those initial alert barks are done.

Aside from ensuring needs are met and establishing yourself as the leader, as covered earlier, there are some things you'll want to have in place:

#1 Have your dog trained to obey a 'Sit'. You may wish to refer to: 'Training: Command Training'.

#2 Training treats. These should be extra delicious, moist, small, and something that is reserved just for training. You may wish to refer to: 'Feeding and Nutrition: Training Treats'.

#3 Helpers that consist of friends, extended family, and/or neighbors that your dog typically barks at.

#4 Have your dog on harness and a short leash. You will want to have full physical control of your dog without accidentally harming him.

#5 Behavior corrector device, if you choose to use this. This is a harmless, but often effective device that lets out a short hiss of compressed air. The noise makes a dog take immediate pause. The Company of Animals Pet Corrector is one such device.

You can then practice how you want your dog to respond to visitors by:

1. Having a helper take the role of visitor.

2. Be inside the house, approximately 10 to 15 feet from the door, with your dog on leash and harness, and some training treats in your pocket.

3. When you know that your helper is about to reach the door, command a 'Sit'.

4. Place the leash on the floor, with your foot firmly on it to prevent your dog from moving about; note that using a harness and not a collar will allow you to do this without causing neck injury.

5. When the doorbell rings or your helper enters (depending on what typically takes place at your home that triggers your dog to bark):

- Allow for a few barks.
- Say 'Okay' in a firm voice, to let your dog know that you appreciate the alert, but that you approve of the visitor.
- Palm and offer a training treat to praise the alert.
- If your dog has risen, order a 'Sit' and give praise when this is obeyed.
- Have the person slowly enter or step forward.
- If your dog barks again, give a firm 'No' and have your helper stop in place. If your dog does not listen to this and keeps barking, consider using a behavior corrector (#5) to cause him to take pause.
- During this pause in which your dog has stopped barking, give reward again, as your helper walks forward and fully enters the house.
- Each bark from this point onward is met with immediate interruption (a firm 'No' or a quick depression of a behavior corrector). Every 20 to 30 seconds in which there is no barking, reward is given.

6. As you go about greeting your helper and settling down for the visit, your dog may be circling you, since it is common for canines to compete with visitors for attention. Have your helper toss a ball a few times or otherwise interact to show that everyone can get along.

Barking While Being Walked

Every dog has a certain level of stimuli that they can handle before they start barking. For some dogs, it takes quite a bit. However, it's not uncommon for a dog to bark at everything that they see. This includes other dogs, people, cars driving by, and even birds in trees.

You can help curb this type of barking by:

• **Starting off with walks on a calm, non-distracting route.** It's near impossible to train a dog to stop barking while walking if there are non-stop triggers. Start taking walks in areas that have very little to no cars, few pets, and a quiet atmosphere. Once your dog learns how to stay composed, you can gradually work your way up to routes that have more activity.

• **Keep your dog on leash and harness.** Use a harness to prevent neck injury and a retractable leash so that you can keep your dog in a heeling position to your immediate left. Note that if your dog is ahead of you, the following steps will not work. Have the leash adjusted to the exact length needed to keep your dog in position. Hold the handle in your right hand, have your left hand holding the cord near your left hip, and your dog to your left side, neither ahead nor behind.

• **When your dog barks, do not tense up, stop, or otherwise respond.** Typically, owners tend to tense up, since they are used to feeling embarrassed that their dog is making a ruckus or there's an immediate increase in stress levels due to frustration over the situation. It's also common for owners to stop, thinking that they are supposed to do something to deal with the barking. But, if you do either of these things, you'll be acknowledging that the barking is warranted. After all, it made you physically react, so you are responding to the trigger too. Instead, stay relaxed and keep walking. You can safely do this because your dog will be wearing a harness and you'll be in control because the leash will be kept short.

• **As you move away from the trigger, barking will naturally cease.** As soon as it does, slow (but do not stop) and palm a reward treat while giving praise (Good dog).

• **Throughout the walk, randomly give praise and reward at times when your dog is not barking.** Slow (but do not stop) and palm a reward treat while giving praise (Good dog).

• **When you feel that your dog is ready,** switch to a route with slightly more distractions and triggers, working your way up to your preferred walking route. Do keep in mind that every dog has their limits, and a route packed with commotion may be too much for any dog.

Jumping on People

It's not uncommon for dogs to be so excited about something or someone, that they jump up against people. This may be jumping on their owners, on visitors, or even those encountered when outside. This happens without much thought; it's instant excitement that triggers a dog to jump, and for this reason, training can be a be a bit tricky and needs lots of repetition.

First, Some Tips to Reduce Jumping

Before we get into the actual jumping itself and how to deal with that, the following can help reduce jumping:

#1 Enough Exercise. When a dog is holding any pent-up energy, it is going to eventually be released. In many cases, all it takes is a trigger, like a person entering a room. So, be sure to walk your dog at least twice per day for 20 minutes each session, along with a daily 15 to 20 minutes of fetch or other cardio activity. If you are already doing this, increase walks by 5 to 10 minutes.

#2 Tone Down the Surprise. The goal is to give a dog time to process that an interaction is about to happen, rather than it being a rush of surprise that triggers jumping. If your dog typically jumps on you when you come home, if there is someone else in the house that can assist, have that person distract your dog with a toy or treat while you are entering. You will want to make a noise and remain standing in blocked view. For example, jiggle the doorknob and position yourself so that your dog would need to navigate around furniture to reach you and greet you.

Training Prep: For this training, you'll want to have some things ready in advance:

#1 Your dog should know the 'Sit' command. While you may think that this won't matter because your dog gets too riled up to listen to you anyway and that he won't obey a 'Sit' when jumping, this is actually a very important part of this training. You may wish to refer to: 'Training: Command Training'.

#2 Have your dog on leash and harness. This is of course if you are outside the house, but also if you are at home and are expecting a visitor.

#3 Have treats in a zipped plastic bag and in your pocket for quick, easy access. Be sure that the training treats are small, moist, extra delicious, and not ones that would be given at any rate.

Training to Stop Jumping on Other People

Many training guidelines to stop dogs from jumping involve having a person turn their body to the side so that a dog does not receive his jumping 'goal'. However, that typically only works with medium and large-sized breeds that can reach close to or up to their owner's face when jumping. So, the following is an alternative training method that can work with smaller dogs.

You'll find that if you and everyone in charge of your dog follow these training guidelines, success can be achieved in several weeks; though, much of this depends on how often you have a chance to train and that depends on how often a dog is put into a possible jumping situation.

1. **As a situation presents itself** that would normally cause your dog to jump up, stop in place and command a 'Sit'. So, this could be seeing someone readying to pass by you, when you are purposefully approaching someone, or if someone is coming into the house.

   While you may not be able to catch all interactions before they happen, such as a child running up unannounced to pet your dog, be very focused that the goal is to stop and command a 'Sit' before jumping would otherwise occur.

2. **The moment that your dog obeys the sit**, immediately give praise (Good sit!) and training treat. Importantly, reel in the leash, so that as soon as your dog is in position, he cannot physically rise. Do not make the leash so taunt that he is aware of this restriction; but rather, this will be used in conjunction with the other components.

3. **In a calm voice**, continue repeating 'Siiiiittt' to keep your dog in position as the jumping 'victim' comes closer. Tell the person that you are training your dog to stop jumping on people and ask that person to bend or lower themselves to say hello.

4. **As your dog is being greeted by the person** and is in a sitting position, give more praise (Good sit, good dog!) and a second treat.

5. **As the greet is ending**, take a step backward while incrementally allowing the leash to unfurl. If at any time your dog tries to lunge forward to jump, tighten the length of the leash and command another sit. If your dog remains calm, give one final praise (Good dog!) and a final treat.

<u>Training Your Dog to Stop Jumping Up on You</u>

As mentioned, the aspect of turning your body to the side to remove a dog's jumping goal cannot be applied to toy breeds. So, training steps are a bit different than with larger dogs:

1. **If you have someone else in the house**, you'll want to have them follow all of the training steps as mentioned earlier, with you playing the role of the jumping 'victim'.

2. **If you are live alone with your dog or if your dog jumps up on you a lot while no one else is around**, allow for a release of initial energy and then command a 'Sit' before any interaction, with obedience rewarded. For jumping during initial 'greets':

   1) Have some training treats in a zipped sandwich bag near key points, so that you can easily grab these on your way into the house or on the way to your dog first thing in the morning.
   2) Greet your dog while he's still in his playpen.
   3) Give a lot of pets and speak to him until it appears that his initial rush of excitement has dissipated.
   4) Only then, open the door and command a sit. Reward this with a training treat.
   5) The elements of having the greeting already take place and commanding a 'Sit' may be all that's needed to prevent jumping due to the excitement of seeing you. However, if your dog does start to jump up after this, keep commanding 'Sits' as needed.
   6) If your dog does not stay within a pen (or gated area), it does make things a lot more difficult; however, order a 'Sit' upon first seeing him, followed by a reward for doing so.

Refusal to Walk While on Leash

You probably know all of the benefits of daily exercise for a dog; so, what do you do if your little one refuses to go for walks? Or maybe, things start out okay, but then your puppy or dog stops every other moment to sniff around. Let's look at how to resolve this:

 # 1. Rule out physical causes. This includes:

- Health issues that may be making your puppy or dog lethargic.
- Burns or injuries to the paws; can be treated at home with a salve or may require vet treatment, depending on the extent.

- Unpleasant walking surfaces that may be causing discomfort (hot summer pavement, freezing and/or slippery winter surfaces). Applying a quality paw wax once per week can help resolve this.
- Overheating (which can quickly lead to heat stroke).
- Overly tired; What may be a good time for you to head out, could be when your dog is ready to take a nap. Dogs often do best in the morning and in the evening after being cooped up all day. But, adjust walking times if you suspect this as one of the causes.
- Some dogs do walk but stop often due to distractions. This will be covered as well.

2. Walks must be done with enthusiasm.
Your dog can, and does, pick up on your vibe. So, if you are feeling frustrated with how walks have gone so far, or are feeling overwhelmed with all you have on your plate, your dog will know that you're not looking forward to the walk. This will severely decrease his enthusiasm.

And, if you truly hate taking your dog for walks and find it to be the absolute worst part of your day, this especially cannot be hidden from a canine. Canines typically refuse to engage in something when it's been made clear it's a horrible activity.

If either applies to you, try to think of taking walks as something beneficial for you regardless of how it goes. Make this a time that you release all worries and enjoy getting fresh air. Even if your dog were to plant himself down and not move at all, you'd still be getting fresh air, so it would not be a total loss (but, don't worry, we'll get your dog moving!).

3. Make walks worthwhile.
A dog will agree to a wide range of activities if he knows that something great is at the end of it all. Sometimes, a special offering (reserved only for walks and given right at the end, before you enter the house) works well. Try a treat that offers a flavor not normally enjoyed, while giving praise ('Good job!').

In other cases, a new toy will do the trick. You do not need to buy a dozen new toys; you can obtain just 2 or 3. At the end of each walk, introduce one new toy. Once all have been introduced, hide away the one that your dog loved best. This will become the one special toy that is only given out when a walk is coming to completion. It is best given outside, at the end of a walk, so that a dog understands he is receiving it as the 'final portion' of the walk. So, stash this in a planter outside your entranceway, etc.

#4 Take your dog to the designated bathroom area before the walk.
Many dogs stop and sniff to find 'the perfect spot' to urinate or defecate. Remove this need. Head to the designated bathroom area before the walk, allowing for plenty of time for bathroom needs. Only then, start the walk.

#5 Have your dog on a short leash or an adjustable leash, and a harness, for a proper heeling position.
The leash kept short will allow you to successfully command a heeling position, which means your puppy or dog will be to your immediate left and no further ahead than the extension of your left foot. You'll hold the handle in your right hand, have the leash cross over in front of you, and you'll grip the cord with your left hand at hip level. With your dog in a harness, not a collar, you can control the pace (see next tips).

#6 To get your dog moving,
circle around him, and then start walking.

#7 You do not need to stop when your dog does.
With a harness (no chance of neck injury), you do not need to stop walking when your dog does. A dog should never control the walk; that is the job

of the owner (Alpha leader).

#8 So, walk with confidence. While following the rules of short leash, harness, and heeling positioning, start the walk going at a pace that is comfortable for your puppy or dog and do not stop to indulge the whims of sniffing every spot. Since your dog pee'd and/or poo'd before the walk (tip #4), there is no valid reason to stop.

#9 Keep your dog on his toes. You are in control of the walk, so make the route a challenging game. Exit the house, go back in, and then go out right back again. Head up new streets, vary the pace from walking to light jogging (short intervals), weave around sign posts, etc. As you do this, speak enthusiastically, as if you're having fun navigating things (and you probably will be!).

#10 Of course, none of this means that you should drag your dog along, so incorporate treats, if needed. If your puppy or dog flat out refuses to walk, sits down stubbornly, adopts a stance of planting himself onto the ground, and you would have to drag him across the ground for him to move at all, reassess '#1, physical causes' and be sure to incorporate '#2 enthusiasm', and '#3 make walks worthwhile'.

If those are addressed:

1) Obtain training treats. These should be something that is reserved just for training, moist (works much better than dry), very small (so that multiple rewards do not cause a dog to feel too full or affect appetite for dinner), and extra delicious.

2) Use those treats to move your dog ahead. Gain your dog's attention, hold the treat so that he can both see it and smell it. Say the cue word of 'Let's go', and toss it 8 to 10 feet ahead in the direction that you want your dog to walk. If you picked a great training treat, your dog will not only want the treat, but want more. Tip: be sure to keep your dog in the heeling position, and not allowed to run ahead to grab the treat.

Keep repeating this, tossing the treat further and further. Once you are successful with this, it will be time to have your dog walk but without a treat for each segment. Hold a treat and let your dog see that you have it. Start walking; he will follow along because he's following what is in your hand. Offer praise (Good dog!) and a tease (Let's.... let's....), walking him a good distance before you say the complete 'Let's go!' while tossing the treat.

In time, treats can be spaced further and further apart. Ultimately, in a few weeks' time, a treat given once at the halfway point and once at the completion of the walk should be all that is needed.

Socialization & Desensitization Training

> Please note that this section is for shy, nervous, or fearful dogs. If your dog is a barker (yet brave), you may wish to refer to 'Behavioral Training: Barking' and if your dog is aggressive, you may wish to refer to 'Behavioral Training: Aggression'.
>
> For socialization and desensitization training, we are going to look again to Faye Dunningham, a popular canine trainer, who has several well-regarded books on Amazon. Ms. Dunningham has contributed this expanded, re-worked, special-edition socialization and desensitization training section.

Before we commence, please note that while I do use the words 'pup' and 'puppy' quite often, and we do touch on puppy behaviors, this type of training can be used for a dog of any age.

What is Socialization?

Socialization is the method of guiding a pup through introductions and interactions with elements in his environment. This includes people, other animals, places, and situations. It is a gradual process, where the trainer leads the pup through one small, first step, and incrementally builds on things from there. If successful, the pup is comfortable and confident in his world, responds in a friendly manner to all those that are worthy of such a response, and handles himself with ease under any circumstance or event.

What is Desensitization?

Desensitization is similar to socialization, in fact, these can crossover quite a bit throughout training. It is the method of gradually exposing a pup to a trigger that normally elicits a negative response. Exposure to the trigger is gradually increased over time, with each negative or positive reaction handled in specific ways. If successful, a pup tolerates a wide range of elements and does not become rattled even with unexpected encounters or exposures.

Is it Normal for a Dog to be Fearful?

It is not uncommon, and while any dog can be afraid of any element, fear is most commonly seen with toy breeds. They understand that some dogs are larger, that people reaching down to pat them are taller, etc. So, this does play into things a bit.

In addition, there is a huge shift in the way that a puppy sees the world between the age of 2-months-old and 4 to 5-months old. When very young, a pup's cognitive abilities are not at full capacity. He may seem aloof and nothing may phase him. He may be fine with being picked up by strangers, saying hello to visitors, and crawling all over children. The 8-week-old puppy is deemed incredibly friendly, and owners feel lucky that they chose such an outgoing, happy dog!

But, this may change. And, owners of new pups that do not know a transition may be coming, can fail to provide socialization during a critical time. Once a puppy has matured and has the ability and capacity to take in *all* that surrounds him, he will start to react to the entire weight of a situation. If he was not socialized to his world, he may start to display fears and phobias.

With this all said, young pup or adult, small dog or big dog, the extent to which a dog fears his world is almost always directly related to three things: Past experiences, level of desensitization, and level of socialization.

Let's see how these 3 things work together to either increase or decrease a fear:

All it takes is one exposure to something in order for fear to develop, particularly if a dog inadvertently learned that he was correct to be afraid (owner coddled him, etc.) or if the experience was truly unpleasant.

The more that a dog experiences events and situations and has interactions, as long as those instances are not perceived as negative experiences, the less that he is going to be afraid of them. Each time that something occurs, if the outcome is either neutral or favorable, a bit of the fear associated with it will be chipped away.

Home Socialization & Desensitization – Build the Perfect Foundation

The Importance of Touch

It cannot be overstated how important touch is. Most dogs without past 'touch desensitization' are very impatient when it comes to grooming (bathing, brushing, nail trimming, ear cleaning, dental care, wiping of the eyes, etc.). And, if a pup is not handled enough, he may never be a dog that naturally cuddles up to humans; the aloof adult dog that shuns close contact with his humans is the grown-up version of the puppy that lacked this important element.

Therefore, touching and handling your puppy is a part of socialization and desensitization. It involves interaction with you and desensitization to all of the aspects of being handled. Begin with small steps; each day (or multiple times per day), simply sit down at floor level, holding your puppy and petting him. Touch the tail, the ears, and the paws. Gently open the puppy's mouth; using a finger, all teeth should be touched: front, back, and tops.

In time, graduate from touching to actions that will be regularly taking place in regard to grooming:

❖ From touching the coat to brushing it
❖ From touching the teeth to using a puppy-sized toothbrush or finger-brush dental tool
❖ From touching the paws to applying paw wax
❖ From touching the ears to swiping the inner flap with a sterile piece of gauze
❖ From touching all parts of the body to swiping them with a grooming wipe
❖ From touching the face to swiping over the eyes with an eye wipe

Speak matter-of-factly while you do this. When a session is complete, give praise. Gradually increase the duration of sessions, from 2 minutes to 5, and then to 10. For dogs that are very reluctant, offer a training treat when done; it should be a special one, reserved just for this so that your dog has something to look forward to.

Your Property – Finding Out Which Exposures Your Puppy Needs

Note that before you bring your puppy outside to any area, including your own yard, be sure that he has had all of his puppy shots or that no wildlife or any other pets could have had access to the property; excluding your own pets that are up-to-date.

If you socialize your puppy to elements encountered while at home, you will have much better success when doing so with elements outside of the home and the property.

With your pup on leash, explore the yard. Allow him to stop along the way to investigate what he wishes as long as it is not harmful. If the weather is pleasant, stay outside for a good amount of time. Sit together and allow your puppy to see squirrels and hear birds chirp. If you live on a busy street, allow him to have short periods of sitting on leash beside you to hear the cars drive by.

If it is raining, put on your raincoat and allow your puppy to become accustomed to raindrops falling upon him. If it is snowing, bundle up (and bundle up your puppy, especially if you have a toy or small breed dog) and allow him to become accustomed to seeing the snowflakes drift down and experience how the ground feels solid as opposed to soft grass.

As you expose your pup to this small section of the outside world, keep in mind what he accepts and what causes him to take pause. Any element that appears to cause nervousness, anxiousness, or wary behavior, should be 'red flagged' as one that your puppy may need to be socialized to.

For example, let's take a look at what to do if your puppy acts frantic in the rain (assuming that the temperature is warm):

Keep the first time spent in the rain short; one to three minutes. Do not immediately bring him back inside, even if he seems bothered. It is important not to offer soothing words during this short, initial discovery. If you say in a comforting voice, "It's okay, calm down, the rain is not going to hurt you", it will send a message to your puppy that he is correct in being upset and that you, his leader, agrees since you are now trying to pacify him.

You will want to act in a very casual way. Just speak in a normal tone. You can say just about anything that you want, aside from "No" or the soothing words of "It's okay", as long as it's said in a matter-of-fact way. The goal is to show your puppy, by your words and your calm actions, that the rain is no bother to *you*.

Each time it rains, make it a *point* to bring your puppy outside. Each time you do this, increase the time increment by 1 to 2 minutes. Each time, act casual as described earlier. Ignore any barking, begging, nudging against you, or any other attention-seeking behavior. As the session time is ending and you are ready to bring your puppy back inside, if he is acting calm take that moment to offer a special treat and praise before entering into the home.

When you do this on a regular basis, your puppy will learn that since you do not mind the rain (or traffic noises, or birds chirping, or snowfall or any other outside element) that neither should he. You will lead by example and he, ruled by canine instinct, will choose to follow your lead.

Socializing a Shy Puppy to Visitors to Your Home

Sudden Rushes of Thought

As we discussed earlier, a very young puppy may appear to be oblivious to guests in your home or may even show very friendly behavior. Fast-forward a few months, and the pup will be more aware of his world, his cognitive abilities will be stronger, and it is then that he may become overly shy or even nervous around people. For an unsocialized puppy, when a guest arrives, this creates a sudden rush of thoughts. He has a lot to think about. Thoughts that run through a puppy's mind are akin to, "Who is this person?", "Is this a friend or foe?", "Am I in danger and should I hide?", and "What is their intention?"

It will be your job to show your puppy, by your words and by your actions, that he has no reason to be afraid, nervous, or feel anything other than confident and happy.

Preparing for Visitors

Prepping in advance is needed since it's nearly impossible to do proper socialization without setting a few things up first.

#1 Enlist the help of one person. This can be a neighbor or friend who is willing to assist in teaching your puppy to interact with guests. As your pup advances his social skills, you can have several people visit at one time; but, for these first steps, one is enough!

#2 Have training treats at the ready. These should be very small, chewy, extra yummy, and something that your pup is not given for regular snacks. Your guest will need to hold onto some as well. You can give these to your helper in advance, or leave a zipped sandwich bag of these near the entrance for them to grab.

#3 Have your pup's area set up and accessible. This will be your pup's indoor exercise pen or gated off area. Have the entrance to this open. This is because forced interaction does not work. You will want your pup to *choose* to interact and have the freedom to retreat as he wishes.

#4 Offer a tranquil environment. You'll want the house uncluttered, calm, and relatively quiet.

Training for Visitors

1. Sit on the floor with your pup, preferably in a comfortable room such as the living room, that has a view of the front door or at least a long view of an entrance point in which your helper can be standing approximately 15 to 20 feet away. Have several training treats in your left hand, with one at the ready in your right hand, cupped.

2. Have your helper start to enter, but stand in place at full viewing distance, at approximately 15 to 20 feet.

3. The moment that your pup sees your guest, open your palm to offer a training treat, while giving praise ("Good, dog") in a calm voice. Then, offer a second one.

4. When your helper sees that your pup has finished the second treat, have them back away, moving out of viewing range.

5. You will stop giving treats the moment that your helper is no longer in view.

6. Both you and your helper will play this 'game' of him/her moving into and out of view, while you do or do not give treats and praise. Each time your guest is in view, your pup gets a treat. Each time your guest is out of sight, the treats stop.

7. If your pup seems to be handling things so far, and he very well may be since the guest will not be close enough to truly illicit a strong response, and the treats will be a distraction to some extent, you and your helper will repeat this 'game', but at 18-feet, then 16-feet, then 14-feet, and so on. Have your helper move closer in a casual way.

8. As your guest approaches the 8 to 10-foot range, have them slowly lower themselves to the floor without

making direct eye contact with your pup. If your pup starts to retreat, allow this. But, have your helper toss a training treat to your pup. Since he just had the taste of the special rewards, he may very well stop to mouth the one just tossed in his direction.

9. Actions will vary, depending on what your pup does:

#1 If your pup finishes retreating and enters his pen or gated area, remain in position with your guest, and talk in a casual manner. At some point, your pup may sneak back, just to check on things, if so, see #2, 3, and 4.

#2 If your pup backs away, but stays in the area to observe things, remain in position with your guest and talk in a casual manner, but take turns tossing treats to your pup every 30 seconds or so.

#3 If your pup remains in place, unsure of what to do, remain in position with your guest and talk in a casual manner but take turns tossing treats every 20 seconds or so.

#4 If your pup comes over at any time, acknowledge him by giving praise with "Good dog" in a happy but not sudden or loud voice. Every 15 seconds, take turns with your guest to give a treat. If your pup will not take a treat directly from your helper's hand, the treat can be placed on the floor at arm's length.

No matter how your pup reacts, limit this first session to about 15 minutes. Try to have as many sessions as possible, preferably several a week. If you start to see improvement, add on 5 minutes, and then 10. As your pup progresses, new elements can be incorporated, such as your guest offering a toy, tossing a ball for a light game of indoor fetch, etc. In time, graduate to having more than one helper at a time. Do, however, know your pup's limits; they all have them. Many puppies and dogs will simply not do well in a crowded room with lots of people, and should always have a quiet area to retreat to.

Established Fears: Desensitization Training Prep

Desensitization requires a purposeful, gradual introduction and exposure to triggers. *There are some vital things to do and to keep in mind:*

1) If a fear came on suddenly, have health issues ruled out. If a normally happy, calm, and friendly dog suddenly becomes fearful, this can point to a health issue that is causing pain or discomfort. Even if you were just at the vet's office, something that was borderline and not showing up on testing may have

just crossed the line.

2) Know that some dogs simply cannot overcome a certain fear. In cases of abuse and other severe circumstances, a dog may not be able to work through a particular anxiety. Emotional scars can linger, even if a dog is far removed from his past. While you should not automatically assume that a fear will last a lifetime, do show understanding if your dog simply cannot tolerate a particular trigger. Forcing exposure may do more harm than good and can exacerbate things even further. For these such instances, avoidance is best.

In addition, it is near impossible to stop a dog from being afraid of thunder & lightening and fireworks. The first is due to changes in air pressure and noise and the second, of course is the noise. With senses, including hearing, vastly superior to us humans, a dog cannot be trained to 'un-hear'. In these cases, the use of a thunder-vest can be helpful.

3) Organize and prioritize. If your dog is afraid of a lot of things, taking on too many triggers at once will be stressful for you and counterproductive for your dog. Fears are best when conquered one at a time.

4) Start with the 'easy' ones. Dogs can be afraid of normal household noises; this happens most often if a breeder did not introduce these elements to the puppy. This may include being afraid of the sound of the washing machine, sink disposal, etc. Anything that can be worked on at home or from home, such as walking passed dogs or walking beside traffic would be on this level.

5) Be sure that everyone in the household is on board. There can be setbacks if another family member is not following along with the guidelines.

The 8 Steps for Training a Dog to Overcome Fears

Now that you've

narrowed down what your dog is afraid of (even if that list seems long), you realize that some things are better left alone, and you've decided what to work on, the following tips can help:

1) The goal is to expose your dog to the trigger in a non-threatening, non-forceful way. In some instances, he can simply start off as an observer. As he gains confidence that nothing bad will actually happen, you can bring him closer to the action.

2) Work with your dog every day, if possible. At the very least, 3 times per day will be needed.

3) Sessions should start off very short. Depending on the fear, just 5 minutes at a time is often appropriate. Each week, add on 5 minutes.

4) Intensity should begin very low with the goal to work up. For example, if a dog is afraid of traffic, you begin on a road where very few cars even drive by. Then, you graduate to a slightly busy road... then a moderately busy road and so on. After one week of handling a certain intensity of traffic in a calm manner, you can then take things up one level.

5) If at any time your dog is acting calm, offer reward. You should not take time to fish into your pocket or go searching for the treat. Have some ready in a sealed, zipped plastic bag for easy distribution.

6) During the window of exposure, your job is to remain calm and matter-of-fact while ignoring the fearful behavior. Canines are amazingly adept at picking up on their owner's cues. So, do not pick your dog up, offer soothing words, or take any actions that could imply you are validating the fear.

7) For any training that takes place outside, keep your dog on a harness. This allows you better control, but most importantly, part of this training is for you to keep walking or performing an action while ignoring any whining/barking/refusal to move and with your dog on a harness and not a collar, this allows you to continue on (slowly yet assuredly) without harming him or causing injury to his neck.

8) Set small goals and celebrate them. Maybe your first goal is for your dog to stay to your side for security instead of running to hide in a closet. Or maybe a reasonable objective is for your dog to quietly watch dogs playing; while he is not jumping in to join them at least he is not cowering. These are all steps in the right direction. Reward for them, be proud of your dog, and be patient as you reach for the next level of acceptance.

Tips for Very Fearful Rescue Dogs
Even if you know the basic background of a shelter dog, it's nearly impossible to truly know what that dog lived through that left emotional scars. Here are some tips to keep in mind:

1) The oddest things can be scary to a formerly abused dog; such as just a specific type of person (this can be gender-related or even height), certain rooms (dark rooms such as the garage or small rooms such as the bathroom), or typical care elements such as baths or brushing that the neglected dog was never able to become used to. Time and patience are needed and do use your judgement; in some cases, catering to a certain fear is not necessarily enabling it; it is just the kind, logical thing to do.

2) Do not take it personally if your dog seems afraid of you. For some dogs, the person who was their 'leader' was the one that inflicted pain and suffering. It can take a while for a dog to learn that his current human is a good one. This can be overcome. When there are more new, good experiences than there are bad ones, there will be a gradual transition to a new life.

Remember, some sources say that dogs do not have good memories. But this is not really true. They have trouble with short-term memory. However, when something is repeated often enough (such as commands, house training, etc.) it then moves from short to long-term memory. And it stays there as long as it is reiterated once in a while. So, if a dog was treated in such a way to induce fear, those memories are going to stay for a while. But, as long as the treatment is not repeated, they will fade away.

3) Give what is really craved, compromise on some things, and be firm with others. If a rescue dog feels best when he makes a little nest for himself in a closet or if he only eats once everyone leaves the kitchen, allow him that as long as it does not interfere or conflict with your own needs. For other elements, compromise; perhaps your dog does well with a few visitors but cannot handle large crowds;

you can have him out to meet & greet when there are just a couple of guests over but have him safe and sound in his canine playpen if you have a large gathering. And when it comes to care necessities such as bathing, brushing, nails, etc. you'll need to perform these for both hygiene and health reasons. Most dogs do best when these tasks are done on a schedule (they will start to learn what to expect) and in an area that is calm and relaxing for both owner and dog.

Specific Training: Strangers, Dogs, and Traffic

It is best to have your pup's involvement in a new activity, exposure to a new environment, or interaction to a new situation be a gradual, incremental experience, even before you learn if it is going to be a problem. If you do this, it most likely will never become an issue at all. If you wait and find out that it is a problem, you will then need to invest time and effort to reverse the behavior. The three most common elements a dog will be exposed to are:

Encountering Strangers – This can occur while taking your daily walks or while out in public in any location.

Other Dogs – Of course, encounters will occur at the dog park or the pet supply store. Your puppy may also need to become used to your neighbors' dogs.

Traffic – Most often encountered while taking a walk with you, but some dogs are also afraid or wary of traffic that passes by the home.

The Process for Meet and Greets with Strangers

For encountering strangers, this will be a matter of showing your puppy how to interact with people, while safe under your leadership. If the route that you take for your daily walks does not often bring you by other people (or does not present an opportunity to engage with them), there are other places you can visit that will allow you to socialize your puppy to strangers. The dog park will certainly be such a place; however, if you still need to teach your puppy how to behave with other dogs, this may be too much since he will need to deal with two new elements: strangers and unknown dogs.

Better would be an outdoor mall, a neighborhood yard sale, a small flea market, an outdoor patio of a coffee shop or ice cream parlor that permits dogs in their outside seating area, a local youth baseball game, a hiking trail, a smaller park that is not an official dog park but does allow pets, etc. Plan on visiting these types of places one to two times per week.

Three things need to be in place before beginning:

#1 Your puppy on a harness. A harness gives you better control than a collar; additionally, if your pup jumps up or tries to run, the harness will prevent neck injury that can otherwise occur with a collar.

#2 Have training treats at the ready. These should be small, chewy, extra yummy, and something that your pup is not given for regular snacks.

#3 Your puppy should know the 'sit' command very well. When you are ready for your puppy to interact with a stranger, you will command him to sit. You may have seen references elsewhere that claim an owner should ask *the stranger* to command the puppy to sit. But, it's a terrible idea to have anyone other than a puppy's direct human leaders to command him. Giving commands shows leadership. If complete strangers, and a lot of them, are giving commands to your puppy, this can rescind all that you were working for to have your puppy see you as his leader.

Start in a Heeling Position

When you are out and about with your puppy, the first step is to simply walk among other people. Your dog should be to your left. This is the standard positioning for proper heeling; and, it is good for your puppy to always understand that your left side is his 'starting' and 'ending' point. When out in public and later on when you are exploring the world together, your puppy (soon to be your adult dog) will feel safer and you will have more control if he is to your left as opposed to anywhere that he wishes.

As you walk with your pup, talk to him in a casual voice, but do not distract him. Let him take in the new sounds, interesting scents, and become familiar with activity that occurs in groups of people. Undoubtedly, there will be people who come up to you to comment on your puppy and ask to pet him. This is your opportunity for one-on-one socialization.

Making a Decision about a Meet and Greet

It is at this point that you must take note if your puppy is ready for one-on-one physical interaction, which we will refer to as a Meet and Greet.

Not all puppies will be ready on Day One. For pups not used to lots of people and noise, just being in a crowd is enough for the first few outings. If anyone approaches your dog and asked to pet him, you can answer politely by saying, "No, I'm sorry, my dog isn't quite comfortable with new people yet, we're working on it!"

Signs of being ready or not ready for a Meet and Greet with a stranger will be how your puppy behaves when the person approaches. If he is calm, this is a good sign. But, if your puppy is anxious (whining, trying to cling to you, excessive lip licking, etc.) you would have to be forcing any interaction. This can increase a dog's fears, and can even lead to a biting incident. If your pup is anxious with just the possibility of interaction, spend more time simply walking in crowds. Typically, after several sessions, a dog will be so accustomed to seeing other people (and has learned that nothing bad comes of it), that he will then be ready to Meet and Greet.

Continuing on with the Meet and Greet

If your puppy is calm when someone approaches to comment on him or asks to pet him, do explain to that person that you are in the process of training your puppy to be socialized and then ask that person to please give your puppy a treat (that you hand over to the person) when it's time to say 'good-bye', *if* your puppy behaves for them. Most people will be more than happy to assist.

Command your puppy to sit, giving praise ("Good, sit"). While you do not want to run off a list of rules for the person who just wishes to say hello, you'll want to mention two quick things, and keep two others in mind:

#1 If all strangers interact with your puppy from a standing position it will cause too much of an intimidation factor. Ask the person to please pet him from the same level as the dog.

#2 Suggest pats to the chest and/or chin, not the top of the head.

#3 A stranger should never pick up your pup. Your puppy needs to trust you that when you both go out in public that it does not equal you allowing strangers to handle him.

#4 You may need to encourage your puppy to remain sitting by saying "Wait…Wait…" as you may have done while training him to sit.

While a person may want to pet your puppy for quite a while, it is best to keep meetings short until your pup is used to interacting with all sorts of people. You will then have a better understanding of his tolerance level; many dogs, even outgoing ones, have one. Therefore, while you do not need to officially time it, a Meet and Greet of 30 seconds to 1 minute is best.

You can explain to the person that you area keeping initial meetings short for now. Ask that person to end things on a good note and have them offer the treat (that you had given to them earlier) to your puppy. Give the release word of 'Okay', to bring your pup out of the sit, and move on to walking among the crowd. Always end things on a good note; the excursion should come to a finish while your puppy is behaving and is not tuckered out or has become frustrated.

Success, and Moving On

Increase Meet and Greets as your puppy learns to handle them. Normally, within 8-10 outings, a pup will become familiarized enough with this aspect of his world that he will be ready to handle strangers in just about any situation. And if so, you can move on to meeting dogs, which will involve a Meet and Greet with both dogs and their owners (and your puppy will already be used to one of those elements). This introduction to other dogs is discussed in the following section.

The Process for Meet and Greets with Other Dogs

While most dogs do not need to be 'friends' with other canines, it is best to socialize your puppy to other dogs. One reason is that if you do so, it greatly decreases the chances that your puppy (and then older dog) will bark or have other negative behaviors upon hearing, seeing, or picking up the scent of another dog. It also cuts down on the chances of your puppy growing up to show aggression toward other dogs. And, if you ever bring another dog into the home, it will make for a much easier transition. Therefore, this is a socialization lesson well worth teaching.

If you live in a neighborhood with other pet owners that frequently walk their dogs, this will provide opportunities for your puppy to learn to be a 'good neighbor'. If your neighborhood does not have a big pet population, a dog park (with separate sections for dogs based on size to ensure safety), can be a good option for Meet and Greets with other dogs.

The 'Canine Hello'

Before you take your puppy to commence Meet and Greets with other dogs, let's go over the 'canine hello', which involves sniffing each other. While a dog may sniff the other's face or entire body, most will sniff near the anus. When dogs greet in this way, they are sniffing each other's scent that is secreted by the anal glands (scent glands); there a pair of glands, located just on the rim of the anal opening.

Via this scent, dogs are exchanging information. The scent tells a dog the gender, health status, and temperament of the other. It even lets dogs know if they have encountered each other before.

Typically, one dog will take the position of the dominant one; he will be the first to engage in sniffing. So, if you have a shy dog, do not be surprised if your dog always goes second; in and of itself, there is nothing wrong with this. When both dogs have assimilated the information received and both are satisfied that a meeting would be beneficial, the dogs will continue on to Meet and Greet.

First, Meet the Neighbors' Dogs and Friends' Dogs – Arranging This

Beginning this training with somewhat 'known' dogs is best, as you will have more control to help your puppy learn this before attempting socialization with unknown dogs encountered at the park, etc. Keeping in mind the way that dogs instinctually and naturally greet each other, an owner does not need to do much, other than to initiate the Meet and supervise the Greet.

With friends or family, arranging a time for this is all that is needed to begin. For neighboring dogs, it is best to plan for this as opposed to having your puppy encounter them while out for a walk. Therefore, if you are friendly with any neighbors who are dog owners, you can agree to meet and allow the dogs to get to know each other.

If you do not know a neighbor very well, this is a good opportunity to get to know them. If this is what you wish to do, it is suggested to say hello and introduce yourself without having your puppy with you. You can let them know that you have a new puppy (or dog), and so that everyone gets along well you wish to bring him or her over for a Meet and Greet at a convenient time. Elsewise, you can wait until encounters occur while out walking in the neighborhood; however, when you plan this out you can be better prepared.

Note: When doing a Meet and Greet with known dogs, if you have an un-neutered male and he will be meeting an un-spayed female, check in advance to make sure that the female is not in heat. If you have an un-spayed female, and she will be meeting an un-neutered male, do not allow this to occur if she is in heat.

The Initial Meet

Always keep your puppy on leash and harness, and never let go of the leash, even if things seem to be going just fine. If opposition develops or any jumping occurs, you can safely reel your puppy back to you without putting any undue pressure on the neck.

Talk to your puppy in a relaxed, calm voice as the dogs first take note of each other. After that, your puppy probably will not be focusing on your voice very much, if at all. Therefore, take that short window of opportunity to relay that you are calm and relaxed, as your puppy will often read your tone of voice and pick up on the vibes that you are sending.

The Greet

Keeping the leash out long enough to permit freedom of movement, allow your puppy and the other dog to sniff each other as described earlier. They will then decide if they wish to continue on to play, etc.

If the other dog backs off and does not show interest in playing, do not take it personally. There are many reasons why another dog may do this. If he or she is an older dog, they merely may not have the personality that wants to romp around with a puppy. No matter what their ages, the dogs may find out during the exchange of information that they are not well-suited playmates. It is best to just be happy that your puppy was successful in saying hello.

Alpha Beta Agreements and Disagreements

When two canines play, they may want to establish which one of them is the Alpha and which one is the Beta, if this was not made clear during their initial exchange of information. With puppies, this may be done with wrestling, in a playful manner. But, keep a close watch, in case things take a turn for the worse.

The result regarding 'Who is Alpha?' may occur without you knowing. However, predominantly with adult dogs, if both wish to be the governing one and if each firmly 'demands' to be Alpha, they may take a fighting posture. You will want to be on the lookout for this so that you can immediately intervene.

Warnings of Imminent Fighting

If two dogs are squaring off over Alpha disagreement, there are usually warnings. The warnings can include growls, bared teeth, standing off to face each other, tensing into a fighting stance, and/or direct staring into each other's eyes. If any of this occurs, immediately separate the two dogs (this is why keeping the dogs on leash is important).

Encouraging Play

If both pups appear to be tolerating each other but are not playing on their own, you can enter the picture and encourage play. Tossing a ball to them works well and if one certain pup is clearly the faster runner, tossing two balls (one to each) should keep both happy.

Ending on a Good Note

End the meeting on a good note, when your puppy is behaving. You can offer treats to both (with the permission of the other dog's owner of course) to show that you are proud that your puppy handled things well.

Encountering Unknown 'Stranger' Dogs

At various times, your puppy will encounter dogs that are 'strangers'. This is inevitable if you will be taking your puppy for daily walks and trying to expand his world by bringing him to other locations. And, of course, it will occur if you bring your pup to places that are meant for pet owners. This is terrific and encouraged; just keep in mind that at some point there may be an aggressive dog that warrants both you and your puppy staying away.

For meeting unknown dogs, much of the interaction will occur as it did when your pup practiced with 'known' dogs. There will be the initial sniffing to exchange information, the dogs will decide if they wish to play, young pups may wrestle if they are not completely sure of the Alpha-Beta ranking, and there is always the chance of a disagreement.

Whenever you head out with your puppy to go somewhere, always bring treats with you. Whenever your pup behaves well around another dog, after approximately 5 minutes, end the session (so that you end on a high note) and give praise and then reward.

After your puppy has built up enough skills to do well with other dogs on a consistent basis, time spent playing and interacting can increase if you wish.

If your pup is not behaving nicely, lead him away and allow him a rest before meeting any other dogs. It may just be a matter of needing to 'regroup', especially if your puppy has already said hello to several dogs during the excursion; he may be feeling a little overwhelmed.

While you are taking a rest, keep him beside you on leash. Do not give a treat when the rest is over. Simply allow him an opportunity to enter the situation again and demonstrate better behavior. Any time that he does prove better behavior than before, offer praise and a treat.

If encounters do not go well at all, this means that your puppy needs shorter sessions. Some owners reverse course and back away from Meet and Greets; they believe that since their pup did not do well, that it is best to stop putting them into a Meet and Greet situation. But this is not the answer. When a dog is unsure how to socialize, he needs more exposure, not less. That exposure should, however, be at shorter intervals, allowing a more gradual experience.

As time goes by, your puppy will gain self-confidence when encountering other dogs. You will have taught your puppy that dogs come in all sizes, ages, and have various temperaments. Your puppy will learn that some dogs are friends, some are foes, and some will be neutral animals that warrant a 'Meet' but you are not forcing a 'Greet'.

If Your Dog is Afraid of Traffic

The Overall Goal

Many puppies and dogs are fearful of traffic if they have not been exposed enough. This is understandable since canines have no real sense of what automobiles are. Even if a dog has seen hundreds of cars pass by, he may still not feel safe that these loud and fast-moving objects do not present a danger.

While it is done with good intentions, one of the biggest mistakes that owners make is to soothe or comfort their dog. It is natural human instinct to comfort; but, in most cases, this will just reinforce a dog's phobia. When an owner has established themselves as a dog's leader, this gives a dog reassurance to follow the lead of that person. Therefore, if an established leader is tense, the dog will become tense. If the leader is calm, the dog will become calm.

Quite contrary to offering comfort, when a dog shows fear of traffic, the owner must show by example that there is nothing to be afraid of. You will always be there to protect your dog; therefore, do not feel that the following method is akin to 'leaving your dog on his own'; it is not. What you will be doing is leading by example and giving your puppy an opportunity to gain self-confidence. This is done by ignoring any displays of fear. A puppy may try to cling to you, cower down, whine, turn and tuck his tail down, and/or shake. It will not matter what your puppy does; your goal will be to walk with confidence despite any of this, which will ultimately transfer that confidence to your dog.

Starting Slow

As with any socialization or desensitization training, begin slow. For fear of traffic, this will be on a street with very little traffic. For a 15 to 20-minute walk, perhaps 1 to 2 cars pass by. Any more than this will be overwhelming. Of course, you cannot control the movement of the traffic; so, you will find that some days bring 1 passing car and another day may bring 3 or 4, and this is alright. Your job will be to find a location to walk that offers the best chances of 1 to 2 cars driving by, on average, during your walk.

Prepping

Be prepared by having your puppy on harness and a short or retractable leash, and have training treats (small, chewy, extra yummy, and not something that is given out at any rate) somewhere that is easily accessible, like a jacket pocket. And, have your pup in a heeling position: To your immediate left no further ahead than the extension of your left foot; the handle of the leash is held in your right hand, you will grip the cord with your left hand, near your left hip.

Walking and Talking

As you walk, talk! Talk to your puppy in a relaxed and matter-of-fact way, keeping in mind that you do not want to sound comforting or soothing. It does not matter what you talk about... you can tell your puppy about your day at work or you can recap your favorite television show; All that matters is that your puppy becomes aware that you are in a calm mood with no trepidation or fear.

During times that the walk is going well, occasionally palm a treat to your dog as you're walking along. You may need to slow down, but do not completely stop. Give praise of 'Good, dog'.

When a Car Passes By

When a car inevitably passes by, do not tense up in anticipation. Continue walking. Your puppy may

attempt to plant himself down firmly or try to lie down. This is one reason the harness comes in handy. Keeping the same steady pace, continue walking as if you are completely and utterly unaware that your puppy is attempting to either stay still or drop down. With the harness displacing pressure across the back, shoulders, and chest (and not the neck as a collar would) you will cause no harm to him as long as you do not run.... Just walk at the normal pace that you established as your walk began.

If your puppy whines, continue talking about the TV show or your work day or whatever subject you were speaking about. Your goal is to entirely act as if you do not notice any change in your puppy's behavior. You will want to continue on as if the car was no more important than a passing butterfly.

As the car drives by and is then gone from sight, your puppy is going to become confused for a moment. The thoughts that will rush through his mind are going to be akin to: "Oh my Gosh, that was *terrifying*, why didn't my human notice that horribly scary thing!", "My leader continued to walk as if that scary object *wasn't* scary... What's happening?"

Then Another Car Will Pass, and Another

When the next car passes, and you are just as nonchalant, your pup will consider things even more. And, by the time 10 or 20 cars pass by, thoughts will eventually become: "Wait a moment... things are starting to become a bit clearer...my leader, the person I depend on for survival, was not afraid of that car at all, in fact she ignored it completely... Perhaps... Yes, perhaps I was wrong to think cars are scary."

And now you're on your way to success. You have taught your puppy to consider the fact the cars do not need to be reacted to. This is a turning point. It will now be time to take things up a notch to a slightly busier road, then even more busy, up to the level of traffic that you desire your dog to be accustomed to.

Behavioral Issues

Image: Cooper; Photo courtesy of YankeeBelle Chihuahuas

Begging

If your dog begs for things on a regular basis, some changes should be made. Not only will it make life easier for you, it can also help a dog become calmer; begging can be a stressful habit that requires a lot of physical and mental work!

Why Dogs Beg: In order to stop this behavior, it's important to understand why it is done in the first place. A dog will beg for one of two reasons:

1. He is unsure of the outcome. He desperately wants something. It has not been established if he is allowed to have it, so he will make every attempt to obtain it.

2. He knows the outcome will be favorable. He knows if he begs hard enough and long enough, he will receive what he desires.

The Physiological Factor:

While your dog begs to satisfy a want, you comply to gain something as well:

o   Love. When we love somebody, we want to make them happy, even if it is temporary and even if it may not be the wisest choice in the long run.
o   Peace and quiet. Begging is not easy to watch or to hear, and surrendering to it immediately calms your dog.

What to Do:

Knowing that the two reasons a dog will beg is that he either is not sure of the outcome or he knows he will eventually win you over, the training to stop this is rather straightforward: You must train your dog that begging will not bring desired results.

Of course, this is easier said than done. It takes a tremendous amount of willpower and it also takes a bit of time. Here are the steps to follow:

1. Decide which foods your dog is allowed and not allowed to eat. Most Chihuahuas do well with 3 small meals per day, plus 3 to 4 snacks in between meals. Training treats are given in addition to this for any sort of training or to reinforce lessons. Decide exactly which type of snacks are allowed and how often they will be given out.

If there are certain foods that your dog begs for that you feel are okay for him to eat, it is best to work these into his meals. For example, if he always begs for a piece of a banana any time you peel one or barks to be given some tuna fish, add a bit of that food into his kibble. Just be sure it is a food that is safe for canine consumption and is relatively healthy. This way, you can stay strong while training to stop begging, since you'll know that your dog is receiving the food in his bowl.

2. Everyone in the house must be in agreement. All people in the household must be on the same page that training to stop begging is about to begin. Dogs are very clever; if there is a weak link in the chain, your dog will find it.

3. Do not give in. It may *seem* that your dog can beg endlessly; however that, of course, cannot be true. While it may, at first, exceed a duration that seems logical and you may be pulling your hair out, it will end. So, no matter what, no matter how much barking, whining or jumping is done, no matter how cute your dog looks or how bad you feel for him, he will not be given what he's begging for. All behavior must be 100% completely ignored.

4. Refocus your dog. Most begging stops once the object of longing is out of view. So, place the object of the begging away, and choose a method of refocusing your dog's attention to something else.

Some good distractions include a reminder of a new toy, heading out for a walk, turning on the TV, refilling the water bowl (if this typically prompts your dog to lap at it), playing a puzzle game together, practicing commands, and brushing the coat (if your dog enjoys this).

Before you Begin:	• Decide what will and what will not be given • Everyone in the house must be on the same page
While Training:	• Do not give in • Refocus your dog • Reward verbally and by touch • Have patience
Additional:	• Offer attention in other ways

5. Reward good behavior both verbally and by touch. During windows of good behavior, reward it, but not with food. Use praise and pets of affection.

6. Have patience. Once you decide to stop giving in, it can take a dog 1 to 4 weeks to believe that you are serious about it and that your say on the matter is final. When a dog realizes that his efforts do not bring about any results, he will no longer put energy into that effort.

7. Step things up a notch in other areas. Since it will be typical for an owner to feel bad for ignoring their dog, it can help to offer fun and happiness in other ways. Head out to explore a new walking route, visit a pet supply store to pick out a new toy, carve out some time to teach a new command, or play a game of fetch. When you feel that you're doing an outstanding job as a caring owner, it will be easier to stay strong when your dog begs.

Clingy Behavior

While owners want their dogs to snuggle up at times and have a close bond, it can be troubling if a dog is too clingy. A dog may constantly shadow his owner or always be trying to wrap himself around an owner's leg. In many cases, this sort of overly dependent personality can make it nearly impossible to leave the house without worrying how the dog will handle himself.

Fortunately, there are some steps you can take to help a clingy dog; these do involve some time, as this sort of behavior cannot be resolved overnight. Do keep in mind that for some dogs, while clinginess can be improved upon, a dog may never be an outgoing, super-independent dog.

Please note that for deep fears, training is covered under 'Behavioral Training: Socialization & Desensitization'.

There are Different Categories of Clingy Behavior

New puppy: Once the initial period of heaps of attention wanes (brand-new puppy) and things transition into regular interaction (older puppy), owners may notice that their pup does not handle being alone very well. As a pup learns his place in the household, and the schedule of when he receives attention and when he does not, and certainly with the help of the upcoming steps, things will even out.

Sudden and unexpected clingy behavior, any age: There are several possible reasons why a dog may suddenly act clingy. This includes:

- **Being traumatized in some way, often an event the owner is not aware of.** The dog walker did not report that a dog barely escaped an attack by another dog, a friend didn't admit to stepping on a dog's tail, or a visit to the groomer may have involved something that spooked a dog. This type of short scare is usually overcome with time.

- **Injured or ill.** Many dogs will retreat when they are sick or in pain; however, dogs can act the opposite way as well. If you suspect that your dog may be clingy due illness or injury, this warrants an immediate vet visit.

- **Reduced amount of time with an owner.** A sudden change in schedule that results in a dog having much less time with his human can cause overly clingy behavior in the few moments that they do have together.

Seniors: An increase in clingy behavior with senior dogs may be indicative of vision problems, which is not uncommon for aging canines. When a dog cannot rely on his sense of sight as much, he may tend to become more dependent on his humans. Another issue that may occur with senior dogs is Cognitive Dysfunction Syndrome which is the canine equivalent of dementia. This can cause confusion and anxiety among other issues which in turn can cause a dog to cling to his owners.

Both of these senior issues should be ruled out as possible causes. With each, there are treatments that may control, if not cure, the conditions.

How to Help an Excessively Clingy Dog

The goal is to have a dog that enjoys the time you spend together, but also has enough of an independent streak and self-confidence occupy himself or to be alone at other times. Many dogs, particularly toy breeds that were bred to be companion dogs, are not born this way; it has to be taught. The key is to 1) Create an environment that offers a sense of security, 2) Teach that independent play is not such a bad thing, and 3) Take steps to help your dog gain self-confidence

1) Create an environment that offers a sense of security.

Offer a 'den'. If a dog does not have a defined space, he may cling to owners, in part, simply because he has nowhere else to go. And, by nature, canines find 'dens' to be secure safe places. You can create one using an indoor canine playpen that has a door; within this should be a quality bed, a great selection of toys, water, food (if you won't be home), and pee pads (optional, but a good idea for dogs when home alone). A corner in the living room or kitchen is a good spot for a playpen.

Offer a companion toy. When you get right down to the basics, a dog clings because of not wanting to be alone. So, a toy that offers a sense of companionship can be helpful. Some dogs can take naturally to any sort of stuffed animal. But, some dogs need a bit more than that, and this is where a companion toy can come in. These are designed to mimic a living creature (often a dog) via being a good size, with a realistic heartbeat and body warmth. You can read more about these under 'Care Items - Chihuahuas of All Ages: Toys'.

2) Teach that independent play is not such a bad thing.

Give toys that encourage independent play. It's incredibly hard to expect a clingy dog to go off and play with a toy by himself. After all, what reason does the dog have for leaving his owner's side and going to a toy instead? The key is to offer a few toys that will react to a dog, simulating intelligent interaction.

These are great for when you are home but can't stay focused on your dog, or for when you have to leave the house. The more a dog plays with these, and realizes that fun can happen without his owner right nearby, the closer he will be to learning to be more independent.

One type that works well are those that speak or make noises. Toys with crinkle material and/or squeakers and treat-release toys can all be great as well. If your dog needs extra encouragement to play with toys, add a dab of 100% all-natural smooth peanut butter or a dash of fish oil on the toy, to make it super-enticing. You can read more about these toys under 'Care Items - Chihuahuas of All Ages: Toys'.

3) Take steps to help your dog gain self-confidence.

Encourage exploration. The more that a dog sees of the world, the more experiences he has, and the more that he interacts with various elements, the more he will gain a sense of self. And as a dog becomes more aware of what exists outside his 'bubble', and when these are positive experiences, the less he will fear stepping outside his 'safe zone' (which is right by your side).

So, take your dog to different places. Head to a new dog park. Visit your local pet supply store. Drive to the beach. Take a new route for daily exercise. See what's at the end of that forest path. Treat the two of you to the offerings at the nearest dog-friendly restaurant.

And have your dog do some new things. If it's summertime, see if your dog likes a pool, or a sprinkler, or chasing after bubbles. If it's wintertime, get your dog dressed up warm and play in the snow for a little while (keep it under 20 minutes). Play new games, hide a toy in the yard that's scented with fish oil or bacon drippings and teach your dog to 'hunt'. Stop and say hello to neighborhood pets.

Teach your dog a command. This is a fantastic way to boost a dog's self-confidence. When done correctly, every session will make a difference, since 'good tries' are rewarded. And once a command is mastered, every time a dog obeys it (which brings about praise and sometimes a treat), it makes him feel great about himself.

Dogs that are well-versed in all basics commands of sit, stay, come, and down, are often confident, poised, and well-behaved. This has the added benefit of establishing you as the leader, which often prevents other behavioral issues such as aggression or stubbornness. For this, look to 'Training: Command Training'.

Do not inadvertently encourage clingy behavior. Dogs are typically very in tune to their human's emotions, and they can pick up a person's vibe quite easily via tone and body language. You can't really hide anything from a dog! If your overall vibes says, 'Oh, you poor little thing, let me cuddle you right up and take care of my precious baby!', you can guess that this won't help a dog be more independent.

But, maybe your actions and words are not quite so literal. Even so, it can have the same effect. When you get home, do you rush over to your dog? Doing so can send the wrong message and cause a dog to become clingier than ever. When dogs are home without their owners, they are metaphorically thinking, 'Will she ever come back?' and 'What if I never see him again?'.

Then, when an owner finally arrives, flings the door open, runs over to the dog, picks him up, and hugs the breath out of him, it is akin to the human saying, 'Oh, my Gosh! I didn't think I'd EVER be back! It's a miracle!'

Clingy dogs do much better with a calm, relaxed atmosphere where essentially nothing is a huge deal. Keeping things on an even keel and not getting excessively excited yourself (though you should still have enthusiasm to do things with your dog with an upbeat manner) can gradually teach your dog to accept things and 'go with the flow'.

React the right way to excessively clingy behavior. It is extremely important to have interaction with your dog; but, if you always pick him up and hug him when he's clinging to your leg, you are teaching him that clinging brings about hugs. It's better instead to direct your dog's attention elsewhere. You can do this by giving a quick, friendly pat (to say hello and give acknowledgement), but then lead your dog to a toy or activity. You can call him over to snuggle up later when you have time to do so.

Depression

Clinical depression is a real medical condition that can affect canines much in the same way as it can affect humans.

Symptoms of Depression in Dogs: This will include loss of interest, retreating, decreased appetite (often leading to weight loss), lethargy, and/or sleep changes.

What Can Cause Canine Depression: Triggers for canine depression include:

1) Loss of a pet. This is a major life event that can severely affect a dog's state of mind. If your dog has experienced the loss of a canine playmate, as to not repeat text, please refer to 'Situational Issues: Having More Than One Dog: Loss of a Pet in a Multiple Pet Household'.

2) Loss of a human family member. This is undoubtedly one of the most common reasons for moderate to severe depression with canines. The bond between owner and dog is strong and this situation can make a dog feel hopeless, sad, despondent, and unable to rise from the sadness without some help.

3) An addition to the family. Whether this change is a new human family member or a new animal family member, a dog may take this as a negative experience.

4) Moving to a new home. This can cause a dog to feel out of place and unsure of why he is there and where he fits in. In many cases, this is an acute depression that will ebb away as the dog acclimates to the new environment; but, see 'Prevention' up ahead. In addition, moving can be stressful and a dog may be picking up the hectic vibe from his owners. Take time to stroll through the new neighborhood and play some light-hearted fetch in the yard; this can offer both you and your dog a break from this often busy event.

5) Longer time periods alone. Many dogs already need to work through some separation anxiety issues when their owners are gone for the day, so if there are circumstances that lead to a dog being alone for even longer periods of time than normal, this can have an effect on the dog's mood. As to not repeat text, please also refer to 'Situational Issues: Separation Anxiety'.

6) Illness or Injury. During the beginning stages of many diseases, health issues, and injuries there may not be any other symptoms aside from acting withdrawn. Therefore, you'll want to have health issues ruled out.

7) After surgery. While rare, a dog can have depression after surgery, and spaying and neutering are the two most common surgical procedures that are done to pets. This is usually related to the anesthesia that was given, though pain medications can also cause behavioral changes. Depression due to anesthesia can take 1 to 2 months to resolve on its own.

8) During the winter. Some dogs can develop Seasonal Affective Disorder (SAD), due to fewer hours of sunlight for the long duration of the winter months. Like humans, some dogs are sensitive to changes in melatonin production that occurs during this time. Less time outdoors and/or less exercise can add to this. Dressing your dog for the weather and increasing outdoor activity can help improve mood. In severe cases, owners can speak to the veterinarian to discuss the use of light boxes; which can simulate sunlight.

9) After giving birth. Due to huge hormonal swings, a female dog may experience some post-partum depression after giving birth. This does not happen to all dams and the severity of the depression can range from mild to severe. In most cases, this will naturally resolve as hormones level out.

Prevention: If you know that a change is coming, try to have your dog become accustomed to the new element ahead of time. If you will be moving, visit the new home as many times as possible, before you officially move in. Bring his favorite toys. Walk around both the entire inside and outside of the home. Take time to play in the yard. Take your dog for a short walk on what will become his new walking route. When it is time to make the move permanently, try to set up all of the dog's favorite items in the same places as before. For example, the food dish in the right corner of the kitchen, the toys in a toy basket in the left corner of the living room.

If a there will be an addition to the family, do not push your dog to become immediate and best friends. This takes time. You may want to start familiarizing your dog to the new smells of a baby or the new aspects of having another pet in the home. Offer the same amount of attention, if not more. It is easy to get caught up in the excitement of your new change, but making sure to give an overdose of attention will make transitions easier.

At-Home Treatment: Barring any possible health issues, if a dog is depressed due to an event (loss of a family member, moving, too much time alone, etc.) there are some things that you can do at home to help:

1) Introduce a New Element. It is very common for a depressed dog to have no interest in normal activities. He may be completely unenthusiastic to go for a walk or play with his toys. However, introducing a new activity can do the trick.

One of the most effective methods is to choose an activity away from the house. Just the sights and sounds of someplace new can help make a depressed dog more alert and allow him to focus on something other than the element that was causing the depression. Some ideas include exploring a new 'easy' hiking path or an outing to a beach or other shoreline (pond, lake, etc.). If you notice some improvement, try to bring your dog to this new location and enjoy spending time together there 1 to 3 times per week.

2) Keep up with Exercise. Unless there is a health issue that is causing a dog to feel down, regular exercise is an important part of an overall treatment plan. While most depressed dogs will not be rearing to go when it's time for a walk, it's important to try to stick with your dog's normal exercise routine or even bring things up a notch by adding another short walk to the day. Exercise releases endorphins (a 'feel good' chemical) and coupled with exposure to light, this can help ease depression.

3) Limit Changes for Some Elements. Now is not the time to bring a new pet into the home, make changes to the furniture, or bring your dog to a new groomer.

Medications and Veterinary Treatments: In cases of chronic depression where at-home treatment methods do not work, a veterinarian may prescribe an antidepressant medication. Unlike with humans, canines often do not need to take anti-depressants for long periods of time for there to be improvement.

With paroxetine, sertraline, and fluoxetine, most dogs respond very well in as little as 1 week and can usually be taken off after 6 months with the depression cured. Another option is clomipramine, which is an FDA approved medication for separation anxiety. It is a non-tranquilizing calming medication that has also been found to work effectively for depression. Side effects of antidepressants may include lethargy, depression (ironically), vomiting, diarrhea, elevation in liver enzymes, confusion, increased thirst, increased heart rate, convulsions, and more.

Digging

This is not a classic 'digging' breed; however, some Chi will indeed develop a habit of digging just about anywhere that has sand, dirt, or gravel. A dog may enjoy making many small holes in the ground or work each day on a larger one. Another element is 'digging' indoors, when a puppy or dog scratches at carpeting or other flooring, seemingly trying to 'dig it up'.

How to Stop Unwanted Outside Digging: There are 4 things that should be done:

1) Control digging access. A dog cannot dig holes in a yard if he is supervised and not allowed to dig. And, allowing unsupervised jaunts outside is unsafe. Toy dogs can be swiped at by hawks or attacked by larger dogs that jump the fence. And, there are always the dangers of eating toxic weeds, ingesting grass or feces, swallowing pebbles, being stung by bees, escaping through a small hole in the fence, and more.

2) Distraction techniques. If a dog begins to dig and then is offered something deemed to be of more value (i.e. more fun), they will change course. Typically, this means an interesting toy or chew or a bout of playtime. This can make a dog forget why he was digging in the first place.

3) Offer a specific area. If you enjoy digging yourself (if you like to garden) and spend a lot of time doing this, you may wish to allow your dog to have his own spot to dig so you can do so together. Some owners use a small children's sandbox for this. You can encourage your dog to use the designated spot by burying some treats and goodies that he can find.

4) Reward for good behavior. Nothing teaches a dog faster than a reward for good behavior. If your dog is digging and you command an authoritative and firm 'No' and he stops digging, offer great praise, pats, and a small reward treat.

How to Stop Indoor Digging: Digging inside is caused by the same canine instinct to dig and bury, even if it is not physically possible. You can:

1) Block off access via baby gates.

2) Use a deterrent spray on the flooring. Deterrent sprays are typically a bitter apple flavor. Do note that these do not work for all dogs; oddly some do not mind the bitter taste.

3) Interrupt and refocus. Just as discussed in 'Behavioral Training: Barking', the goal is to cause your dog to take pause, and the redirect his focus on something else. Sometimes, a loud hand clap and a quick firm 'Hey' or 'No' works. If not, you may want to incorporate a canine training tool that releases a short hiss of compressed air. These are designed to produce a particular sound that usually works very well to cause a dog to stop and take pause. One such device is The Company of Animals Pet Corrector.

When you have your dog's attention for a moment, you'll want to redirect his focus elsewhere. You can work on a few commands, play a game together, or direct your dog to an intriguing toy.

Eating Feces

Can a Dog Get Sick from Eating Feces?
Depending on whether a dog eats his own or that from another animal, there are health concerns:

Eating his own feces: May lead to upset stomach and/or intestinal distress, may suggest a lack of proper nutrition (which in itself can lead to both short and long-term issues), and any dog being treated for worms may re-infect himself via eggs found in feces during the 'shedding' process.

Eating feces from other dogs: There are many parasites and disease that can be spread if a dog eats another dog's feces. Top concerns include worms (roundworms, whipworms, tapeworms, hookworms) and disease including Campylobacter, coronavirus, cryptosporidiosis, giardiasis, parvovirus, and salmonella.

Eating cat poop: A dog can contract worms from a cat, if she has worms and even if she is being treated for them, via eggs found in feces during the 'shedding' process. Additionally, 3 diseases a dog can most commonly contract from eating cat feces are clostridium, salmonella, and Campylobacter.

Possible Reasons a Dog Eats Feces: The reasons behind coprophagia fall into 3 categories: Health, nutrition, and behavioral.

1. Health. While there are quite a few illnesses that have coprophagia as a symptom, it is important to note that with most of these, there will be other, much more pronounced symptoms that let you know that a dog is ill. Health conditions in which coprophagia may be present include by are not limited to:

- Inflammatory bowel disease. Symptoms include diarrhea, vomiting, weight loss, gas, and/or abdominal pain.
- Intestinal tumors or cancer. Symptoms include diarrhea, vomiting of blood or feces, abdominal swelling, black or tarry stools, and/or hypoglycemia (low blood sugar) which causes confusion, trouble walking, and/or weakness.
- Intestinal bacterial overgrowth. Symptoms include larger or more frequent stools in comparison to food intake, vomiting, gas, weight loss, abdominal pain, and/or increased appetite.
- Parasitic infection (includes worms and some fungal infections). Signs of worms are very varied depending on the type, but include vomiting, diarrhea, coughing, low energy, swollen abdomen, changes in appetite (increase or decrease), weight loss, poor coat texture, skin irritations, and worms that can sometimes be seen in the dog's stools.
- Lymphangiectasia (intestinal tract disease). Symptoms include weight loss, diarrhea, abdominal pain, swelling in the limbs, vomiting, and/or cough.
- Age related (young or old) nutrient absorption issues. Without any precise health issues, very young puppies or older senior adult dogs may simply have troubles absorbing nutrients.

2. Nutritional. This revolves around fillers, which are 'empty' ingredients meant to bulk up dog food (commonly employed as a cost-saving tactic by the manufacturers of cheap, inferior dog foods). Fillers include corn, corn bran, soy, wheats, hulls, husks, some 'meals', by-products, certain oats, mill runs, and more.

If a dog eats 1/2 cup of superior wholesome food, he'll receive the benefits (fuel and nutrients) of 1/2 cup of food.

If a dog eats 1/2 cup of inferior food with fillers, he'll be full at first (he *technically* ingested 1/2 cup of food), and he'll be receiving *some* fuel and nutrients, but also a lot of ingredients that the body cannot process. A good portion of fillers will pass through the body, providing nothing. So, while it may appear the dog is eating enough, he can be severely lacking in carbs, healthy fats, protein, and a wide range of vitamins and minerals. This can cause a dog to seek out another food source. And, a dog's own feces can be a tempting food source; if the food contained fillers, much of those were not even digested by the body; they are food bits (albeit, low-value ones) mixed within the feces.

In addition, there is a theory that a vitamin-B deficiency may lead to coprophagia, though other vitamins or minerals are suspected as well.

3. Behavioral. This includes:

- o **Boredom.** Lacking stimulation, boredom can set in quickly, leading to a dog inspecting and ultimately eating his feces.
- o **Stress.** This may include separation anxiety, a chaotic environment, a move to a new home, or any other event or situation that a dog finds to be overwhelming.
- o **Unintentional training.** The hubbub that occurs when a dog eats his feces (rushing over, inspecting the dog, speaking a mile-a-minute) may cause him to repeat the behavior to gain attention.

Note: Though some sources will claim it as factual, there is no proof that a dog will eat feces due to 'hiding' an accident. There is also no proof that coprophagia is a continuation of puppy behavior, as young pups do not eat their own feces.

How to Stop a Dog from Eating Feces: With some time and effort, most cases of coprophagia can be reduced or completely stopped. There are 3 main things that you'll need to do: **#1** Offer top-quality filler-free meals and snacks, **#2** Limit ability to eat feces, and **#3** Try a deterrent supplement or aid (if it's a matter of your dog eating his own feces)

#1 Offer top-quality filler-free, well-rounded meals and snacks. Avoid kibble with corn, wheat, soy, hulls, husks, and other fillers. Be sure that food offers all vitamins and minerals. You may wish to refer back to 'Feeding and Nutrition: All Meal Feeding Details' and 'Snacks' and/or visit the Supplies page of the PetChiDog.com site for the most current recommendations.

#2 Limit ability to eat feces. There are several things you can do:

In your yard/outside:

- o **Clean up feces in your yard.** This involves both stools belonging to your dog and those belonging to any others (neighbor dogs, etc.). This can be done with traditional poo bags. Attaching a poo bag container to your dog's leash helps make this convenient. Or, you may wish to use a 'pooper scooper'. Weather permitting, you can use a hose to spray down feces; however, do keep in mind that if feces contains worms this can contaminate the soil.
- o **Supervise.** Toy dogs like the Chihuahua should not be outside alone. There are countless dangers including hawk attack, larger dogs jumping the fence, finding a hole in the fence to escape, ingesting toxic weeds or plants, swallowing pebbles, and others.
- o **Leash control.** When you take your dog outside, do so on leash and harness. As leader, you are in charge of where your dog goes and what he does. While there should not be any old feces in the yard, if your dog does head toward some, immediately give a 'No' and direct him away.
- o **If you do see it happen, stay calm.** If your dog eats feces due to the heaps of attention that comes along with it, do not allow this goal to be achieved.

When home alone:

- o **Work to create an engaging environment.** These steps help with separation anxiety as well.
  - **Have lots of interactive toys to keep your dog busy.** This includes interactive toys that respond to a dog's touch, such taking toys, squeakers, and/or crinkle toys. Additionally, treat-release toys are always helpful.
  - **Leave on a TV** (some cable providers offer channels specifically for dogs to enjoy) **or have music playing.**

o **Adjust breakfast time.** Generally, when a dog eats, this will trigger a bowel movement a certain amount of time later. If you can move breakfast time up by an hour, this can result in your dog having a bowel movement an hour later than normal. In other words, a smaller time window for the poop to be deposited and then ingested.

#3 Try a deterrent supplement or aid. Only *some* deterrents work, and for those that do, they do not work for all dogs across the board. What may work for one dog may not work at all for another. In addition, a tolerance can be built up; what works great now may lose its effectiveness later on. So, you may need to change methods over time. Therefore, let's go over what to not waste your time with and which ones may be worth trying:

Issues Related to a Dog Eating His Own Feces:
1. Possible sign of lack of sufficient nutrients
2. Possible upset stomach
3. Lingering feces smell on a dog
4. Embarrassment for owners
5. Reinfection of worms (if being treated for them)
Risks of a Dog Eating the Feces of Other Dogs:
1-4 from above, PLUS:
5. Risk of catching worms (roundworms, whipworms, tapeworms, hookworms)
6. Risk of disease (Campylobacter, coronavirus, cryptosporidiosis, giardiasis, parvovirus, salmonella)

Do not use:

☹ **Hot sauce.** The idea of this is to inconspicuously dribble this over a dog's stools so when he later comes across it and tries to eat it, the hot sauce will burn his mouth and repel him. This method does not fix any underlying issues and does not help if a dog eats his feces when home alone. Additionally, hot sauce can cause burns to the mouth, upset stomach, and startle a dog, making this unethical.

☠ **ANY supplement or aid with MSG (monosodium glutamate).** This can cause minor to severe allergic reactions. It is included in MANY coprophagia supplements and is in many meat tenderizers (a home remedy). Read the ingredients on the packaging of any supplement you are thinking of using!

What may work:

✓ **Pineapple.** This contains bromelain, an enzyme that aids in the absorption of protein and helps with digestion. More protein absorption can potentially decrease the urge to seek other food sources. There is anecdotal evidence that this can cause stools to taste bad, thus acting as a deterrent. If you try pineapple, obtain crushed pieces. Serving size is generally 2 tsp per meal for a puppy and 3 tsp per meal for an adult.

✓ **Pumpkin.** 100% real pumpkin is a great food to keep on hand since it can help with intestinal issues such as constipation or diarrhea. Since it works with digestion, it may aid in the absorption of nutrients, thus potentially decreasing urges to seek other food sources. Only use real pumpkin, not canned pumpkin pie filling. Puppies can have 1 teaspoons per day and adults can have 2 to 3 teaspoons per day.

✓ **Adolph's Meat tenderizer with No MSG.** This is one of the few meat tenderizers that does not contain MSG, but it does contain papin, a protein-digesting enzyme derived from the papaya fruit. Since it works with digestion, it may aid in the absorption of nutrients, thus potentially decreasing urges to seek other food sources. There is anecdotal evidence that this causes stools to taste bad, thus acting as a deterrent. Dosing is not set, as this is an off-label use. We'd suggest nothing more than a light sprinkle.

✓ **Prozyme powder.** This is a supplement that can help puppies and dogs that have trouble absorbing nutrients (and may also struggle to maintain weight). It can also help with issues such as loose stools. More nutrient absorption can potentially decrease urges to seek other food sources. Read the labeling for dosing instructions.

✔ **Potty Mouth.** This is a supplement chew designed to taste just fine, but cause stools to taste terrible. It is effective for some dogs, and may be worth a try. As of the time of this writing, there is no MSG and ingredients are brewer's yeast, cayenne, biotin, vitamin B1, vitamin B2, vitamin B6, niacinamide, iron, and copper. Serving size is 1 piece per 10 pounds.

✔ **NaturVet Coprophagia Deterrent Soft Chews.** This also is designed to taste good, but cause stools to taste terrible. It is effective for some dogs and may be worth a try. As of the time of this writing, there is no MSG and ingredients are yucca schidigera (a flowering desert plant, used in holistic remedies), parsley leaf, an enzyme blend, and chamomile. Read the labeling for dosing instructions.

<u>How to Stop a Dog from Eating Cat Feces:</u> Though a cat may be the same size as a Chihuahua or even larger, and this prevents you from doing some of the tricks that can be done with medium or large sized breeds, one thing remains: a feline can climb. Therefore, your best bet is to move the location of the cat litter box to a height that your dog cannot reach. Many people find that the top of the washing machine is a good place.

Eating Grass

<u>Can a Dog Get Sick from Eating Grass?</u> There are health concerns:

1. Digestive issues. Eating grass can cause vomiting (more ahead regarding if dogs eat grass on purpose to self-induce vomiting), which can lead to dehydration; even just a 3 to 4% decrease in normal water levels can cause mild dehydration, disrupting a dog's focus and cause lethargy.

Also, since grass is not easily digested it can cause discomfort and other issues as it passes through the intestines. In some cases of high grass ingestion, intestinal blockage can occur which is considered to be an emergency, often needing surgical treatment. ***Image: Zara, photo courtesy of YankeeBelle Chihuahuas***

2. Possible ingestion of lawn care chemicals. Ingestion of pesticides or insecticides can lead to toxic poisoning. Even if you don't use these, a neighbor may, and rain can bring this onto your property. Also, parks and other public areas may be treated; warning signs can be removed while traces of chemicals still remain.

Ingestion of grass recently treated or long-term ingestion of grass previously treated but with residue can lead to allergy-like symptoms, breathing problems, fever, eye pain, vomiting, abdominal pain, inflammation, vision issues, incontinence, anxiety, irregular heartbeat, dizziness, and/or hyperactivity. Long-term effects include kidney and/or liver damage, neurological issues, weakened immune system, and cancer.

3. Possible bug bites. There is always the risk of red ant bites; however, the most common danger is wasps, bees, and other stinging insects. It is not uncommon for a toy breed dog to have an allergic reaction to a sting.

4. Disease. There's the chance of contracting disease from contaminated grass (from feces of animals). This includes Campylobacter, coronavirus, cryptosporidiosis, giardiasis, parvovirus, and salmonella.

Commonly listed, but invalid or unproven reasons for eating grass:

Countless sources touch on this topic; however, with two of the reasons most sited, there is actually no scientific data to back up those claims. In fact, a multi-step study disproved one of them.

X To induce vomiting. The texture of grass and edges of the blades can trigger a dog to throw up. So, it's a popular thought that dogs will deliberately seek out grass if they want to induce vomiting to clear the stomach. Interestingly, a multi-step study showed that this really isn't true in many instances.

In 2008, researchers at the University of California, Davis conducted a couple of studies[1] on this. First, they polled 25 veterinary students who were also owners of dogs that ate grass on a regular basis. Only a small percentage (8%) attested that their dog threw up afterward and none of them reported that their dog appeared to feel ill before eating the grass.

Going a step further, 47 dog owners that routinely brought their pets to the university for outpatient vet services were polled. The majority of those people did say that their dogs ate grass or other plant-like elements from the outdoors (79%). However, only 12% of those pets vomited afterward and only 6 % appeared to have some sort of stomach distress beforehand.

The final step in the study was to expand questioning regarding grass consumption to a large group of pet owners. Out of 1,571 dog owners, 68% stated that their dog ate grass at least once a week. Out of that group, the results on this were similar: Just 1/3 of those dogs vomited afterward and just 8% showed any signs of feeling sick beforehand.

Risks from Eating Grass:
1. Possible sign of lack of sufficient nutrients
2. Upset stomach
3. Vomiting, possibly leading to dehydration
4. Internal blockage
5. Poisoning due to chemicals
6. Bug bites
7. Certain diseases

From these polls, it would seem that only a small number of dogs may seek out grass when feeling sick, and of those dogs only small percentage will actually vomit afterward.

X The body needs 'greens'. There is a theory that if a dog is not receiving certain nutrients, that he will instinctively seek out those nutrients by eating grass. While a dog *may* very well be needing certain nutrients, if he's looking to grass for them, his instincts would be wrong. Grass is not an easily digested food and it has very little nutritional value. The main nutrient that it holds is crude protein, and it lacks nutrients commonly found in vegetables such as vitamins A, B-6, C, and K, magnesium, and iron.

Actual Reasons Why a Dog May Eat Grass:

✓**Hunger, along with possible nutrient deficiency.** This mainly revolves around fillers. As mentioned in 'Eating Feces', fillers are 'empty' ingredients meant to bulk up dog food (commonly employed as a cost-saving tactic by the manufacturers of cheap, inferior dog foods).

If a dog eats 1/2 cup of superior wholesome food, he'll receive the benefits of 1/2 cup of food. Ingredients will be digested. Carbohydrates will be turned into glucose to provide energy. Healthy fats will be condensed and stored for later use as an energy source, as needed. Amino acids from proteins will maintain and repair muscle. Fiber will aid in slow digestion and help the body absorb nutrients. Vitamins and minerals will be used for a variety of functions. The dog will be sufficiently satiated.

But if a dog eats 1/2 cup of inferior dog food that contains fillers, he will not receive 1/2 cup of useful ingredients. A good portion of the fillers will pass through the body, providing nothing. The dog will be satiated for a short time, but then become hungry again soon afterward.

✔ **Boredom.** An unsupervised dog may munch on grass to pass the time. And, if an owner is present, but there is limited interaction, the same reason applies.

✔ **Curiosity.** Blades of grass can look interesting to a dog, especially a toy breed that is mere inches from it. And canines of any breed or size will use their mouths to figure out what something is, even if there is no intention of eating it. Once it is in the mouth, a dog may chew and then decide to swallow it.

✔ **Habit.** Dogs may resort to a habit even if they do not gain much from the action. And dogs can rapidly transition from an action done out of exploration to a pattern of repeated behavior, particularly if there are no better alternatives at any given moment.

How to Stop a Dog From Eating Grass:

#1 Offer high-quality food and snacks. Since low-quality dog food can lead to both hunger and

nutrient deficiency, and of course since a well-balanced diet is vital for a dog's overall health, you may want to reassess both meals and snacks. As to not repeat text, please refer to 'Feeding and Nutrition: All Meal Feeding Details'.

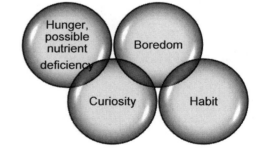

#2 Supervise. As with many behaviors that a dog

may display when outside, supervising your dog can resolve them. Do not allow your dog to be outside alone; this is risky for a toy breed for many reasons including hawk attack, larger dogs jumping the fence, finding a hole in the fence to escape, eating toxic weeds or plants, eating feces, swallowing pebbles, and more.

When you are on walks (and your dog is on leash and harness), you, as the leader, will control where he goes and what he does. You may also wish to refer to 'Behavioral Issues: Refusal to Walk While on Leash', which covers a dog's behavior of stopping a lot along the walking route.

Out in the yard but on leash, if your dog starts to eat grass, give a firm 'No'. This may need to be done alongside a loud clap to gain your dog's attention. As soon as he pauses, refocus his attention elsewhere, by commanding a heel and walking several paces away.

Out in the yard but off leash, if your dog starts to eat grass, give a 'Hey!', not a 'No', and a loud clap to gain your dog's attention, then call him over to you. If you say 'No', your dog may not want to come when called.

1 Sueda, K.L.C., Hart, B.L. & Cliff, K.D. (2008). Characterization of plant eating in dogs. Applied Animal Behavior Science, 111, 120-132.

Fear of Thunder and Lightning

Thunderstorms bring a lot of disturbance and it is not uncommon for a dog to react to this. Many dogs have a heightened sense of awareness during storms. A percentage of dogs are absolutely terrified of them and for good reasons.

Commonly Seen Behaviors: In general, there will be panicked behavior. This may include attempts to hide, shaking, whining, pacing back and forth, excessive drooling, excessive barking, lip licking, and/or chewing on items normally not chewed on. In some cases, a dog may lose all control; some have been known to ram into walls.

What Causes This Reaction: There are **5** main elements that a dog may be reacting to:

1) **Flashes of light.** A dog may feel he is losing his sense of security and control over his normal environment.
2) **Noise of the thunder.** This can be exceedingly loud to a canine's superior hearing.
3) **High winds.** Canines hear on a frequency of 40 to 60,000 Hz, compared to our 20 to 20,000 Hz; therefore, dogs may react to high-pitched winds not perceptible to the human ear.
4) **The sound of the rain hitting the roof.** The continual pounding of rain can be quite aggravating.
5) **Changes in air pressure and static electric field.** Canines can sense drops in barometric pressure as well as sense shifts in the static electric field; both of these occur alongside thunderstorms.

How to Help:

#1 A compression shirt (also known as a thunder shirt, thunder vest, or thunder jacket) can be quite helpful. This is a form-fitting, structured 'vest' based on the concept of swaddling. It gently compresses key points on a dog's body to offer a sense of security during times of stress. This method is effective for up to 70% of dogs (depending on the dog and which brand is used).

Many of these are marketed to help with anxiety in general, including separation anxiety; however, that would require long-time wear, and this is something you may want to avoid. Compression is typically meant to help a dog during short, stressful periods, not for extended hours. At the time of this writing, our top recommendation is the ThunderShirt Classic Dog Anxiety Jacket. This starts at size extra-extra-small for dogs under 7 pounds and size extra-small fits dogs 8 to 15 pounds.

#2 Remain calm. Any worrisome or rushed behavior by you can make thing worse. Don't run over to windows to slam them shut or run across a room to close a door. Keep your actions casual.

#3 Allow your dog to hide if he wishes. If a dog wants to huddle down somewhere, being prevented from doing so will add to stress levels. While this isn't encouraged for every fear, make an exception for thunderstorms. And, don't take the urge to hide as a personal insult; curling up in a small area is canine instinct. If there's a favorite spot, like a closet, set this up in advance with a small blanket, a favorite toy, etc.

Other Aides: Typically, the aforementioned methods work; however, you may find that your dog needs some additional help. Other options include:

✔**Calming supplements.** Since canine calming supplements are not regulated by the FDA, there few real studies to show if these work. Ingredients common to these include a colostrum complex (thought to have a calming effect on animals), L-theanine (found in many teas and said to provide a calming effect), and vitamin B (said to help manage stress). If you want to try this, at the time of this writing we recommend Pet Naturals of Vermont Calming for Small Dogs, which has both L-theanine and colostrum. However, do keep in mind that thunderstorms can roll in fast and pass by quickly and by the time this works, the storm may be over.

☺ **Prescribed anti-anxiety medication**. Some veterinarians may suggest a mild anti-anxiety medication. However, we do not recommend this unless a compression shirt did not help *and* you live in an area that receives substantial thunderstorms on a regular basis.

☺ **Desensitization.** Before the popularity of compression shirts and calming supplements, some owners would employ the technique of desensitization. This can take a LOT of time, just the training alone can be stressful for a dog, and it does not help with flashes of light nor changes in air pressure or the static electric field. So, this is not the ideal answer in most cases. This said, if you are curious about this, it is done via a recording of thunderstorms. It begins by playing this at a very low volume, for a short amount of time, typically 5 minutes. As the days and weeks progress, both the volume and duration are gradually increased.

Humping

Humping is an act of canine masturbation. This said, the reason for humping is not always related to hormonal urges to mate. And both genders may do this. A dog may mount another dog or, most commonly, an inanimate object such as pillows or toys. A dog may also hump against a human by latching onto the person's ankle and other reachable body parts.

Males do not necessarily hump until they ejaculate; though this may very well happen.

Humping behavior often starts early; as young as 5 to 6 weeks old when a pup is still with his littermates. Puppies may hump each other during play even though a pup of that age is far from puberty.

Reasons Why a Dog of Any Age May Hump

Sexual Behavior. Even dogs that are neutered may hump a female, as they can still get an erection; this is because though the testicles have been removed, the body does still produce some testosterone via the adrenal glands. Do note that even if a male dog ties with a female, she cannot become pregnant as long as the neutering procedure was properly performed.

Play behavior. It is considered normal canine behavior to hump during play. In some cases, this is tied to dominance and submission; the dominant dog (or the one trying to establish that he is dominant) will hump the other to show that he is the 'leader'.

Improper Hierarchy. If a dog is always humping his owner's leg, this is often linked to improper understanding of hierarchy. Just about all owners assume that their dog sees them as the leader; however, in some cases, the dog has other ideas. If a dog believes that he is in charge or even thinks that he has a chance to claim that title, all sorts of behavioral issues can start to develop, humping included.

Stress. This is not always related to a 'bad' event; such things as moving to a new home or even a visit to the groomer can affect a dog. This said, stress that leads to humping is often due to such issues as separation anxiety or high levels of tension in the household (children running in and out, blaring TV's or music, yelling, arguing, etc.).

Compulsive issues. A lot of different things can become habit for a dog, and when you take an issue like humping, something that feels very good, this can quickly become a compulsive problem. A dog may become 'stuck' in a pattern of constant humping, unable to control their urges. When this occurs, humping may not even be pleasurable any longer; a dog may simply be acting on the compulsion drive and this can actually cause a dog to feel stress.

Health issues. Whenever a dog is paying particular attention to a certain body area, this can point to a health issue. What may appear to be humping may actually be a dog trying to scratch an itch or otherwise find relief for discomfort emanating from in or around the genital area. This may include urinary tract infections or allergies that are causing severely itchy skin.

Should You Stop a Dog from Humping? There are a few key points to keep in mind:

1. Humping can be due to a health issue (UTI, skin issues, allergies, etc.) and for this reason, humping should not be ignored. It is something to bring up to the vet during your next wellness check. And, of course, if there are any signs of illness, bring your dog to the vet right away. Signs of UTI include difficulty urinating, blood in the urine, cloudy or smelly urine, and/or incontinence. Symptoms of allergies include but are not limited to chewing at the paws, dry skin, hot spots of red irritated skin, possible breathing issues such as wheezing or coughing, and/or red, bloodshot eyes.

2. Humping can be due to stress and for this reason, it should not be ignored. An assessment of the household environment should be taken and if needed, steps taken to reduce anxiety.

3. Since this can become a compulsive habit for some dogs and not even pleasurable at that point, and excessive humping can be quite distracting and take time away from normal interaction, you may want to intervene.

4. Humping is not always welcomed by other dogs. So, if your dog tends to hump other dogs, this may not always end well. Another dog may become disturbed and act out in defense.

5. Finally, since a dog may hump against his human if he does not understand proper hierarchy, this as well is a reason to make some changes.

How to Help Stop a Dog From Humping Please note that the following is done AFTER a dog has been cleared of any possible health issues.

1) Spay/ neuter. While spayed and neutered dogs technically may still hump, it is rare. The decrease in hormones that occurs after the procedure usually leads to an abrupt stop in humping behavior. It is also considered an effective method to help a dog calm down in regard to trying to run away, not listening and other such behaviors. And of course, spaying and neutering can help a dog live a longer life by eliminating or reducing the chances of developing certain cancers.

2) Interrupt and re-focus. The key is that you must not only interrupt your dog but also offer something that will be seen as more pleasurable than the humping. Canines will always choose an action that brings about the most favorable outcome. For this reason, you will want to A) Distract with a loud noise (a clap, a shake of coins in a can, your firm voice, etc.) and then B) Offer something of value that is not food related (as food signals a reward). It is best to offer a new toy.

Note that this does not mean that you have to continually purchase new toys. It is always suggested to keep 2 toy bins so that a dog has a 'new' set every few weeks. This said, if your dog is due for some newer toys, you may want to obtain 3 or 4 tempting ones that are only used when addressing humping behavior.

3) Teach commands. A well-trained dog will stop what he is doing to obey a command such as 'Sit'. Give a reward for obeying and at this point a dog will often move on to other things.

4) Make sure your dog understand hierarchy. This is a major reason for so many different unwanted behaviors and it is always a good idea to follow rules not only so that your dog learns that you are leader, but is also reminded of that fact on a daily basis. While the full details are under 'Training: Teaching Proper Hierarchy', the basics of this is that you will want your dog to obey the 'Sit' command before any food is given (both meals and snacks) and that you will always be the first to enter or exit the household.

5) If your dog tends to hump against people, such as visitors to your home, you can try the distraction method. However, if this does not work, it may warrant a firm 'No', followed by a short 5 to 10-minute time-out in a gated-off area or canine playpen.

It will be important to not yell or otherwise act as if your dog did something truly terrible; but rather segregate him to stop the humping, allow him to 're-set', and then bring him back to the fray for interaction. If he humps again soon afterward, keep repeating until he learns that humping equals no fun and no attention from his human or the visitors.

6) With other dogs, sometimes play can start off just fine, but as it intensifies and escalates, it leads to humping. If your dog has a habit of mounting other dogs, be sure to always have your dog on leash and harnesses. It will be important to use a harness and not a collar, so that injury to the neck does not occur. On harness, you will lead him away, give a firm 'No', and give a for a 'time-out'.
While it does take many sessions of doing this, eventually the lesson will be learned that humping another dog means that all fun stops.

7) If you believe that your dog is humping due to stress, take every step possible to reduce stress and allow your dog to be relaxed, confident, and happy. Socialization training can be extremely helpful with this and well as taking steps to reduce separation anxiety, if applicable. See also: 'Behavioral Training: Socialization & Desensitization' and 'Situational Issues: Separation Anxiety'.

Hyper Behavior

When Does Hyper Puppy Behavior Calm Down? Puppies are bundles of pure energy and it is normal for them to have surges of high activity followed by periods of rest. A pup will scamper all over the house, pounce on toys, and act silly, only to crash and fall asleep without much warning.

There tends to be a leveling-out that occurs; as a pup grows a bit older he needs fewer and less frequent naps, but also has learned some restraint in how he acts when he is awake. In addition, as a puppy learns about his world, there is less that is 'new' and this can help calm him down as well. Expect to see some calmer behavior gradually beginning around the 6-month mark, and a much more noticeable difference by the 1-year mark.

Things That Can Make a Puppy or Dog Hyper

1) Encountering new elements. Every time that a dog comes into contact with, sees, or even hears something novel, this can trigger an inquisitive response. There may be jumping, barking, running around, and otherwise being on high alert as the answer to 'what is this?' is figured out.

2) A high energy household. Most often, a dog will act in a way that correlates to his environment. It is rare to find a mellow, calm dog in a loud chaotic household. In cases of older dogs acting hyper, typically the house has too much foot traffic, loud noises (arguing, blaring TV's, etc.), and other stimuli that is too overwhelming for the dog to relax and calm down.

3) Reliance on owners to provide entertainment. When a dog thinks that his only form of entertainment is to play with his owner, this can lead too much reliance on this interaction. Depending only on his human to bring about fun, a dog may act super-hyper in an almost begging sort of way... jumping up, barking, and essentially demanding attention.

4) Not enough healthy ways to release energy. When dogs are inside too much, they can suffer from the canine equivalent of cabin fever. This can happen if owners are gone at work all day and after arriving home are distracted by household obligations such as cleaning, cooking, and childcare. Other factors include weather-related issues such as rain or snow that limit how often a dog is taken out.

Rare, but possible: Hyperkinesis (hyperkinesia). With this, a dog will have clinical hyperactivity problems; however, this is exceedingly rare and owners should be on guard for misdiagnosis. Most dogs that do suffer from this have a high intolerance for any noises or activity and can be set off into a hyper state by seemingly mundane elements such as the noise of a dishwasher. They will also typically have a rapid heartbeat and heavy breathing even when at rest. If suspected, testing at a veterinary clinic for 2 to 3 days is generally done. The dog's heart rate and respiratory responses are monitored both at rest and while stimuli is introduced. If this is found to be the cause of exceedingly hyper behavior, medications can be given.

<u>How to Help a Hyper Dog Calm Down</u>
There are things that you can do that can lead to a calmer, more restrained dog.

1) Gradually expose your puppy or dog to all sorts of outside elements. Dogs that have not learned how to respond to stimuli may always respond in a negative way. Just about every element will be perceived as 'new' the first 20 or so times that it's encountered. After that, these elements eventually become a tad boring and will not elicit a major response.

The key is to do a slow and gradual introduction to the world. Short sessions are best, and this is built upon in both frequency and duration. A dog that is walked alongside traffic, sees other dogs, interacts with cats, hears birds and other woodland animals, sees a wide variety of people, and has his world expanded will have a better tolerance for these things. For more details regarding barking at elements while out on a walk, see 'Behavioral Training: Barking'.

2) Offer a peaceful vibe in the house. Dogs that do not feel safe in regard to their territory or their belongings can have a near constant unnerved feeling that can translate into acting oddly hyper. A dog's eating area should be in a quiet corner where no one walks by or otherwise makes him feel as if he is being encroached upon.

A resting and sleeping area, in a room that allows for seeing the family but not so close that a dog is bombarded with activity and noise, should be provided as well. Alternatively, do not have your dog in a spot that makes him feel too isolated; the stress of that can also alter behavior.

Toys should be kept in a bin and not played with by children in the house. These are a dog's prized possessions; if the toys are disturbed this can cause agitation.

3) Teach independent play. While playing with your dog is a very important part of care and helps create a strong bond between owner and dog, it's just not possible to spend every moment keeping your dog busy and entertained. A dog needs to learn how to keep himself occupied. Since options are limited with canine family members, the best method is to offer a good collection of a wide variety of toys. This should include chewers, treat-release, and interactive toys that will offer different playing experiences. See also: 'Care Items – Chihuahuas of All Ages: Toys'.

4) Meet exercise requirements. In just about all cases of hyper dogs, there is a need to increase daily exercise.

Exercise allows a dog to release pent-up energy. It gets the heart pumping, the blood flowing, and the muscles moving. In addition, taking walks outside allows a dog to put his canine senses to work. He uses his exceptional hearing to pick up noises that humans don't even notice. He uses his remarkable sense of smell to pick up scents that we are not even aware of. He is also taking in his surroundings.

When a walk is complete, a dog feels an inner satisfaction. The body has had a bit of a workout and canine senses were put to use. This alone often brings about a more relaxed, calmer state of well-being. Dogs that are regularly active in a controlled way are able to rest, focus on tasks at hand such as commands and toy interaction, and also sleep much better at night.

At a minimum, head out for two 20-minute walks per day, done at a pace that is brisk for your particular dog, and have a 20-minute session of fetch or other such activity that allows your dog to run around. If you are already meeting that requirement, up each walk by 10 minutes and add on an extra session of fetch or 10 minutes to the one session.

Unless there are severe weather conditions, do not allow cold temperatures or stormy skies to disrupt this schedule. Toy breeds do have a low tolerance for cold and/or wet weather; however, by placing the right outdoor gear on your dog (lined vest for the cold, water-resistant jacket for the rain) and paw wax (plus dress appropriately yourself as well), rain or snow does not need to be an obstacle.

Licking and/or Chewing at the Paws

Licking or chewing at the paws is a common issue seen with dogs, though one that many owners struggle over. The key to fixing this is to be very thorough in addressing all possible triggers and following every step to resolve them. The 3 steps are:

#1 Identify the trigger. Reasons can change over time. In addition, multiple triggers may be happening simultaneously. Go through every possible cause, taking note of those that could be applicable.
#2 Work to reduce or eliminate it. Unless the trigger is addressed, healing treatments can only work so much.
#3 Treat the paws. If the paws are dry, peeling, cracked, excessively itchy, have developed sores, or are otherwise damaged, there are treatments that can help. This includes an anti-itch spray and/or a soothing lotion or wax to stop irritation and repair any damage.

#1 Identify the Trigger and #2 Work to Reduce or Eliminate It

While you may have tried to figure this out in the past, it's prudent to take the time to work your way down the list. Reasons may have changed, or signs that point to certain causes may be more obvious than the last time you put effort into sleuthing this out. In addition, it is entirely possible that your dog is licking/chewing due to more than one reason. Note that each cause has multiple steps to resolving it, and each should be followed to the best of your ability.

Stress: While most paw licking or chewing can be traced to an irritant, some dogs compulsively lick their paws as a soothing mechanism to deal with stress. Unfortunately, this can lead to all sorts of damage, including open sores (referred to as lick granuloma or acral lick dermatitis). Triggers of stress include a wide range of issues including severe and long-lasting boredom, separation anxiety, a chaotic household, or changes in the family dynamic such as a new person or pet moving in, or the loss of a loved one.

Resolving this:

Dogs that are overly bored need to have two things: A fuller schedule and the means to keep themselves occupied.

Be sure to take your dog for at least 2, and perhaps 3 walks per day, and try to have a daily 20-minute session of interactional play such as fetch. Once a week, head out to explore, such as going to a new dog park or a visit to a pet supply store. Work on commands or play games together. If other family members are not very involved in spending time with your dog, now may be the time to remind them how rewarding it can be to brighten up a dog's day with some interaction.

That said, even the most loving, studious owners only have so much time in the day; and this is where certain toys can really help. Those that react to a dog's motion, speak, make funny sounds, or otherwise interact with a dog can be great ways to keep a dog busy. See also: 'Care Items - Chihuahuas of All Ages: Toys'.

Dogs that have separation anxiety can be helped in a multitude of ways, including creating a secure and safe 'den', playing calming music, using an interactive pet cam, offering interactive toys, and offering a companion toy. More details are in 'Situational Issues: Separation Anxiety'.

Dogs that are stressed due to commotion in the house will appreciate a calmer atmosphere, and for the times that that is not possible, a quiet corner to retreat to. Be sure that this is not too isolated, as that would cause stress as well. But, a bed that is away from foot traffic and loud noises is always appreciated.

Changes to the family take some time to get used to. With the addition of a new pet, try to give both animals their own private spaces for eating, resting, and sleeping. Supervise them to ensure there is no rough play. With the loss of a family member, time is the best cure. However, exploring different surroundings (the beach, a new 'easy' hike trail, etc.) to offer new sights, smells, and sounds, can help perk up a dog.

Once you have identified the trigger and have worked to resolve it, damaged paws many need topical treatments; See ahead for '#3 Treating Paw Issues'. Note that open sores (often moist with coat loss) will need to be treated by the veterinarian; an antibiotic gel is given and in severe cases, laser treatment. Stress that cannot be resolved by making changes may need to be treated with antidepressants and/or calming medications.

Environmental Issues:
Between walking on different surfaces (rough, coarse, rocky, grassy), paws need to stand up to a lot. When you add irritants to this (frozen ground and/or ice melt in the winter, heat in the summer, small pebbles, lawn chemicals, etc.) and weather-related aspects such as arid air, this can be a recipe for dry paws. And dry paws typically equals itchy paws. Note that if the paws are very dry, there may also be an all-over issue with dry skin.

Resolving this:

Work to resolve elements that cause damage and/or dryness:

- When walking your dog on surfaces that are new (for example, rocky paths), start with short sessions, and work your way up.
- Protect the paws against heat, cold, pebbles, ice, and other outdoor elements. This can be done by applying a quality paw wax. This is usually done once every 1 to 2 weeks, depending on how much outdoor walking a dog engages in.
- Encourage proper hydration; you'll want to keep the bowl clean, keep water cool and fresh, and bring along water for your dog to drink when out on walks.
- In the winter, when air typically lacks moisture, humidifiers can help combat dry skin.
- As always, use a top-quality shampoo with soothing ingredients like oatmeal and/or aloe that helps prevent dry skin.

Once you have identified this trigger and have worked to resolve it, damaged paws many need topical treatments; See ahead for '#3 Treating Paw Issues'.

Yeast Infection:
Some degree of yeast (fungi) is always present on a dog's skin. However, it can start to reproduce in greater than normal quantities, in certain areas, and under certain conditions. Yeast thrives in warm, dark, and moist areas, and this is why a yeast infection between a dog's toes is a common problem.

It may be that a dog starts to chew at his paws due to one reason (acute injury, stress, allergies, etc.), but then a yeast infection develops due to the paws being constantly moist from saliva. Alternatively, a yeast infection can be the single root cause of itching, having developed due to areas between the paw pads or between the toes staying moist after baths and/or becoming wet from walking outside.

Dogs with a lower immune system can be vulnerable to yeast infection. And, there is some thought that a diet containing sugars like honey or corn syrup and/or carbs (which are broken down into sugars) like potatoes or sweet potatoes may lend a role.

Signs: Itching, and subsequent licking, chewing, or biting at the paws may be the only sign. However, in many cases, and particularly once yeast has had time to multiply enough, there will be an odd smell. This may be a powerful corn chips odor or a sour, moldy, or musty smell. With severe yeast infection on the paws, skin sores can develop; these may be raised and/or crusty.

Resolving this:

1. Reassess kibble and snacks to see if they contain honey, high fructose corn syrup, or high amounts of potatoes or sweet potatoes.

2. Use anti-fungal products. This is a 2-step process: Give baths with a medicated anti-fungal shampoo and apply a medicated anti-fungal topical (spray or cream) to the area.

- *About the shampoo:* While just a topical may work, baths with antifungal medicated shampoos are an opportunity to soak every nook and cranny on the paws, and this can go a long way in curing things. Look for a quality shampoo with ketoconazole (typically 1%), which is one of the most effective antifungal medications for dogs. A ketoconazole shampoo may also contain chlorhexidine gluconate (typically 2%), which is an antibacterial. With this combination, a shampoo can resolve a wide range of skin infections.

  This is typically used twice per week. You'll want to massage this in well, and let it soak in for 10 minutes. Since symptoms can resolve before a fungal infection is completely gone, you may want to do one more bath after signs are no longer apparent.

- *About the topical spray or cream:* While baths with an antifungal shampoo will allow your dog's paws to get nice thorough soakings, another part of this is to offer daily, round-the-clock treatment. We recommend a spray since it is very easy to apply, and for dogs whose paws are sensitive, this allows a no-touch application. Look for one with 1% ketoconazole and 2% chlorhexidine gluconate, but also with soothing ingredients such as aloe which helps with itching and heals sore skin. Spray the paws 3 times per day, with 1 application at night right as your dog is falling asleep, and continue using this 5 to 7 days past the date that the paws seem to be back to normal. Note that this can resolve yeast infections on paws as quickly as 4 to 5 days.

  To stop this from being licked off, you'll want to prevent your dog from touching the paws for 1 hour as the product dries. You can use a 'recovery collar' or you can slip socks over the paws. With either, take these off after that first hour.

Note: Oral ketoconazole may be prescribed by the veterinarian, and is needed in cases of very stubborn yeast infections that do not respond to the topicals.

Allergies: At the root of many licking/chewing issues with the paws is food, environmental (seasonal), or contact allergies.

Signs: In some cases, itchy paws are the only symptom. In other cases, it is one of the first symptoms, with more to follow. And for other dogs, it is seen alongside other signs including rash, hot spots, dry skin, itchiness on other areas of the body, thinning fur (in places where a dog licks or chew at), wheezing, coughing, runny nose, and/or irritated eyes.

Resolving this: Work to reduce or eliminate allergens. There are tests (ELISA blood test or intradermal skin test) that can help to pinpoint triggers; but, these are not entirely reliable. With or without allergy testing, you'll want to clear the house and your dog of as many allergens as you can. Here are some quick tips:

1. Regularly vacuum the entire house (all flooring surfaces) with a vacuum cleaner that uses HEPA filtration.
2. Clean the air via a central air system with HEPA filters or using stand-alone air purifiers with HEPA filtration.
3. Wet-dust the house.
4. Wash all bedding, pillowcases, dog bed covers, etc. in hot water (at least 140° F).
5. Cover mattresses and pillows with mite-proof coverings.
6. Once the house is cleared, keep windows closed.
7. Have everyone remove their shoes upon entering the house.
8. Each time your dog enters back inside, wipe him down with hypo-allergenic grooming wipes and rinse the paws off in the sink.
9. On high pollen days, avoid taking your dog out during the middle part of the day when pollen is at its peak.
10. Feed 100% all-natural kibble and snacks that have ZERO grains, corn, soy, wheat, chemical preservatives, artificial flavoring, or by-products.
11. Do not use plastic bowls.

You may also wish to refer to 'Health - Other: Allergies', for all details.

Once you have identified the trigger and have worked to resolve it, damaged paws many need topical treatments; See next for "#3 Treating Paw Issues'.

#3 Treating Paw Issues

Treatments for paw issues will work best when used concurrently with resolving the underlying causes. If the trigger(s) of a paw problem (allergies, etc.) is not fixed, results with these remedies will be limited, as you will be fighting an uphill battle. Let's see what can help, depending on precisely what is happening:

Paw wax. A quality paw wax can do quite a bit. It will protect the paws from heat, cold, snowballing, rough surfaces, and drying. It can also help heal overly dry paws. A good one will create a protective barrier while allowing the paws to breathe, and contain ingredients that will moisturize and help heal minor problems.

For prevention of paw issues, apply this every 7 days between the pads and between the toes (a Q-tip can help with that). For healing minor issues, apply this up to once per day. See next for moderate to severe issues.

Healing cream. To treat excessively dry paws, peeling, irritation, and/or minor to moderate cracking, a restorative cream is a good option. Look for ingredients that will be absorbed into the skin, soothe, and prompt regeneration of skin cells. This includes aloe vera, manuka honey, coconut oil, olive oil, hemp seed oil, shea butter, certain blue-green algae, and vitamin blends (A, B, C, and/or E). This can be massaged into the paws 1 to 2 times per day, and you may see results in as little as 3 days.

Anti-itch spray. For itchy paws, you can offer immediate relief with an effective anti-itch spray. Since licking or biting is a major problem as well, we recommend an all-natural spray that is non-toxic. Ingredients that can relieve itching right away include colloidal oatmeal, baking soda, and wheat germ. The spray should also contain certain vitamin, such as A, B, C, and/or E.

If the paws are in *terribly* bad shape, and itching is to the point of painful, consider opting for a medicated spray with hydrocortisone (for itch and inflammation) and lidocaine (numbing agent for discomfort). However, do note that you will then need to slip a sock over the paws(s) or place a recovery collar on your dog so that he cannot lick the applied spray.

 Since pet care products such as waxes, creams, and sprays are always evolving, yet this book is static, current recommendations can be found on the Supplies page of the PetChiDog site. You can reach this by entering any page of PetChiDog.com; look to the navigation which is in alphabetical order, and choose 'Supplies'.

When to See the Veterinarian

If you've followed all of the guidelines here but still cannot pinpoint the reason for your puppy or dog's paw issues, if you've tried all available treatments but there is no improvement, or if there is severe cracking and particularly if there is bleeding and/or pus-like discharge, a veterinarian visit will be warranted to check for underlying health issues and prescribed medication, including antibiotics.

Nipping

There are very few things more frustrating than when a cute and adorable puppy nips. Whether or not it breaks the skin, this very serious behavior needs to be addressed in a serious way.

Young nipping behavior and reactions: Nipping behavior often begins when a puppy is very young and playing with his littermates; it is part of normal play. If a puppy nips too much or too hard, the 'victim' lets out a loud yelp. If the nip was strong enough, the puppy that was bitten will ignore the offender. In some cases, the dam will also exclude the offender for a while as well.

This works to a great extent because of how canines automatically process things. To canines, they live in a pack. The pack has a leader, the 'Alpha'. While you will be your pup's leader once he is in your home, it is the dam who is the leader when the pup is young. When the pack (siblings) and sometimes the leader (dam) ignores him - essentially banishing him - he quickly learns that it was wrong to nip.

The banishment is temporary of course, and after a few minutes, he is allowed back in to play. If he nips too hard again, he is banished again, and it continues this way until he learns that nipping simply will not be tolerated.

The transitional phase: When a puppy transitions from his old home (dam and littermates) and moves to his new home, his 'pack' changes. However, it takes him a little while to figure this out. Usually, if you are housebreaking your pup, teaching commands, and making it clear that you are the one giving him food, in a few weeks, he learns that you are the leader. Pups often see other adult humans as leaders too. Young children may be seen as equals in the 'pack'; this is one reason why a puppy may nip at a child, but not an adult.

Reacting to nipping: You will want to teach your puppy to stop nipping in the same way that he learned before. Therefore, if he nips and his 'pack' ignores him and temporarily banishes him - or more specifically the leader of the pack (you) does so, he will get the message loud and clear. Here are some methods to send the message that it is not acceptable (note that if nipping is done in a very aggressive way, you'll want to refer to 'Behavioral Issues: Aggression').

1) Say 'No' loudly and firmly.

2) Immediately move into a position of authority. If you were both sitting on the sofa, place your puppy on the floor. If you were both sitting on the floor, immediately rise and either sit on the sofa or stand. The idea is to show that you are the leader and the one in charge by being physically superior.

3) Temporary banishment. This can be done with the pup free in the room. However, if the pup is hyper and threatening more nips, place him in his pen or behind a gate as a 'time-out'.

For this, you must 100%, absolutely and without wavering, completely and utterly ignore the puppy. Any other humans in the house must join in as well because he won't learn a thing if he nips at you, but can move on to play and interact with another human. This type of ignoring must be *very* clear. Everyone must behave as if the puppy is invisible. No speaking (it's suggested to not even speak with other people, in case the puppy thinks you are speaking to him), no looking at him…nothing.

4) It will take a puppy anywhere from 1 to 10 minutes to actually understand that he is being temporarily 'banished'. When he realizes it, he will become a bit nervous. He may whine for attention, bark, and/or pace around. *Only then* will you know that it is working.

5) After a full 5 minutes of time in which the pup *knows* he is being ignored, speak to him but do not pick him up.

6) After a minute or so, only if he does not try to nip again, return to the exact same positioning as you both were when the first nip occurred. For example, both on the floor or the sofa, etc.

7) Do not act overly happy, but interact as you were before the nip. Only if he does not nip again, rev things up a notch by petting him and offering words of praise.

8) If at any time he nips again, immediately start over by giving a sharp 'No', physically positioning yourself higher and giving temporary banishment (steps 1, 2, and 3).

9) Most puppies need to have this done 4 to 5 times to fully understand that banishment happens due to nipping.

Note: For maximum results, be sure that your puppy sees you as the leader. For details, refer to 'Training: Teaching Proper Hierarchy'. And again, for very aggressive nipping, look to 'Behavioral Issues: Aggression'.

Rolling in Feces

Why Dogs Roll in Poop: This is a common, long-established canine behavior. Yet, there are only theories about why dogs do this. While some reasons may hold more weight than others, none of these can be completely ruled out, as they all make sense in some way, at least to dogs.

Reasons for rolling in the feces of other dogs may include:

1. To mask their own scent. Taking steps to mask scent is linked to a dog's 'pack' behavior. And, while it may seem as if this might only apply to large breeds, all breeds are dictated by canine rules. To say that any toy dog, inside dog, or lap dog will not behave in *any* canine way is essentially saying that they are not a canine. So, this is something that has to remain on the table as a possibility.

Rolling in the feces of other animals *is* a valid method of a dog masking his scent, and this has benefits (at least in regard to pack mentality) of not announcing a dog's presence to prey and to bring the scent of the prey back to the pack.

2. To mark the poop with their own scent. While this may seem like a bit of a reach, some animal behavioral experts suggest that a dog may roll in the feces of another dog or animal to leave their scent on it and override the existing scent. If a dog does this within the yard, this may be a way of claiming territory.

A Reason for rolling in their own feces may be:

Self-advertising. All dogs have a 'calling card'. Their scent glands (anal glands) hold a fluid that via chemical process lets other dogs know their gender, health status, mood, and level of interest to interact.

Some dogs, and particularly intact dogs with strong mating urges, may feel that they want to advertise themselves in a stronger way than just their scent glands. One way to do this is to roll in their own feces, thus spreading their scent over their entire body.

Reasons for rolling in any sort of feces may include:

1. The dog is fascinated with the smell. While this is a common theory, it can be off-putting to owners who put time and effort into keeping their puppy or dog nice and tidy. The coat is healthy, hairs are soft and shiny, there's a nice fresh fragrance. Why on earth would your dog ruin that by thinking that poop smells better than the cherry blossom or warm vanilla cookie coat spray that you've spritzed on?

Well, it is suggested that this all correlates to a dog's incredible sense of smell. While we humans rely mainly on our sense of sight, sense of smell is a dog's top focus. Canines have 250 to 300 million olfactory receptors in their noses, compared to our 5 to 6 million. For this reason, dogs are captivated by all sorts of smells. They interpret scents and odors in ways that we cannot even imagine.

2. It feels good. This seems odd but is an accepted suggestion. And, while pressing the body into both feces and grass could, hypothetically, feel good to a dog, this may actually not be related to the poop. A dog may enjoy lying down on grass and wiggling around on it. If there are feces on the grass, getting it on the coat may just be an unfortunate consequence of enjoying a nice 'grass massage'.

3. Attention seeking mechanism. What do you do when your pup rolls in poop? Do you let out an 'Oh my Gosh!' and rush over? Most likely. Do you hover over your dog to inspect just how bad the damage is?

Probably. And then, do you make a nice bubbly bath and clean your puppy or dog all off? We hope so. And while those are all expected reactions, and the bath is a required one, they all have one thing in common: The dog gets tons of attention! What dog doesn't want that?

How to Stop a Dog from Rolling in Poop: Since the reasons for rolling in feces can vary, address as many of these that are applicable.

1. Spray or neuter. To owners who had not considered having this done, it may seem like an extreme measure; however, there are many benefits to having a dog fixed, including overall better behavior (less marking, trying to run away, better listening skills, etc.) and health benefits including decreased risks of some types of cancer.

2. Stay calm, if it happens. Though against human instinct, try to remain calm. If your dog rolls in feces due to the heaps of attention that comes along with it, do not allow this goal to be achieved.

3. Keep the yard clean. Cleaning up poop in the yard prevents people from inadvertently stepping in poop, keeps flies away, and of course, foils a dog's plan to roll in any piles of it. Just as you pick up your dog's poop while at the park or during walks in the neighborhood, do this at home. Attaching a poo bag container to your dog's leash helps make this convenient.

4. Supervise. For reasons including reinforcing housebreaking lessons and limiting danger, toy breed dogs should always be supervised when outside in the yard. Keep your dog on leash and harness (not collar). Take your place as leader, and control where your dog walks and what he does. At the first motion of sniffing a poop pile, interrupt by saying your dog's name, then redirect focus elsewhere.

5. For rolling in poop while you're not home: *1) Work to create an engaging environment.* These steps help with separation anxiety as well.

- Have lots of interactive toys for staying busy and focused. This may include those that speak in response to being nosed, those with crinkle paper inside, and/or squeaker toys.

- Leave on a TV (some cable providers offer channels specifically for dogs to enjoy) or have music playing.

- Offer a treat-release toy. Often, a mixture of dry kibble and 100% all-natural smooth peanut butter makes this type of toy tempting. Use one that lets you adjust the difficulty level for an inviting challenge.

2) Adjust breakfast time. Generally, when a dog eats, this will trigger a bowel movement a certain amount of time later. If you can move breakfast time up by an hour, this can result in your dog having a bowel movement an hour later than usual. In other words, a smaller time window for the poop to be deposited and then rolled in while you are not home.

Running Away

Most attempts to take off are due to strong canine instincts; so, never take this personally. The key to fixing this issue is to help a dog with canine urges to run and, remove as many opportunities as possible.

Help a dog with canine urges to run:

Spay or neuter. Many dogs that run are running *to something*, not away from something. And for intact dogs, this 'something' is often another dog of the opposite gender or even the possibility of another dog. Both intact males and females can, and often do, have strong mating urges. Intact males can act on this urge at any time. Intact females act on this urge during the heat cycle. For this reason, having your dog spayed or neutered can significantly resolve the issue.

Increase exercise and activity. Dogs can become very restless and/or have quite severe cases of 'cabin fever' if they do not get outside enough. They can be both physically and emotionally frustrated, feeling trapped and confined, with increasingly strong urges to be outdoors. These dogs, just barely holding themselves together, will often try to run off at the first opportunity. And that is usually when the front door opens. Who can blame them?

For this reason, be sure to meet the minimum exercise requirements of two 20-minute walks and a 20-minute session of fetch or other cardio each day. And, if your dog is already meeting these requirements, add an extra 20-minute walk (for a total of 3) or increase walking and/or cardio session duration by 10 minutes each.

Remove the opportunities: If dogs were allowed to be free off leash and able to do whatever they wished, all owners would be in big trouble. Part of responsible pet ownership is putting in an effort to control and supervise your dog. With dogs that try to run off, you'll need to be extra diligent:

- The leash should never come off when outside.
- Even family members should ring the bell or knock, so someone can either place the dog in his playpen or hold onto him.
- If your dog is home alone and tries to dash out of the house when you come home, do not allow him to have free reign in the house. Use a playpen or gate off a room.

How to Bring Back a Dog that Ran Off: Hopefully, you will follow the aforementioned guidelines, thus resulting in your dog never running off. However, should this happen, there are some ways to bring a dog back in:

- Strongly and with the conviction of leadership, order a 'Sit!'. Do not screech it, even if you are terribly worried that your dog is in danger, as a screech does not offer as much authority as a deep, serious command. And, if you yell out 'No!', your dog may keep running; some dogs do not want to stop and face the consequences of doing something wrong. But, a loud and firm 'Sit!' that instantly reminds a dog of learned commands, may cause him to take pause.
- The moment that your dog hesitates, change your voice to a friendly, playful tone. The goal is to have your dog chase after you, not the other way around. You'll encourage a chase with a teasing, "Bella, can you get me? Try to get meeeee!" while dancing in place and jogging slightly away. If your dog takes the bait, jog slowly, circling a bit to make it engaging. When your dog finally 'catches' you, swoop him up.
- Never scold your dog for coming back to you. After all, running was due to instinct but your dog reigned that all in to listen to you and return.

Shaking or Trembling

It may be common for Chihuahuas to shake; but, this does not mean that it's a 'normal' event that should not be addressed.

Top 3 Reasons for Shaking without Other Symptoms:

1. Being cold. This may sound too simple; however, it is one of the most common reasons. Fat works as an insulator and muscle helps generates body heat; the Chihuahua has a low percentage of each. **How to Help**:

1) When it's cold outside, check your dog's normal resting areas for any drafts.

2) In the winter, if the core body is keep warm and dry, a dog will handle the cold much better. Place a sweater, vest, sweatshirt, or jacket on your dog.

3) During the summer, ensure that cool air from an AC is not directly focused on your dog.

4) Keep the house above 68°F (20°C). Many Chihuahuas feel most comfortable with a room temperature of at least 72°F (20 and 22°C).

5) Do not let your dog rest or sleep on the floor; a quality bed offers proper support as well as providing warmth. And, for dogs with low tolerance to the cold, a self-warming bed may be best.

6) Layer baby blankets on your dog's bed.

7) If the shaking continues, you will want to have your dog evaluated for other possible causes.

2. Stress or high levels of emotion. Feeling anxious, nervous, fearful, or overly stressed can cause a dog to shake. Also, a sudden rush of emotion can cause shaking; this can include anticipating a meal (particularly if dinnertime is running late), or even in anticipation of being brought outside.

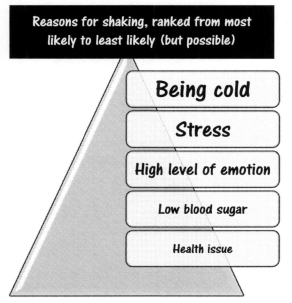

Reasons for shaking, ranked from most likely to least likely (but possible)

- Being cold
- Stress
- High level of emotion
- Low blood sugar
- Health issue

How to Help:

1) Work to evaluate the exact trigger of any stress, and take appropriate steps. See also 'Behavioral Training: Socialization & Desensitization'.

2) Keep a schedule for meals and daily walks.

3) If the shaking continues, you will want to have your dog evaluated for other possible causes.

3. Low blood sugar (hypoglycemia). This is seen much more often with puppies than it is with adults; however, it can happen to a dog of any age. Other signs include weakness, trouble walking, and confusion. This can be triggered by not eating frequently enough, though stress may play a role as well. Minor cases may be remedied by rubbing a dab of honey onto the pup's gums. And, this can be prevented, in part, by ensuring a pup eats small yet frequent meals and snacks. See also: 'Health – Other: Hypoglycemia'.

Other Less Common Reasons for Shaking: If shaking continues and the listed remedies do not resolve the issue, there are other less common health issues to consider. A wide range of illness from distemper to liver disease can cause shaking, typically along with other symptoms including, but not limited to changes in weight, changes in appetite, coughing, wheezing, weakness, fever, eye or nasal discharge, excessive sleeping, and/or restlessness. In rare cases, shaking may be due to seizures. If you suspect any health issues at all, do not delay seeking veterinary assistance.

Sleep

How Much Sleep is Normal:

Newborns. Newborn puppies, from 1-day-old to 3-weeks-old, sleep just about all of the time, up to 22 hours per day. They will mainly only be awake to nurse. The age of 3-weeks-old is a huge turning point; at this time both hearing and vision are working well and with this comes a new-found curiosity. A heightened interest in exploring his world and for playing with siblings will cause a pup to stay awake a bit longer now. From 3 weeks to 8 weeks, a puppy will sleep anywhere from 20 to 21 hours per day.

Puppies. The first few months in a new home, age 2-months-old to 5-months-old, a puppy will sleep from 18 to 20 hours per day; this includes both nighttime sleep and naps. A puppy may be so interested in his world, that he struggles to stay awake. A pup may zonk out in the middle of playing, or even eating, resting his head on the rim of the bowl because he just couldn't make it to his bed. Each month that a pup matures, he will sleep a bit less and stay awake for longer periods. By the age of 6-months-old, puppies are close to the sleeping schedule of adults.

Adults. Adults sleep roughly 12 to 14 hours per day; this includes both nighttime sleep and naps. This may seem like a lot (especially when compared to how much we get); however, most of this will be done during the night. When you subtract 8 or 9 hours of nighttime snoozing from 13 average hours of sleep, this leaves 4 to 5 hours of on-and-off-again naps. The amount of naps an adult takes depends in part on whether or not he gets more or less of those 8 to 9 hours, and most will shadow what their owners do. Dogs that are overly bored will take more naps than they would if they had activities to keep them busy.

Seniors. As a dog ages, there are many changes: decreased metabolism, joint issues, and/or muscle loss that leads to reduced activity, etc., and the more time a dog has to rest, the more he may nap. In addition, the production of melatonin (which regulates sleeping patterns) slows as a dog ages; this can lead to disrupted sleep at night, thus more naps during the day. Having trouble getting comfortable due to osteoarthritis can cause issues with sleeping as well. Generally, each year after age 8 brings another 20 to 30 minutes per day of sleep. You may not notice this right away, but as the years pass, this adds up.

When a Puppy or Dog Has Trouble Sleeping:

Puppies can take a while to accept their schedule; many may seem downright nocturnal. It can take a couple of months for a pup to understand the cues of a day winding down, and overcome feelings of isolation that may cause him to stay awake whining or barking. Also see 'Behavioral Training: Barking', for barking at night issues.

For seniors, be sure to stick with twice-per-year geriatric vet visits to reevaluate treatment for osteoarthritis and other possible issues. There may be a need to change dosing for joint supplements or other medications. See also: 'Feeding and Nutrition: Supplements'.

For dogs of all ages, there are some elements that can help provide a good night's sleep:

Quality of the bed. The right supportive mattress can help a dog settle down, stay warm, and provide the right cushioning for the body. Even if you've already obtained an excellent bed, it may be time to reassess it. Beds don't last more than 4 years or so; cushions will lose buoyancy and won't be as supportive as they once were. A puppy may be outgrowing his smaller bed, and seniors may need a better orthopedic mattress than when they were younger.

Location. While it is a good idea to give your dog his own space, especially if you want him to get used to that area for when home alone, it should be in a quiet corner of a normally active room, and not isolated away.

Drafts. What may have been a good sleeping area in the summer may not be good in the winter and vice versa. Drafts from cold weather or cold spots due to AC's may cause interrupted sleep.

Exercise. There's a balance that must be achieved. You'll want to be sure that your dog meets daily exercise requirements; this helps prompt better sleep at night. However, exercise too close to sleepy-time can cause a dog to have trouble settling down. It's often best to have the last walk of the day 2 to 3 hours before intended bedtime.

Cues. It's difficult for a dog to go from fully alert to deep asleep without cues to let him know that the day is coming to a close. About one hour before intended bedtime, start to dim lights and lower noise levels.

Melatonin; given with care. It is vital for all possible health issues to be ruled out first. Then, to also incorporate all of the previously listed suggestions. At that point, if a dog has insomnia for unknown reasons, you may wish to speak to your vet about offering melatonin. Melatonin is produced by the body at night and works to regulate sleep patterns. While low melatonin levels are seen mostly with senior dogs, a melatonin supplement can work as a sleep aid for dogs 1 year and up.

It can sometimes interfere with medications, so you'll want your vet to give you the 'okay' for this. Dosing for dogs under 10 pounds is 1 mg per day, given at night. There is typically no difference between melatonin packaged for humans and those packaged for pets, though there can be a huge difference in quality. Be sure to obtain just melatonin and not one that has Valerian root or any other additions. Nature's Bounty is a reliable brand and offers 1 mg tablets.

Reasons a Dog May Sleep Too Much: Dogs will vary the amount of time that they sleep by an hour or so, and this small change is not typically a concern. However, if there is a marked increase in sleep, this warrants taking a closer look. Possible reasons include:

Mimicking. Even if you don't sleep much, if you spend a lot of time watching TV or zoning out with video games, etc. your dog may take that as a sign that it's time to stop all activity and rest. After all, very few dogs will run around and stay super-active if the owner is plopped on the sofa.

Lack of Stimulation. If a dog has nothing better to do, he'll often do one of two things: get restless (pacing, barking) or get tired. Dogs need interaction, challenges, sights to see, and scents to smell. Reassess things to see if you can add some sessions of fetch, work on commands, or head out together to explore new settings.

Illness or Injury. A sudden and drastic increase in sleep is a red flag that there may be a health condition. If you suspect this, contact your veterinarian as soon as possible.

Should my dog sleep in my bed? This is tempting; after all, it's so nice to cuddle up; what could it hurt? Well, there *are* some things to consider:

- If a dog sleeps in his owner's bed, he may have trouble getting used to his area that he's placed into during the day if home alone.
- Toy sized dogs can be inadvertently rolled over and/or fall off of the bed.
- If your dog is having any behavioral issues in which part of the resolution is to instill proper hierarchy (the human is the leader), allowing a dog to sleep in the bed works against this.
- Once you let a dog sleep in your bed, it can be challenging to reverse the decision.

Situational Issues

Afraid of Other Dogs

The Chihuahua breed, in general, gets along well with other canines. As seen in 'About the Chihuahua: PetChiDog's Chihuahua Survey', only 8% of owners checked off 'Getting along with other dogs outside the house' as an issue seen with their puppy or dog, and for all elements, 9% of owners reported that their Chihuahua has trouble with being scared or nervous.

This said, if you're reading this section, chances are that your dog is among those that need some help in this regard.

Please note that if your Chihuahua simply barks at other dogs, you may find the 'Barking While Being Walked' section under 'Behavioral Training: Barking' to be of help. This section will cover fear of other dogs, which makes socializing with them nearly impossible. This can affect many things; most typically this will be issues with daily walks and outings to public places.

Some Things to Keep in Mind:

#1 While there are methods of improving a dog's confidence in greeting other dogs, a dog may always have a fear of certain types of dogs. A toy breed may learn to do well with other toy breeds, or even medium breeds, but his limit may be large breeds. Dogs are able to sense when another dog does not make a good playmate, so refusal to interact with much larger dogs is not necessarily a bad thing; in some instances, a small dog's fear of a large breed may be justified.

#2 Throughout training and beyond, never push your dog to do anything. Dogs do best when training is done in short increments. To work, a dog needs to believe that it's his idea to become a bit braver, and therefore, it must be his decision to learn to say hello or interact in any way. No one (canine or human) can truly learn to have courage if forced into a situation to 'deal with it'. When the decision to do something is voluntary, there is a foundation of determination and intent.

#3 Never act upset at if your dog displays fear. Fear is an uncontrollable and powerful emotion whether or not it makes sense to you. Any sort of scolding or even a 'bad' vibe from you can make your dog feel worse.

Prep to Do Before Training: There are a few things to have in place before you begin:

#1 Establish Proper Hierarchy. As with any sort of training, you'll want your dog to view you as his leader. If so, he will feel more secure and be better able to take cues. As to not repeat text, please refer to 'Training: Teaching Proper Hierarchy'.

#2 Your dog should know the 'Sit' command very well. Many types of training require a dog to obey a 'Sit'. If your dog does not yet have this mastered, work on this first. You may wish to refer to 'Training: Command Training'.

#3 While you are working on training, it is best to avoid other instances of running into other dogs, such as on walks or at parks. For now, avoid areas that typically have dogs, and if possible, adjust your walking route.

#4 Prepare to do this with your dog on a short leash and a harness. A harness is always recommended; but, especially for this, there may be instances when you want to be able to quickly pull your dog to you without causing possible injury to the neck.

#5 Have training treats. These should be small, extra tasty, moist, and something that is reserved just for training.

#6 You will need to enlist the help of someone (friend, family member, neighbor, etc.) that has a dog with a proven history of getting along well with other dogs. This is best done with another dog of the same breed or at least the same size.

Training:

The idea is to offer safe short sessions in which your dog will be in the presence of another, but without forcing interaction.

Enough short sessions without bad experiences will allow for longer more frequent sessions. When a dog has enough accumulated good experiences, he may be ready for interaction, and for some, even playtime.

#1 Initial sessions should take place outside in your yard or another quiet area. If done inside, your dog may feel that the other dog is invading his space and territory, which can make things worse.

#2 With training treats in your pocket and BOTH dogs on leash, casually walk to the meeting area. Plan to arrive first.

#3 Upon arriving, order a 'Sit'. When your dog obeys, give praise (Good dog) and a training treat.

#4 When your helper walks up with his dog, do not tense up. Your dog will sense that. Speak in a matter-of-fact manner. Ignore any attempts to cling to your leg.

#5 After greeting your helper, crouch down for a moment to the other dog's level to pet him and say hello. This will show your dog that you are accepting the other and that you do not see him as a threat.

#6 Allow your dog to rise if the other dog initiates the typical canine greeting of sniffing each other.

#7 Your goal, for now, is to chat with your helper, while your dog is simply in the presence of the other dog. If your dog wants to curl up near your foot, whine, tug at your ankle, etc., ignore it and converse with your helper in a casual, upbeat manner. Chat for 5 to 10 minutes, thank your helper, and leave. As you are turning to walk your dog back, give praise (Good dog) and another training treat.

#8 Consider this a success, no matter the extent of nervous behavior. You have just completed the 1st of many planned, short, and as stress-free as possible exposures to other dogs. On the 15th, or perhaps on the 30th session, your dog will have had enough exposures that he'll learn it's not so bad after all. He may even start to interact; that will be the final goal. This is something you cannot force; it must be your dog's idea.

#9 Over the course of the following weeks, have as many sessions as possible (up to twice per day). When your dog shows improved behavior, up the sessions by 5 minutes. If your dog does not show any signs of improvement, it may be time to bring in a professional canine trainer for one-on-one coaching.

Having a Chihuahua and a Cat

For this sort of mixed pet household, size is a plus. Unlike quite a few other dog breeds, many Chihuahuas will be the same size or slightly smaller than many cats. As seen under 'About the Chihuahua: PetChiDog's Chihuahua Survey', 46% of adult Chihuahuas were 6 lbs. or under and 54% were 6.5 lbs. and up. The typical house cat is 8 to 10 lbs. This is beneficial and can lead to both pets getting along nicely.

That said, there are some general guidelines to know and some elements to keep in mind, if you'd like to have both a cat and a Chihuahua living together in the same house.

Before Mixing the Two Pets:

With your dog: If your dog barks at or shows intolerance toward cats, you'll want to think twice about bringing a feline into the house. If on the other hand, your dog shows curiosity or even indifference, this is a good sign.

With that in place, be sure of your ability to control your dog with commands. Should there be any moments of tension or instances where you need to step in, all basic commands of Sit, Stay, Down, Come, and Heel will be invaluable. Work with your dog until all of these commands are down pat before proceeding. If you have a friend, neighbor, or friend that owns a cat, ask for them to visit with their pet to test your dog's ability to follow commands when the distraction of a cat is present.

With a cat: If your plan is to rescue one from a shelter, you'll want to inquire about the cat's history of living with dogs. Even so, before making a commitment to bring her home, you will want to allow the cat to smell something that has the scent of your dog on it. A blanket or small pillow are two items that hold in scents quite well and can easily be taken to the shelter or other location where the cat currently is. Some cats, just upon smelling a dog, will hiss and this is a red flag. Indifference is the behavior that you'll want to look for.

Introducing the Two Pets: There are some things that you can do to make the transition a bit easier, though it should be pointed out that when two different animals meet, behavior cannot be fully predicted. For this reason, both pets need to be supervised until you are more than satisfied that there will not be any problems.

The main element is to make the introduction a gradual one. In fact, each pet should be slowly made aware of the other before they even meet face-to-face.

Here are some tips:

1. Whichever pet is the established one should be cordoned off into a room while the new pet is brought into the house. If you will be confining your dog, be sure not to give the impression that it is some sort of punishment and if needed, have one family member stay with the dog to keep him company. If that is not possible, be sure to give him a new toy (or two), a snack, and water to stay happy and occupied.

The new pet should be brought in and taken throughout the house for a good 20 to 30 minutes, being led to locations that the first pet has left scents, such as playing and sleeping areas. After this time, do the reverse and allow the established pet to smell the scents that the newer one has just left as he/she explored.

2. Once this is complete, if both have acted calm during their investigations, with the dog on leash, introduce them to each other. Be sure that this happens in a spot that the cat can escape if needed. Cats do not like to be cornered and if she gets spooked, you'll want her to be able to climb her post or jump free to feel safe.

While it would be great if they immediately acted like best friends, this may not happen. Interest is normal and indifference is just fine. When two animals act as if the other does not exist, this is a good sign that neither sees the other as a threat. Do keep in mind that this may be fleeting; once they figure out that the other is there to stay, feelings may change so you'll want to keep an eye on them until behavior has been established.

Tips for Helping a Dog and Cat Get Along: It takes 2 to 3 weeks to truly know how any one cat and any certain dog will get along. These tips can help facilitate this:

1. Never force interaction. Animals need to approach, interact, and retreat as they wish. Placing both in the same room to force them to learn to like each other is a sure way to increase tension.

2. Maintain separate areas. It may very well turn out that your dog and your cat become best friends, always wanting to be near each other, and even sleeping together. And, there can be plenty of 'family times' when both pets roam around and pass by each other. However, at all times, each should have their own spot to retreat to, should they wish to have some space. This is especially important for times that you will not be at home.

In regard to food, you'll want to make sure that your dog does not eat the cat's food. Most cat food contains a much higher percentage of protein and different levels of fat than dog food; for this reason, many dogs are attracted to it. While eating a little bit is not a reason for concern, long-term consumption can cause all sorts of issues including diarrhea and upset stomach.

Beware of a dog getting into a cat's catnip. While catnip acts as a stimulant to felines, it has the opposite effect on canines; it can work as a sedative. It can also cause a dog to lose water, as it acts as a diuretic, and finally, it can cause moderate to severe stomach upset.

Until the two are getting along very well, try to have them eat meals at separate times; this is because simultaneous eating, initially, can be interrupted as a high-stress event where one or both pets feels as if their food is under threat from the other.

With the litter box, keep this out of your dog's reach. If given a chance, a dog may ingest cat feces. One way to avoid this happening is to place the litter box where a dog cannot reach it. The top of the washer/dryer is often a popular choice.

For sleeping, until you know if the two will tolerate each other, it is best if the cat can jump up to her sleeping area and out of the way of the dog. If the cat has a small scratching post that can be placed up high, this would be advantageous as well.

3. If things seem to be going well, after a week or two, you can try to have both pets eat at the same time. Eating a meal together tends to create a close bond with animals and over time will help establish the idea that they are both members of the same 'pack' (household). It is best to start with the cat's food still up on the counter, but with both pets called in at the same time.

4. Give your dog praise when getting along nicely with the cat. You may think that praise is not needed for 'expected behavior'; however, if your dog behaves nicely, letting him know that you're happy about it can only be beneficial. Our canine family members need to hear that they are doing a great job and behaving well, not just when being trained, but throughout their lives.

If Your Dog and Your Cat Do Not Get Along:

Serious problems - After the initial 2 to 3-week phase in which the animals are gradually getting accustomed to each other, if there are serious issues of chasing and fighting and certainly if either receives any injuries, this is a huge red flag that the two will not get along.

While most Chihuahuas do okay with cats, there are always going to be some instances where it just does not work out. Of course, it is best if you plan for this rare but possible circumstance in which the only answer is, unfortunately, to keep them separate at all times or to find a new home for one of them.

Minor problems - It is not uncommon for a dog and cat to play well but then one tires of the other while one is still going strong. There can also be issues when there are significant age differences and a senior animal does not have the tolerance for lots of hyper play from a young one.

If your dog is really bothering the cat or the two are starting to fight, you'll want to give a stern 'no' and separate them, giving each a 'time out' from each other. While this temporarily fixes the problem, when this is done each time, over time, it can lead to a clear understanding of what will and will not be tolerated.

If the cat tries to scratch at your dog, a product such as Soft Claws can help. These are small plastic hollow caps that fit over a cat's claws. They are the feline equivalent of human glue-on nails if you will, yet with the purpose of stopping destructive scratching. They are considered humane, are said to be very tolerable, and are not as sharp as the claws that they are covering. These can be applied at home, come in an array of colors, and last up to 8 weeks.

Having More than One Dog

You may be thinking about bringing another puppy or dog into your family, and in most cases, this works out very well. Lots of dogs appreciate having a playmate. And, for many owners, the more the merrier; having multiple dogs and a 'full house' offers lots of extra love.

But, there can be a period of adjustment as well as some common hiccups.

<u>Are You Ready for the Commitment?</u> If you're only thinking about adding another dog to your family, be sure that you are prepared for this. First, there is the time aspect. While some things can happen simultaneously, such as going for walks, other care tasks like giving baths, trimming nails, and brushing the coat means double the work. Then, there is always the element of money. Two dogs means twice as much food, care products like shampoo, heartworm protection, dental treats, and of course vet visits.

<u>The Element of Hierarchy Among the Dogs</u>: As we've covered several times throughout this book so far, hierarchy is the status and ranking order of every member of the household, both humans and pets.

To dogs, the order of hierarchy is very clear: Within the den (house) lives the pack (all humans and animals), and that pack has a leader (the Alpha). Everyone under the leader is a follower (Beta) since they follow the leader's commands. Yet, in households with multiple dogs, among the subset of dogs, there is *also* a leader: The Alpha Dog. He or she is the boss of the dogs and sets the tone and pace for them.

When a new dog enters into the family, this disrupts the ranking. Where does he/she fit in?

This brings about the need for the dogs to establish which one of them will be leader of the pets. You may wish for all of your dogs to simply see each other as equals; however, this goes against canine instinct. Until hierarchy is established, there can be unrest.

You can help by establishing and/or showing agreement with which dog is the Alpha Dog. This can be beneficial for dogs that would otherwise fight over the position. And, if the dogs are having a hard time deciding, you can settle the matter relatively fast. Here are some tips:

First, identify the Alpha. The Alpha dog is usually the oldest. If close in age, and of different genders, it will be the male. If there is a much older female and very young male, it will typically be the older female. Still, there can be exceptions. If you are not sure, take note when the dogs are playing. Is one more outgoing? More 'pushy'? Who runs to their food first? Typically, the Alpha tries harder in all aspects.

Once you know, you can then help both dogs. Keep in mind that the Beta dog is just as important and loved as the other. Not being Alpha Dog is not a negative thing. Both will be less stressed, knowing their place in the 'pack'. Essentially, you will do everything for the Alpha Dog first, reinforcing that you agree with his ranking. This includes setting down dinner bowls, giving out snacks, placing on harnesses, giving out toys, exiting the car to have fun at the park, etc.

Boundaries: Typically, for two dogs to get along, and especially when introducing a new puppy to an established dog, there is a need for clear boundaries. This does not mean that your dogs will not interact or play with each other. This simply allows each of them to have their own designated areas for what is most important to them. Later, if the dogs decide to share space, that is just fine.

Eating areas. Dogs can eat in the same room and at the same times; however, each should have eating 'areas' a good distance from each other. When food and water are too close, this can cause dogs to feel as if they have to compete.

Resting/Sleeping areas. This is especially important if you have an older dog and a younger dog in the house together. Many older dogs require a private area to retreat to when a younger one is wearing him out. As with eating areas, this can be in the same room, but in separate corners.

Toys. While it is difficult to keep all toys separate, each dog may have a few favorites that they are not happy about sharing. It can help to have toy bins for each dog, placed near their beds.

When an Older Dog Corrects a Younger Dog:
It is completely natural for an older dog to discipline a puppy. It is not acceptable if aggression is shown and the pup is injured. However, for the home to run smoothly, you should allow the older dog to 'put the younger dog in his place' via nose nudges, etc. For example, an older dog may nose a puppy away if he gets too close to his toys.

When Dogs Ignore Each Other:
It can be upsetting to see two dogs ignoring each other when the whole goal was to bring in a second dog to be friends with the first. Often, this is just a temporary transitional phase. It can take an established dog several weeks to become accustomed to an addition to the household. Ignoring is a much better sign than aggression; it means that a dog is tolerating the other; he is just not quite ready to be friends.

Mood Changes with the Introduction of a 2nd Dog:
When a new dog is brought in, the established dog may become moody in reaction to a change in the household. This may include acting withdrawn or mopey. It's hard to not take it personally, and the best thing to do is to not ignore him back. Give a few extra hugs and some extended play time.

If an Older Dog is Bothered by a Puppy:
An established, older dog may struggle with the hyper nature of a new puppy. You can help following the rules of the aforementioned 'Boundaries', and never forcing interaction.

If There is Fighting Between Dogs:
Actual fighting that involves biting often requires the services of a professional canine trainer; this said, this sort of severe aggression is rare. For growling, snapping, and other signs of intolerance, the offending dog should be removed from the situation and given a 'time-out'.

While you *can* use a playpen, if it is used for 'home alone' times, it's best to avoid it being associated with something negative. So, it is preferable for the time-out to be behind a gated area. During this time, the offender should be completely and utterly isolated socially, which means no eye contact, no touching, and no speaking to him.

The duration of the time-out will depend on how long it takes the offender to notice that he's receiving it. After all, it will not have much impact if the dog takes a short nap and then is let out. Signs of noticing the social isolation include whining, barking, and/or pacing.

After 5 minutes, *of noticing he is being ignored,* he may be let out to prove he has learned his lesson. Good behavior is rewarded with praise and occasional treats, and bad behavior leads to another immediate time-out. Note that socially isolating a dog works best when an owner has already clearly established himself as the leader. You may also wish to refer to 'Training: Teaching Proper Hierarchy'.

The Need to Spay/ Neuter in Multiple-Dog Households:
With multiple intact pets, there is often an increase in marking, humping, and other hormone-driven issues. Spaying/neutering can help resolve these behaviors and has many health benefits. You may wish to refer to 'Health – Other: Spaying & Neutering'.

Loss of a Pet in a Multiple Pet Household:
When two pets live under the same roof, they become part of each other's lives. When one passes, this can be a terribly sad time for the remaining pet. Dogs coping with such a loss may become withdrawn and depressed. There may be changes in sleep and/or eating patterns. It can be just heart-wrenching.

If you know a pet will be passing - As sad as it may seem, the best way to help a dog cope with this is *before* another pet passes. If a pet is ill or very old, and you know that he or she is going to pass away relatively soon, having more one-on-one time with the dog that will be remaining can help.

This involves just the two of you going for walks, having playtime in the yard, and/or heading out to parks and other settings. It is sad to just think about doing this; instinct tells us to let them spend as much time together as possible. However, we must remember that canines are different than humans, and creating this sort of gradual separation can help with the shock that comes at the time of loss.

If there is little time to prepare, this can be quite a dreadful time for everyone. There are some things that you can do to help. It is recommended to allow a couple of weeks to pass to just allow the situation to sink in. Everyone will be feeling sad and you may not feel up to taking on new things. However, do cuddle as often as you can; extra hugs and petting will offer both of you some much-needed comfort. Do not take it personally if your dog wants to retreat. It is a form of mourning and part of the process that canines go through.

After a week or two, it can help to engage your dog in a new activity never experienced before. This can be something as simple as blowing bubbles to your dog, or as involved as teaching him an agility activity (weaving in-between poles or cones, running through a tunnel, etc.) Anything new to take his mind off things for a bit and have fun for a while.

When is the best time to get a new puppy or dog? It's great if you are thinking of adding a new puppy or dog to your household. Typically, it's best to wait at least 2 to 3 months. Some owners can feel a tinge of guilt; they don't want to feel as if they are 'replacing' the pet that they've lost. It's best to wait until you feel that this is not a replacement, but rather an addition, and one that your former canine family member would be happy to know about.

Rescued Dogs

A good number of Chihuahuas are adopted into new homes. As seen under 'About the Chihuahua: PetChiDog's Chihuahua Survey', 23% of owners obtained their puppy or dog from a shelter or rescue.

Maybe you are thinking about adopting a dog, or perhaps a rescue is already part of your family. If so, that is fantastic. It is a gratifying and rewarding experience to take in a pup that is just waiting to be loved by someone who can show him that the world does not have to be so bad. This does not come without some challenges; yet, they can certainly be overcome.

Issues to Be Ready For: Even though a shelter, rescue, or foster home will be caring for your dog before he finds his way to your home, some things may need to be addressed by you.

The coat may be in poor shape. Longhaired Chi may need a trimming if matting is present. For all Chi, baths with superior products, a good food to provide the right nutrients, and an omega-3 fatty fish oil supplement can help restore coat health. For thinning, additional steps may be needed. Also see the 'Grooming' chapter, the 'Fur and Coat' chapter, and 'Feeding and Nutrition: Supplements'.

Dental issues. If there's been a lack of dental care for some time, there may be tooth loss which may result in trouble eating hard kibble. If so, since dry food is recommended over wet, try drizzling warm low-sodium chicken broth over food, mix well, and warm it in the microwave, or offer a 50/50 mixture of wet and dry (try to use the same brand).

In addition, never assume that the shelter was able to have all current issues taken care of. Poor dental hygiene in the past could have caused decay and infections that you'll have to have addressed now or in the near future. It is not uncommon for rescues to need to have several teeth extracted. When you bring your rescue for his first veterinary visit, be sure to ask that the teeth be examined. You may wish to refer to 'Dental Care' for more details.

Food transitions. Chances are slim that a rescue was properly fed in a formerly neglectful home. And shelters, due to budget restraints, often cannot afford top-quality kibble. You may want to rush your new adopted dog onto a great food right away; yet, a sudden change can lead to stomach upset and even vomiting and/or diarrhea.

Find out the exact food that your rescue has been eating, and obtain both that and your new chosen food. Make a gradual transition over the course of 3 weeks. Week one: 3/4 'old' to 1/4 'new', week two: 1/2 and 1/2, and week three: 1/4 'old'; to 3/4 'new'. Week four is fully on the new diet. Also, refer to the 'Feeding and Nutrition' chapter.

Leash issues. A rescue may not have much experience walking nicely on leash. It's a good idea to start off right away with heeling. The more you walk your dog incorrectly (leash pulling, jumping, refusal to walk, etc.) the harder things will be later. You may wish to refer to both 'Training: Heeling' and 'Behavioral Training; Refusal to Walk While on Leash'.

Fears and Phobias. It's impossible to say what fears a rescue dog may have; however, chances are that the dog associates at least one element with his former life that can bring back bad memories. This can include fear of small spaces, big dogs, other people (sometimes just certain people like tall men or women with black hair, blond hair, etc.), cars, certain noises, and so forth. Fear of being alone (separation anxiety) is common as well.

Accommodate what you can, never force a dog to interact with a fear-trigger, and start on socializing him to elements that you do feel he will need to get accustomed to. You may wish to refer to 'Behavioral Training: Socialization & Desensitization Training', 'Behavioral Issues: Clingy Behavior', and 'Situational Issues: Separation Anxiety'.

Care Items to Have: Your rescue will need all of the same care items as other puppies and dogs when first going to a new home. However, a playpen (or other designated area), a quality memory foam bed, and superior grooming products are among the top necessities. For more information on all supplies, look to 'Puppy Care: Supplies to Have' (many items are applicable to adults new to a home as well) and 'Care Items - Chihuahuas All Ages'.

The Environment, Vibe, and Expected Interaction: It is human instinct that you'll want to mother your new adoptee, offering tons of hugs and spoiling. If your new dog is receptive, that is wonderful. But, a newly re-homed puppy or dog may not be ready for that yet. Depending on what the dog has seen and lived through, it can take a while to get settled in. The most important thing is that you have him safe under a loving roof. His journey to you is complete. Allow plenty of time for your dog to gain his bearings and realize that no harm will come to him.

Don't walk on eggshells, but refrain from being overly hyper or excited. Once your rescue is used to you and his new home, more of your spirited personality can come out!

Separation Anxiety

One of the biggest concerns that owners have is leaving their dog home alone. Our survey (see also 'About the Chihuahua: PetChiDog's Chihuahua Survey'), in which 3,272 owners responded, 14% reported issues with separation anxiety.

And, one of the biggest missteps that an owner can make is skipping over steps to resolve this. For example, we are going to talk about creating a safe, secure, and defined area for your dog, and what to place inside of it. If you scan over the bullets points that cover the 3 types of toys to have and just think 'okay, toys, got it!', you may miss some very important elements. And, if you have the right toys to keep your dog occupied and comforted, but the house is dead quiet, there may be little improvement.

So, moving forward, please realize that every single recommendation is listed here for a valid reason. And all elements work together to fully resolve separation anxiety.

Signs

Before You Leave: Many dogs are able to pick up on visual or even auditory cues that let them know an event they consider to be distressing is imminent. Behavior may include nervousness, pacing, excessive clingy behavior, stubborn behavior, and/or trembling.

While you are Gone: Much of this behavior is a result of overwhelming feelings of isolation and loneliness. This may manifest with excessive barking, curling up, continual despondent whining, urinating or defecating due to stress, and/or self-licking due to stress. Some dogs may also have panicked behavior and/or restless behavior. This may manifest as destructive chewing, ripping things apart, excessive pacing, trying to escape, or even ramming into walls.

No matter which signs a dog outwardly displays, separation anxiety can be exceedingly physically and emotionally exhausting.

When You Arrive Back: Some dogs cannot instantly recover when an owner arrives back home and may need time to recuperate from feeling so distraught. Signs include trouble calming down, obvious emotional exhaustion, a rapid release of pent-up energy and emotions (jumping, circling you, etc.), excessively clingy behavior, and/or depression. Since owners are not home to see what is happening while they are away, often it is a dog's behavior at this time and/or signs of disturbance in a dog's area that lets them know there are separation anxiety problems.

FAQ

Does the amount of time I leave my dog alone affect this? This can vary. With some dogs, reaction will be the same regardless if they are alone for 1 hour or 5. With others, it is only when they reach a 'tipping point', that separation anxiety will begin.

Is this more common with certain ages? The age that a dog can develop separation anxiety is broad reaching; it can begin at any age at all, even if the environment or duration of time left alone has not been altered. In some cases, a puppy will do just fine home alone, but as he matures and becomes more cognizant of his surroundings, realizing that he's truly alone, separation anxiety can develop. Senior dogs can develop separation anxiety as well. This is often due to issues commonly seen with older dogs, including decreased vision and hearing, joint pain, etc., that cause feelings of vulnerability.

Why do some dogs have this and others don't? There is a wide range of factors that can be at the root of this issue. As mentioned, age is an aspect in some cases. Elements that used to keep a dog calmed, soothed, or busy may have stopped working. Other stress-inducing issues such as loss of a family member or moving to a new house might trigger this. A significant change in schedule that results in more extended periods of being home alone is certainly a factor. For some dogs, there was always some level of stress, but unnoticed by owners; as time went by, feelings of frustration accumulated and finally spilled over.

Would it help to have my dog go to doggie daycare? It all depends on your particular puppy or dog. Some love the company of other dogs and will enjoy that time. Others are not yet socialized to other dogs enough to enjoy play time and/or find being away from home more stressful than being home alone.

If you are thinking about this, try it for a half-day, and see how your dog does. It's best to choose a daycare that offers webcam views; never take a worker's word for how your dog did; after all, it is a business that wants customers. You can locate one near you by doing an online search for 'doggie daycare near me with webcams'.

Should I get another dog to provide companionship? In most cases, two dogs will keep themselves busy and provide each other with companionship. However, it should be noted that in some cases, both dogs will be unable to cope with the absence of their human and/or the dogs may have a period of adjustment in which they are not getting along with each other well enough yet to offer companionship and comfort. Since there is no guarantee, you may not want to take on the huge responsibility of having a second dog for this reason alone.

Resolving Separation Anxiety

Fortunately, there are very effective methods to help with even severe cases of separation anxiety. A huge element of this is to follow as many steps as you can, not just a few. It is a combination of all aspects that work together; so, each tip is important. Even something that may seem insignificant (like lighting or sounds) can make a big difference.

#1 Create a secure, calming 'den'

There are some fundamental canine truths that so profoundly instinctual, a dog's response is automatic. And one of these is a dog's response to a 'den'.

- o It immediately triggers feelings of safety and security. This is why some dogs run to hide in closets during thunderstorms and expectant dams seek a nesting area. This instinct is also very prevalent in wolves; they have even been known to claim dens of previous occupants (some date back over 700 years).
- o When a dog is left to roam an empty house or has an entire room to himself, this is the opposite feeling of a den and can increase feelings of isolation.
- o Without a designated, defined area, a dog's separation aids (more ahead) may end up too far away for him to find during a frantic moment and/or be too far away to be effective.

An effective method of creating a den is via an indoor canine playpen. Place this in a room often used by the family. **Within this**, have a quality bed (aids in 'den' feelings, and allows the right support for resting and sleeping), 'stay busy' toys (more ahead), food and water, a companion toy (if you opt to obtain one), an article of your clothing that has your scent on it (can offer some level of comfort), and pee pads for bathroom needs.

Even if your dog is not trained to go on pee pads, since the area will be defined, and a dog rarely soils on his own belongings, chances are that urine and stools will be deposited on the pads.

#2 Provide methods to stay busy

Your dog home alone, with nothing to do, is the last thing you want. There are ways to help keep a dog busy:

- o An assortment of engaging and interactive toys that speak or make noises in response to touch (talking toys, squeakers, and crinkles).
- o Chew toys; often flavored ones (bacon, cheese, etc.) make the chew toy enticing.
- o A treat-release toy that tempts your dog with his normal dry kibble mixed with 100% all-natural smooth peanut butter. Alternativity, a dash of wild fish oil can work excellent as well.

#3 Provide a companion toy

These are intended to mimic a living creature (often a puppy). This is done via accurate sizing, and two elements that make a toy 'alive': a heartbeat and body warmth. It will be as close to another dog that you can get without actually bringing home a new puppy. This serves as both a dog's 'friend' and source of comfort. For more details, refer to 'Care Items - Chihuahuas of All Ages: Toys: #6 Companion Toys'.

#4 Make environmental changes

There are several things you can do to create an overall pleasant and secure environment:

- o Leave on lights. Even if you think you will be home before dark, stormy weather or approaching dusk can darken a house, which can increase feelings of isolation.

- o Assess sun glare from windows. On days you are home, check to see how the sun shines in during the day into your dog's 'den' area. If it is glaringly bright, this can be disturbing. Move the 'den' or adjust curtains, as needed.
- o Assess the 'den' being too close to AC or heating vents.
- o Don't have the house be dead quiet. There are some fantastic music CDs (or digital streaming) that are specifically designed for canine ears. Some are calming, others are to keep a dog interested (animal sounds, etc.). Alternatively, some television service providers offer channels just for pets to watch (these may be found under 'On Demand' or an equivalent feature).

#5 Break up the day

If a dog can have a break from his time alone, even if it's a short break, this can be very helpful. When provided with this, some dogs are able to 'reset', and this can resolve issues that develop due to too much accumulated time alone. There are three very different, yet effective, methods to provide this.

- o If possible, go home during lunch time. Even a 10-minute session of play and a bathroom break can be very helpful.

- o Hire or enlist a dog walker. This can be a professional dog walker, or a friend, family member, or neighbor that is willing to help out; don't be shy about asking, you may be surprised. If you choose this option, have that person visit your home several times in advance, so that your dog can become used to them. This is also your opportunity to show and go over handling and care instructions.

- o Use an interactive pet cam. This is not for every budget, as these can be a bit pricey. However, interacting with your dog while you are away from home is a great option. While these can vary with their features, most work in this way: The cam is a sturdy device that sits on the floor; there is a camera at the top, and within the center is an area that holds dry treats. You control the pet cam with an app that you've downloaded to your phone. Through the app, you can see your dog and speak to him. Some have two-way audio so that you can hear your dog. And, with a tap on your phone, the device will toss out a treat.

#6 Reverse the cues regarding your departure

Most dogs are able to sense that their owner is preparing to leave the house and are very aware that some actions such as putting on shoes, handling your house keys, etc., mean that you're readying to go. And certainly, placing your dog in his pen and opening the front door is an obvious cue. This can cause a dog to start worrying much earlier than he needs to. So, it can help to show that doing these things does not *necessarily* mean that you are leaving for a long period of time, or leaving at all.

On days that you will not be leaving, perform one (or some) of these actions, randomly throughout the day and then simply go about your home, tidying up or otherwise casually staying busy (but within sight). For example, if you are planning on reading a book, pick up your keys, jingle them, and then sit down to read as if nothing just happened.

Randomly, place your dog in his playpen, and go to another room, out of sight. No matter his behavior, stay out of sight for 5 minutes and then very matter-of-factly, re-enter the room. Wait for 3 to 5 minutes and then open the door to the pen or take him out. Vary these times of leaving the room; for example, 5 minutes one day, 15 the next, 10 the next. Open the door to inspect the weather but then go back to whatever you were doing inside. In some instances, open the door, actually go outside for varying times of 5 to 15 minutes, and then come right back in.

#7 Follow departure guidelines

Please note that these are in order:

o Wake up early enough that you do not need to rush around; just this vibe alone can cause a dog to get tense, and you'll want plenty of time to follow the next steps.
o Bring your dog outside for bathroom needs, allowing a good 15 minutes for this.
o Go for a morning walk; a minimum of 20 minutes is best.
o Place your dog in the playpen well in advance of leaving.
o Do not shower your dog with hugs and kisses to say goodbye; this is the most obvious departure cue of all; though it goes against instinct, leave quietly.
o Try not to spend your day worrying. If your dog is safe (tip #1), has separation anxiety aids (tips #2 and #3), and the environment is pleasant and secure (tip #4), there should be improvements. If you're providing a way to break up the day (tip #5), all the better.

#8 Keep your arrival back home calm and casual

When you finally come home after a long day at work, it is natural to want to greet your dog and offer hugs, kisses, and tons of attention. However, when a dog suffers from separation anxiety, making a big deal out of arriving back home can be counterproductive. If you rush inside and then rush over to your dog to really pour it on thick, this can be the same as sending a message that says 'I can't believe I made it back home! This is a miracle!', and this can tell a dog that they were correct to be worried.

Rather, it's best to casually enter, walk to the kitchen for a drink of water, thumb through the mail… and then after 1 to 3 minutes, calmly approach and in a matter-of-fact manner, say "hello". After this, bring your puppy or dog outside for bathroom needs. Once that business is taken care of, it will be time for lots of attention.

Supplements and Medications

OTC Supplements: Some OTC supplements are marketed to help calm dogs down; these work to varying degrees, but typically never so well that they are effective on their own without implementing most or all of the aforementioned steps.

This includes those that contain L-theanine or colostrum. L-theanine is an amino said to increase dopamine which regulates mood; it typically does not cause drowsiness. It is not without side effects, which may include dizziness and headache. Colostrum is the initial milk produced by mammals; For canine supplements, this is usually bovine (cows) colostrum, and is said to have relaxing properties that may reduce stress. This has very few reported side effects but may cause constipation and/or stomach upset.

Melatonin may help a dog relax; this is sometimes prescribed by veterinarians for sleep issues since it does cause drowsiness; but, may be used to help reduce stress. You'll want to discuss this with your vet first, since it can interfere with some medications, and should not be given to dogs with certain health issues. In addition, dosing must be done carefully; it is one thing to give a dog something to relax, but quite another to knock him out.

Prescribed Medications: These are customarily a 'last resort'. In many instances, the side effects are not worth the benefits in all but the most severe cases. The two types of medication most often used are:

Benzodiazepines (tranquilizers) - These can have some negative side effects including sleepiness, increased appetite, and the possibility of increased anxiety. Studies have found that these may interfere with memory and the ability to learn.

Antidepressants - This may include buspirone; side effects may include loss of appetite, restlessness, nausea, headache, dizziness, aggression, and hyperexcitability. Some MAOI antidepressants can have dangerous side effects in dogs that have recently ingested cheese products. A commonly prescribed antidepressant for canines is clomipramine, which is a tricyclic antidepressant; but can cause lethargy, depression, vomiting, diarrhea, elevation in liver enzymes, confusion, increased thirst, increased heart rate, and/or convulsions.

Since pet care products are always evolving, yet this book is static, our most current recommended separation anxiety aides including playpens, 'stay busy' toys, companion toys, music for dogs, and pet cams, can be found on the Supplies page of the PetChiDog site, which is updated as new products emerge. You can reach this by entering any page of PetChiDog.com; Look to the navigation which is in alphabetical order, and choose 'Supplies'.

Your Chihuahua and Children

A household with young children is not necessarily the best environment for a Chihuahua. As noted under 'Age: Life Expectancy of the Chihuahua', trauma is the 2nd leading cause of death for puppies of all breeds, and is the 2nd leading cause of death for the Chihuahua. Part of this involves improper handling and fatal injury from being stepped on, etc. In addition, aggression, though only seen with 9% of Chihuahuas (see also 'About the Chihuahua: PetChiDog's Chihuahua Survey'), having a Chihuahua nip at a toddler is certainly not an ideal situation.

This all said, there are plenty of households with both young kids and Chihuahuas; planning ahead and following certain guidelines can help things run more smoothly.

Hierarchy in a Home with a Dog and Children:

What's at play: As we've covered many times in this book already, dogs are acutely aware of hierarchy. Within the den (house) lives the pack (all humans and animals), and that pack has a leader (the Alpha). Everyone under the leader is a follower (Beta) since they follow the leader's commands. This makes sense when it's just you and your dog (you are the Alpha), you and your spouse (you are both Alphas), or you and several dogs (you are Alpha, the dogs are Betas). But, what about when there is a young child?

A dog will usually either think of children as his Beta peers (the equivalent of his litter-mates) or he will consider them to be part of his Alphas (the humans in the house who are his leaders, and therefore he will listen to commands, behave well in order to receive praise, etc.). Rarer is for a dog to perceive a child as an Omega (ranking lower than the canine and making for a terrible household environment in which the dog tries to rule over the child).

For a happy and peaceful household, we will want to eliminate any chance of children being seen as fellow Betas or as Omegas. If a dog is shown in a loving and gentle way that a child is an Alpha, that puppy or dog will then behave as such: He will not nip at, will not bark at, will walk beside, and will gently protect, play with, and respect the child.

How to achieve this: The methods of accomplishing this are similar to how adult humans should approach this. Let's look at some aspects that children can be involved with:

- **Feeding.** The dog should be taught to sit before a meal is given. Only after the command is obeyed, the bowl is placed down. A child can most certainly take turns being the one to do this. However, once the bowl is down, the dog should be given plenty of personal space to eat without being disturbed. Many kids love to watch a dog eat; for some reason, they are amazed by this. However, a dog may feel as if his personal space is being invaded and his food is at risk of being taken away if anyone is too close at feeding time. Instruct children to give your dog a bit of 'alone time' during meals.
- **Commands.** Working together, you and your children can teach a puppy the basic commands that are the foundation for a well-trained, well-behaved dog. 'Sit', 'Stay', and 'Come' are 3 easy commands that a child of any age can help train. Remember to let a child know that training is not accomplished in a day or even a week, but rather is a gradual process, much like a semester in school; little pieces of information are absorbed during each 'class' resulting, at the end, in a dog that 'receives an A'.
- **Entering/Exiting.** All humans, including children, should enter and exit the house first, followed by the dog. It's quite normal for kids to 'chase' after dogs, and therefore your child may trail behind your dog when it's time for everyone to head outside. Help your children learn to order a sit, cross the threshold, and then give the 'okay' for the dog to follow.

Safety Tips: Rough play can cause injury to a Chihuahua and teasing behavior can cause a dog to either become overly shy or act out aggressively. Please remind children of some simple rules:

1. Show your child how to pick up a puppy: Approach from the side, kneeling down to cradle the pup, one hand on the rump, the other gently yet firmly holding the tummy /chest area.

2. A child should never run, spin, or jump when holding a dog.

3. A child should never point a finger at, poke at, or pull the tail of a puppy or dog.

4. Supervise grooming. There is no reason why a youngster cannot be part of grooming care, especially brushing the coat and helping to give baths; however, please do teach the steps of proper grooming techniques. As your child grows, you may just have a helper who can take over these tasks.

5. Remind your child that they must never give a piece of their own food to a dog. Onions, a highly toxic food to canines, can be found in so many dishes: Pizza, subs, spaghetti, and many more. And, as you may know, grapes, raisins, the cores of many fruits, and chocolate are exceedingly toxic.

6. Have your child (or any visiting children) be very aware that toy-sized dogs are 'under-the-foot' dogs, meaning small and quick; This breed can go from being across the room to being underfoot in the blink of an eye, where young children can trip over or accidentally step on the dog.

Your Chihuahua & Your Baby

Having a new baby will be a big adjustment for everyone. However, by implementing some elements both before and after your new arrival, everything can run very smoothly. Those who have issues with their dog and baby are usually those who did not plan ahead of time.

Before Baby Arrives: There are several things you'll want to have in place and several things you'll want to do.

#1 Your dog should know basic commands. You'll want to be able to control your dog's movements by verbal command. At the very least, your dog should know 'Sit' and 'Heel'. Ideally, he'll also know 'Stay', 'Come', and 'Down'.

#2 Introduce baby-related smells. If you know which diaper rash or bathing products you'll be using, play daily games of applying some of these to a paper plate or other item, and allowing your dog to sniff them. Just don't let a quick mouth swipe it from you. Just before bringing your baby home from the hospital, send over a blanket that the baby has been wrapped in, to help your dog get used to your baby's particular scent.

#3 Introduce baby-related sounds. If you have a baby mobile or other baby toys that make noise, sit down with your dog daily and turn these on for him to hear. Some owners like to desensitize their dog to the sound of crying babies, since this can be disturbing at any rate, and especially so for a dog that is not used to hearing this.

If you wish to do this, an online search of 'crying baby' will produce many results for you. At first, play the recording at a very low volume. As your dog becomes used to the noise, you can then play it louder each week. The goal, though a lofty one, is to reach the point of being able to play the recording at its natural volume.

#4 Make any furniture layout changes now. If you believe that you will be changing the layout of your home, do this as soon as possible. Dogs love consistency. If a baby highchair is going to be in the spot where a dog's food bowl once was and his bowl is going to be moved to another corner in the kitchen, give your dog time to get accustomed to this before the baby is home.

If your dog balks at the idea of having his food and water moved and you absolutely must change the location of his dishes, you can try to do this slowly. Each day, move the bowls a foot or so. After a while, you will reach your goal!

#5 Teach toy lessons. It is best to choose a designated area for your dog's toys and if possible, a designated area for your baby's toys (and where you expect the soon-to-be toddler's toy bin will be). Spend as much time in advance helping your dog understand the difference between his toys and the baby's toys. Each time your dog goes over to the baby's toys, clap your hands loudly and then immediately direct your dog one of his own toys. When he mouths his own toy, give pets and praise. Done in this way, you are not reprimanding your dog for being curious.

#6 Make adjustments for care-handlers now. Discuss with other household members if there will be a need for some or all of them to take over care tasks in regard to your dog. This includes going for walks, grooming, feeding, etc. If there will be changes, have them start now.

#7 Bring your dog to the vet for a wellness check. Since a baby's immune system is not strong, ensure that your dog is healthy and is up-to-date with de-wormings before the baby arrives. Humans cannot catch such disease as heartworms, parvovirus, or distemper from canines; however, Campylobacter (symptoms in dogs includes runny diarrhea, lethargy, and/or fever) can be passed to humans, as can ringworm.

After the Baby Arrives: Associate the baby's presence with positive things. Give your dog treats and lavish praise for desired behavior around the baby. Do not place the baby on the floor with your dog without supervision.

Even with meticulous planning, months in advance, some dogs may be a bit jealous or become clingy once the baby is home. If your dog is extremely clingy, do acknowledge him by giving a quick pat and then do what you must to care for your baby. All three of you can snuggle if you are sitting on the sofa feeding your baby and all three of you can head outside when you are taking the baby for a walk in the stroller. In time, your canine family member will become used to having a little brother or sister.

Seasonal Care

Summer Care

If you live in an area that experiences seasonally hot temperatures or year-round steamy weather, there are important care elements to follow. This will ensure that your puppy or dog is safe, comfortable, and happy no matter how hot it may get.

#1 Help Your Dog Be Comfortable Indoors

There are just a couple of things to keep in mind:

1) **Evaluate windows.** If your dog has a playpen or other defined area inside the house, evaluate the amount of sunshine that is coming through windows and shining in. This may have changed since you initially set things up. In the summer, the sun's rays hit the Earth at a different angle and of course, it shines for almost twice as long than it does during cold, dark winter months.

2) **Take note of any strong AC currents.** While you'll want to keep the house cool, this toy breed does not do well with cold air pouring directly on him. Gated areas or playpens should be situated where your dog will benefit from the cooling system but not in the direct path of cold air being cycled out.

#2 Follow Summer Exercise Tips

While the Chihuahua does better in the heat than some other breeds (like brachycephalic dogs that can have breathing issues or Spitz-type dogs with double-thick coats of fur), Chihuahuas can indeed overheat during the summer. But, do not let this fact stop you from offering daily exercise; a season spent indoors will be an unhealthy one. You can keep your puppy or dog active yet safe by having some precautions in place:

1) **Avoid heading outside during the hottest parts of the day**, typically from 10 AM to 4 PM.
2) **When you do go for walks, bring along water.** Bring a small insulted thermos, which will work well to keep water cold and a collapsible dog bowl, or a canine travel water container, in which the lid serves as the bowl. At the halfway point of the walk, find a shady spot for a break to rehydrate.
3) **Know the signs of heat stress.** No matter how many safeguards an owner puts in place, you can never be entirely sure how a dog is going to react to summer heat. And once heat stress occurs, steps must be immediately taken to cool the dog off; if not, this can lead to heat stroke which can be fatal. Signs include rapid panting, bright red tongue, red, pale, or blue gums, thick sticky saliva, weakness, dizziness, vomiting (sometimes with blood), diarrhea, and/or slow capillary refill time (CRT).
   - **In many cases, testing the capillary refill time (CRT)** of blood flow to the gums can let you know if your dog is in distress. Press a finger onto your dog's gums. When you release

it, the pink color should return within 2 seconds. If it takes longer than this, this is red flag sign of heat stress.

- o **If you are not sure about signs,** take your dog's temperature, also refer to 'Safety and Happiness: First Aid'. A temperature of 103°F (39.4°C) means to take steps right away to cool your dog down, 106°F (41.1°C) is a life-threatening emergency.
- o For full details regarding heat stress, please refer to 'Exercise & Activity: Heat Stroke'.

4) **Take advantage of dusk.** In the summer, when it can be light until 8 or even 9 PM, it can be hard to figure out when, exactly, to take a dog for a walk. You want it to be 2 to 3 hours before bed, but at the same time, meals and exercise should be spaced one hour apart. So, that hour or so of dusk can be the perfect time for a dog to be walked or to run around.

#3 Help Your Dog Stay Cool

The top priority is to have your dog enjoy the season, with methods to stay cool and hydrated, even when the temperature soars.

1) **Bring water to any destinations.** Whether you are going somewhere by foot, car, or other, it's always smart to bring along water anytime you venture out in the summer. This is to keep your puppy or dog hydrated and to use in emergency instances of heat stress to cool down the body.

2) **Encourage your dog to drink once an hour.** Summer is not a time for a dog to play 'catch up' with water. Keep the bowl filled with fresh, cool, and preferably filtered water, and remind your dog to drink.

3) **Offer a cooling mat.** These are incredibly helpful; a canine cooling mat absorbs a dog's excess body heat. It is self-activating. A special gel inside is triggered when a dog sits or lies on it. This it does **not** radiate out cold (like an ice pack), *it absorbs heat*; so, it will not feel cool to you if you place your hand on it. These are great to use outdoors when in the yard and are also effective for helping a dog cool off once he comes inside. Another reason to have a cooling mat is to use as an emergency measure in the event of loss of electricity.

4) **Offer a raised cot.** Also referred to as an elevated pet bed, these are typically a breathable fabric stretched over a steel frame. Both the fabric and the fact that it's off the ground means great air flow and it will help a dog stay cool. Some are designed with umbrellas that offer shade as well.

5) **See if your dog enjoys playing in water.** Sprinklers and small kiddie pools are great ways for toy breeds to stay cool and have fun in the summer (more on full-size swimming pools ahead).

#4 Protect Certain Body Parts

1) **The paws.** A dog's pain threshold on the paws is 125°F. At 130°F, paws can receive burns. Asphalt surfaces (blacktop, pavement), red brick, and cement can easily reach well past these temperatures, even hitting 140°F starting at 12 noon. Aside from these risks, walking on somewhat hot surfaces over the course of weeks and months can cause accumulative damage that results in overly dry paw skin. Itching, peeling, and/or cracking may not be too far behind.

What to do: Apply a quality paw wax once per week to protect the paws (should be done year-round). Choose a good wax that adds a layer of protection, but still allows the paws to breathe. In addition, test the pavement; if you cannot hold your hand to it for a count of 10, it's too hot for your puppy or dog.

2) **The nose.** While dogs should have some exposure to sunlight (it helps a nose maintain its pigmentation), too much sun can lead to sunburn (hard to notice on a dog's nose). Once the top

layer is damaged by the sun, this causes drying, peeling, and/or cracking. Not to mention, the nose is one of the most common areas where skin cancer develops on canines.

What to do: At the first signs of dryness, apply this, and continue to apply this weekly. For nose issues like peeling or cracking, 1 to 3 applications daily may be needed.

3) **The coat and skin.** Summer sun exposure can dry out both skin and coat. And, sun exposure can cause dark spots to develop on the skin.

What to do: Use a good leave-in coat spray. Depending on how much your puppy or dog is outside, you may want to consider using one that contains a sunscreen, (see below for belly-specific issues).

4) **The belly.** Not every dog needs to have their belly protected; but, some do. The stomach can get sunburned from UV rays reflected from ground surfaces (and from bodies of water) and the skin on this area is usually very sensitive. Additionally, sun exposure on the belly can cause dark spots to develop. While these are generally an aesthetic element, it should be noted that canines can and do develop skin cancer. Any dark spots appearing on your dog's tummy during the summer is your cue that the area may be receiving too much sun exposure.

What to do: If your dog is prone to sunburn, has dark spots appearing, spends a lot of time outside, and/or like to lie belly up when outside in the summer, apply a canine sunscreen to the belly about 20 minutes before heading outside. Note many sunscreens for humans contain zinc, and this is toxic to dogs; use a product designed for pets that does not contain zinc.

#5 Use Care and Caution When Driving

When it's hot out, you'll need to follow a few extra rules:

1) Anytime you are going to enter into your car with your dog, ***first*** open windows to release heat, then turn on the AC to cool it off. Cars can become overwhelmingly hot when parked.
2) Check your dog's car seat to make sure it's not hot (similar to how a steering wheel can become super-hot to the touch in the summer).
3) While driving, keep the car cool; however, the AC blowing directly on your dog may be overwhelming.
4) To prevent motion sickness, have a window partially opened in conjunction with the AC running.
5) Depending on the height of your puppy or dog's car seat, you may find that using car shades can be helpful in keeping sunlight out of his eyes which can cause a dog to be quite uncomfortable and also increase motion sickness.

#6 Follow Swimming Safety Tips

Chihuahuas, like most dogs, can swim; however, it is a myth that canines are automatically excellent swimmers. It can take time to understand how to feel comfortable in the water and how to best stay afloat. Here are some safety steps:

1) Start off with a kiddie pool to allow your Chi to work on building up his swimming skills.
2) Never just toss a dog into a pool or other large body of water. While a dog will 'doggie paddle' out

of survival instinct, this is certainly not a method that will convey swimming can be fun.

3) Always closely supervise. In big pools, a dog may swim out too far and have trouble getting back. Just like humans, they can tire out.

4) Most swimming pools have high levels of chlorine to keep the water clean. This can be an eye irritant, so routinely check your dog's eyes for signs of redness. A canine saline rinse can help clear up bloodshot eyes. Also, if it is left on the coat, chlorine can severely dry out both the skin and fur. Once done swimming, you'll want to rinse the coat off thoroughly.

#7 Protect From Summertime Insects

In regard to fleas, while this is indeed thought of as a 'summer insect', dogs need year-round protection as it is very arduous not only to rid a dog of fleas, but to remove them from the house as well. You may wish to read more under 'Health – Other: Fleas'.

For mosquitoes, you may want to consider using safe mosquito repellent for any time your dog is out after dusk in the summer when these pesky bugs are in full force. Ahead, you'll see that some tick repellants also work for mosquitoes.

Now, let's cover ticks: While you may know about Lyme disease, there are 7 main tick-borne diseases in total that infect thousands of dogs every year, across the US, Canada, and all over the world.

1. **Lyme disease is caused by the deer tick.** The deer tick is also known as the blacklegged tick in the US and Canada, the sheep tick in Europe, or the Taiga tick in Asia. Unlike most other ticks, the deer tick can be active year-round. They are not killed off in the winter and can be active on any day in which the ground is not frozen or covered with snow. In the US, they are most typically found in the northeast from southern Maine through Washington, D.C. and the northern Midwest.

2. **Canine ehrlichiosis is caused by the brown dog tick**. The brown dog tick is found in many states in the US, but is most prevalent in the southwestern US and has a high population in Florida. This tick almost exclusively latches onto dogs and is the tick most often found to live

indoors. Outside, they live in grasses, wooded areas, and shrubbery. If inside, they can be found living in indoor potted plants.

3. **Canine anaplasmosis ('dog fever' or 'dog tick fever') is caused by the deer tick.**
4. **Rocky Mountain Spotted Fever is caused by the American dog tick and the lone star tick.** The American dog tick is found in the Pacific Northwest and on the entire eastern half of the US. The lone star tick is found in southeastern states and along the east coast.
5. **Canine babesiosis is caused by the American dog tick and the brown dog tick.**
6. **Canine bartonellosis is caused by the brown dog tick.**
7. **Canine hepatozoonosis is caused by the brown dog tick and the Gulf Coast tick.** This disease is caused by tick bites, but can also be contracted if a dog eats a disease-carrying tick. Despite its name, the Gulf Coast tick is found along the Gulf Coast states of Texas, Louisiana, Mississippi, Alabama, and Florida, but also has been found in Maine, Iowa, Delaware, Maryland, Oklahoma, Arkansas, and Kansas.

For most tick-borne diseases, there is a 24-hour window of time to find and remove a feeding tick before it transmits an infection.

How to check for ticks: If you live in any of the states in which ticks are known to be, anytime your dog was in an area in which there may have been ticks (grassy areas including your yard, fields, shrubbery, leaf piles, and wooded areas), it is a good idea to check him over. With proper lighting, feel for tiny bumps and also look for small dark spots. Check all areas: head, chin, neck, both sides of the ear flaps, legs, between the toes and paw pads, armpits, belly, chest, back, and tail.

How to remove a tick: Ticks should not be removed by hand because some diseases can be contracted to humans via secretions from the tick. Also, burning a tick is not a good idea since this can burn a dog and/or trigger the tick to vomit into the bite site. There are tick removal tools that can do a good job and if you live in an area with a high tick population, you may wish to obtain one. If you do not have this sort of tool, the best option is to use tweezers. Here are the exact steps:

1. Using tweezers, firmly grasp near the head that is buried in the skin.
2. Pull straight and slowly, using steady, even pressure. The goal is to not allow the head to remain, and this can be tricky since the mouth has inverted barbs.
3. Treat the site by washing it with a mixture of your dog's shampoo and warm water. Then, apply an antiseptic such as Betadine (this should be in your dog's first aid kit, see also 'Safety and Happiness: First Aid').
4. Keep the tick for 1 month (in a zipped plastic bag). This is for identification purposes if your dog were to become ill.
5. If any part of the tick remains or if the tick is buried too far for you to remove it, have the veterinarian assist with this within the 24-hour window of disease transmission.

How to help keep your yard free of ticks: Maintain the grass, keeping it cut short at all times. Seal cracks and crevices around the house. Do not allow leaves or other lawn debris to collect. Since ticks love damp, shady areas, prune low-lying bushes to allow more sunlight to enter. Remove any fallen fruit, keep barbecue areas free of food droppings, do not build up wood piles, and do not spread bird seed, as all of these things can encourage mice or other rodents (that carry ticks) to enter onto your property. If you live on a property that abuts a wooded area, create a 3-foot barrier on that line using woodchips, mulch, or gravel.

Using Tick Prevention: The heartworm protection that you use for your dog may also work to repel ticks. So, check the labeling. If you are using Advantage Multi (which toy breeds seem to tolerate well), this *can* work to repel ticks (even though it is not advertised as so) in low population areas.

For areas of high tick infestation, you'll have a choice between an insecticidal medication or an all-natural one. Insecticidal medications can cause side effects, ranging from allergic reaction to seizures and even death. For this reason, you may wish to opt for a spray or balm that works to repel mosquitoes, ticks, and more, via plant and other natural extracts.

Since many manufacturers of these products keep their exact formulas a proprietary 'secret', you may only see ingredients listed as 'essential oils', along with moisturizing elements such as shea butter. However, some ingredients that may be among those oils include apple cider vinegar, rosemary, lemon, and eucalyptus.

Each dog's body chemistry is different and each location in which someone lives has diverse populations of fleas, ticks, and mosquitoes; so, if you try a no-chemical product and find that it does not work well enough for your particular dog, you may need to use an insecticidal product.

Stinging Insects: Another element to keep in mind is the issue of hornets, wasps, bees, and other stinging insects. Dogs are prone to get stung since they tend to stick their noses into areas where these insects may be, such as in bushes and such. Dogs are often stung on the face and while this is painful enough, some may also suffer an allergic reaction which can be dangerous.

If your puppy or dog is stung by a bee or other stinging insect, keep an eye on him for signs of an allergic reaction; this includes swelling around the face, breathing difficulty, and/or signs of weakness. ***If a Chihuahua is stung 3 or more times, he should be taken to the vet regardless of how he seems***, since toy sized dogs can have severe reactions and it can take up to 45 minutes for these to develop.

You will want to check your dog to see if the stinger is present. Do not try to remove it with tweezers, since this can release more venom. It's best to use your license or a credit card to scrape it out. A mixture of water and baking powder made into a paste can be applied to help with swelling and pain. You may also wish to refer to 'Safety and Happiness: First Aid: Bees, Wasps and Other Stinging Insects'.

Winter Care

Winter care revolves around three main elements:

1) Keeping your dog active enough 2) Helping your dog tolerate cold-weather conditions and 3) Preventing issues with coat, skin, paws, and nose, which are very common in the wintertime.

#1 Do Not Allow for a Drastic Decrease in Exercise

What happens: Though it can be a challenge in the winter, meeting exercise requirements is important year-round. A significant decrease in exercise over the winter can lead to changes in appetite, and your dog will miss out on the many cumulative benefits of regular exercise including heart health. In addition, without enough physical activity to release pent-up energy, dogs can become frustrated, which can manifest as excessive barking or destructive behaviors.

What to do: Unless there is below freezing temperatures and/or dangerous snow conditions, commit to maintaining your dog's daily walks. Upcoming tips will help with that. On days that it's not wise to head out, offer indoor activity via playing fetch down a hallway or rousing games of hide n' seek. Be sure to time this to at least 15-minute intervals, 2 to 3 times per day.

Other options include working on commands, or even just encouraging your dog to follow you around the home to pick things up (you carry the basket, your dog picks up the items) can be fun if you use an excited tone of voice and offer praise as you go along.

#2 Protect Your Dog From the Cold

What happens: Small dogs like the Chihuahua can have trouble tolerating the cold. This can make it difficult to meet exercise requirements and can interfere with housebreaking. Overexposure to the cold can lead to 'the chills', which is actually the beginning stages of hypothermia, and full hypothermia is a concern. If the coat becomes wet and cold, this can lead to hypothermia much faster.

How much cold tolerance a dog has depends on a few factors: Body composition plays a big role. As mentioned under 'Behavioral Issues: Shaking or Trembling', fat works as an insulator and muscle helps generates body heat; the Chihuahua has a low percentage of each.

In addition, overall size is an aspect. In the winter, the temperature near the ground can be much colder than just several feet above it, so toy dogs that are close to the ground are often exposed to colder temperatures than larger breeds. In addition, toy dogs are in more contact with snow than larger breeds just by body height alone.

Type of coat matters as well. Some Chihuahuas have a single coat of fur and some have a double coat; however, in either case the coat is not extremely dense as it is with Spitz-type dogs nor is it water-resistant as it is with some Retrievers.

Finally, a dog's age and health status affect his ability to withstand the cold.

What to do:

1) **Place outerwear on your dog when appropriate.** In general, if it is 32°F (0°C) or lower (taking into account wind chill factor), this may warrant a layer of clothing (lined vest or coat) on the core body. If snow is actively falling, a waterproof vest or coat may be needed.

2) **Know the signs of hypothermia:** Shivering is often the first sign and is your cue to bring your dog inside. Without treatment, the next sign is listlessness. This can spiral into a coma and eventual death. A dog's normal temperature is between 101 and 102.5°F (38.3 to 39.2°C). A temperature of 99°F (37.2°C) requires at-home treatment. Below 98°F (36.7°C) requires immediate veterinary treatment.

3) **Know how to treat hypothermia:** Warm towels in the dryer or on a radiator, and place over your dog. Place a warm hot water bottle in a towel, and place against the abdomen. Encourage your dog to drink warmed water. Check your dog's temperature every 10 minutes. If it is not rising to normal ranges, this warrants immediate veterinary treatment. Once it is at or above 100°F (37.8°C), you can stop the blankets and water bottle.

#3 Work to Keep Coat, Skin, Paws, and Nose Healthy

Coat and Skin | **What happens:** Whether or not it's snowing, the air in the winter is much drier than other seasons. Cold air cannot hold much moisture and therefore humidity levels drop. The air inside the house can be worse than outside; when arid air meets the warm temperatures of a heated house, it dries out even more. Over the course of the winter, arid air can lead to itchy skin and poor skin and coat health.

What to do:

1) Keep giving your puppy or dog a bath every 3 weeks; though dogs often stay cleaner longer in the winter, the bath serves more purposes than just washing off debris. Body oils are still accumulating, which can lead to blocked skin pores and stinky odors. And, baths are your opportunity to thoroughly soak your dog in moisturizing products to help prevent and heal dry skin, and add moisture to the coat.

2) Use a quality daily leave-in coat spray. This will help protect against dry air, contact friction, and static, and as an added bonus, it will help keep your dog smelling nice.

3) Control the humidity level in the house. The best method is to use humidifiers. Keep in mind their capacity. Most units will only work for one or two rooms. If you only have one humidifier, consider placing it near your dog's sleeping area. Remember that humidifiers must be regularly cleaned to

keep them free of bacteria. There are some home remedies to increase humidity levels, though these are not as effective as quality humidifiers. This includes:

- Placing metal bowls of water on top of heat registers or heaters.
- Leaving the door to the bathroom open during and after showering.
- Taking a large plastic zipper-bag and punching roughly 20 holes in it, placing a large wet sponge inside, and then placing that on counters and other areas. You may need 5 to 10 of these spread out over the house.
- Obtaining houseplants, since they release moisture after they are watered.

Paws | What happens:
Frozen ground surfaces can dry out paws, 'snowballing' can occur (which is when snow between a dog's paw pads and/or toes melts, refreezes into ice, and stretches or splits the skin), ice and salt chemicals can cause chemical burns and/or problems with the nail beds, and loss of traction on slippery surfaces can be a concern.

What to do: Apply a quality paw wax on a regular basis. This will add a layer of protection from the aforementioned elements, and give your dog good traction. A good wax can heal minor drying issues and a restorative lotion may be needed for more severe peeling and/or cracking. For maintenance and protection, apply once per week. To heal issues via a wax or lotion, apply 2 to 3 times per day.

Nose | What happens:
Dry winter air can quickly dry out a nose. And before you even notice that it's dry, there can be cracking and/or crusting issues. And, since a puppy or dog licks their nose quite a bit, even a few minutes outside in the winter can cause chapping.

What to do: Apply a quality nose balm once per week to add a protective layer on the nose. Bad chapping, peeling, cracking, or crusting may require 2 to 3 applications per day.

#4 Follow Snow Safety Tips

Playing: Some dogs love to play in the snow, and this is just fine as long it is above freezing, you supervise, and keep the time to under 20 minutes. Once inside, use an absorbent towel to dry the coat (pat, do not rub). If needed, slip on a t-shirt on your dog to help the body warm back up.

Bathroom issues: Some dogs do not do well with walking even a few feet in the snow. You'll want to be diligent about keeping the pathway shoveled. Since typical ice-melt products contain chemicals that can burn a dog's paws, use pet-friendly ones. As of the time of this writing, SafePaws is recommended; it is environmentally friendly and safe for pets (and children).

#5 Anticipate Changes

Some dogs can feel as if their schedule is thrown off when days are shorter and sunlight is limited. This can lead to wanting to go to sleep much earlier than normal. It can help to perform some grooming tasks *after* the sun sets such as brushing the teeth or the coat. This sends a message that even though it got dark out, the day is not quite over yet.

Senior dogs may have increased aches and pains due to arthritis flaring up. Reevaluate your dog's bed to see if it is time for a better orthopedic one. If there seems to be a significant amount of increased discomfort, do not hesitate to bring this to the attention of the vet.

Health & Care – Body Part Specific

Anal Glands

Anal glands (also known as scent glands or anal sacs), are located right on the rim of the anal opening; one on each side. These hold a very foul-smelling, oily substance that is released in tiny amounts when one dog meets another (the scent allows the dogs to communicate important information including gender, health status, and even mood), and when stools are pushed out (as long as they are firm enough).

What can happen: Because this scent oil is gradually released and replenished, there is not usually a problem. However, if a dog rarely encounters another dog and/or if his stools are very soft, the glands may not release much oil at all. If so, several things can happen:

1) **Anal glands may become engorged, swelling with excess oil.**

   o   This stretches the skin in this sensitive area.
   o   A dog may scoot his rear across the ground in response to the discomfort.
   o   Friction when the dog scoots may cause the glands to burst open. If so, all of the oil will spill out at once. The smell of this can be overpowering, to say the least, often worse than skunk spray.
   o   Note that the color of the oil can vary (clear, yellow, yellow-brown, reddish-brown) and should not be confused with the discharge of un-spayed females during the heat cycle.

2) **If glands do burst open, the broken skin will then be vulnerable to infection.**

   o   You can give your dog a bath; however, do not rub the area, gently pour water over it instead.
   o   This can be followed by dabbing antibiotic ointment on the area to help prevent infection.
   o   Keep an eye on this for several weeks.
   o   If there is inflammation, red skin, pus, or any other signs of infection, this warrants veterinary care. The vet will flush the area, possibly close any open skin with stitches, and prescribe antibiotic medications.

3) **In some cases, engorged glands do not burst open, but instead become impacted, also referred to as 'anal sac disease'.**

   o   The oil hardens into a thick paste-like substance that has a consistency of peanut butter.
   o   Dogs with impacted anal glands may still make the scooting motion, will be more prone to licking the area, may hold the tail funny, and/or may show signs of pain when sitting.
   o   In these instances, a veterinarian will need to perform a minor surgical procedure. Dogs are first given a sedative. A small incision is made to remove the impacted material and flush the glands. Most veterinarians will then inject an antibiotic ointment into the glands to protect against any possible bacterial infection. A prescribed oral antibiotic may be given for 7 to 10 days afterward.

Prevention: A dog's stools should be somewhat firm, akin to the consistency of playdough, where if you picked it up, it would hold together for a bit before a piece would break off and fall down. If your dog's stools are not as firm as this, consider adding 1 teaspoon of 100% pure pumpkin to each meal to firm them up. Be sure to use real canned pumpkin and not the pie filling.

If you notice your dog scooting his rear along the ground, this is your cue that the glands need to be expressed. Expressing anal glands is similar to 'popping a pimple' and will prevent issues with engorged and/or impacted glands. The vet or a groomer can do this, generally with reasonable fees.

Ears

The two main issues of concern regarding the ears are 1) keeping them clean and 2) resolving ear infections. These aspects are often related; dirty ears can lead to an infection, and cleaning the ears can, in many cases, clear up an infection.

Ear Care

#1. Inspect the ears. It's a good idea to routinely inspect your dog's ears. This can let you know if they need to be cleaned and give you early warning of an ear infection. You'll want to have a look at the inner flap of the ear and the entrance of the ear canal; the skin should be pink. Some level of odor and/or excess wax are signs that the ears need to be cleaned. Redness, inflamed tissue, and/or crusting, often along with a foul odor, are signs of an ear infection.

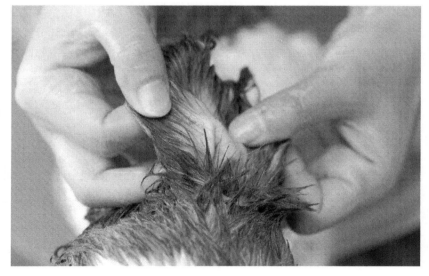

#2 Clean the ears. Cleaning the ears every 6 weeks is an effective method to prevent ear infections. And, if your dog has a history of ear infection, no doubt the vet has recommended this. It is a relatively easy task to do. The goal is to loosen compacted wax and dirt with a solution. Some of this will move up toward the outer ear canal, where you can swipe it away.

Ear cleaning supplies: A quality ear cleaning solution and sterile gauze pads or sterile cotton pads.

Instructions:

1) Fully do one ear before moving on to the next.

2) Hold the ear and gently dribble the solution into the ear canal. Do not go deep. You will see the solution, so only place enough so that it does not overflow. The solution will slowly make its way down; however, you do not need to watch and wait. It will be time for Step #3 as soon as you have

dribbled the solution into the canal.

3) Massage the base of the ear for 30 to 60 seconds. This is done by having your thumb on one side of the ear and your forefinger on the other side. Gently press your fingers toward each other and move them around in a gentle circular motion. During this time, you may hear the solution swish around.

4) Use the cotton to wipe out the ear. Place your finger in the middle of the gauze to keep it firm. Do not attempt to clean out the inner ear, the solution is just meant to loosen compacted wax and debris, so just wipe as far as you easily can. Rotate the cotton pad several times and then remove it. Do not be surprised at what you see after removing the cotton pad. The color of the debris that you clean up may be anywhere from a yellow to a dark brown, and there may be small black bits of matter.

#3 Pluck the ears, if applicable. Seen primarily with longhaired Chihuahuas, long hairs can grow inside the canal and can lend toward clogging the ear, as wax and other debris cling to them. If you see long hairs sticking out of the ear canal, you can use an ear powder (to make it easier to grab the hairs) and a small ear forceps tool that latches onto the strands, allowing you to pluck them out quickly. Do not over-pluck, just remove those that are obvious.

Ear Infections

The medical term for an ear infection is otitis externa, and this is a top health issue seen with puppies and dogs. In fact, most dogs will have at least one ear infection in their lives. Some dogs, unfortunately, are plagued with chronic infections, which keep reoccurring, even with proper care.

Types of Ear infections

1) Bacterial: This is the most common type of infection. Of this, there are two subcategories:

- ○ **_Non-pathogenic_** - This is the most common type of bacterial ear infection, in which the body overproduces staph bacteria. Many things can cause this, including a foreign body stuck in the canal, allergies, or a stressed immune system.
- ○ **_Pathogenic_** - With pathogenic forms, an outside source of bacteria reaches the ear canal. This can happen in countless ways; however, one example is a dog lapping water from a contaminated source such as a dirty puddle.

2) Yeast (fungal): All dogs have some level of yeast growing on their skin and in the ears. One particular yeast, of the Malassezia species, can be triggered to reproduce uncontrollably, leading to overpopulating, and in turn, an infection. In some cases, the trigger for this is unknown. However, some things that can cause yeast to overpopulate include being in a hot, humid environment, excess water in the ears, and certain health issues in which the immune system is compromised.

3) Mites: Technically, this is not an infection, it's an infestation. Mites are very contagious, so it's easy for them to transfer from one dog to another during any sort of contact; though, these miniscule pests also can jump short distances. Though mites may first take up residency in the ears, in most cases, they will travel to other parts of the body as well.

Symptoms of Ear Infections

Whether due to yeast, bacteria, or mites, most symptoms are the same:

- o Itchiness and/or pain that leads to scratching or pawing at the ears, shaking the head, or rubbing the head against surfaces.
- o Red, inflamed tissue on the ear flap and/or the outer canal.
- o Discharge. This is typically thick and yellow. If dirt or debris is mixed in, there may be specks of brown or black, or the debris may cause the discharge to be a yellow-brown color.
- o Pus (only in some cases).
- o Crusting of discharge, usually seen overnight.
- o A bad odor.
- o Dizziness or loss of balance (usually seen if the infection travels down to the middle ear).
- Left untreated, ear infections can lead to temporary or permanent hearing loss.
- ◆ Specific to mites: debris that resembles coffee grounds in the ears and/or reddish-brown or black crusting along the outer ear, and/or itching on other parts of the body (mites may spread).

(handwritten note: Coffee gra)

Treating Ear Infections

❶ **In *some* cases, you can successfully treat an ear infection from home; but, not always.** It depends on the exact type of infection (bacterial vs. yeast vs. mites) the extent of the infection, the treatment you choose, and how your particular dog responds to that treatment.

❷ **If your dog does not respond, has overwhelming symptoms that are causing distress, and/or has reoccurring ear infections, these are reasons to bring your dog to the veterinarian.** Severe, long-lasting, or chronic ear infections can lead to permanent damage and hearing loss, so this must be taken seriously.

Treatment at home involves applying an OTC ear cleanser, in the same way that you regularly clean the ears (apply into the canal, massage the base of the ear, wipe out excess solution and debris from the

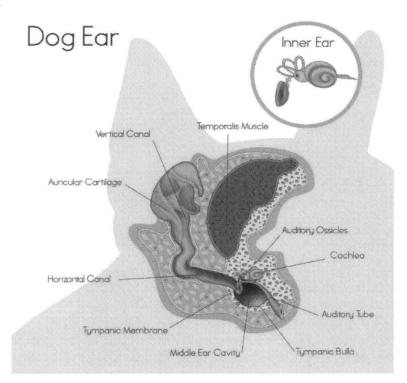

outer ear canal). The differences will be 1) the product you use and 2) frequency; this is done up to 2 times per day, for up to 14 days.

Some of the following ingredients can make for an effective ear infection solution: Acetic acid (antibiotic for bacteria and fungus), isopropyl alcohol (antibacterial properties), hydrogen peroxide (an antiseptic), tea tree oil (antifungal and antibacterial properties), and rosemary extract (antibacterial properties).

Some ear infection solutions will have stronger medications; this includes hydrocortisone (1%) which can really give a dog much need relief and/or lysozyme, which is an enzyme that breaks down and destroys bacteria.

Mites can be much harder to treat than bacterial or yeast ear infections. With infections caught early, a product with some of the aforementioned ingredients, along with vinegar may kill mites.

Prescribed treatment may be needed, and should be sought for a full-fledged, raging infection in which a dog is in distress and/or a dog does not respond to at-home treatment. The veterinarian should take a sample swipe of the outer canal to confirm the cause: bacteria, yeast, or mites. For dogs that have chronic ear infections, other tests should be run as well such as looking for thyroid issues or allergies.

After cleaning the ears, an antibiotic (gentamycin, tobramycin, amikacin, etc.) may be prescribed for a bacterial infection, an antifungal medication (ketoconazole, fluconazole, etc.) for a yeast infection, or a parasite medication (pyrethrin-based products) for mites. Note that for mites, all pets in the home will need to be treated, and this type of medication can be harsh on a dog; follow instructions very carefully.

Be sure to follow through with all doses, even if your puppy or dog appears better. *Just a trace* of bacteria left in the ear can grow back into a widespread infection.

Chronic Ear Infections

It can be frustrating to work to clear up an infection, only to have it come back again and again. Each time that the ear is assailed in this way, it can cause small amounts of damage. In time, this will add up and can lead to permanent damage including loss of hearing. **Guidelines to follow in these cases include:**

o   The veterinarian should look for an underlying cause. One of the most common reasons for reoccurring ear infections is allergies. Signs may include watery eyes, wheezing, coughing, and/or skin and coat problems.
o   When you are given a prescribed medication for your dog, be very careful to follow instructions to a tee.
o   Follow all ear infection prevention tips at all times (see below).
o   Dogs with chronic ear infections should not be allowed to swim until the condition is under control.
o   Hygiene is vital; be sure to regularly clean the ears to remove excess wax and pluck any long hairs (seen primarily with long coat Chi) as these may contribute to the issue.

When a dog does not respond to antibiotics and is nearing the point of permanent damage (bone degeneration that can be seen via x-rays), surgery may be recommended as a last course of action.

Often, it will be total ear canal ablation (TECA) and bulla osteotomy (BO). Antibiotics are given pre-surgery. With TECA, the vertical and horizontal ear canals, down to the level of the middle ear, are removed. With the added BO, the middle ear is opened and cleaned. Note that hearing structures remain. After the procedure, pain medication and another round of antibiotics are given.

Rare but possible complications include but are not limited to hearing loss, facial nerve paralysis (up to 20%, but can be temporary), bleeding, balance issues, and healing complications.

Prevention of All Types of Ear Infections

There are some things that you can do to help prevent ear infections:

1)   **Keep the ears dry.** When giving baths, place cotton in the ears beforehand.

2) **Routinely inspect the ears.** Look for discoloration, excess wax, long hairs (seen primarily with long coat Chi), and any odor. Catching problems early offers the best chance at a speedy recovery.

3) **Do routine cleanings,** even if there are no problems. A cleaning will remove excess wax, dirt, debris, and may pull out yeast or bacteria in the very beginning stages.

4) **Do not allow your dog to drink from any potentially contaminated water source**. This includes lapping at puddles and ponds.

5) **If your dog is going to swim**, be sure to dry the ears right afterward.

6) **If an allergy is suspected** to be the cause of chronic infections, take steps to resolve the allergy issues. See also, 'Health – Other: Allergies'.

<u>Ear Set</u>

The Chihuahua has interesting ears! Puppies are born with floppy ears; as the pup matures and the muscles at the base grow stronger, the ears stand up. With adult Chi, the ears are large in comparison to the body, naturally stand erect, and change positioning depending on how the dog is feeling. When alert, they are held high. When relaxed, they can flare to the side. This is seen in the AKC breed standard with *'Large, erect type ears, held more upright when alert, but flaring to the sides at a 45 degree angle when in repose giving breadth between the ears.'* In addition to this, the ears can go straight back.

Chi on the left; alert with erect ears

Chi on left: relaxed, ears at 45° angle

Chi on the left; alert with erect ears

Chi on left: relaxed, ears are fully back

This said, not all Chihuahuas are able to hold the ears fully erect. As we covered in 'About the Chihuahua: PetChiDog's Chihuahua Survey', in a poll of 3,272 owners, 75% reported that their Chihuahua had two erect ears. But, other things can be happening, such as one or both ears folding down halfway (also known as 'half-ear'), flopping once in a while, or one that is up and one that is down.

Ears on a puppy: Chihuahua puppies are born with folded or flopped ears. This is because puppies do not have the proper muscle strength at the base of the ear in order to hold them erect. For most, as the pup matures, the ears will gradually stand.

The age that this happens varies from pup to pup. It can be as early as 6-weeks-old or as late as 6-months old. As the ears make this transition, one ear may stand up before the other. And there may be a lot of flip-flopping going on until they fully stand. If by 6 months, the ears are still down or are 'half-ears', most likely they will not stand.

Ears during the teething phase: Teething, which starts around the 4-month mark can somewhat affect the ears, causing them to lose a bit of strength. If so, once teething subsides, the ears can bounce back up.

Methods to help the ears stand up: Having erect ears is possible when there is sufficient muscle strength, which for the most part is due to genetics. If the muscle strength is not there yet, it may develop over time (up to 6 months old). There are a couple of things you can do; however, this will only work in some cases:

1. Massage the base of the ears 1 to 3 times per day for several minutes to help increase blood flow to the muscles.

2. Another method that can work nearly overnight (BUT, it only works if the muscle strength is *virtually* what it needs to be) is to shave the fur on the ears. You would think that the weight of those hairs would not make much of a difference; however, if the ears are right on the 'borderline', removing just that small bit of weight can allow struggling ears to blossom.

Note: You may have heard about 'taping', a method of literally taping the ears into a 'stand'. There is no proof of that method working. If a pup's ears were taped and then stood, this was most likely a coincidence of the ears naturally gaining strength while they happened to be in the taping process.

Eyes

The Third Eyelid

The third eyelid (nictitating membrane) is involved in some of the eye issues that this book covers, so it's a good idea to be reminded what this is. Canines have an upper eyelid, a lower eyelid, and a third eyelid that closes *across* the eye (rather than up and down). This transparent third lid serves to lubricate the eye and produces 1/3 of a dog's natural tears.

Inflammation

This is a general disorder that covers inflammation due to irritation.

Signs: Excessive blinking or squinting, sensitivity to bright lights, discharge, dull coloring of the iris, bloodshot eyes, and/or swelling of the upper and/or lower lid.

Causes: Most commonly, this is due to small matter caught in the eye. Rare, but possible, are certain diseases.

Diagnosis: The eye will be examined with an instrument that allows the vet to see the interior of the eyeball. Blood tests may need to be performed if the cause is not apparent.

Treatment: Initial at-home treatment can involve rinsing the eyes with a canine eye rinse. If there is no improvement after 3 days or worsening symptoms, this must be treated by a veterinarian. Anti-inflammatory medication will be given for any swelling, antibiotics will be given if there is an infection or reason to believe an infection may develop, and eye drops may be given to help with pain. If a disease is deemed to be the underlying cause, treatment will vary according to the health issue.

Prognosis: Very good, for inflammation caused by acute issues. If an underlying disease is the cause, the prognosis varies.

Dry Eye

Dry eye (keratoconjunctivitis sicca, also referred to as 'brown eye'), can be a very painful condition, in which the clear film that naturally protects the eye (tear film) develops an abrasion. It most commonly affects middle-aged and senior dogs.

Signs: Excessive blinking, bloodshot eyes (sometimes to the point of completely covering the sclera - the white part of the eye), thick yellow discharge or pus from the eye, prominent third eyelid showing, inflammation around the eyelids, and/or vision impairment. If not treated, scarring can occur, which can lead to complete loss of vision in the eye.

Causes: The most common causes include dehydration, excessive dry air, or poor nutrition. Other less common causes include reaction to certain medications, canine distemper, canine diabetes, and some neurogenic diseases.

Diagnosis: A Schirmer tear test will be performed; this measures the level of tear production. A low level points to dry eye. A test using fluorescein stain and a Wood's light can check for abrasions or ulcerations. Testing may be done to check for bacterial growth.

Treatment: This must be treated by a veterinarian. This will include artificial-tear medication, eye drops for lubrication, medication to reduce pain and inflammation, and in some cases, antibiotics. In rare cases, surgery must be performed if a tear duct is damaged. The Schirmer tear test will be performed again 4 weeks later, and then at 6 weeks, to check for improvement. Some dogs may need artificial-tear drops indefinitely.

Prognosis: Very good, if caught early. If caught late, once scarring has developed, this can lead to partial or total vision loss.

Cherry Eye

Cherry eye refers to when a dog's third eyelid (nictitating membrane) slips out of place and bulges out. It is important to have this treated as soon as possible since the longer the gland remains out of place, the more swelling will occur, potentially leading to other, more serious problems.

Signs: A pink or red bump that significantly protrudes out over the sclera (the white part of the eye). *In addition to this*, there may also be excessive blinking or squinting, bloodshot eyes, discharge, swelling around the eye, and/or vision impairment.

Causes: It is thought to develops due to a weakening of connective tissues. It very rarely happens to both eyes at the same time; however, once it happens to one eye, it is common for it to occur in the other eye within a few months.

Diagnosis: Fairly straightforward; the veterinarian is able to clearly see the issue.

Treatment: This must be treated by a veterinarian, and is resolved with a relatively simple surgery. While the appointment is being scheduled, the vet will prescribe topical antibiotics and anti-inflammatory medication. During surgery, a small section of the nictitating membrane will be removed, then stitches will secure the remaining tissue back into its proper place. Since its very common for the other eye to develop the same issue soon afterward, many veterinarians will recommend securing the other eye's nictitating membrane in place as well, to prevent it from slipping out.

Prognosis: Very good, eyes will most often return to normal.

Distichiasis & Ectopic Cilia

In regard to distichiasis, this occurs with 5 to 6 % of Chihuahuas. Ectopic cilia is not as common, but can occur. These are conditions in which the eyelashes, sometimes just one or two, grow abnormally. **With distichiasis**, a lash(es) will grow in an odd place on the lid itself. **With ectopic cilia**, the lash(es) will grow through the inside of the eyelid, inward toward the eye. This can be a very painful condition and can lead to corneal ulcers (next section).

Symptoms, distichiasis: Eye pain, abnormal twitching of the eyelid, excessive tearing, bloodshot eyes, change in iris pigmentation.

Symptoms, ectopic cilia: Eye pain, abnormal twitching of the eyelid, excessive tearing.

Diagnosis: Fairly straightforward; the veterinarian is able to clearly see the issue.

Treatment: This must be treated by a veterinarian. In some cases, the eyelash(es) can just be plucked out. However, it is imperative to note that they can, and most often will grow back within 4 to 5 weeks, at which time they will need to be removed again. A minor surgery can be performed to remove both the eyelash and the follicle to prevent any reoccurrence. Any secondary corneal ulcers will be treated (see next).

Endothelial Corneal Dystrophy

Corneal dystrophy is a condition in which the cornea (the clear, shiny membrane that makes up the surface of the eyeball) clouds over. Of the three types: Epithelial corneal dystrophy (affects the outer layer of the cornea), stromal corneal dystrophy (affects the middle layer of the cornea), and endothelial corneal dystrophy (affects the inner layer of the cornea), the Chihuahua breed is prone to endothelial corneal dystrophy. Typical age of onset is between the 6 and 13 year mark.

Endothelial corneal dystrophy affects the deepest cells, which serve the purpose of clearing excess fluid out of the cornea. In turn, the cornea remains transparent. With this disorder, these cells deteriorate. There is then a buildup of fluids, internal swelling, a clouding of the cornea, and impaired vision. Small ulcers/blisters can form, which can make this condition quite painful.

Signs: Discoloration (appears opaque, white, or blue and usually starting in the corner of just one eye) that spreads towards the center and often moves to the other eye, signs of pain (often only once this progresses) which may include excessive blinking and/or pawing at the eye, and vision issues (often only once this progresses), which can lead to total blindness.

Causes: It is thought that this is heredity; however, as of the time of this writing, the gene responsible for this has not been identified, and therefore there is no genetic test for this.

Diagnosis: A special microscope called a slit-lamp can identify corneal dystrophy. In addition, a fluorescein stain test will be performed to check for corneal ulcers.

Treatment: Medicated eye drops are given to help remove excess fluid, as well as medicated drops to help heal blisters and/or ulcerations. If pain levels are very high, a surgery called thermokeratoplasty may be performed to reduce pain; however, this does not reduce any of the clouding and can make vision worse. This is a laser surgery that flattens the cornea to help prevent the formation of ulcers.

Another option to help reduce pain due to ulcers is grafting surgery in which a portion of the conjunctival tissue (the lining of the eyeball and the back surface of the eyelid) is moved to cover the area where ulcers can form. As with thermokeratoplasty, this can impair vision further.

Cataracts

Cataracts are a common condition seen with canines; however, more so with certain breeds. This is seen with approximately 8% of Chihuahuas. This involves a clouding of the transparent lens over the eye. This is a progressive disorder that can lead to blindness. If the cataract has less than 30% opacity (cloudiness), it may not cause any issues. However, once it reaches 60% or more opacity there is often vision issues.

Signs: A blue, grey, or white layer that clouds over the eye. Note that older dogs can have this very same symptom; yet, it is due to nuclear sclerosis, an age-related clouding of the lens, which is not as serious. For this reason, any clouding should be diagnosed by the veterinarian. Other signs include excessive blinking, eye irritation, and/or signs that vision is impaired including hesitancy to navigate around objects and/or trouble seeing at night.

Causes: Many cases are hereditary, and if so this can develop in a dog of any age at all. Another common cause is canine diabetes (about 75% of diabetic dogs develop cataracts and these can occur literally overnight). Cataracts are also linked to trauma, old age (most often seen with dogs 8+ years old), and low levels of calcium (hypocalcemia).

Diagnosis: There are several testing options; a common one at this time is electroretinography, which measures the response of cells in the retina. Pressure tests may be done to rule out glaucoma. Blink tests and other vision tests are often done as well.

Treatment: If a cataract is near, at, or over 60% opacity, surgery must be performed as soon as possible to help save a dog's eyesight. One technique that has a 90% success rate is phacoemulsification. This involves using a special ultrasonic tool to break up the cataract while aspirating the pieces out with suction. A special lens is then implanted.

Prognosis: It varies; if the cataract is caught in time and surgery is performed and goes well, vision will be improved, but not perfect, due to the implanted lens not having focusing abilities and some level of scar tissue. However, with surgery, a dog's vision will be saved and another cataract will not be able to develop in the eye.

Nose

<u>Wet or Dry, Cold or Warm</u>

Many people take note of both the tactile temperature of a dog's nose and its level of perceived moisture to determine if the dog is healthy. No doubt, countless owners have heard that the nose should be wet and cold. However, there is a lot more to it than this.

In many cases, both a wet *and* a dry nose are considered normal, and a cool and a warm nose are considered normal, to a certain degree. In just one day, a dog's nose can change from one to the other.

However, a drastic swing in either direction may point to a problem. For example, an overly wet nose may be an indication that a runny nose is developing, and a chronic dry nose can spiral into peeling and/or cracking. If the nose fluctuates from moderately moist to slightly dry, and cool to warm, without any other issues, this would be considered normal.

Some elements that can cause temporary dryness or are a precursor to more severe drying issues, and that can cause a nose to feel warm include:

- Sun exposure.
- Being situated close to a heat source (heating vent, radiator, etc.), due to both the heat and the dry air.
- When just waking up; one of the leading causes of a nose feeling wet is that a dog licks it throughout the day; since this doesn't happen overnight, it may be dry when he first wakes up.
- Slight dehydration. A loss of just 3 to 4% of body fluids can cause the nose to feel dry (and warm) along with possible trouble in focusing, irritability, and/or headache (the dog may rub his forehead against surfaces).
- Arid air (most common in the winter).

If your dog's nose is regularly dry and warm *without* any peeling, cracking, or signs of illness, it's recommended to:

1. Protect the nose with balm or butter to guard against sun exposure in the summer and chapping in the winter.

2. Protect the nose with balm or butter to guard against sun exposure in the summer and chapping in the winter.
3. Move your dog's resting area away from heat sources, if applicable.
4. Encourage adequate water intake.
5. Use a humidifier if the air in the house is very dry; this is most common in the wintertime.

Overly Dry, Peeling, and/or Cracked Noses

Note that crusting is a separate issue, covered in the next section

The nose has only 3 layers of skin as opposed to the 5 layers that cover the body. This is one reason why a dry nose can quickly escalate into a peeling or cracking issue. The outer layer, called the stratum corneum, has grooves that give it texture. Being very thin, any problem that causes this layer to peel away or develop cracks will expose the pink layer underneath.

These sorts of issues can be very painful for dogs, so it is important to treat this as soon as possible and to take steps to prevent issues from developing in the future.

Causes: Some of the most common causes include those that bring about temporary dryness (sun exposure, too close to heat source, slight dehydration, arid air - but triggers were not resolved), with the addition of a few other reasons:

- Sunburn. An overexposed nose, left to endure more exposure, can become sunburned. This is not always easy to see on a dark-pigmented nose.
- Chapping from winter weather (arid air). Chapping causes a dog to lick his nose, which leads to more chapping. If there's no intervention, the nose can become terribly raw.
- Allergies. Generally, if just the nose is affected, without other allergy symptoms, it is due to contact allergies, as opposed to food or environmental and is often seen alongside nose discoloration (fading).

Rare but possible: ◆ Autoimmune disease ◆ Cancer

At Home Treatment of Dryness, Peeling and/or Cracking:

1. Address any allergy issues. See also: 'Health – Other: Allergies'.
2. If there is pus, bleeding, discharge, swelling, or very deep cracks, this warrants veterinary treatment. Underlying causes will be determined and antibiotics (topical and/or oral) may be prescribed.
3. Encourage proper water intake.
4. Apply a quality nose butter or balm that is designed to treat dryness, peeling, and/or cracking. This will protect the nose from the sun, arid air in the winter, chapping, and other issues that lead to problems, while it moisturizes, and restores nose health.

   o Use an organic product, since a puppy or dog will lick at the nose.
   o Opt for scent-free, as a scented product may cause a dog to resist having it applied.
   o Apply this liberally each evening right before your dog goes to sleep for the night.
   o Also apply 1 to 2 more times, during the day. Near meal times, apply after your dog eats.
   o Once the nose has healed, routinely apply the nose balm to prevent future issues.

Crusts or Sores

Crusting that appears after drying, peeling, or cracking: Small crusty flakes can be a sign of healing. These are often red or brown, and can simply be the body's method of protecting the sensitive skin from germs while the skin cells rejuvenate. If so, allow these to flake off when they are ready to; do not pull or pick at the crusts.

For crusting alone, without the precursor of drying, peeling, or cracking: There is always a good chance that you simply did not notice drying, peeling, or cracking, and only just noticed the crusting. If you believe so, refer back to 'At Home Treatment of Dryness, Peeling and/or Cracking', as those steps will help with crusting. This said, there are some conditions that can cause rather severe crusting over the nose. This includes:

- **Discoid lupus erythematosus.** This is a type of skin disease that also affects the lips, ears, and eyelids. In some cases, there will be open sores on the genitals. With this disease, there can be discoloration of the nose as well. Treatment involves both corticosteroids and immunosuppressive medications. Since sunlight exposure can worsen the condition, owners are often instructed to apply sunscreen to the dog's nose for any outdoor activities.
- **Pemphigus foliaceous.** This is an autoimmune skin condition. Symptoms include crusty skin lesions along with boils that most often develop along the bridge of a dog's nose. These frequently grow into large pustules that easily rupture and then turn into dried crusty scabs. With some dogs, this can spread over the entire muzzle and even up to the ears. In rare cases, it will develop on the paw pads. Minor cases are treated with topical hydrocortisone. Moderate to severe cases are treated with prednisone. It should be noted that as a dog is tapered from this, the disease may flare up again.
- **Distemper.** This is rare and is typically only seen in puppies that have not been vaccinated. Changes to the paws is a more common symptom; however, with some pups there will be crusting and a hardening of the nose. Other signs include sneezing, coughing, discharge from the eyes and/or nose, fever, lethargy, vomiting, and/or diarrhea.
- **Solar dermatitis.** A very rare condition in which the nose is affected by sunlight, causing blistering. This can be prevented with canine sunscreen applied all year-round 20 minutes before the dog goes outside. Some cases will need to be treated with antibiotics due to infection.
- **Zinc responsive dermatosis.** This occurs when a dog's body is unable to properly absorb zinc. There are several types, many of which are only seen with certain breeds (the Chihuahua is not among them). Zinc responsive dermatosis related to food intake is the one that can be seen with this breed, though rare. Signs include nose scaling and crusting, and is often accompanied by fever, depression and/or swollen lymph nodes. It can be treated very effectively with zinc supplements.
- **Nasal hyperkeratosis.** This can be inherited, idiopathic (cause unknown), or seen in conjunction with one of several nose disorders (the aforementioned pemphigus foliaceous, distemper, and zinc responsive dermatosis), in which the body overproduces keratin. With this, the body over-produces keratin, which leads to the nose skin becoming thick, dry, calloused, crusted, and often cracked. Open skin is vulnerable to infection. In some cases, it can affect the paws as well. At the time of this writing, there is no known cure, but there are treatment options. Once all possible underlying conditions are ruled out, an experienced veterinarian can trim away excess keratin. The nose may also be treated with propylene glycol.

Runny Noses

Many dogs naturally have a small degree of a very thin, clear nasal discharge; however, this is often not noticed due to the dog licking the nose before owners take notice. If discharge is runny enough that fluid leaks out soon after wiping the nose with a dry cloth, if the discharge has any color to it (yellow, gray, green, brown, etc.), or if the discharge is thick, this will need to be addressed: Possible reasons include:

- **Allergies.** This is by far the most common reason for a runny nose. With allergies, a runny nose *can* be the only sign. There are 3 types of allergies: food, environmental, and contact. Resolving this involves quite a few steps to reduce or eliminate allergen triggers. For details, please refer to 'Health – Other: Allergies'.

- **A blockage.** A wide range of items can be sucked up into the nose when a dog is sniffing around. This includes blades of grass, seeds, random things such as pencil erasers, and other small items. In some cases, you may be able to spot the culprit and remove it with tweezers. If you are unsure about doing this, seek vet assistance.

  In some cases, an object can be lodged further up the nasal canal, where it cannot be seen but can cause quite a bit of discomfort. Signs are odd breathing, snorting, pawing at the nose, and/or slight bleeding, along with discharge that may be leaking out of just one nostril. The veterinarian will be able to remove the obstruction; though this sometimes needs to be done with the dog under sedation.

- **Tooth infection.** The roots of the upper teeth are located close to nasal passages and for this reason, a dental infection can trigger a runny nose. Even if you are spot-on with at-home dental care, infection can still occur. Signs include eating less, and/or anxious or distressed behavior. This is treated on a case by case basis, with possible extraction.

- **Less common causes.** There is a wide range of diseases and conditions that can trigger a runny nose. Rare, yet possible include but are not limited to cryptococcosis (a fungal disease), nasal growth (polyps, tumors), distemper, and pneumonia.

Bloody Noses

A bloody nose (epistaxis), is understandably worrisome. Let's look at some possible causes:

- **Trauma.** Even if you did not see it occur, it only takes a split second for a dog to bonk his nose against something hard enough to cause an acute bloody nose. **Let's go over what to do if your dog gets a nosebleed:**

1) **Try to remain calm,** since your dog will pick up cues from you, which can cause him to become stressed as well and this can increase the rate of blood loss.
2) **Gently apply a soft ice pack** (wrapped in a washcloth) to the bridge of the nose, while you are seated and have your dog cradled in your arms. Apply a light, steady pressure more so to the nostril that is bleeding.
3) **If the bleeding does not stop after 15 minutes**, it will be time to take your dog to the vet.

If you do not know what caused the trauma to the nose, it may also involve other parts of the body. For example, if a dog fell from the sofa and landed wrong, there may be injury to the hips, back, neck, etc. Always look for any signs of distress (limping, whining, resting in an odd position, etc.) and bring your dog to the vet clinic if you suspect there are any other injuries.

- **Other less common reasons.** The list of what can cause an acute bloody nose or chronic nose bleeding is very wide-ranging. This includes random events such as a rattlesnake bite, serious issues including cancer or even Rocky Mountain spotted fever, or something like nasal polyps.

Bloody noses caused by minor trauma that do not respond to at-home treatment or those without obvious causes need to be treated by the veterinarian.

Nose Color

Natural nose color: Many puppies are born with pink noses. For those with pink noses that are predetermined to have a darker nose, this will happen gradually. For a good number of Chi, the nose will transition even before the pup goes to a new home at the 8 to 10-week mark. However, for some this can take much longer, even up to a year or so for the nose to fill in completely.

Once coloring has come in, black is a common nose color. However, there is also chocolate (brown), blue (a diluted, faded black), and spotted (only seen with merles, which are only accepted by the AKC). For a few select Chi, the nose will remain pink (though this may transform into a darker pink); this happens primarily with light-colored Chi such as fawn, cream, etc.

In most cases, nose color will match other skin pigmentation (eye rims, lips, and paw pads). So, if your Chi has a nose that is transitioning, if you look to those skin points you can get an idea of what to expect with the nose.

Nose color changes: While a light nose can transition to a darker one, it does not naturally happen in the opposite way. If the nose starts to fade or turn pink, there are elements to address:

- **Plastic bowls.** Even those that are PBA and/or PVC free can cause the nose to gradually fade, typically over the course of 6+ months. This is due to dyes and/or contact reaction to the plastic. You can help reverse this by only using stainless-steel or ceramic bowls.
- **Lack of sunlight.** Canines need some level of sun exposure for the nose to maintain normal pigmentation. Staying indoors too often can lead to 'winter nose' or 'snow nose' in which lighter patches develop. You can reverse this by bringing your dog outside for the recommended 2 daily walks plus one 20-minute outdoor play session, and refrain from using a nose balm unless nose issues such as drying or peeling are present.
- **Nasal depigmentation (Dudley nose/vitiligo).** While uncommon with this breed, this is a condition in which the nose fades. It can be minor or dramatic. A dark nose can fade to brown, pink, or in some cases, even white. Because this is seen as an aesthetic issue, no treatment is given. A nose faded in this way should be protected with nose balm since it can be very sensitive to sunlight.

Protecting Your Dog's Nose

There are a few things that you can do to keep your dog's nose in good health:

1) Nose balm. In the summer, it protects a dog's nose from the sun, which can cause everything from dryness to burns. In the winter, it prevents chapping, drying, and cracking. If there is a current issue with drying, peeling, cracking, or crusting, it can heal this. Look for organic, scent-free balms of high-quality (they will be thick enough to stay on despite some licking) and will have natural ingredients to moisturize, nourish, and restore.

2) Add humidity. Arid air, most typically a problem during the cold winter months, can wreak havoc. It can affect the nose, but also skin over the entire body, and cause eyes to dry out. Add moisture to the air by running a humidifier near your dog's sleeping area. Other home remedies include adding houseplants, setting up open water containers on radiators, and leaving the bathroom door open when showering. See also: 'Seasonal Care: Winter Care'.

3) Hydration. Don't assume your dog will automatically meet water requirements for the day. Dogs can become distracted and/or may not drink stale water. Wash the bowl daily, replace water (not just top-off) often, offer filtered water, and bring along some H20 when you take your dog out for walks and exercise.

4) Supervise outdoor sniffing. Noses can find a lot of trouble outside. From red ant bites to bee stings, to snorting up a pebble. While sniffing around satisfies a natural canine instinct, keep an eye on this.

 Our most up-to-date recommended nose care products can be found on the Supplies page of the PetChiDog site, which is updated as new products emerge. You can reach this by entering any page of PetChiDog.com; Look to the navigation which is in alphabetical order, and choose 'Supplies'.

Paws

General Paw Care

How Tough are Paws? Most dog owners think of dog paws as being tough and strong, and in a way, like shoes for a dog. However, there is much more to consider. The paw pad is made mostly of keratin, which is an exceptionally thick protein. This is a type of skin, albeit a thick one, and therefore vulnerable to many of the issues that 'normal' skin is vulnerable to.

The thickness of a dog's paw is directly related to how often he walks outside and the roughness of those outdoor surfaces. Puppies will have much softer (and more sensitive) paws than older dogs. And older dogs that are routinely taken for walks outside on a variety of surfaces (sand, cement, grass, etc.) will have thicker, more resilient paws than dogs that are kept inside more often.

So, in general, as your dog matures, the paws will become thicker and more durable; however, all dogs, of any age, can benefit from paw protection. Note that paw wax, the most common form of paw protection, does not prevent paws from becoming more durable; just the opposite, in fact. It conditions the paw skin to be healthy and strong, and the protection it offers from certain elements will lend toward more outdoor walking, which in turn leads to stronger paw skin.

This is one reason why athletic dogs and sled dogs, that always have paw wax applied, have extremely durable paws.

What Can Damage the Paws? Many of the elements that your dog encounters during everyday life can affect the paws. Minor to moderate exposure can accumulate into issues such as drying, peeling, or cracking. Severe exposure can cause almost immediate damage.

- Hot walking surfaces. In the summer, pavement, red brick, cement, and other terrain can easily surpass 130°F (54°C), which is the temperature at which paws will receive burns.
- Pebbles, sand, and other small debris can wedge between pad pads.
- Frozen surfaces can dry out paw skin.

- Snow can cause 'snowballing', which is when snow between the pad pads and/or toes melts, refreezes into ice, and then stretches the skin.
- Ice melt/salt products can cause chemical burns and/or irritation to the nail beds.
- Lawn care chemicals can cause allergic reactions, irritate the paws and/or cause chemical burns.

How to Protect the Paws:

1) **Regularly apply a quality paw wax**; this is typically done once per week. It will keep paw skin healthy and resilient, offer excellent traction, and add a breathable layer of protection that prevents damage from hot surfaces in the summer, cold surfaces in the winter, irritation from small bits of sand and pebbles, and lock in moisture to help prevent drying. Additionally, if your dog has some skin damage there (dryness, peeling, irritation), a good canine paw wax can help heal these issues.

2) **Give the paws a quick rinse** in the sink after coming back inside (this is a must for dogs with allergies), to remove any outdoor irritants (pollen, lawn care products, etc.) that can cling to paws.

3) **When walking on rough terrain**, stop now and then to check the paws. You'll want to look for cuts, cracks, or other signs of injury. Dogs may only begin limping once inflammation from an injury develops and the pain is overwhelming.

4) **Do not allow the paws to stay wet for long periods of time.** This can lead to yeast infection. After baths or walking on wet surfaces, dry off the paws and make sure to get the area in between the toes (a cotton swab can work well for that).

Paw Issues

Licking and/or chewing at the paws, **including related itchiness, an odd smell, thinning fur, and/or sores.** These are all common paw issues seen with both puppies and dogs. Information on this is quite extensive. Please refer to 'Behavioral Issues: Licking and/or Chewing at the Paws'.

Rare Issues: Nasodigital hyperkeratosis. This disorder can affect a dog's paws, nose, or both, and is a condition that can be inherited, idiopathic (cause unknown), or seen in conjunction with one of several disorders (see previous section, 'Nose'). The Chihuahua is not one of the breeds most commonly affected by the inherited form. With this disorder, the body overproduces keratin, which leads to paw pads becoming thick, dry, calloused, and often cracked. There is no cure, but there are treatment options. An experienced vet can trim away excess keratin and the paws may be soak-wrapped in a propylene-glycol solution.

Auto-immune disease of the skin (pemphigus). This is a canine disease in which a dog's immune system goes off balance, mistaking healthy skin cells for unhealthy ones and begins to attack them. Symptoms include sores (usually with a pus-like substance in them), crusty sores (which happens after the pus-like sores break open), and sometimes along with sores on a dog's nose and/or ears. This is diagnosed with a skin biopsy. Treatment is with immune-suppressing medication.

When to Treat at Home vs. Going to the Vet:

- **For peeling or minor to moderate cracking**, you can often heal this at home by applying a quality paw wax or a restorative lotion. This should be addressed asap, since paw issues can spiral out of control very quickly. The wax or lotion should be applied 1 to 3 times per day, with one of those applications being at night right as the dog is falling asleep. For all applications, a sock can be slipped over the paw to prevent licking; however, some dogs will be experts in removing it. This is why one application will be at night. If your dog requires daytime applications but pulls at the sock, consider a pet protection collar.

You may also wish to refer to 'Seasonal Care: Summer Care' and/or 'Seasonal Care: Winter Care'.

- **If cracks are deep, with any active bleeding or pus-like discharge, moderate to severe swelling, and/or pain that causes limping,** this warrants a vet visit to rule out any possible infection and/or for antibiotics to prevent or treat infection.

- **For small superficial cuts or moderate cuts,** you can clean the wound with warm, soapy water and then pat it dry. Inspect the area for any possible slivers. Once cleaned, you can dab topical antibiotic ointment on the cut and then cover the paw with a clean sock. If possible, keep your dog inside until the paw has healed. Keep an eye on the area for any redness, swelling, or worsening condition, which would warrant a vet visit.

- **Severe cuts or cuts that do not stop bleeding** must be looked at by the veterinarian. Deep cuts such as this may need to be flushed and stitched. The vet may prescribe oral antibiotics, as well as topical treatment. The paw will need to be protected to allow it to heal and healing can take some time.

- **Any time issues do not respond to treatment.** If you do not see any results with at-home treatments after 3 to 5 days or if symptoms worsen, do not hesitate to contact the veterinarian.

Tail

Hold and Set: The Chihuahua's tail is one of his defining features. Per the AKC breed standard, it is *'Moderately long, carried sickle either up or out, or in a loop over the back with tip just touching the back. Never tucked between legs.'* Sickle means curved, and for this reason, it can indeed loop over the back; however, this is the preferred way of a dog carrying the tail in the show ring; outside of that, a Chihuahua can carry his tail in just about any position and it is considered to be normal.

Long coat

Smooth (short) coat

Today's AKC breed standard also makes it clear that a docked tail (surgically shortening the tail) or a bobtail (a dog is born with an unusually short tail or the tail is missing entirely) is never allowed: *'Disqualifications - Docked tail, bobtail'.* **Why even mention this?** Well, it's because a bobtail was permissible until 1953. When the AKC breed standard of **1923** was written, it was not uncommon for this breed to have a 'kink' at the half to three-quarter point of the tail. This led to a number of Chihuahuas being born with a bobtail in which the tail did not develop past the point of the kink. The **1923** standard worded this as *'Tail- Moderately long, upper portion meaty and break or kink is felt midway or near end, below which tail finishes to a rat end carried cycle or loop-fashioned. Born bob tails are common and not disqualifying.'*

The **1933** breed standard used the exact same wording regarding the tail. In **1942**, the wording changed, but still allowed for the bobtail and even a completely tail-less Chihuahua: *'TAIL – Moderately long, carried sickle either up and out, or in a loop over the back with tail tip just touching the back. Never tucked under. Hair on tail to be in harmony with the coat of the body, preferred furry. A natural bob-tail or tail-less permissible if so born, and not against a good dog.'*

Then, things changed in **1953**; the word 'bobtail' was removed entirely: *'Tail- moderately long, carried cycle either up or out, or in a loop over the back, with tip just touching the back. Never tucked under. Hair on the tail in harmony with the coat of the body, but preferred furry.'* A shortened tail (via docking and not as a trait seen from birth) was only mentioned under disqualifications with *'Disqualifications- cropped tail'*.

This continued with the **1972** breed standard; the only change to the tail section pertained to longhaired tails being long and full which was taken from the coat section and added into the tail section: *'Tail: moderately long, carried sickle either up or out, or in a loop over the back, with tip just touching the back. Never tucked under. Hair on tail in harmony with the coat of the body, preferred furry in smooth coats. In long coats full and long as in a plume.'* The word 'bobtail' reentered the standard under disqualifications with: *'Disqualifications: cropped tail, bobtail'*.

In **1990**, the details of fur on the tail were moved up into the coat section of the standard, leaving the tail section as so: *'Tail – Moderately long, carried sickle either up or out, or in a loop over the back, with tip just touching the back. (Never tucked between legs.)'*. The disqualification remained the same, with *'Disqualifications – Cropped tail, bobtail.'*

The gene that causes the kink and the bobtail is still within the Chihuahua breed today; however, it is recessive and rarely appears.

If the Tail is Held in an Odd Way: The 4 most common issues at play are:

1. **Engorged anal glands.** This pair of small glands (one located on each side of the anus rim) hold oils (commonly referred to as scent oil). Miniscule amounts are released when one dog encounters another and some is also released when a dog has a firm bowel movement. Sometimes, the oil will build up, causing the glands to become swollen with excess fluid. This can lead to somewhat intense itching (a dog may scoot his bottom along the ground in response) and/or hold his tail in a funny way. You may also wish to refer to 'Health & Care - Body Part Specific: Anal Glands'.
2. **Back problems.** Since the tail is a continuation of the spine, issues in the back can radiate down into the tail. Issues can range from a muscle spasm to a herniated disk.
3. **Age-related posture.** With age, there can be muscle loss, weakened tendons, and some level of osteoarthritis. All of these may cause a senior to have a weakened tail hold. It can be mistaken for an injured tail (see next point).
4. **Tail injury.** Many types of accidents can happen to a dog's tail. Common ones include the tail being accidentally stepped on, caught in a car door or house door, or injured during rough play with another dog. Injury can range from a bruise to a break. If you suspect tail injury, this warrants a vet visit. The tail and spine will be examined and x-rays will be taken. Since the tail consists of bone, either a bruise, sprain, or break will be determined. Anti-inflammatory medication may be given, which also helps with pain. In most cases, rest ranging from 2 to 6 weeks will allow the tail to heal. Often, even breaks will heal on their own without a need to set the tail; however, if the fracture is at the base, surgery may be needed to prevent nerve damage.

Health- Stomach, Intestinal

Vomiting

Vomiting may be acute or chronic and may present by itself or with other troubling symptoms such as diarrhea. In many cases, this can be treated at home but close observation is required for possible red flags warranting veterinary treatment. Symptoms can change quickly, and dehydration is always a top concern. Other instances will require immediate veterinary treatment.

When to Take Your Dog to the Veterinarian

This list is not arbitrary, and these are not exaggerations. As you'll see further along, many vomiting-related symptoms can be treated at home, with instructions for a vet visit if things do not improve. However, if your puppy or dog has any of the following, this warrants immediate veterinary intervention and treatment:

➢ Violent, projectile vomiting - Vomit is expelled from the mouth, and sometimes the nasal passages, with extreme force
➢ Blood - Seen in vomit and/or stools
➢ Severe weakness
➢ Refusal to drink
➢ Bloated stomach
➢ Excessive drooling
➢ Any signs of distress - pacing, restlessness, panicked behavior
➢ High fever - anything above 103.5°F (39.7°C)
➢ If vomiting episodes continue for more than 24 hours
➢ If you suspect any form of poisoning

Again, if your puppy or dog has any of the above symptoms, read no further. Any of the above signs warrants an immediate vet visit and should be considered an emergency.

Vomiting Scenarios

Sudden, Acute Vomiting

Acute vomiting will pass quickly; however, during the time that the dog is ill, it can be physically exhausting. Keep in mind that after 72 hours, 'acute' cases will be deemed 'ongoing'.

The 2 most common reasons for this are:

1) **Ingestion of a food or non-food element that causes irritation.** This includes ingesting grass, weeds, other outside plants, or a food (usually taken out of the trash) that irritates the stomach. The element may be toxic or non-toxic.

What to do: If your dog just ate grass or something from the trash that he shouldn't have, there's a good chance that he'll vomit a couple of time and quickly recover without further issue. However, if you suspect that your dog may have ingested something toxic, even if you are not sure what it was, call the vet ASAP.

If you know what was ingested, but are not sure if it is toxic to dogs, call the vet. The most common elements toxic to canines include (but are not limited to): Any food sweetened with xylitol (most often found in sugarless candy & chewing gum), chocolate, coffee (both the grounds and the beans), grapes, raisins, the core of most fruits, any beverage with caffeine, macadamia nuts, onions, garlic (only in large quantities), certain moldy walnuts, leaves and stems from the tomato plant, and raw potatoes.

2) **Eating or drinking water too fast**. If a dog gulps down a large amount of water at one time or swallows a meal too swiftly, this can cause one quick episode of vomiting, and then the dog can be fine afterward.

What to do, water: As long as there are no other troubling signs (see 'When to Take Your Dog to the Veterinarian'), this should be acute, without further vomiting. To prevent this, encourage your dog to drink throughout the day so that he never reaches the point of deep thirst. After exercise, offer water in smaller amounts (1/2 bowl, then 1/2 bowl).

What to do, food: As long as there are no other troubling signs (see 'When to Take Your Dog to the Veterinarian'), this should be acute, without further vomiting. To prevent this:

o Serve smaller but more frequent meals.
o Use a slow-feeder bowl or place a stainless-steel portion pacer in the existing dish.
o Avoid giving meals when your dog is revved up since food can be eaten with too much enthusiasm if it's presented during a state of excitement. If your dog is hyper but dinner is overdue, offer a small snack, allowing him time to calm down before the full meal is offered.

Vomiting and Diarrhea

When diarrhea occurs along with vomiting, this points to a more serious issue. It is not just a quick stomach irritation since the digestive system and intestinal tract is now involved. **There are several reasons for this including:**

1) **Viral causes.** This can range from a mild virus that can clear up in a few days to more serious parvovirus or coronavirus. Vaccinated puppies can contract parvovirus before all puppy shots are complete. With dogs of any age, the vaccine for coronavirus *may* not be included in vaccinations.

What to do: If your dog has any of the signs under the aforementioned 'When to Take Your Dog to the Veterinarian', take your dog to the veterinarian. Elsewise, look ahead to 'Treating Vomiting'.

2) **Eating a certain food.** This can include table scraps, and most often something too greasy. If this is the case, both symptoms of vomiting and diarrhea will pass rather quickly; usually within 2 to 12 hours. It can also include a sudden switch to a new food (with or without irritating ingredients).

What to do: If your dog has any of the signs under the aforementioned 'When to Take Your Dog to the Veterinarian', take your dog to the veterinarian. If you just switched your dog to a new food, assess if that food had inferior products (see 'Feeding and Nutrition: Main Meals'), and if a fast change was made, look ahead to 'Treating Vomiting', followed by a more gradual transition to the new kibble.

3) **Parasites.** A dog can catch one of many parasites, mostly due to ingesting contaminated soil or the feces of other dogs. Many parasites cause diarrhea, and some cause both diarrhea and vomiting. This includes coccidia, giardia, hookworms, whipworms, roundworms, tritrichomonas, cryptosporidium, and tapeworms.

Signs to watch out for: Some worms can be seen in a dog's feces, though not always. You'll want to look for fever, dehydration, weakness, vomiting and/or diarrhea that does not clear up after 12 hours, abnormal behavior, signs of distress, or any other clinical sign that seems out of the ordinary. If so, this warrants veterinary care.

4) **Bacterial infection.** A dog can become sick from certain bacteria by ingesting the feces of other dogs or from ingesting spoiled food. This include clostridium, Campylobacter, E. coli, and salmonella.

What to do: If your dog has any of the signs under the aforementioned 'When to Take Your Dog to the Veterinarian', take your dog to the veterinarian. Elsewise, look ahead to 'Treating Vomiting'.

Vomiting Yellow Liquid and/or Foam

It should be noted that yellow vs. white liquid is very different. Yellow fluid with or without foam is indicative of stomach bile. Bile is a substance that works to neutralize acids in the stomach before it works its way to a dog's small intestines and it counteracts microbes that may be in any digested food. Bile will vary from watery to thick. It may be interlaced with foam or a foamy substance may form around the edges of the puddle.

Reasons for vomiting yellow liquid include:

1) **The stomach is too empty**. This is the most common reason. When the stomach is completely empty, bile can churn and be vomited out.

What to do: Change the feeding schedule to include smaller, more frequent meals and more frequent dry snacks.

- o Most toy breeds do best with 3 small meals per day, plus 4 to 5 small snacks.
- o Take care to not overfed at any one meal, which can affect appetite for other meals; look at what your puppy or dog requires over the course of the entire day, and split this up accordingly.
- o Check the labeling on the kibble for feeding guidelines; these are based on weight and are pretty spot-on.
- o Also, note that the serving size suggestions assume that you are offering additional snacks; but, if your dog does not have the appetite for snacks, decrease meal portions *slightly*, so he will accept dry treats in between meals.
- o To encourage eating while you are away, place kibble (or a mixture of kibble and 100% all-natural smooth peanut butter) in a treat-release toy. See also: 'Care Items - Chihuahuas of All Ages: Toys'.
- o As always, be sure that you are offering a superior food.

2) **Gastritis.** Rare, but possible, is gastritis (inflammation of the stomach). With gastritis, vomiting of yellow foam may come and go or be chronic. Other signs of this include black tarry stools, a green color in the vomit (which indicates bile from the gallbladder), flecks of blood in the vomited fluid, and/or bits of undigested food mixed throughout the yellow foam. This warrants veterinary care.

Vomiting Clear or White Foam, Mucus, or Liquid

White foam *may* be an issue of an empty stomach as with yellow foam, or it can be a random acute case that does not lead to anything. However, it can also point to one of several very serious and sometimes fatal issues.

Serious Reasons for vomiting clear or white foam or liquid include:

1) **Blockage.** If a dog swallows a non-food item or a chunk of food that is too large to pass, this can cause a partial or full blockage in the stomach and/or intestines. In some cases, the first symptom may be vomiting clear or white fluid, sometimes hours before any other clinical signs.

What to do:

1- Search over areas of the house that your dog had access to, looking for anything that was disturbed as a possible clue that he may have gotten into something that he should not have.

2- Closely watch for any other developing signs. Other red flags include straining to eliminate a bowel movement, restlessness, acting panicked, whining, non-interest in eating or drinking, retreating, and/or any signs of discomfort. **With any of these signs, this warrants an immediate vet visit and this is considered an emergency.**

2) **Bloat.** This exceedingly serious condition involves the stomach rotating or twisting and then filling with gas. This is often linked to eating and exercising too closely together or eating or drinking too fast. However, if you see the warning signs of bloat, always seek help even if you do not believe that your dog did either of those two things. Other symptoms include bloated abdomen, heavy panting, dry heaving, restlessness, pacing, not able to sit or lie comfortably, retreating, anxiousness, and/or hunched-over positioning. **With any of these signs, this warrants an immediate vet visit and this is considered an emergency.**

3) **Other possible causes.** There are many other possible causes. This includes kennel cough, diabetes, kidney disease, infection of the digestive tract, food allergy, hepatitis, and even rabies.

What to do: 1- If your dog has any of the signs under the aforementioned 'When to Take Your Dog to the Veterinarian', take your dog to the veterinarian **AND 2-** *Only then*, if bloat and blockage have also been ruled out, look ahead to 'Treating Vomiting'.

Vomiting Right After Eating

This is technically regurgitation, which means that the food is expelled before it begins to digest. Fortunately, the most common reason for this can easily be resolved at home. It typically happens if a dog eats too fast or too much. You'll want to:

o Serve smaller but more frequent meals.
o Use a slow-feeder bowl or place a stainless-steel portion pacer in the existing dish.
o Avoid giving meals when your dog is revved up since food can be eaten with too much enthusiasm if it's presented during a state of excitement. If your dog is hyper but dinner is overdue, offer a small snack, allowing him time to calm down before the full meal is offered.

Less common, but a possibility is collapsed trachea; other signs include a hacking cough and/or breathing issues. See also: 'Health – Other: Collapsed Trachea'.

Vomiting During or Immediately Following Exercise

This can happen if a dog is allowed to run around or is taken for a brisk walk right after eating, before the food has had a chance to digest. Canines have a much more sensitive gag reflex than humans; therefore, allow for 1 hour between meals and exercise. This is also a standard guideline to prevent bloat, which can happen to any breed.

<u>Treating Vomiting</u>

Here is what you can do from home, as long as there are no red flag symptoms that warrant a vet visit:

1. Stop all food for 12 to 24 hours. Once a dog vomits, any more food will most likely trigger another episode. In addition, if there is also diarrhea, it can be very beneficial for the body to have a rest. For these reasons, it is recommended to withhold food for at least 12 hours. Depending on when you start this, and sleeping patterns, you may withhold food for up to 24 hours, as long as your puppy or dog is drinking.

2. Keep your dog hydrated. This is important, so encourage your dog to slowly drink water. Offer just a bit at a time. Be sure to offer filtered or spring water, not unfiltered tap water.

If you feel that your dog is not drinking enough, ask your veterinarian if you can offer a blend of water and unflavored Children's Pedialyte®, which is a drink designed to replace electrolytes that may have been lost when vomiting. If you offer this, it must be plain Pedialyte and not with any other added ingredients. When given in moderation, this is generally considered safe for canine consumption. Double-check with your vet; however, dosing is relatively small; just 1/8 of a cup for each 10 lbs. of body weight, every 1 to 2 hours.

3. If drinking triggers more vomiting, offer ice cubes. Ice cubes can be made from filtered or spring water or mixed with 50% water and 50% pure apple juice, or mixed with Children's Pedialyte (under vet supervision).

4. After 12 to 24 hours, start your dog on a bland diet. This is typically just 1 protein and 1 starch. One of the most tolerated combinations is plain, white, skinless chicken breast diced small and plain white rice. However, lean beef and sweet potato are other good options.

5. After 3 days, start to transition back to a regular diet or a new, better food if that was decided. By then, the body should be well-rested.

If vomiting lasts for more than 24 hours, this warrants an immediate vet visit.

Diarrhea

When to Take Your Dog to the Veterinarian

This list is not arbitrary, and these are not exaggerations. As you'll see further along, many diarrhea-related symptoms can be treated at home, with instructions for a vet visit if things do not improve. However, if your puppy or dog has any of the following, this warrants immediate veterinary intervention and treatment:

➢ Diarrhea along with violent, projectile vomiting - Vomit is expelled from the mouth, and sometimes the nasal passages, with extreme force
➢ Explosive diarrhea – Almost pure water, shot out with force
➢ Bloody diarrhea
➢ Diarrhea along with blood seen in vomit
➢ Severe weakness
➢ Refusal to drink
➢ Bloated stomach
➢ Excessive drooling
➢ Any signs of distress - pacing, restlessness, panicked behavior
➢ High fever - anything above 103.5°F (39.7°C)
➢ Trouble breathing
➢ If moderate to severe diarrhea lasts for more than 24 hours or mild diarrhea lasts more than 3 days
➢ If you suspect any form of poisoning

Again, if your puppy or dog has any of the above symptoms, read no further. Any of the above signs warrants an immediate vet visit and should be considered an emergency.

Acute vs. Chronic vs. Intermittent Diarrhea

▪ **Acute diarrhea** will be a short episode, typically lasting 2 to 5 days that responds to at-home treatment and does not reoccur again within the next 3 months. *Steps seen here may help.*
▪ **Chronic diarrhea** lasts more than 5 days. It may appear to get better once a dog is treated at home, but resurfaces soon afterward. *For this, diagnosis and treatment at the veterinarian's office is needed.*
▪ **Intermittent diarrhea** is bouts seen often throughout the year. It comes and goes. It may be a week or a month between occurrences. *For this, diagnosis and treatment at the veterinarian's office is needed.*

Reasons for Diarrhea are Often the Same as Reasons for Vomiting

Many of the same triggers that cause vomiting will cause diarrhea; this includes ingestion of a certain food or non-food element, viral causes, parasites, bacterial infection, and other health issues. So, do please refer to the previous section, 'Vomiting'.

In addition to those causes listed under 'Vomiting', diarrhea may also be due to:

1) **A food intolerance.** Milk-based products are at the top of this list. Some dairy foods such as cottage cheese and whole white yogurt are tolerated well (and can actually be helpful for some stomach and digestive issues); however, many other types of dairy products such as ice cream, milk, and cheese (such as deli cheese, etc.) can cause diarrhea. It should be noted that large quantities of cheese can have the opposite effect and cause constipation. Other foods include table scraps such as very fatty meats or greasy foods.

Dairy allergy [handwritten annotation in left margin]

What to do: If your dog has any of the signs under the aforementioned 'When to Take Your Dog to the Veterinarian', take your dog to the veterinarian. Elsewise, look ahead to 'Treating Diarrhea'.

2) **Food allergy.** Many cases of food allergies pertain to a dog suffering an allergic reaction to a chemical found in manufactured food such as artificial coloring, flavors, or preservatives or to fillers such as corn or brans, manifesting as skin rash, itchiness, etc. *However,* some dogs can have trouble with certain 'real' foods, and this can lead to diarrhea. This can be in response *any* 'real' food including any protein or eggs.

Aside from diarrhea, other signs may include moderate to severe itching around the anus, and/or flatulence.

What to do: With diarrhea caused by a specific food, once steps have been taken to treat the diarrhea, a dog may recover but almost immediately have troubles again once his normal food is introduced back into his diet. If you suspect a protein, change your dog's protein base; for example, from fish to chicken, or chicken to lamb.

If you find yourself completely baffled as to what food could possibly be the culprit, you may wish to use a method of trial and error. With this, a dog is put on a bland diet for 2 weeks, which is typically just 1 protein and 1 starch. One of the most tolerated combinations is plain, white, skinless chicken breast diced small and plain white rice. However, lean beef and sweet potato are other good options. Then, every 2 weeks, 1 new food is introduced to ascertain which ingredient is causing distress.

3) **Stress.** Diarrhea can happen if a dog is suffering from overwhelming stress. This can include severe cases of separation anxiety or a chaotic or negative environment (loud noises, yelling, domestic upset, etc.). Other times, a certain situation may cause temporary intestinal distress such moving to a new home, the introduction of a new pet or being transported or traveling when not accustomed to it (car or airplane).

What to do: Resolving this is quite detailed; you may wish to refer to 'Puppy Care', 'Situational Issues: Separation Anxiety', or 'Safety and Happiness: Traveling'.

4) **Inflammatory bowel disease.** This is a catch-all term that is given if a dog has ongoing, chronic diarrhea linked to one of several conditions including allergies, parasites, lowered immune system, and some diseases including colitis. Signs include persistent diarrhea, low-grade fever, weight loss, lethargy, and/or vomiting. This is more commonly seen in dogs that are 5+ years, though it can happen to younger dogs as well.

Diagnosing this includes blood testing, urinalysis, stool testing, and other tests. Antibiotics, corticosteroids, and medications to protect the lining of the intestines may be given. In many cases, a change to a different food which includes a switch in both protein and carb sources can help.

5) **Other less common reasons for diarrhea include:** Kidney disease, liver disease, cancer, lymphangiectasia, pancreatitis, and hemorrhagic gastroenteritis.

Treating Diarrhea

Here is what you can do from home, as long as there are no red flag symptoms that warrant a vet visit. Note that these instructions are nearly identical to treating vomiting, with the exclusion of offering ice cubes. And, there is additional treatment related to a sore anus.

1. Stop all food for 12 to 24 hours. It can be very beneficial for the body to have a rest. Aim for at least 12 hours; but, depending on when you start this, and sleeping patterns, you may withhold food for up to 24 hours, as long as your puppy or dog is drinking.

2. Keep your dog hydrated. This is important, so encourage your dog to slowly drink water. Offer just a bit at a time. Be sure to offer filtered or spring water, not unfiltered tap water.

If you feel that your dog is not drinking enough, ask your veterinarian if you can offer a blend of water and unflavored Children's Pedialyte®, which is a drink designed to replace electrolytes that may have been lost when vomiting. If you offer this, it must be plain Pedialyte and not with any other added ingredients. When given in moderation, this is generally considered safe for canine consumption. Double-check with your vet; however, dosing is relatively small; just 1/8 of a cup for each 10 lbs. of body weight, every 1 to 2 hours.

3. After 12 to 24 hours, start your dog on a bland diet. This is typically just 1 protein and 1 starch. One of the most tolerated combinations is plain, white, skinless chicken breast diced small and plain white rice. However, lean beef and sweet potato are other good options.

4. After 3 days, start to transition back to a regular diet or a new, better food if that was decided. By then, the body should be well-rested.

5. Tend to a sore/burning anus area. Diarrhea can burn as it is expelled due to its often high level of acidity, and therefore, repeated bouts of diarrhea can cause a dog's anus to become sore, red, and very irritated. Here is what you can do:

o *Keep it clean* - Gently wipe the anus after each episode of diarrhea with a doggie tushie wipe or canine grooming wipe. If you do not have any on hand, a non-scented baby wipe can be used.
o *Apply a barrier cream or gel* - Dab an ointment, cream, or gel onto the anus area to create a barrier against stinging diarrhea that passes the skin as it is expelled. Be careful regarding what you use; some human facial creams or creams for dry skin can cause more burning. Petroleum jelly is one of the best choices; if you do not have this, vitamin D ointment can be used as a substitution.
o *Check for skin damage/infection* - Skin may break open and then be vulnerable to infection, so keep an eye on this area. This is a reason to contact the vet, and a topical antibiotic may be needed.

Constipation

While constipation may involve the inability to push out stools, there are other, less severe signs included with this. For each, these will occur for at least a 24-hour period. This includes straining, fewer bowel movements, hard consistency, and/or smaller size (small tiny pellet-type pieces). Fortunately, many cases of constipation can be treated at home.

Causes of Constipation

Some basic, common things can trigger constipation:

1) **Inadequate water intake.** If a dog is not drinking enough, this can cause stools to harden, which leads to constipation. In general, canines need a minimum of 1 ounce of water for each 1 pound of body weight. This amount increases for very active dogs, and in the summertime.

2) **Decrease in exercise.** Exercise prompts food matter to travel through the large intestines. If there is a sudden decline in activity, bowel movements may slow down.

3) **Change in food.** This can lead to temporary issues including upset stomach, runny stools, or constipation. Too fast of a switch can cause problems, even if the new diet is a better food. It can also be a matter of the newer diet containing less fiber than before. Cheese or red meats can make stools sluggish as well.

4) **Stress.** Common stress issues include a sudden addition to the family, moving to a new home, or a drastic change in routine such as more time home alone.

5) **Habit of holding in bowel movements.** This can happen if a dog does not want to soil inside the house. It's also common if a dog is in a new place, like a boarding kennel or when traveling.

Red Flag Health Issues that Can Cause Constipation

It is always wise to be aware of certain health issues that have constipation as one of the symptoms. If treatment at home does not resolve the issue or if there are other signs as described, it will warrant a visit to the veterinarian.

➤ **Engorged anal glands.** If glands are swollen and engorged, due to their positioning, these can act as a sort of barrier, making it more difficult to push out stools. See also 'Health & Care – Body Part Specific: Anal Glands'.

➤ **Internal blockage.** This is a very serious condition where an object or hard-to-digest matter (food or non-food) causes partial or full blockage. In addition to straining to push out stools, other signs include drooling, panicked behavior, loss of appetite, vomiting, and/or dry heaving. This should be considered an emergency and requires immediate veterinary care.

➤ **Enlarged prostate gland.** Relevant for males, this can develop due to age-related hormone changes (80% of intact males 8+ years have some level of this), but this can be due to bacterial infection or even cancer. Other signs aside from constipation include trouble urinating, blood in the urine and/or the stools (will appear bright red), and/or stools shaped like thin strips (often equated to ribbon).

➤ **Other causes.** While rare, an array of other conditions can cause constipation; this includes trauma to the pelvic area, rectal tumors, and certain neurological disorders. For seniors in particular, arthritic pain in the hips or back can lead to trouble with finding a comfortable stance to push out stools. This hesitation can cause stools back up.

Treating Constipation

Some home remedies can usually resolve minor to moderate cases of constipation. For quick results, follow as many as are applicable.

1. **Encourage increased water intake**. Ways to do this include:

   o The water bowl should be stainless-steel or ceramic. Plastic bowls do not keep water cool and dogs like cool water much more than warm.
   o Refill the water often. Dogs often balk at stale water or water with bits of food floating in it.
   o But, another option is to obtain a canine water fountain, as opposed to just a bowl. The sight and sound of the flowing water are great for attracting dogs and encouraging them to drink.
   o Bring water along with you whenever you head out for walks or outdoor activity. Stop every 15 to 20 minutes for a short break and a sip of water.
   o Offer fruits high in water content; this includes blueberries (85% water) and raspberries (87% water); both of these are packed with antioxidants and are low-calorie, which makes them healthy as well.

2. **Add fiber.** Soluble fiber typically works well to relieve constipation, and pumpkin is the standard go-to remedy that works well for many dogs. Obtain 100% real canned puree pumpkin and not the pie filling. Start with 1 teaspoon per day and increase to 2 teaspoons if needed. Alternatively, kale and spinach can be effective (though too much can cause flatulence). When ground, these can easily be mixed into meals.

3. **Exercise.** Exercise helps move fecal matter through the large intestine faster, which leads to less water being absorbed by the body and therefore facilitating bowel movements. Also, the increased breathing and heart rate triggers natural contraction of intestinal muscles which can also prompt a bowel movement. Add an extra 20-minute walk or 10 minutes to each walk.

Note: At-home remedies to be wary of include coconut oil, supplements containing acidophilus, folic acid and/or vegetable enzymes, milk of magnesia, bran, mineral oil, organic apple cider vinegar, and psyllium husk powder. These can cause upset stomach and other issues.

When Constipation Needs to Be Treated by the Veterinarian

Chronic constipation lasting 2 weeks or more can lead to impacted feces that cause the large intestine to become unnaturally stretched. This can lead to a serious condition, megacolon, that often requires surgery. Therefore, veterinary care is needed if any of the following apply:

➢ If your dog has not had a bowel movement for 48 hours
➢ If constipation (in which there are some stools) lasts longer than 1 week
➢ If there are any other signs including but not limited to labored breathing, panicked behavior, marked lethargy, signs of pain, bloated stomach, dry heaving, vomiting, fever, marked decreased appetite, and/or trouble drinking.

Treatment will involve laxatives or stool softeners, and in some cases, an enema may be given.

Health – Other

Allergies

Signs and Symptoms

Don't let the long list fool you. A dog can have just **ONE** of these symptoms, and suffer terribly. For example, continual licking at the paws to the point of severe irritation and even open skin sores. Also, symptoms can change over time; for example, a dog may lick at his paws in the spring and summer, and then have bloodshot eyes in the winter. The full list of possible symptoms includes:

- Excessive dry skin
- Itching
- Rash
- Skin sores
- Skin scabs
- Hot spots
- Thinning coat
- Chronic ear infections
- Eye discharge
- Bloodshot eyes
- Wheezing
- Coughing
- Sneezing
- Runny nose
- Exercise intolerance due to breathing issues
- Upset stomach and/or vomiting (if seen, will most likely be due to food allergies)
- Licking, scratching, or chewing (often the paws) and/or rubbing the body against surfaces

Types of Allergies and Specific Allergens
A dog can be allergic to a wide range of allergens that can be placed into 3 main categories, and there are certain allergens within those groups that are the most common triggers.

1. Food Allergies. It is often additives in dog food that cause a problem; far too many brands are guilty of adding these. This can also include certain foods that are known for triggering allergies, including 'filler' foods that manufacturers add as a cost-saving method.

The following dog food ingredients can be allergens:

- Chemical/synthetic preservatives: Butylated hydroxyanisole (BHA), butylated hydroxytoluene (BHT), tert-butyl hydroquinone (TBHQ), ethoxyquin, and propylene glycol (PG).

ethoxyquin

- Artificial coloring dyes: Blue 2, Red 40, Yellow 5, and Yellow 6.
- Artificial flavoring: MSG (monosodium glutamate). Look out for soy extracts and soy concentrate; these contain MSG.
- Corn and grains: For corn, this also includes corn germ meal, corn gluten meal, and corn bran. For grains, this includes wheat, oats, barley, and other cereal grains (may be listed as hominy feed). * Rice can be an exception; with rice, the hull, bran layer, and cereal germ are removed and for this reason, rice is often tolerated very well.
- While it is rare, dogs can be allergic to such things as eggs or even any protein such as chicken (normally very well tolerated), beef, lamb, bison, rabbit, fish, or any other meat.
- Soy: This can be listed as soy, soybeans, or soy meal.
- Other fillers and additives: There is almost an endless list; however, some to avoid include wheat mill run (may be listed as wheat middlings - is what is swept up from the floor of wheat factories), peanut hulls, and menadione.

Toxins in tap water can be a source of allergens. There are literally hundreds.

2. Environmental Allergies. This includes airborne allergens such as seasonal pollen (from trees, weeds, and grasses), plus those found in your home.

Trees. *Some trees release a lot of allergens in the spring*, including aspen, beech, birch, maple box elder, cottonwood, elm, hickory, mountain elder, oak, pecan (but can go into June), and willow trees (but can go into July). *And some trees release allergens at other times*, such as ash and elm that can release allergens in both spring and fall (depending on your location), the mountain cedar which releases pollen from December to March in southern states, and mulberry trees which release pollen in the winter right into the spring.

Weeds. This includes ragweed, which starts in the summer and reaches its peak mid-September, ryegrass which creates pollen in May and June, and pigweed that is worst early spring through the summer.

Grass. This top pollen producer is everywhere; but some of the top pollen-producing grasses include Bermuda grass, Johnson grass, Kentucky bluegrass, orchard grass, sweet vernal grass, and Timothy grass.

Dust mites and their droppings are a major source of allergies and asthma year-round. Mites don't bite; their food source is the dead skin flakes of people (or pets), but they do leave pellet droppings, and that is what some people and canines are allergic to. Dust mites live in dust (a 1/2 teaspoon contains up to 1,000 mites and over 25,000 droppings), in carpeting, and in bedding such as mattresses and pillows.

The American Lung Association warns that 4 out of 5 homes have detectable levels of dust mites in at least one bed. A used mattress can have hundreds of thousands of mites inside it. And, a substantial amount of weight of old pillows can be comprised of mites and their droppings.

They multiply rapidly; a male dust mite lives 19 days, at the most. But, a female lives up to 70 and can lay 60 to 100 eggs during that time.

Mold spores. Mold grows year-round, both inside and out, in moist areas. If a house has an unknown water leak, moisture in the basement, a slightly leaky window, or any damp areas under rugs and such, mold can quickly grow there. This is more common in locations that tend to receive a lot of rain.

Finally, such things as aerosol cleaners or air freshener sprays that are used in the house can contribute to a dog's allergies.

3. Contact Allergies.

This is the least common type of allergy with canines, but should not be ruled out. This refers to something that a dog is coming into physical contact with. High on the list are plastic bowls. But, this could also include carpeting and fabrics such as bed linens. In some cases, even rubber toys can cause an allergic reaction.

In most cases, there will be a localized skin reaction on the area that touches the allergen element. For example, with bowls, this will often be on the nose and may be around the mouth. If a dog is allergic to carpeting or even laundry detergent that used to wash throw rugs, a dog bed cover, etc. there can be a full body rash.

So, as you can see, there's quite a lot for a dog to be allergic to, year-round; however, knowing what the main culprits are is half the battle.

Diagnosing Allergies

Testing at the veterinarian's: We certainly encourage you to take your dog to the veterinarian for help with allergies. However, it must be noted that the 2 main types of allergy testing for canines are not without their drawbacks:

- **Blood testing.** The most commonly used type of blood test to check a dog for allergies is known as ELISA (enzyme-linked immunosorbent assay), which checks the blood for antigen-induced antibodies. It is more accurate in determining food allergies than it is for environmental or contact triggers. Because this test was specifically designed for humans, it is not entirely precise for canines and is known to produce false positives, which can send you down the wrong path.

- **Intradermal skin testing.** Of the two, this is the more reliable. However, it is not without some downsides. A section of a dog's coat is shaved, and tiny amounts of the most common allergens are injected just under the skin. One con of this test is that a dog must be sedated for it. In addition, for the test to work to any degree of certainty, antihistamines and other allergy medications cannot be given for 1 to 3 months beforehand. You can expect accurate results approximately 75% of the time. This is because it is up to each veterinarian to determine what qualifies as a true skin reaction, and only a limited number of allergens are available to use with this testing.

Testing at home: While you cannot run an actual test, you can eliminate common triggers, thus determining for yourself which changes are helpful in clearing up your dog's allergy symptoms. Do note that with some triggers, especially food allergies, significant improvement may not be seen for up to 12 weeks.

Vet vs. at home: Whether you decide to handle this at home, or see the vet for testing, a vet visit is warranted when a dog is having quite severe reactions. Other issues that mimic allergies can be ruled out and the vet can prescribe antihistamines, anti-inflammatories, and other medications if needed. You can work side-by-side with the vet to truly tackle allergy issues.

The 3 Steps to Resolve Allergies Effectively and Permanently

As with many things in life, shortcuts will get you nowhere. When it comes to allergies, you will find very limited or temporary success if you try to circumvent the steps to resolve them.

This is due, in part, to the fact that a dog can be allergic to more than one trigger. Remove one, but not the other, and your dog will still be exposed. In addition, for every trigger, there are multiple steps that you'll want to follow. Skip one, and all your other work may be done in vain. So, to truly resolve allergies, there are 3 steps:

1) Significantly reduce or completely eliminate allergens.
2) Use effective allergy treatments to resolve symptoms.
3) Continued avoidance of allergens and good care management to help prevent re-occurrence.

Step 1: Significantly Reduce or Completely Eliminate Allergens
It is best if you do not automatically discount any of these. And keep in mind that your puppy or dog may have more than one type and more than one subset of allergies. For example, both a sensitivity to synthetic preservatives (food) and reaction to dust mites (environmental).

Step 1, Part 1 Eliminate Food Allergens: Main meals and all snacks should be assessed.

Meals:

1- **Start by choosing a kibble that has NONE of the most common allergens.** You'll want to offer a wholesome, all-natural, quality food that has zero corn, corn germ meal, corn gluten meal, corn bran, soy, soybeans, soy meal, wheat, barley, or hominy feed. * Rice *can* be an exception (the hull, bran layer, and cereal germ are removed and for this reason, rice is often tolerated very well), but, if you want to be thorough, choose 100% grain-free. It should also have no chemical or synthetic preservatives, artificial coloring dyes, MSG or other artificial flavorings, or menadione. See also: 'Feeding and Nutrition: Main Meals'.

2- As mentioned earlier, it can take up to 12 weeks for food allergens to completely clear out of the body. **So, if after 12 weeks, you still suspect a food allergy or if you already know that your dog is sensitive to a certain protein, change protein bases, while sticking to the rule of ZERO common allergens.** Chicken is the most widely tolerated protein; in fact, this is what veterinarians most often recommend as part of a 'bland diet' to help dogs recover from intestinal issues. However, this is not to say that a dog cannot be allergic to poultry, it does happen.

Other protein bases to choose from include lamb, beef, fish (salmon, whitefish, etc.), rabbit, duck, turkey (a chicken allergy does not necessarily equal a turkey allergy), and bison.

Snacks: **Every snack and training treat that you offer should be held to the same high standards as main meals.** If you switch to a wholesome kibble, but continue to feed your puppy or dog snacks or treats that trigger symptoms, allergies will not be resolved.

Water: Tap Choose a method to offer filtered water. Tap water across the US is filled with over 100 known contaminants that are regulated by the EPA, meaning that they may be present in small amounts. This includes rocket fuel, factory run-off, and pesticides. Methods to offer toxin-free water include offering bottled spring water, installing a filter to your kitchen sink, or using a filtering water pitcher.

Step 1, Part 2 Reduce Environmental Allergens: Pollen, mold, dust mites, and aerosols.

Since these particles are minute yet powerful, just missing one of these steps may allow allergies to continue. So, you'll want to follow as many of these steps as you can:

1. Vacuum all rooms of the house, no matter the type of flooring, with a vacuum cleaner that has HEPA filtration. HEPA is certified to trap 99.97% of particles as small as 0.3 microns; therefore, it will trap dust, dust mites, pollen, mold spores, and other allergens. This will remove these elements from the floor and can clear the air to some extent as it cycles through the machine. Use a hand-held model to vacuum furniture such as sofas and cushioned chairs.

2. Filter the air. If you have a central air system, run this (just the fan setting is okay) while using either HEPA filters with a MERV rating of at least 9, or a filter with an FPR of at least 9. These will filter out pollen, mold, dust mites, and other microscopic allergens. If you do not have central air, consider obtaining free-standing HEPA air purifiers for your home.

3. Consider adding some plants to your home. Studies by the American College of Allergy, Asthma & Immunology[1] have proven that the English Ivy removes 78% of airborne mold in a room within just 12 hours. A spider plant can remove as much as 90% of airborne toxins in a room in 48 hours. And, the Boston Fern, Chinese Evergreen, and Peace Lilly are great at removing airborne toxins as well.

4. Wet-dust the house often. Use a 'dust and allergen' spray to pick up dust (and in turn, mites and their droppings).

5. Routinely wash bed linens, pillow covers, toss pillows, throw rugs, and every other washable in a hot water cycle, as allowed. This is to kill dust mites; only water that is at least 130°F (54°C) can destroy them.

6. If you have old pillows, mattresses, or other items that you don't need, and they have not been protected with dust-mite protection covers, consider tossing them.

7. Protect all current mattresses and pillows with dust-mite protection covers. These are made with a special allergen-blocking fabric that zippers up securely. The mattress cover will encase all sides of the mattress (top, bottom, and sides). Note that this traps existing mites inside the mattress or pillow (they *are* there), and will prevent them from triggering allergies or moving about the house.

8. As you are clearing the house of allergens, keep windows closed so that pollen and other airborne allergens cannot re-enter the home.

9. Have everyone remove shoes before they enter the home. Keep these up and out of reach.

10. Keep the grass in your yard cut short.

11. But when it's being mowed, be sure to keep your puppy or dog inside.

12. The person who mows the yard should remove as much clothing as they can while still outside, wash those clothes right away, and promptly shower.

13. Routinely apply paw wax to your dog's paws to help create a barrier between them and outdoor triggers on grass and walking surfaces. A bonus is that a quality paw wax can help clear up irritated paw skin and other issues that often manifest due to allergies.

14. Keep track of high pollen-count days. You can see this information alongside most local weather reports. The best time for daily walks on these days is early in the morning and then again later in the evening. This is because pollen usually reaches its peak right around noontime.

15. Wipe your dog down each time your puppy or dog comes back into the home. This is regardless of whether it was a 2-minute bathroom trip or a 20-minute walk. Use a hypo-allergenic grooming wipe.

16. Rinse off your dog's paws after coming back inside. The paw wax will have created a barrier, but you want to wash off what is now clung to that barrier, so it is not tracked into the house. The kitchen sink is often the most convenient method. Don't worry about the paw wax coming off; water will not remove it; it takes about 1 week for the wax to slowly wear away.

17. Brush the coat often. Regardless of coat length, brush the entire body 3 to 5 times per week.

18. Limit the use of chemical cleaners including aerosol air freshener sprays and carpet deodorizing powders. When you are using strong cleaners, such as when scrubbing the bathtub, keep your dog away from the area.

19. Inspect the house for any water leaks. Check the basement and around all visible plumbing.

Step 1, Part 3 Eliminate Contact Allergens: Bowls, carpeting, detergent, and toys.

For this, you'll want to rule out certain items and elements that your dog may be coming into contact with. This includes:

Bowls. One of the most common contact allergens is plastic bowls; even those that are BPA and/or PVC free can be to blame, and this is often due to heavy color dyes, but can be the plastic material itself. Use stainless-steel or ceramic bowls.

Carpeting. Certain carpet fibers can cause allergic reactions, and rough texture just adds to the problem. If you have wall-to-wall carpeting and suspect this to be one of the culprits, encourage your dog to rest and sleep in his bed and/or place down small blankets that have been washed in hypo-allergenic detergent.

Detergent. Stuffed toys, blankets, etc. that have been washed in heavily perfumed detergent may cause a reaction. Always use a hypo-allergenic detergent that is free of perfumes or dyes.

Toys. Certain toys, and particularly inexpensive ones that you may find at dollar stores, may be made from cheap rubbers or plastics, and often with heavy coloring dyes. Check your dog's toy collection and remove suspect toys.

Step 2: Use Effective Allergy Treatments to Resolve Issues

Here, we will look at all options, including those that work very well and those that are iffy at best and carry certain risks.

Treatments Through the Veterinarian:

Prescribed medications. We know that many owners would prefer to treat their dog's allergies at home, and not have to visit the veterinarian. However, with moderate to severe cases, a vet visit is often warranted so that strong medications can be given. This may include an antihistamine such as hydroxyzine. This is not FDA approved for veterinary use, but is given by some vets. It can make a dog very sleepy; other possible side effects include change in behavior, dry mouth, vomiting, and even seizures.

There are also prescribed anti-inflammatories and anti-itch medications. One is Cytopoint, which is engineered antibodies meant to specifically target proteins that send an 'itch' signal to the brain. It is given every 4 to 8 weeks via injection by a veterinarian, so it can be rather expensive. This does not help with any symptoms other than itching and does not resolve the cause. Also, very little testing was done before being approved (for itching related to atopic dermatitis). At the time of this writing, only 36 dogs were tested for 7 months.

Alternatively, corticosteroids such as prednisone may be given for itching; this can only be given short-term without risk of severe side effects. Even short-term, there may be changes in thirst or appetite, and risk of susceptibility to infections. A dog will need to be carefully monitored.

Immunotherapy. Also known as hyposensitization, and commonly referred to as allergy shots, ***these have some major drawbacks and risks that you should know about:***

- With this, a small amount of an allergen(s) is given to a dog with the goal of being able to build up a tolerance. This does not work for food allergies, only has a chance of working if the exact culprit allergens have been identified, needs to be given every day (oral) or once a week (injected), symptoms may worsen during the first few months, it can take years to work, and it may need to be given for life (though less frequently).
- This type of allergy treatment is only effective about 75% of the time, and most importantly there can be very serious side effects including hives, trouble breathing, and even anaphylactic shock.

OTC antihistamines. This should ONLY be given under veterinary supervision. With an over-the-counter allergy medication such as diphenhydramine (Benadryl), there are important things to keep in mind:

1) Antihistamines like this are typically only effective 30% of the time.
2) This must be used cautiously with dogs with certain health conditions including but not limited to glaucoma, cardiovascular disease, hypertension, enlarged prostate, and bladder obstructions.
3) Dosing must be exact. Dosing is 1 mg per 1 lb. (.45 kg) of body weight, given 2-3 times a day; it's dangerous to inadvertently give too much.
4) If it *does* work for itching, it will not resolve severe skin issues including hot spots, nor will it cure an allergy. The best method is to follow the steps of working to reduce or remove all possible triggers, and use effective treatments (coming up next) to cure itching and bring relief or see the vet for severe symptoms.
5) There are possible side effects including but not limited lethargy, dry mouth, sleepiness, decreased appetite, and vomiting.
6) Any formulas of diphenhydramine mixed with cough syrup or other medications can be toxic to dogs. If this is used, it must be diphenhydramine only.
7) This should only be used after checking with the veterinarian.

At Home Treatments:

A combination of two or more of these can be very effective. However, note that if you do not work to reduce or eliminate the allergens, these can only do so much. It'll be an uphill battle.

1. Sprays. A good allergy spray can offer immediate relief, as well as work long-term to help resolve severe itch, hot spots, irritated skin, and/or rash. These are great for targeting specific areas on a dog that are troublesome. And, these are a good choice if a dog's skin is very sensitive and it would be best to not touch those areas.

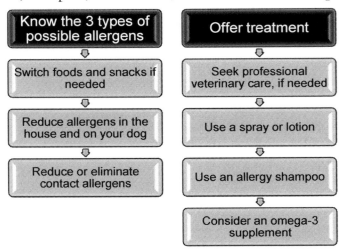

There are both medicated and non-medicated spray. An anti-itch *medicated* spray is typically for severe cases; but, should not be used on areas that a dog can lick or chew unless you will be placing a recovery collar on your dog or slipping on socks (if it is the paws being treated). This will be a spray with hydrocortisone (for itch and inflammation) with or without lidocaine (numbing agent for discomfort).

There are also *non-medicated* allergy sprays that can be quite effective. These are a good choice if the itchy areas are those that a dog may lick or chew. Also, non-medicated is best if skin is broken open. Typically, these will work with a combination of ingredients such as colloidal oatmeal, wheat germ, and/or baking soda (for itch) and vitamin blends, aloe vera, and/or shea butter for soothing the skin.

2. Lotion. Lotion, like spray, puts help directly where a dog needs it. Lotion is often best if a dog has itchiness just about everywhere. It'll be easier to apply than trying to spray the entire body. But, something to keep in mind is that with lotion, you will be touching your dog to apply it.

So, if your dog is so sensitive that you can't imagine massaging a lotion in, one of the aforementioned sprays will be better. Lotions with a blend of anti-itch and restorative ingredients can offer immediate relief while improving skin condition. This would include manuka honey, aloe vera, coconut oil, olive oil, shea butter, hemp seed oil, and vitamin blends.

3. Allergy shampoo. A good allergy shampoo allows you to thoroughly saturate your puppy or dog in a healing product, reaching every single area of the body. Once massaged in, allow it to soak in for a good ten minutes; this can provide ultimate relief, healing, and restoration. So, whether you use a spray or a lotion, you'll want to have a superior allergy shampoo.

There are both medicated and non-medicated specialty shampoos. A *medicated* shampoo can offer what the medicated spray does, which is hydrocortisone (for itch and inflammation) and lidocaine (numbing agent for discomfort); but, you'll also want it to have something to soothe at the same time; aloe vera and/or colloidal oatmeal are good choices for this.

A *non-medicated* shampoo can be very effective as well, using natural, organic compounds to stop itching, soothe sore skin, and restore skin cells. Bentonite clay can be particularly helpful for clearing skin up. And other natural ingredients such as aloe vera, colloidal oatmeal, shea butter, olive oil, hemp seed oil, and coconut oil are also excellent.

4. Omega-3 fish oil. While a quality dog food will have omega-3 in it, an extra supplement of omega-3 DHA and EPA can help improve both skin and coat health. A liquid fish oil is recommended, preferably derived from wild fish, not farmed.

Step 3: Continued Avoidance & Good Care Management

Once your dog is no longer suffering from allergies, and symptoms have cleared up, you'll want to do all you can to avoid future problems. There are just a few things to keep in mind:

1. Canines can grow in and out of allergies, and allergens can change all throughout the year (for example, pollen in the summer, ragweed in the fall, and mites in the winter), so always be on guard. It's easier to treat things like irritated skin or rash at the beginning stages.

2. Don't fall behind in keeping both your house and your dog allergen-free. It's normal to dive enthusiastically into getting rid of allergens when your canine family member is really suffering badly. But, then as time goes by, and a dog is feeling better, it's common for owners to let things slack a bit. Before you know it, you're a week overdue in vacuuming, you haven't changed the filters in the purifier in months, and that container of grooming wipes ran out weeks ago. Keep a schedule and recruit other members of the household to help out.

3. When a dog's skin, coat, paws, and nose are in tiptop shape, these areas will be less prone to issues. Bathe your dog on time using a quality shampoo and conditioner, use a daily coat spritz, regularly apply paw wax, and use nose balm if the nose tends to get dry.

1 American College of Allergy, Asthma, & Immunology's annual meeting, Anaheim, Calif., Nov. 4-9, 2005. News release, American College of Allergy, Asthma & Immunology]

 Since pet care products are always evolving, yet this book is static, current recommendations for allergy shampoos, sprays, and lotions, and more, can be found on the Supplies page of the PetChiDog site, which is updated as new products emerge. You can reach this by entering any page of PetChiDog.com; Look to the navigation which is in alphabetical order, and choose 'Supplies'.

Arthritis

There are four types of arthritis with canines: Osteoarthritis (this is the most common form and the one that we will cover here), immune-mediated, infective, and idiopathic (cause unknown). With osteoarthritis (also known as degenerative joint disease) a dog's joints become inflamed and painful.

What Happens Cartilage serves as a cushion between bones. It allows the body to move fluidly and without pain. Several elements keep cartilage healthy, including glucosamine and chondroitin. However, as a dog ages, the body produces these compounds in decreasing amounts. This leads to cartilage becoming thin and wearing down. When it does, bones start to rub together. This causes joint pain, stiffness, and inflammation. With progression, bones can become structurally damaged.

Causes   Unfortunately, this is a common part of aging; 80% of dogs 8+ years are affected by some level of arthritis. There *are* some contributing factors. Dogs that have had luxating patella or other joint-related issues are more prone to develop arthritis in those areas (knees or hips).

Weight plays a factor as well; the Chihuahua is certainly not a breed that is prone to being overweight; however, some older adults and seniors may carry a few extra pounds, especially if they have become sedentary. The more weight a joint must bear, the more stressed the joint becomes, and the more susceptible it will be to damage.

Symptoms

- Steady onset of weakness in one or more limb
- A general 'slowing down'
- Lethargy, easily tiring out
- Joint stiffness (difficulty rising from a down position, navigating stairs, etc., this is usually worse in the morning and may improve as the day goes on)
- Discomfort (may manifest as retreating, depressed behavior, fidgeting when resting, and/or trouble sleeping)
- Symptoms may flare-up in the winter and on cool, rainy days

How This is Diagnosed

- X-rays are currently the best method to access the severity of arthritis
- As a second step, joint fluid may be collected and analyzed

Prevention   If you are proactive about this, you can reduce the chances of your dog developing arthritis, or at the very least, reduce the severity of it:

1. **Keep your dog at a healthy weight.** Though weight issues are not at all common with this breed, even a pound or two can make a big difference. See also: 'Feeding and Nutrition: Helping an Adult Chihuahua Lose Weight'.
2. **Keep your dog on a daily exercise routine.** This should be 2 to 3 walks per day, for a minimum of 20 minutes per walk, at a pace that is brisk for your dog, and ideally, a 20-minute session of cardio, such as fetch. See also: 'Exercise & Activity: Exercise Requirements & Restrictions'.
3. **Limit actions that can cause injury.** This particularly includes jumping from too high of a height such as leaping off sofas or other furniture. For favorite spots, place pet steps or a ramp. Use gates at the top of stairways, if it makes sense to do so.
4. **Supplements.** Starting at 8-years-old, offer a glucosamine and chondroitin joint supplement. At 10+ years, it may be a good idea to offer one that also contains MSM and Coenzyme Q10. See next, under 'Treatment'.

Treatment

At Home: There are several things you can do to help your older dog in terms of mobility and comfort.

1. **Steps and ramps.** Place pet steps and/or ramps up against sofas, chairs, and other furniture that your dog likes to rest on.
2. **Provide a proper orthopedic (memory foam) canine bed.** Dogs with arthritis require proper support for sore joints. Add up 12, 14, or more hours each day on an inferior mattress vs. a proper

one, and this can mean the difference between a dog limps about the house or one that joins you for a walk.

3. **Ensure that your dog does not rest or sleep near cool drafts.**
4. **Prevent slipping**, by placing skid-free rugs on hardwood floors and routinely applying a quality paw wax to help with traction.
5. **Keep up with exercise.** When a dog is feeling stiff from arthritis, staying house-bound can exacerbate the problem. With your vet's 'okay' one or two 'easy' walks per day can help loosen up joints and improve mobility.
6. **Body manipulation.** This may include massage (a certified canine massage therapist can show you the technique to perform at home), and/or gentle placement of warm compresses to the affected areas.
7. **Offer daily supplements.** While supplements cannot reverse structural damage to bones, glucosamine and chondroitin with MSM and Coenzyme Q10 (CoQ10) can help the body repair cartilage, attract proper levels of fluid into tissue around the joints for good shock absorption and lubrication, supply nutrients to the cartilage, maintain proper function of blood vessels, and reduce pain and inflammation. Additionally, omega-3 fatty fish oil (DHA and EPA) can help with pain and inflammation. See also: 'Feeding and Nutrition: Supplements'.

Veterinary Treatment: There are medications and other alternative treatments, so be sure to discuss all of these with the veterinarian:

- **Adequan® injections.** Adequan is an FDA approved injectable disease-modifying osteoarthritis drug (DMOAD) for canines that helps repair cartilage. It can be expensive, and typically needs to be injected twice per week, for up to 4 weeks. However, many owners report improvement with few side effects.
- **NSAIDs** (non-steroidal anti-inflammatory drugs, such as Rimadyl®) can help with pain and inflammation. This will need to be overseen by the veterinarian for proper dosing and careful monitoring of potential side effects, including but not limited to organ damage.
- **Steroids** such as prednisone may be given; this can only be given short-term without risk of severe side effects. Even short-term, there may be changes in thirst or appetite, and risk of susceptibility to infections. A dog will need to be carefully monitored.
- **Analgesics** such as tramadol (a synthetic opioid); this is typically reserved for instances of severe pain and after other treatments and medications have proven ineffective. Gabapentin (a medication for nerve pain) can help as well.

Alternative treatments:

- **Class IV therapeutic laser** is an alternative treatment that works to stimulate blood flow to tissues.
- **Acupuncture.** This may help with pain management and is a widely accepted alternative treatment. Many canine acupuncturists will use scented oils and soft lighting to help a dog relax. Then, tiny needles are inserted just barely below the skin into key points of the body; most dogs tolerate this well. A session can last from 5 to 20 minutes.
- **Prolotherapy** involves regular injections of dextrose (sometimes with lidocaine and/or vitamin B 12), meant to stimulate cell growth and strengthen joint tissue.

Bad Breath

Bad breath (halitosis) is not uncommon with canines, and reasons for this can vary. Because some of the causes are quite serious, never ignore significant bad breath issues.

Reasons for Bad Breath that Should be Confirmed or Dismissed

Teething. It is not uncommon for teething puppies to have sweet-sour smelling breath, sometimes equated to sour milk. This is due to mild bleeding that occurs in the mouth that mixes with saliva and bacteria that is normally present.

What to do: Provide at-home dental care; this is important even for young pups as it sets up a foundation for a lifetime of proper dental hygiene. In addition, brushing the teeth can temporarily relieve itching related to teething. Look ahead to 'The #1 Top Reason for Bad Breath - What to do'.

'Dog food breath'. A dog's breath may have an odor that resembles his kibble, but stronger and with an odd trace of smelling 'old'. This can happen when fine particle dust on kibble mixes with saliva; it forms a chalky 'paste' that clings to teeth and/or on the inner pockets of the cheeks.

What to do: Any food that has gone stale will be more apt to chalk up, so if you tend to buy large bags of food, you may want to downsize to smaller containers that are finished off faster or transfer kibble to airtight plastic containers. It can also help to encourage your dog to drink right after eating. In addition, providing regular at-home dental care will remove any chalked-up food and keep breath smelling fresh. Look ahead to 'The #1 Top Reason for Bad Breath - What to do'.

Breath that smells like feces. The most common cause is literal: eating feces. Much rarer, but possible, is intestinal obstruction.

What to do: If you suspect that your dog is ingesting feces (his own or that of another animal) look to 'Behavioral Issues: Eating Feces'. In addition, look ahead to 'The #1 Top Reason for Bad Breath - What to do'. Signs of intestinal obstruction include straining to push out stools, drooling, panicked behavior, loss of appetite, vomiting, and/or dry heaving; this is a very serious health issue and requires immediate veterinary care.

Foreign object stuck in teeth/mouth. There are many things that a dog can mouth that can get stuck between the teeth or even pierce the inside of the cheek or tongue. If so, there will be localized inflammation and possibly infection that can cause bad mouth odor. The most common item is a small wooden splinter.

What to do: In some cases, you can remove a foreign object with your dog's toothbrush. In the case of a splinter in the mouth, this is something that the vet should handle to make sure that the entire object has been removed and to prescribe antibiotic medication if needed.

Certain health issues (non-dental related).

o Very sweet (fruity) or acetone (like nail polish) mouth odors may point to diabetes. Other signs include changes in appetite, excessive thirst, weight loss or gain, lethargy, changes in urination, and/or reoccurring UTI's.

o A urine, fishy, ammonia, or 'mousy' mouth odor may point to kidney issues. Other symptoms include vomiting, diarrhea, constipation, loss of appetite, weight loss, increased thirst, and/or lethargy.

o Chronic bad breath that does not respond to at-home treatment and is not related to dental issues can be due to other health conditions including but not limited to liver issues, lung disease, or gastrointestinal issues.

What to do: If you suspect any of these non-dental related conditions, this warrants an immediate vet visit.

The #1 Top Reason for Bad Breath

Dental Issues. This is often overlooked if a dog is not showing any signs of pain and the teeth look okay. However, the leading cause of bad breath with dogs revolves around the teeth (either unclean teeth or some level of decay).

As covered in 'Dental Care', plaque is constantly being produced. This clear, sticky substance clings to teeth. It is not fully removed from chewing on toys or treats. Within 3 days, it starts to harden into tartar (also referred to as calculus), which is much more difficult to remove.

As these substances grip a dog's teeth, they eat away at the enamel. Tartar can also travel *under* the gum line where it eats away at teeth, unseen. This often leads to tooth decay, gingivitis (gum disease), periodontal disease, and eventual tooth loss. There can also be tooth infection(s), infection that travels up into the sinuses, and the risk of full-body sepsis which can be fatal.

What to do:

1. If you are not sure if your dog's teeth are without issues, schedule a veterinary exam. The vet will examine the teeth and any current issues will be resolved. Then, you can implement an at-home program of proper dental hygiene to prevent any future problems.

2. Implement an at-home dental care program to keep the teeth clean and healthy. Full details can be found in the 'Dental Care' chapter; however, a quick summary is as follows:

1. Brush your dog's teeth daily, using a quality canine toothbrush or finger-brush and an effective canine toothpaste.
2. Alternative to that, and only reserved for dogs that simply do not tolerate brushings, use a dental spray or dental wipes.
3. Offer a daily dental treat.
4. Use a canine dental supplement that is added to water.

If these steps do not resolve bad breath issues, this warrants a vet visit to rule out dental issues (tooth decay, gingivitis, and/or periodontal disease) and any other possible health conditions.

Collapsed Trachea

This is a painful and difficult condition that is more common with toy breeds than any other size breed and, therefore, is seen far too often with Chihuahua.

The windpipe (trachea) is surrounded by rings of cartilage that allows the neck to be flexible. If a ring(s) structurally collapses inward, partially obstructing the breathing passage, this is referred to as collapsed trachea. Weakened tracheal rings can be genetic; collapse may occur at any rate but can be triggered by pressure and stress placed on the neck (collar). Or, this can be acquired. The acquired form is linked to chronic respiratory disease, Cushing's disease, and heart disease. Any minor issues of a weakened trachea or collapsed trachea can be severely exacerbated by wearing a collar while on leash.

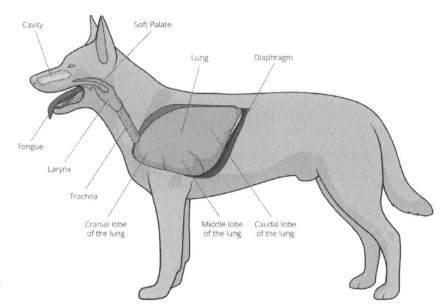

Though this condition can develop or occur at any age (and as young as 6-months old), the genetic type typically leads to collapsed trachea by the age of 6-years-old.

Symptoms

- A distinctive cough, often referred to as a honking noise (like a goose) This is the #1 sign and can be one of the most troubling symptoms. A dog may take a stance of extending his neck and spreading his elbows apart as if trying to cough something up. Generally, coughing progressively worsens.
- Noisy breathing (gasping, rattling, or wheezing noises)
- Gagging
- Breathing difficulties (trouble catching the breath, etc.)
- Exercise intolerance
- Symptoms may be more apparent during or after exercise, when excited, or when breathing in cold air
- Cyanosis (low oxygen levels in the blood may cause gums to turn blue) (in very severe cases)
- Collapse, fainting (in very severe cases)

How This is Diagnosed

Experienced veterinarians will immediately suspect this by the particular honking-type cough. X-rays are then taken to confirm. In some cases, x-rays will not show a tracheal collapse; however, a dog may still be treated for it. If you desire confirmation and x-rays are inconclusive, you can ask for a fluoroscopy, which allows real-time visualization of the trachea as a dog inhales and exhales.

There are four degrees (grades) of collapse:

Grade I: The tracheal membrane is hangs slightly, cartilage maintains normal shape, the tracheal opening (lumen) is reduced approximately 25%.

Grade II: The tracheal membrane is widened and hanging, cartilage is partially flattened, the tracheal opening (lumen) is reduced approximately 50%.

Grade III: The tracheal membrane is almost in contact with dorsal trachea (the opposite side of the windpipe), cartilage is nearly flat, the tracheal opening (lumen) is reduced approximately 75%.

Grade IV: The tracheal membrane is lying on dorsal cartilage (is completely touching the opposite side of the windpipe), cartilage is flattened and may invert, the tracheal opening (lumen) is essentially closed.

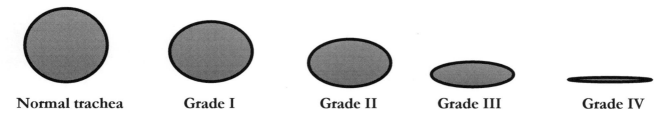

| Normal trachea | Grade I | Grade II | Grade III | Grade IV |

Treatment, Non-Surgical
Studies, though ongoing, have shown that approximately 70% of dogs respond well to non-surgical treatment. And, all of these options should be explored, since surgery is quite drastic. This includes:

1. **Immediate discontinuation of a collar.** A collar should never be worn again; a harness will be used when on leash (this is also recommended to help prevent this issue). See also: 'Care Items - Chihuahuas of All Ages: Leashes, Harnesses, Collars & ID Tags'.
2. **Limit exposure to cold air.** Take care on below freezing days to limit outdoor activity.
3. **Limit over-excitement.** Keep things low-key, offer introductions to fun activities in a casual manner.
4. **Avoidance of exercise during heat/humidity.** Moderate to heavy activity in hot (and especially humid) weather can make breathing difficult. Follow general care tips to limit exercise during the hottest parts of summertime days. See also: 'Seasonal Care: Summer Care'.
5. **Weight loss, if applicable.** Though excess weight is certainly not a problem typically seen with this breed, some older adults and seniors may carry a few extra pounds, especially if they have become sedentary. Even a couple of extra pounds can compound the condition. See also: 'Feeding and Nutrition: Helping an Adult Chihuahua Lose Weight'.

Treatment, Medications

• **Cough suppressants.** Cough medications such as hydrocodone or dextromethorphan can help.
• **NSAIDs** (nonsteroidal anti-inflammatory drugs) such Rimadyl® or Etogesic® can help with pain and inflammation.
• **Corticosteroids** such as prednisone may be given to help reduce pain and inflammation. This may be given via an inhaler. This can only be given short-term without risk of severe side effects. Even short-term, there may be changes in thirst or appetite and risk of susceptibility to infections. A dog will need to be carefully monitored.
• **Antibiotics.** Secondary lower respiratory tract infections are a concern. Antibiotics will be prescribed as needed.

Treatment, Surgical
If non-surgical treatment does not produce any relief and if a dog is having severe breathing difficulties and/or is in a lot of pain, surgery is often recommended. This involves using a mesh-type sleeve to reinforce the trachea, along with prosthetic polypropylene rings to form a tube that will not collapse.

The success rate of this surgery is 75% or higher, though it is extensive and there are risks including bleeding, paralysis of the larynx (voice box), and/or severe internal swelling that can lead to death. This surgery is most often successful with dogs under the age of 6.

Coughs and Other Noises - Quick Reference

There are many types of coughs and other noises that a dog can make; this quick reference may help you sort things out. This covers those discussed in this book in more detail, as well as other types of coughs and noises.

Sudden episodes of loud, quick, consecutive inhales, often rhythmic in the way that hiccups are. May sound like snorting: This points to reverse sneezing. A dog may take a stance of extending his neck and spreading his elbows apart as if trying to cough something up. Episodes are often short, with normal behavior afterward. May be random or repeating episodes. Triggers include breathing in very cold air, having a rush of excitement, breathing harder due to physical activity, wearing a collar that is too tight, and/or breathing in an airborne irritant. See also: 'Health – Other: Reverse Sneezing'.

A honking-type cough: This can be due to collapsed trachea. A dog may take a stance of extending his neck and spreading his elbows apart as if trying to cough something up. It is not random; it happens on a regular basis and may worsen with time. May also include gagging when eating, noisy breathing, breathing difficulties, exercise intolerance, and symptoms may worsen during or after exercise, when excited, and/or when breathing in cold air. In severe cases, gums may turn blue and/or the dog may collapse. See also: 'Health - Other: Collapsed Trachea'.

A dry cough: This can be due to allergies. If so, this is often alongside *one, some, or all* of other allergy symptoms: Excessive dry skin, itching, rash, skin sores, hot spots, thinning coat, chronic ear infections, eye discharge, bloodshot eyes, wheezing, sneezing, runny nose, exercise intolerance, and/or upset stomach. See also: 'Health - Other: Allergies'.

Deep, dry, hacking cough: This can be a sign of kennel cough, a highly contagious disease affecting the upper respiratory system (windpipe and voice box). This usually causes a very deep, dry cough, but some dogs will have a honking cough, similar to that of collapsed trachea. Other signs include vomiting or dry heaving, coughing to the point of watery nasal discharge, loss of appetite, weakness, and/or fever. Mild to moderate cases may be left to run its course. With severe coughing and/or trouble breathing, anti-inflammatory medication, cough suppressants, and antibiotics may be given (since this can morph into pneumonia).

A dry, persistent cough, *without* **most signs of allergies** (skin issues, itching, thinning coat, chronic ear infections, eye discharge, bloodshot eyes, sneezing, runny nose) **but alongside** *some* **of them** (wheezing, exercise intolerance) *and in addition* there may be gagging. This may point to chronic bronchitis (chronic obstructive pulmonary disease - COPD). In severe cases, there may be cyanosis (low oxygen levels in the blood may cause gums to turn blue) and/or collapse. Treatment involves corticosteroids and bronchodilators. Antibiotics may also be prescribed.

Coughing alongside flu-like symptoms (sneezing, fever, nasal discharge which may be yellow or green, difficulty breathing, loss of appetite, and/or lethargy) may be due to the canine flu, also known as canine influenza virus). This is different than the flu that humans can catch in the fact that it occurs year-round without a specific 'flu season'. It is very contagious and often spreads from dog to dog at doggie daycares, boarding facilities, dog shows, and of course, when there are multiple dogs in the same household. It is treated with cough suppressants and antibiotics. Severe cases may require IV intervention. There is a vaccine for this; however, it is only recommended when a dog will regularly be spending time with lots of other canines.

A dry, *occasional* cough may point to parasites. Other signs include vomiting, diarrhea, distended abdomen, and/or weight loss. See also: 'Health – Other: Worms'.

Wet, mucus cough: This may point to pneumonia, which tends to strike very young puppies or senior dogs, though adults can develop this as well. A wet cough in which thin mucus is expelled is a top sign, along with fever, rapid breathing, and/or rapid pulse. Without treatment, coughing may become so severe that a dog may take a stance of extending his neck and turning his elbows, done in an attempt to breathe. This needs to be treated with antibiotics.

Prolonged coughing seen more often while lying down: This may point to congestive heart failure. In early stages, coughing will be random. In later stages, coughing may be near constant. Diuretics and certain heart medications will be prescribed, along with lifestyle changes that include a low sodium diet. See also: 'Health – Other: Heart Issues'.

Fleas

❶ It's very easy for a dog to catch fleas, even if both the dog and the house are kept clean. Fleas transfer from one animal to another via physical contact, but can also jump several feet; so, just being near an infested dog (or a cat) can lead to a flea infestation. Fleas also live on indoor surfaces like carpeting, bedding, etc., so they can be transferred this way as well.

❷ Fleas burrow down through the coat and live on the skin; they may not be seen at all with a cursory look.

❸ A dog can develop a very fast severe reaction to flea saliva, so there can be intense itching even without a huge infestation.

<u>Symptoms</u>

1) **Itching.** Often continual and intense. May be concentrated on the ears, but can be anywhere or everywhere on the body.
2) **Small black specks.** Fleas can be hard to spot; but, these small specks, which are flea droppings, are easier to see.
3) **Irritated skin and/or coat loss.** May develop after a dog scratches or chews at himself repeatedly.

<u>Confirming if a Dog Has Fleas</u>

1) **Do a very close inspection of your dog.** Part the coat and look down to the skin. Also check the groin area, armpits, and tummy. You will be looking for at least one of two things. Small black specks about the size of a pencil tip are flea droppings, commonly referred to as flea dirt. This may be all that you see since fleas can move incredibly fast, crawling or jumping out of the way before

they can be spotted. Fleas themselves are about the size of a half a grain of rice and are brownish-red. If you see one flea, there will be more (hundreds or thousands).

2) **Inspect the house.** If fleas have been on a dog for more than a few days, they are most likely also in the house. These will be on your dog's bed, on carpeting where your dog rests, or throughout furniture in the house. One method is to take a white paper towel and run it over a rug; if you then see tiny red specks, this is the blood from fleas that were just killed.

3) **If you are still not sure**, do not hesitate to have your veterinarian confirm this.

Why Fleas are So Hard to Kill

Fleas are resilient and repopulate quickly. They like a warm, moist climate best, but can go into a dormant state for as much as a year, waiting until conditions for survival and reproduction are ideal. They live (or lie dormant) indoors (in carpets, furniture, bedding, indoor plants), outside (in yards), and even inside cars.

With a typical full-out flea infestation there can be upward of 4,000 fleas on a dog. These tiny insects, with 4 different life cycles, will have created an entire civilization on a dog's body.

There will always be 4 things within that flea civilization:

1. Adult fleas. These feed on a dog's blood and are the main source of itching.
2. Eggs. Just one female adult flea can lay 50 eggs per day. Most will fall off a dog and settle into bedding, rugs, etc.
3. Larvae. When the eggs hatch, larvae emerge. After 5 to 20 days, they spin tiny cocoons.
4. Pupae. While inside the cocoons, fleas are referred to as pupae. They spend anywhere from 3 days to 1 year inside, emerging as adult fleas when conditions are ideal. For every flea you see, there are approximately 100 others in various stages of this life cycle.

Your 3-Point Plan of Attack to Get Rid of Fleas

1) Thoroughly eradicate fleas, eggs, larvae, and pupae from your dog and any other household pets
2) Thoroughly eradicate all four stages of fleas in your home
3) Thoroughly eradicate all four stages of fleas in the yard and/or car (if applicable)

Definitive host

LIFE CYCLE OF DOG FLEA

Flea eggs

Flea larva

Flea pupa

Flea adult

1) Eradicate All Four Stages of Fleas on Your Dog

You'll need:

1) A flea comb (with a sturdy double row design).
2) Flea spray. Beware of harsh flea dips; some of these are chockfull of chemicals that can cause terrible reactions. Consider using an effective all-natural plant-based product. There are some with peppermint oil and eugenol (an oil made from clove plants) that work very well for both dogs and inside the house (furniture, bedding, etc.)

Instructions are:

1) Pour flea spray into a bowl and dip the flea comb in.
2) Or part the coat and spray by section.
3) Comb every section of your dog slowly and carefully, being sure to reach down to skin level.
4) After every swipe through the coat, dip the comb in a bowl of soapy water (to remove fleas, eggs, larvae, and/or pupae), then wipe dry with a small towel or paper towel.

Unless you have helpers working to remove fleas in the house, yard, and car (see below) at the same time, you may need to go over your dog in this way several times. Now, the next day, and the day that the house, yard, and/or car has been properly dealt with.

2) Eradicate All Four Stages of Fleas in the House

Fleas spend a lot of time on a dog (feeding off of blood), but also time *off* a dog. They may be in the crevices of furniture, on sheets and bedding, in rugs and carpeting, and just about anywhere in the house. To fully rid the house of fleas:

1) Launder everything that is washable (cushions, sheets, blankets, pillow coverings, clothes, etc.) in hot water, if possible, and dry on a hot setting.
2) Sprinkle flea powder or use a flea spray (preferably an all-natural product) on carpets, floors, chairs, sofas, beds, curtains, etc., and then vacuum.
3) With severe infestations in the house, it may be necessary to use a flea bomb. This will send a light mist into crevices that typical cleaning cannot reach. Read the labeling for safety instructions.
4) If you opt to use a traditional exterminator, ask about the chemicals they use and their effects on pets, and check out the company's credentials and ratings.

3) Eradicate All Four Stages of Fleas in Your Yard and Car, if applicable

1) If your dog was in your car (even for a short time), sprinkle flea powder or use a flea spray (preferably an all-natural product) on all interior areas then vacuum.
2) If your dog spends time outside in your yard, it's a good idea to ensure any fleas there are killed as well. They typically hide away from bright sunlight, so you'll want to concentrate on sheltered areas. You can do this yourself with flea products designed for yards (preferably an all-natural product) or hire a professional. If you opt to use a traditional exterminator, ask about the chemicals they use and their effects on pets, and check out the company's credentials and ratings.

Protect Your Dog From Fleas
The heartworm medication that you give to your dog may work for fleas; so, check the label. If you need to obtain flea protection, choose wisely. Dogs can have adverse reactions to chemical flea products. There are all-natural products such as those that contain cinnamon, cedar wood, clove oil, peppermint oil, lemon grass oil, and/or thyme oil that can work well.

Heart Issues

Cardiovascular disease (meaning related to the heart and blood vessels) is the leading cause of death for the Chihuahua breed. As detailed in 'Age: Chihuahua Life Expectancy', a 20-year study showed that 18.5% of Chihuahuas succumbed to this.

The heart conditions that the Chihuahua is prone to are considered to be mainly acquired diseases; therefore, these are seen primarily with adult and senior dogs. This said, heart murmurs, which are often the first sign of these issues can be found with dogs of any age, including puppies. It's important to note that a heart murmur does not necessarily lead to cardiovascular disease.

Heart Murmurs
A heart murmur is an abnormal sound that can be detected via a stethoscope. There are 3 types:

1. Systolic. The murmur occurs when the heart beats.
2. Diastolic. The murmur occurs in between beats.
3. Continuous. The murmur occurs at both times.

And these can be caused by one of two things:

1. Abnormal heart valves or structures within the heart that cause blood to flow abnormally through them.
2. Blood flowing through normal valves and heart structures, but at an abnormal rate.

Diagnosis: An echocardiogram (ultrasound) can determine the cause of the murmur. Using a stethoscope, the murmur will be graded on a scale of 6/1 to 6/6, and is as so:

6/1: Very soft and barely detectable; may only occur once in several minutes.
6/2: Easier to detect, but still soft; typically in only one area of the heart.
6/3: Moderate and easily detectable, may occur in more than one location in the heart. Murmurs that cause heart issues are at least a 6/3.
6/4: Moderate to loud and can be detected in several areas and on both sides of the chest.
6/5: Moderate to loud and there is a precordial thrill, which is a vibration on the skin that is over the heart and lower chest; this can be felt by holding a hand against the area.
6/6: A very loud murmur that can even be heard with the stethoscope held slightly away from the body. There an easy-to-detect precordial thrill.

Treatment: Murmurs graded 6/1 or 6/2 may resolve on their own, or if not, many dogs can live with these minor murmurs without further issues. However, since the Chihuahua is prone to mitral valve disease (details ahead), the vet should be keeping a careful eye on things. A dog with 6/3 or higher murmur will be referred to a specialist who will determine the underlying cause and then prescribe treatment. Possible causes of lasting murmurs include heartworms, hyperthyroidism, endocarditis (an infection of the heart valves), tumors, and a range of heart conditions including mitral valve disease which is covered next.

Mitral Valve Disease
Of the various possible heart diseases, the Chihuahua is predisposed to acquired mitral valve disease, as are several other toy breed dogs.

The mitral valve: There are four chambers of the heart: the right and left atrium and the right and left ventricle. Each chamber has one-way valves connecting them, through which blood flows. The valve that connects the left ventricle to the left atrium is called the mitral valve.

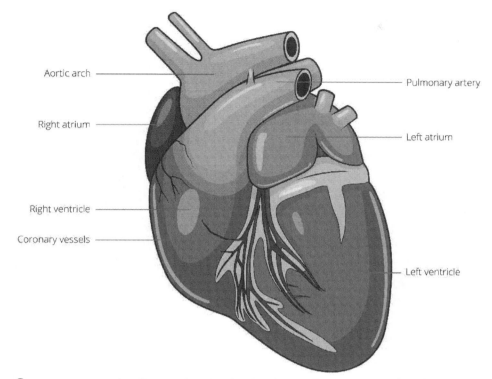

Aortic arch

Right atrium

Right ventricle

Coronary vessels

Pulmonary artery

Left atrium

Left ventricle

Details of mitral valve disease: With this condition, there is a 'wearing out' of the mitral valve which leads to the valve leaking. This causes some of the blood to flow *backward* into the left atrium.

The noise of this occurrence can be detected with a stethoscope and is designated as a heart murmur (also see previous section, 'Heart murmurs').

In most cases, the stress and strain put on the heart eventually leads to congestive heart failure.

Symptoms: The first and only sign in the beginning stages is a heart murmur. As this progresses, pressure builds in the lungs, leading to fluid accumulation. Other signs include coughing, exercise intolerance, and heavy breathing. In severe cases, there can be fainting and even sudden death due to heart failure.

Age of onset: Since this is acquired, it is most often seen with adult and senior dogs age 6-years and up. Incident rate increases with age.

Diagnosis: X-rays, electrocardiography (ECG), and ultrasound.

Treatment: When this disease happens to humans, the valve can be replaced with a mechanical or biological valve. Unfortunately, this is not an option for canines due to the expense and the lack of replacement valves. Rather, this is managed with medication and dietary changes to help slow the progression. This includes:

- Diuretics, to help remove excess fluid from the lungs.
- Angiotensin Converting Enzyme (ACE) inhibitors, which helps to lower blood pressure and facilitate better blood flow.
- Beta-blockers, to lower blood pressure.
- A low-sodium diet, to help reduce fluid buildup.

Prognosis: Once mitral valve disease causes a detectable murmur, a dog may have anywhere from several months to several years before succumbing to congestive heart failure. The sooner a dog responds to the medications, the better the prognosis.

Hernias

A hernia is a tear or a weakening of muscle or connective tissue in which internal organs and/or fatty tissue spill through the opening. There several types:

Umbilical hernia. This is the most common type seen with canines. It can be congenital, meaning present at birth, but it can also be acquired during or directly after the whelping process. Therefore, it is most often seen with young puppies age one day to 6 months old.

When a pup is in the womb, the umbilical cord passes through a small opening in the abdominal wall. Usually, this closes soon after a pup is born. With an umbilical hernia, it does not close, either due to a congenital defect or due to how the umbilical cord is severed; it is most often seen when the dam bites the cord as opposed to the owner cutting it. In these instances, it leads to a portion of the abdominal lining, a portion of the intestines, and/or fatty tissue to protrude through the tear.

There are two types: With a reducible hernia, the protrusion can be pushed back into the abdominal cavity. This is a sign that only fatty tissue is involved. With an irreducible hernia, it cannot be pushed back in; this is a red flag of the intestines being involved and is a serious issue that can threaten the blood supply to the area (known as a strangulated hernia or complicated hernia).

Signs: The main sign is a soft protrusion (bump) on the belly button (just below the ribcage). It may protrude more when the pup is standing, barking, or having a bowel movement. The size of a hernia can range from very small (less than 1/4 inch) to large (more than an inch). Typically, there is a thickened 'ring' of skin around the protrusion.

Diagnosis: X-rays and/or ultrasound.

Treatment: Small umbilical hernias that do not involve the intestines, but rather just fatty tissue, may resolve on their own. If so, this will usually be by the 4 to 6-month mark. Those that do not close or those that are larger or involve the intestines protruding require surgical correction. This involves stitches to close the tear or reinforce the strength of the muscle. If a puppy is due to be spayed or neutered, surgical repair of the hernia is performed at the same time so that anesthesia is only given once.

With an umbilical hernia that involves the intestines (which can threaten the blood supply to the area), this is considered an emergency and will require immediate surgery.

If your puppy has an umbilical hernia and the veterinarian has recommended to wait and see if it resolves on its own or you are waiting for it to be repaired during the spay or neuter procedure, the vet may prescribe antacids and/or medication to help prevent straining during bowel movements, recommend dietary changes, and/or place a removable elasticized band on the area to secure it.

Inguinal hernia. The Chihuahua is one of the breeds predisposed to this type of hernia. This can be congenital (present at birth) or acquired. This can affect both genders and dogs of any age, but it is seen a bit more often with females that have not been spayed, tending to develop during heat or pregnancy. Note that neutered males can develop an inguinal hernia, though it is rare.

This is a hernia located in the abdominal wall of the inguinal canal through which fatty tissue and/or intestines protrude through the tear. For both genders, the groin has a small opening, which is called the inguinal canal. With males, the inguinal canal contains blood vessels and the spermatic cord which leads to the testicles. With females, the inguinal canal contains a cord of fat that runs down.

Inguinal hernias can appear just on one side (unilateral) or both sides (bilateral). In most cases, the inguinal canal is a small enough structure that only fatty tissue can protrude through a hernia. However, in some cases, intestines will spill through as well.

There are two types: With a reducible hernia, the protrusion can be pushed back into the abdominal cavity. This is a sign that only fatty tissue is involved. With an irreducible hernia, it cannot be pushed back in; this is a red flag of the intestines being involved and is a serious issue that can threaten the blood supply to the area (known as a strangulated hernia or complicated hernia).

Signs: With males, the most obvious sign is swelling of the scrotum (skin surrounding the testicles) and/or inner thigh area. With females, the most obvious sign is a soft protrusion in the groin area and/or inner thigh area. Moderate to severe cases are painful; other signs may include lack of appetite, bloody urine, frequent urination, and/or vomiting.

Diagnosis: Contrast study and x-rays.

Treatment: Small inguinal hernias that do not involve the intestines, but rather just fatty tissue, can resolve on their own. If so, this will usually be by the 4 to 6-month mark. Those that do not close or those that are larger or involve the intestines protruding require surgical correction. This involves stitches to close the tear or reinforce the strength of the muscle. If a puppy is due to be spayed or neutered, surgical repair of the hernia is performed at the same time so that anesthesia is only given once.
With an inguinal hernia that involves the intestines (which can threaten the blood supply to the area), this is considered an emergency and will require immediate surgery.

If your puppy has an inguinal hernia and the veterinarian has recommended to wait and see if it resolves on its own or you are waiting for it to be repaired during the spay or neuter procedure, the vet may prescribe antacids and/or medication to help prevent straining during bowel movements, and/or recommend dietary changes.

Diaphragmatic and hiatal hernias. This can be congenital, meaning present at birth; however, most cases are acquired, often due to severe trauma. With a diaphragmatic hernia, there is an internal tear the diaphragm which leads to abdominal organs (liver or stomach) spilling into the chest area. With a hiatal hernia, there is an internal tear the diaphragm which leads to the stomach spilling into the diaphragm and the esophagus spilling into the stomach.

In mild cases, signs include slight breathing difficulties and/or gastrointestinal upset. With hernias due to injury, there are typical signs of trauma including bruising, shock (severe lethargy, hyperventilation, etc.), and/or abnormal heart rate. These types of hernias are corrected with surgery.

Perineal hernia. The cause of this type is unknown; however, it is seen most often with adult dogs in the 7 to 9-year-old range. This involves the muscles that surround and support the pelvis, which gives rectal support. A perineal hernia leads to abdominal contents (small intestine, rectum, prostate, bladder) and fatty tissue to spill into the perineum (region around the anus). Signs include swelling around the anus, straining to urinate and/or have bowel movements, carrying the tail in an odd way, and/or lethargy. This type of hernia is corrected with surgery.

Hypoglycemia

What This Is: This refers to a rapid drop in blood sugar levels. Blood sugar (glucose) is a canine's direct source of energy. When glucose levels drop below normal, it causes a decrease in the body's ability to function normally. In severe cases, this can be life-threatening. It is very important to know the signs of hypoglycemia, how to prevent this, and treatment steps.

Susceptibility: This is a common issue seen with Chihuahuas and other small toy breeds; and while it can happy to a dog of any age, it is most often seen with young puppies.

What Causes this to Happen:

- **With puppies,** the body's ability to regulate glucose levels is not fully developed, which can lead to imbalances.
- **Stress.** This can include 'good' stress such as the first days in a new home.
- **Over-activity.** Using up a lot of energy in a short amount of time.
- **Infrequent feedings.** Missing a meal or sometimes just missing a snack.

Symptoms:

At the onset, symptoms include: Weakness, listlessness, confusion (bumping into walls), incoordination, trembling, muscular twitching, staggered gait (appearing to be 'drunk'), dilated pupils, and/or a sad, droopy look on the face.

Without treatment, the progressive signs will include: Fainting, seizures, and/or possible coma.

If you are not sure about the signs, stand your puppy up and see if he can walk normally.

Treatment: For minor onset signs, you can choose one method below to help raise the puppy's sugar levels:

- Rub a dab of <u>honey</u> on the puppy's gums or roof of his mouth
- Have the puppy drink water with a bit of sugar mixed in
- Offer a children's sugar-coated breakfast cereal if you do not have honey or sugar.

Note: <u>Do not use corn syrup;</u> many sources list this as a treatment method; however, it can have a laxative effect.

Veterinarian Care: If the steps you take at home do not rouse your puppy back to normal, or if you suspect a moderate or severe case of hypoglycemia, do not hesitate to bring your puppy to the veterinarian. Remember, this can be life-threatening. Stablizing a dog may require IV intervention.

Prevention:

1) Keep stress to a minimum. What may seem fun and exciting to you or children in your home can be stressful for a young puppy. As discussed in 'Puppy Care: Introducing your Puppy to Family & Home', you'll want to keep things calm. Lots of commotion can be overwhelming.

Once your pup matures a bit, you can gradually incorporate interaction with people outside your home, more handling, and more activity.

2) Encourage your puppy to take breaks. Puppies are usually revved up with energy, and it's not uncommon for them to keep going far past the point of when a break is needed. Every so often, lead your pup to his resting area. If you believe that your puppy needs to take a nap, but is too hyped up to do so, it can help to draw the blinds, dim the lights, lower the volume on the TV, and other such steps to create a relaxing vibe.

3) Ensure that your Chihuahua is eating every couple of hours. Here are some tips:

- New pups up until the age of 3 months should be free-fed, which means leaving food out at all times; but, this does not mean that a puppy will know to go to his food. Keep track of this, and lead your pup to the bowl every 2 hours, if needed.
- Puppies 3 months and older (and even most adults) do best with 3 meals, plus 3 to 4 snacks per day. In addition to this will be training treats, which offers small boosts of nutrition as well.
- Do not fill the bowl to the brim, as unfinished food can quickly go stale and become unappealing; rather, slowly disperse it as needed.
- If your puppy will be home alone for a number of hours, have him in his playpen with:
  - A bowl of kibble. Being in a defined space with a bowl will ensure that the food is close by. It can also help to place a dab of 100% all-natural smooth peanut butter along the rim of the bowl to make it extra tempting.
  - A treat dispensing toy; use kibble or kibble mixed with 100% all-natural smooth peanut butter or a bit of 100% all-natural liquid fish oil, and/or dab peanut butter or fish oil along the opening of the toy to make it tempting.

Itching – Quick Reference

There are several reasons for itching; this quick reference may help sort things out.

Fleas: Signs are intense itching, irritated skin, possible coat loss (if scratching has ongoing), and flea droppings which are seen as small black specks on the skin when hairs are parted. Often, if a dog has fleas, there are fleas in the house. You can test this by running a white paper towel over a rug; any tiny red specks is blood from fleas that were just killed. See also: 'Health – Other: Fleas'.

Allergies: Itching is a top sign and may be the only sign; other symptoms may including dry skin, rash, skin sores, hot spots, thinning coat, chronic ear infections, eye discharge, bloodshot eyes, wheezing, coughing, sneezing, runny nose, exercise intolerance, upset stomach and/or vomiting (seen with food allergies), licking, scratching, or chewing (often the paws) and/or rubbing the body against surfaces. Allergies may come and go or be near continual. See also: 'Health – Other: Allergies'.

Fungal/Yeast Infection: Itching is a top sign of this, along with an odd odor (musty like old wet socks, or sour like spoiled milk). A dog may smell bad even right after a bath. This can be treated with anti-fungal shampoos, but severe cases may require prescribed oral anti-fungal medications. See also: 'Health – Other: Smells and Odors'.

Mange: With Sarcoptic mange, the main symptom is *intense* itching, that can be so severe, it can make a dog frantic. Other signs include rash, skin that crusts over, and fur loss on the affected areas. Two other types of mange are Cheyletiella mange and Demodectic mange, which involve itching as well. See also: 'Health – Other: Mange'.

Ringworm: This is rare, but possible. There will be a round hairless lesion that may expand in size, remaining circular or becoming irregular. It may scale over and/or become red or inflamed. See also 'Health – Other: Worms'.

Dry Skin: For itching without any other symptoms that align with the aforementioned issues, it may be a matter of excessively dry skin. It's common in the winter due to cold arid air, in the summer due to the drying effects of the sun, or year-round due to low water intake, grooming-related elements, and more. See also: 'Health – Other: Skin Problems'.

Lethargy

Puppies: Puppies have lots of energy and curiosity; but most simply cannot handle staying up for all they want to do and see. Puppies sleep about 18 hours per day (both nighttime and naps), so it's normal for them to tire out and doze several times during the day. This type of tiredness should not be mistaken for lethargy.

With this said, it's a good idea to be on alert for hypoglycemia (rapid drop in blood sugar levels). Some cases are due to young age; however, this can develop from infrequent eating or stress (feeling overwhelmed in a new house, etc.). Signs include confusion, weakness, dizziness, and trouble walking. Minor cases can be treated at home by rubbing a dab of honey on a pup's gums. Moderate to severe cases require immediate veterinary intervention. See also: 'Health - Other: Hypoglycemia'.

Seniors: Sudden lethargy is never normal; older dogs will have a gradual 'slowing down'. Starting at about the 8-year mark and moving forward from there, there will be a bit less 'pep in the step' and a bit more sleeping.

Any age: Whenever a dog acts out of character, lethargic, mopey, or otherwise showing signs of being drained, this should not be ignored. While a dog can just be having an 'off' day, if this continues for more than 24 hours, it can point to one of the following:

- **Health issues.** The majority of health issues have fatigue or lethargy as a symptom. It can be an *initial symptom* that manifests before any others. The list of other symptoms for health issues is, of course, long and varied. However, at least one change in food intake, weight, sleep, urination, bowel movements, breathing, digestion, or sensory organs (eyes, ears, mouth, nose) are often in play.

  Dogs will have more successful treatment and better prognosis the earlier that issues are diagnosed; therefore, do not delay a vet visit if marked lethargy, even without other symptoms, lasts for more than 24 hours or if sudden lethargy that interferes with normal daily activities occurs for any length of time.

- **Situational factors.** When a dog is lethargic, and all health issues have been ruled out, it's time to look at what may be happening in a dog's world. This can be anything that has disrupted a dog's normal routine. This may include changes in family structure, moving to a new home, or longer hours home alone. See also: 'Behavioral Issues: Depression', 'Situational Issues: Having More than One Dog', and 'Situational Issues: Separation Anxiety'.

- **Mirroring vibes.** Canines are known to mimic the general mood of their owners and mold their behavior to the atmosphere of the home, often picking up vibes even if no words are spoken to them. If there are stressors, health problems, or other issues that are affecting an owner, this can eventually cause a dog to react to that with altered behavior. Another possibility is domestic problems such as lots of arguing or yelling. This can be very upsetting to a dog and the response may be retreating and curling up in reaction to the turmoil.

Luxating Patella

The patella (kneecap – located on rear legs) is held together by tendons and tissue. With luxating patella (also known as subluxation of the patella, floating patella, floating kneecap, or patellar luxation), the kneecap slips loose of its normally secure surroundings. It may slip out and right back in again, intermittently slip back and forth, or remain out.

Luxating patella can be due to genetic disposition for weak tendons and/or shallow kneecaps (common with toy and small-sized breeds, and very common with the Chihuahua breed) or can be caused by injury (often jumping down from too high of a height or a fast, awkward twist of the leg). With dogs that have a genetic disposition, a rapid run or a jump can trigger the patella to slip out. Some studies show that females are 1.5 times more likely to have this than males.

Occurrence Rate
The Orthopedic Foundation for Animals (OFA) keeps statistics of this and several other issues. Note that this only includes dogs whose records are submitted to OFA. At the time of this writing, the Chihuahua ranks at #22 out of 128 breeds, with patella luxation identified in 5.5% of dogs.

Symptoms

At the moment it occurs:
- ➤ A dog may let out a loud yelp, but then continue to run or play without issues until inflammation sets in, leading to other signs.
- ➤ Or, a dog may suddenly stop in the middle of running or playing, sit, and hold the leg in an odd position.

Once inflammation sets in, a dog may have one, some, or all of these signs that may come and go or remain steady:

- Limping or an odd skipping gait (sometimes referred to as a 'bunny hop')
- Difficulty rising
- Limb weakness
- Signs of pain when in motion

How This is Diagnosed
This is diagnosed via x-rays, though ultrasound may be done as well. There are four degrees (grades) of luxation:

Grade 1: The knee only slips out when manipulated.

Grade 2: The knee slips occasionally when walking or running. It usually slides back by itself as the dog continues moving. Or, it can be slipped back manually (the veterinarian may do this or may show you how to do this, if you wish).

Grade 3: The knee slips frequently. Even when it is put back into place, it slips again soon afterward.

Grade 4: The knee slips out of place, stays that way, and it cannot slide back into its socket.

Treatment, Non-Surgical   At Home and Veterinary Treatment:

Bed Rest. With the patella positioned into place, bed rest is always part of initial treatment to allow tendons, ligaments, and connective tissue around the area to heal. This involves not letting your dog walk at all, and therefore will require a very small crate. This is a vital treatment step, and should not be ignored by owners who feel bad for their dog being confined as so; it is certainly preferable to surgery, and at least gives things a chance to heal. Length of time for bed rest will depend on the severity of the issue and can range from 1 to 6 weeks.

NSAIDs (non-steroidal anti-inflammatory drugs. These are often given for pain and inflammation. This will need to be overseen by the veterinarian for proper dosing and careful monitoring of potential side effects, including but not limited to organ damage.

Weight Loss. While the Chihuahua is certainly not a breed that easily becomes overweight, weight loss will be recommended, if needed, since even a pound lost is less strain on the knees. If your veterinarian suggests this, you may wish to refer to 'Feeding and Nutrition: Helping an Adult Chihuahua Lose Weight'.

Additional Pain Medication. Often, NSAIDs will be sufficient to bring discomfort to a tolerable level, at least for Grade 1 or Grade 2; however, if a dog is experiencing severe pain, analgesics such as tramadol (a synthetic opioid) may be prescribed.

Anti-inflammatory steroids such as prednisone may be given; this can only be given short-term without risk of severe side effects. Even short-term, there may be changes in thirst or appetite and risk of susceptibility to infections. A dog will need to be carefully monitored.

Medications to help prevent arthritis. The knees are prone to arthritis and if a knee has slipped, it is even more so. For this reason, some veterinarians will suggest monthly Adequan® injections (or a similar medication). Adequan is an FDA approved injectable disease-modifying osteoarthritis drug (DMOAD) for canines that helps repair cartilage, and in these cases can help prevent the onset of trauma-induced arthritis.

Continued Treatment:

Knee-strengthening exercise. After bed rest is complete, it will be time to strengthen the muscles around the knee. First, normal walks will resume. Then, when the veterinarian feels that a dog is ready, knee-strengthening exercise will involve walking up inclines. This will start off with slight inclines for short durations, working your way up to steeper inclines for longer durations.

Supplements and Vitamins. A combined glucosamine, chondroitin, MSM, and CoQ10 supplement, as well as an omega-3 EPA and DHA should be given. These can control inflammation, help with mobility, and are used to help prevent arthritis. In addition, certain vitamins are often prescribed. This includes vitamin C, E, B1, and B6, which can all work to heal and strengthen connective tissue.

Treatment, Surgical

Grade 1 does not require surgery. Grade 2 is a 'grey zone', where some vets suggest it and others suggest waiting to see if bed rest and anti-inflammatories will work. For Grade 3 and certainly for Grade 4, surgery is needed. In these cases, delayed treatment can lead to bone deformities, arthritis, and other complications.

There are several types of surgeries for Grades 2 and 3, all revolving around securing the patella into place. This may be trochleoplasty (deepening the groove where the patella sits), tibial tuberosity transposition (moving the placement of the patella ligament and the tibial tuberosity, which is a bony ridge normally supporting the ligament), or lateral imbrication and medial release (tissue around the patella are tightened/loosened to secure it).

Grade	Treatment	Surgery
Grade 1: Only slips when manipulated	Bed rest, NSAIDs, weight loss (if needed)	Surgery is not needed
Grade 2: Slips occasionally, can be slipped back	Above, PLUS stronger pain meds and/or anti-inflammatories	A 'gray area', surgery may be needed
Grade 3: Slips frequently	Same as above	Surgery most often needed
Grade 4: Slips permanently	Same as above	Surgery is needed

During recovery, a dog will be given anti-inflammatory medications, and you will be shown how to apply alternating ice packs and hot compresses, massage the quadricep muscles (above the knee), and do range-of-motion exercises to the limb. By the end of week one, most dogs are taken for short (10 minute) slow walks 2 to 3 times per day.

Two weeks after surgery, the veterinarian will evaluate how your dog is recovering. By week 4, slow walks will increase to 20 to 30 minutes, along with other exercises such as being directed into a 'sit', being led through figure-of-eights, and doing circles. If it is feasible, swimming rehab is recommended at this time.

By week 6, there will be another evaluation with the veterinarian and walks will still be slow but will involve inclines and/or steps. Full recovery is seen by week 9 to 12.

For Grade 4, a different type of surgery is needed, which involves straightening bones and making cuts into them, often with plates attached to stabilize them. Recovery is about 12 weeks as well and prognosis is good. Most dogs fully recover and can go on to lead active lives.

Prevention

1. Limit jumping. Since trauma can cause this or can be the trigger for a knee that is weak, do not allow your dog to jump from a height that is any higher than your dog is tall. Consider obtaining ramps or steps for favorite resting spots like the sofa.
2. Keep up with daily exercise to keep supporting muscles strong.
3. Never ignore limping or other signs of luxating patella. Bed rest ASAP is an important treatment step.
4. Bring your dog to the veterinarian once per year (twice per year for seniors) for wellness checks. The knees will be examined during the visit.

Mange

Demodectic mange (demodicosis, and also known as red mange, follicular mange, or puppy mange) is a particular type of skin disease caused by the Demodex mite. This is most often seen in puppies, although it can develop in older dogs as well.

A certain number of Demodex mites live on the body of both humans and canines alike (and other animals, too). They are incredibly tiny, just 1/4 of one mm, residing inside hair follicles and on the skin surface (especially certain creases like eyelids and noses). The life cycle of a mite is 1 month; it reproduces, dies, and new ones take over.

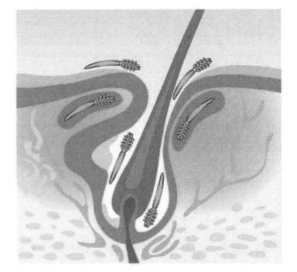

So, a mange infection is not an infection of a new mite being transferred onto a dog. They are there all along. It becomes a problem when there are more mites than normal, beyond what a dog's body can handle or if a dog's body starts to respond differently to them.

More mites than normal can be introduced if a dog is in an unclean environment where there are a lot of Demodex mites (like an overcrowded kennel). Also, if a dam has a high number of mites and delivers a litter, these can be transferred to the new pups (that have none yet) and their bodies may react badly to this sudden onslaught (hence the term 'puppy mange'). Reasons for the body responding differently to the normal amount present include, but are not limited to, lowered immune system during times of illness or due to side effects of medication, and poor nutrition.

Symptoms

- Patches of coat loss in one area or several on the face (sometimes just around the eyes), trunk, and/or legs
- Exposed skin under thinning or balding areas is pink
- Possible odd, unpleasant odor
- Possible itching
- Skin lesions that may appear red and/or crusty, often starting on the head (around the muzzle or eyes); with young pups, lesions may first appear on the legs
- Skin may appear moist and/or look greasy

How This is Diagnosed   The veterinarian will do a deep skin scraping that is observed under a strong microscope to identify the mite.

Treatment   If this is limited to just one spot, it may clear up on its own. If there are multiple areas affected, and symptoms are moderate to severe, the veterinarian will prescribe a lime-sulfur dip. These can be obtained OTC; however, it's highly suggested to have this done under vet supervision, since many other

skin mites and other skin disorders can mimic Demodectic mange, and you'll want to be sure that you're treating your puppy or dog for the right issue.

Sarcoptic mange (canine scabies, or also just referred to as 'mange') is an entirely different type of skin infection, with the Sarcoptes scabiei mite to blame. This is not a mite normally found on dogs. It moves from animal to animal and is extremely contagious, to both other animals and humans. These tiny creatures burrow deep into the skin, causing highly intense itching.

Symptoms

- Intense itching * This is the #1 sign; itching can be so severe that a dog can become frantic
- Thinning or balding areas
- Possible skin sores
- Scabs or crusted areas on the skin

How This is Diagnosed
The veterinarian will do a deep skin scraping that is observed under a strong microscope to identify the mite.

Treatment
If this is even suspected, the dog should be quarantined until treatment is complete. This can very easily spread to other pets and to humans. If a healthy person catches sarcoptic mange from a dog, it usually manifests as a purple-colored rash; it will typically clear up on its own.

This needs to be treated by the veterinarian. Strong scabicidal shampoos will be prescribed for up to 6 weeks, and it is important to follow instructions carefully. In some cases, oral medication will be given as well. Other pets in the house should be treated at the same time. And, steps taken to kill mites in the house will be needed. This can be done with products such as dry diatomaceous earth along with vacuuming, and all washables should be washed in hot water. Note that foggers do not typically work on mites.

Cheyletiella mange (cheyletiellosis, also referred to as 'walking dandruff') is yet another type of skin infection, caused by the Cheyletiella mite. These are easily transferred from one type of animal (wild or tamed) to another. The big difference between this and the aforementioned Demodex mite and Sarcoptes scabiei mite, is that this one can be seen.

Symptoms

- Clear view of the mite. * This is the most obvious method to identify these mites. When you lift sections of the hair, you may see small white flakes that, at first, may appear to be dandruff. However, if you look long enough, these 'skin flakes' will be moving (hence the term 'walking dandruff'). What you see will either be the mites themselves, or it will be mites just under pieces of dry skin.
- Tends to be on the truck of the body, less so on the head or legs
- Mild to severe itching
- Raised red bumps
- Licking that may lead to skin sores

How This is Diagnosed The veterinarian will do a deep skin scraping or take a sample via tape, that is observed under a strong microscope to identify the mite.

Treatment This needs to be treated by the veterinarian. A lime-sulfur dip or pyrethrin shampoo will be prescribed, for up to 6 weeks. It is important to follow instructions carefully. Other pets in the house should be treated at the same time. And, steps taken to kill mites in the house will be needed. This can be done with products such as dry diatomaceous earth along with vacuuming, and all washables should be washed in hot water. Note that foggers do not typically work on mites.

Reverse Sneezing

When a dog has a 'normal' sneeze, air rushes out of the nose; and with this, air rushes *in*. Though it can be troubling to see and hear, and can make a dog anxious, reverse sneezing is typically not harmful to a dog.

Symptoms: There will be sudden episodes of loud, quick inhales. It's often rhythmic in the way that hiccups are. While it can be mistaken for the honking noise of collapsed trachea, with reverse sneezing there will be consecutive snorting sounds. Yet, like collapsed trachea, a dog may take a stance of extending his neck and spreading his elbows apart, as if trying to cough something up. The episode will generally be short, lasting only seconds to a few minutes. As soon as it is done, breathing will return to normal, and a dog will typically behave as if nothing is wrong. These may be random episodes every now and then or repeating episodes.

Triggers: It may happen out of the blue; however, some triggers include breathing in frigid air, having a rush of excitement, breathing harder due to physical activity, wearing a collar that is too tight, and/or breathing in an airborne irritant.

Treatment: Since this can mimic other conditions, like collapsed trachea, if your dog has breathing spasms, take a video of this to show to the vet. If it is indeed reverse sneezing, there are some things may stop an episode:

- Gently cup your hand over the mouth and nose area (allowing room for breathing!) for 15 to 20 seconds. Reverse sneezing can cause too much carbon dioxide to be released, so this can restore it to normal levels.
- Place a small dab of peanut butter on your dog's nose. It will prompt your dog to stick his tongue out, which can relax the throat and in turn, stop reverse sneezing.
- Gently massage the throat area with soft downward strokes, which can relax the throat and in turn, stop reverse sneezing.
- Encourage your dog to drink or offer a small snack. Sometimes, if the reverse sneezing can be interrupted, it stops the episode.

Skin Problems – Quick Reference

There are many types of skin issues; this quick reference may help you sort things out. This covers those discussed in this book in more detail, as well as other types of skin-related problems.

Dry skin: Dry skin can morph into other, more serious issues; yet, just dry skin alone can make a dog uncomfortable. Many of the causes for dry skin also affect the coat, so dry skin and poor coat texture often go hand-in-hand. The most common causes include arid air in the winter, too much sun exposure in the summer, low water intake, and inferior shampoos and coat products.

Steps to take to resolve dry skin include:

1. **Use superior shampoo, conditioner, and leave-in coat spray.** Choose products with proper pH balance and restorative ingredients such as vanilla, almond, tea tree oil, shea butter, colloidal oatmeal, and/or aloe vera, and with a coconut-based cleanser, not soap.
2. **Certain restorative skin lotions** can be very effective as well. Organic ingredients can improve skin (and coat) health. This includes aloe vera, coconut oil, hemp seed oil, shea butter, honey, and tea tree oil. Depending on the severity of dry skin, lotion may need to be applied anywhere from once per week to twice per day.
3. **Let the coat air dry.** Do not use a blow dryer, just towel dry by patting (not rubbing).
4. **Provide cushioning.** Do not allow your dog to lie on the floor. Provide a quality bed.
5. **Omega-3 fish oil.** Omega-3 EPA and DHA fatty acids can really boost skin and coat health. We recommend a liquid omega-3 fish oil derived from wild fish. This is given once per day, with the allotted amount (1/2 to 1 pump, depending on your dog's weight) added to one meal.
6. **In the winter**, add moisture to the house via humidifiers. If you only have one, place this near your dog's resting/sleeping area.
7. **Encourage water intake.** Keep the bowl clean with fresh, cool, and preferably filtered or spring water. Don't top off the bowl, rinse it out and refill it. If your dog really needs prompting, try a canine water fountain; the moving water is often a strong attraction. Bring water along with you wherever you take your dog, including daily walks. Offer healthy fruit with high water content, such as blueberries and raspberries.

Since this book is static, yet skin and coat products are always evolving, you will find current recommendations for lotions and shampoos to help resolve dry skin on the Supplies page of the PetChiDog site. You can reach this by entering any page of PetChiDog.com; look to the navigation which is in alphabetical order, and choose 'Supplies'.

Flaky skin: If you see white flakes on your dog's skin or coat, this can be due to one of several things:

1. Dry skin (see previous skin issue).
2. Cheyletiella mange (Cheyletiella mites, 'walking dandruff'). Upon close inspection, the flakes will be moving. See the previous section of 'Health – Other: Mange: Cheyletiella mange'
3. Dandruff. There will be flakes (that don't move!), typically seen alongside minor to moderate oily skin and/or an odd odor. There may be some itchiness and/or irritated skin.
4. Seborrhea (seborrheic dermatitis). It's easy to mistake this for dandruff but is typically more severe. There are flakes, along with red irritated skin, scaling skin, oily skin (some areas may be dry, some may be oily), and often a strong musty-oily odor. Affected skin is mainly on the back, sides, and face.

Causes of dandruff are quite varied and can be linked to dry skin, food allergies, cold weather, and even age.

Treatment for dandruff includes ensuring your dog has a superior dog food without additives and fillers that can cause issues, brushing the coat often (every 3 days for a short coat, every 2 days for a medium coat, and every day for a long coat), addressing any aspects related to dry skin (see previous skin issue), and using quality, moisturizing shampoos. Since this can easily be mistaken for seborrhea (see next), you may wish to look into that as well.

Causes of seborrhea are often unknown (idiopathic); however, in some cases, this can be linked to allergies, environmental elements (temperature, humidity), poor nutrition, and hormonal imbalances, among other things.

Treatment for seborrhea. This can be treated at home, in many cases, via a medicated shampoo with coal tar, salicylic acid & micronized sulfur. However, if you are unsure of your at-home diagnosis, it is best to have the veterinarian provide one, since there is such a wide range of skin issues and disorders, and you won't want to treat for one issue when it's another one at play.

Hot spots: Hot spots are somewhat circular lesions on the skin that are moist and quite irritated. They are also very itchy and/or painful, so it's common for a dog to lick at these, which just makes them worse. The #1 cause of hot spots is allergies. For this, see 'Health – Other: Allergies'.

Itchy skin: This is a common issue with many dogs. The 'Itching – Quick Reference' section found in the 'Health – Other' chapter points the way. However, a summary is as follows:

- **Itching only, no other signs:** Points to dry skin or allergies. See previous 'Dry Skin' or 'Health-Other: Allergies'.

- **Itching with a musty odor:** Points to skin yeast infection (see 'Health – Other: Smells and Odors') or seborrhea (see previous under 'Flaky skin').

- **Very intense itching to the point of a dog almost frantic, along with skin crusting and/or fur loss:** Points to Sarcoptic mange (see 'Health – Other: Mange') or to fleas, in which intense itching may be the only sign since fleas may not be visible to the eye (see 'Health – Other: Fleas').

Smells & Odors

Smells after going outside:

Reason 1: 'Wet dog smell'. If a dog heads outside during any sort of precipitation, if the grass/ground is wet from dew or previous rainfall and the dog sits or lies down, or even on high-humidity days, this can cause a 'wet dog smell', produced by water coming into contact with an accumulation of body oils.

How to prevent this: The body is always producing oils which serve to naturally moisturize the skin and coat. At about the 3-week mark, there is enough that a dog needs a bath to rinse off oils and 'start fresh'. So, bathe your puppy or dog every 3 weeks with a quality shampoo, even if he looks clean. See also: 'Grooming: Baths'.

How to remove the smell: You can bathe your dog a bit early as long as you are using quality products that will not dry out the skin or coat. If your dog has just recently had a bath (within the past week), give the coat a good brushing instead. This will allow moisture to air dry as you brush and will pull out dead hairs that that are covered in the water/oil combination. Removing those hairs may remove the odor.

Reason 2: Feces. If a dog has a bowel movement, some feces can be stuck on the fine hair around the anus.

How to prevent this: Overly soft stools tend to stick more. Stools should have the consistency of playdough (if you held it up, it would stay in one piece, before a piece slowly broke off). If stools are softer than this, reevaluate the diet and if needed, offer 1 or two teaspoons of 100% pure pumpkin each day (mixed into meals). Additionally, for longhaired Chi, longer hairs around the anus can allow feces to cling to them and can be resolved by having that area trimmed or clipped for hygiene reasons.

How to remove the smell: If fecal matter is still moist, wipe this off with a quality canine wipe or canine tushie wipe. Take care to only wipe out and not toward the genital area. While females are more prone to the issue, both genders can develop a UTI if feces travel to the urinary opening. If fecal matter has dried, this can be scrubbed clean with a full or partial bath.

Smells after going to the bathroom:

Reason 1: Urine splashes. If a male urinates against a tree or other object, this may cause urine to splatter back onto the genital area and/or underbelly. Female dogs can have some splash-back as well, depending on their positioning when urinating.

How to remove the smell: Wipe your dog down with a quality canine grooming wipe.

Reason 2: Feces. If a dog has a bowel movement, some feces can be stuck on the fine hair around the anus. Alternatively, if the bowel movement was especially hard, it can cause the anal glands to secrete more scent oil than normal, which has a terrible and overpowering odor.

How to prevent this: For fecal matter stuck on hairs, see previous 'Reason 2: Feces: How to prevent this'. For anal gland secretion due to hard feces, follow guidelines under 'Health – Stomach, Intestinal: Constipation'.

How to remove the smell: For fecal matter stuck on hairs, see previous 'Reason 2: Feces: How to remove the smell'. For anal gland secretion, inspect the area to look for possible tears in the skin; if so, this will be vulnerable to infection. The area can be washed with warm water or a bath can be given, and a dab of antibiotic gel can be applied. Keep an eye on things; if there is redness, swelling, signs of discomfort, and/or if the tear has not healed within 3 days it should be treated by a veterinarian. You may also wish to refer to 'Health & Care - Body Part Specific: Anal Glands'.

Smells even after a bath:

Reason 1: Scrubbing was not deep enough. One of the goals of a bath is to remove accumulated body oils from the skin. If just the coat is washed, without cleaning deep enough, oils will remain. Mixed with the water from the bath, this can produce a 'wet dog smell'.

How to prevent this: Scrub deep, and if you feel that you need it, use a small canine bath scrub brush.

Reason 2: Low-grade products were used. For shampoo to effectively clean away oils and wash away bad smells, it needs to have the proper amount and correct type of cleansing agents. Inferior products will be lacking this.

How to prevent this: Choose bathing products wisely. You may wish to refer to 'Grooming: Shampoo and Coat Products'.

* If these tips do not help, look ahead to 'Smells Bad all the Time'.

Female smells during heat:

Discharge can hold a bad odor. During heat, discharge is a mixture of blood, endometrial tissue, and body fluids. Both blood and endometrial tissue can smell, particularly when dried onto the body or coat. While this is not usually an overpowering odor, some owners will notice it more than others.

How to prevent this: Place a doggie diaper on your dog (should be done at any rate to prevent discharge from accumulating on furniture, bedding, etc.). Depending on how heavy the flow is, a new diaper may need to be placed on every 4 to 12 hours.

How to remove the smell: You can give partial or full baths during this time.

Female a smell coming from the vagina:

Assess if this is a urine or feces smell; If so, see the previous 'Smells after going to the bathroom'. If your female is in heat, see the previous 'Female smells during heat'. If these are not the cause, this may point to yeast infection, UTI (urinary tract infection), or another health issue that should be diagnosed by the veterinarian.

Smells really bad all of the time:

Baths given too infrequently. Most dogs do well with a bath once every 3 weeks. However, if a dog happens to produce natural body oils at a fast rate, baths may need to be given every 2 weeks. Be sure to follow the guidelines under the previous 'Smells even after a bath'.

Skin yeast infection may be to blame. This can cause a musty or sour-like odor that will not go away even with baths. Other signs include oily skin, possible flaking, and possible itching. Addressing this involves several steps; therefore, please refer to 'Behavioral Issues: Licking and Chewing at the Paws: Yeast Infection'; the instructions there will resolve a full-body infection as well.

Paws Smell: The most common reason is the aforementioned yeast infection. Resolving this involves several steps; therefore, please refer to 'Behavioral Issues: Licking and Chewing at the Paws: Yeast Infection'; the instructions there will resolve this.

Smells coming from the mouth: For bad breath issues, please refer to 'Health-Other: Bad Breath'.

Smell coming from the ears: For this, please refer to 'Health & Care - Body Part Specific: Ears'.

How to Keep a Dog Smelling Nice:

1) **Time the baths.** Once every 3 weeks works well since this is the time lapse in which oils are just accumulating enough that if you wait another week, there can start to be a bad odor.
2) **Use a quality shampoo** that will be effective in removing oils.
3) **Use grooming wipes in between baths** to clean away urine, feces, and other elements that can cause bad odors.
4) **Brush often.** Dead hairs can fall back into the coat, make their way down to skin level, and become encased in natural body oils. By keeping the coat free of these dead hairs and by distributing oils with the brush, it can help keep a dog smelling fresh. Aim for every 3 days for a smooth coat Chi and every 2 to 3 days for a longhaired Chi.
5) **Use a nice-smelling leave-in coat spray.** This will give off a clean fragrance as well as protect the hairs from contact friction, sun exposure, and drying effects of arid air. A light misting every few days, while brushing, is all that is needed. See also 'Grooming: Shampoo and Coat Products'.

Spaying & Neutering

Spaying refers to when a female dog's uterus and ovaries are surgically removed. Neutering refers to when a male dog's testicles are surgically removed.

When polled, 73% of owners reported that their Chihuahua was spayed or neutered, 15% answered that they plan on having their Chi spay/neutered, and 12% did not have plans for this. It's encouraging to see that the majority of pet Chihuahuas are spayed or neutered since there are many benefits.

Benefits of Spaying

- Stops the chance pregnancy.
- Eliminates chances of developing ovarian cancer.
- Greatly reduces chances of developing mammary tumors (when done before 2.5 years old).
- Greatly reduces chances developing ovarian infections.
- Nearly eliminates the chances of pyometra (which affects 23% of intact females, with 1% being fatal cases).
- Cuts down on urges to run away when in heat.
- Stops possible hormone-related mood swings.
- Helps with marking issues (90% of the time, if a female is spayed before the first heat).
- May help reduce the chances of inguinal hernias, which the Chihuahua is predisposed to.

Benefits of Neutering

- Eliminates the chance of impregnating a female.
- Eliminates the possibility of testicular tumors.
- Reduces the risk of prostate disease (roughly 60% of intact males 5+ years show symptoms of an enlarged prostate. Some studies suggest the risk increases - more ahead).
- Cuts down on territorial marking.
- Cuts down on urges to run away (males can smell a female in heat 1 to 3 miles away).

Risks

Most veterinarians agree that the benefits far outweigh the risks. However, there are some possible risks that every owner needs to consider:

Known Risks **Urinary incontinence for females.** Of female dogs that are spayed, approximately 20% will develop incontinence sometime during their lifetimes. Incontinence can develop shortly after the procedure or many years later. Many vets suggest that waiting until the age of 3 months will cut down on the chance of later developing this.

Slight delay in growth-plate closure*. This is only a known risk to *a certain degree*. This refers to growth plates closing later than normal, possibly leading to increased risk of bone fractures or to a dog growing a bit larger than he/she would otherwise. The only portion of this that is generally accepted as fact is that growth plates may close a bit later (12 to 18 months later), though this equals a difference of *just millimeters* seen on x-rays.

Possible Risks There are a lot of studies that suggest risks and some that are inconclusive. This is a list of some notable ones; take note that many veterinary experts state that there is not enough supporting research to conclude if any of these risks are valid.

Cardiac tumors. There is much debate on this topic. At the time of this writing, one study[1] concluded that spaying and neutering increased the risk of cardiac tumors; 4 times greater for females and only slighter greater for males.

Increased rate of other cancers. There is much debate about this as well. Many studies show that spaying and neutering prevent certain cancers. Some studies show it increases the risk. Specifically, one study involving Rottweilers[2] concluded that spay/neutering increases osteosarcoma (a type of bone cancer), a 2002 study[3] showed prostate cancer was 4 times more likely to develop with neutered males, a 2007 study[4] showed prostate cancer was 2 to 4 times more likely, and a 2009 study[5] showed a very slight risk of increase of lymphoma for spayed females.

Myths About Spaying and Neutering

1) Neutering will make a male frustrated that he cannot mate. This is a myth. Canines do not mate out of pleasure; it's instinct triggered by hormones. When neutered, this factor is eliminated, and a male is not troubled by this.

2) Neutering causes a male to lose stamina. This is a myth. There are no notable changes to endurance.

3) A dog will automatically become overweight and/or lazy. This is a myth. When given the appropriate amount of food and exercised regularly, there will not be any noticeable changes in weight or activity for spayed or neutered dogs. If a dog does gain weight after being fixed, this is often attributed to less pacing that was formally due to restlessness.

Age to Spay or Neuter

Studies show that a female's best chance for good health and a long life is to be spayed before her first heat; typically, at the age of 3 to 4 months old. The odds of developing mammary cancer increases even after one heat and increases with each subsequent one. However, even if an owner waits, having this done at any age will have benefits. With a male, this is typically done before he reaches puberty, between 4 and 6 months old. This way, bad habits such as marking are not yet in place.

* For those concerned about growth plate issues, veterinarians may propose waiting until the age of 6 to 9 months.

The Procedures

Spaying is performed under general anesthesia. A small incision is made in the abdomen from which both the ovaries and the uterus is removed. Ovarian ligaments and blood vessels are secured. The abdominal tissues are stitched internally and externally.

Neutering is performed by making an incision in the scrotum from which the testicles are removed. Blood vessels are tied off and cut. This will be stitched with either dissolvable stitches or ones which will need to be removed 10 days afterward.

Post-procedure care: Females typically require bed rest for 10 days. Complications to report to the vet include vomiting, tremors, pale gums, or bleeding. A checkup is done about 2 weeks afterward, at which time stitches will be removed. For a male, there is usually swelling (for about 3 days), slight discomfort and/or bruising. This is typically minor and does not require pain medication. Most dogs are ready to play, exercise, and run around as normal even just days later; however, to make sure that the incision heals correctly, it is recommended to limit these activities for 2 weeks.

1 Journal of Veterinary Internal Medicine. Volume 13, Issue 2, March 1999, Pages: 95–103, Wendy A. Ware and David L. Hopper

2 Cooley DM1, Beranek BC, Schlittler DL, Glickman NW, Glickman LT, Waters DJ. Endogenous gonadal hormone exposure and bone sarcoma risk. Cancer Epidemiol Biomarkers Prev. 2002 Nov;11(11):1434-40.

3 Teske E, Naan EC, van Dijk EM, van Garderen E, Schalken JA. Canine prostate carcinoma: epidemiological evidence of an increased risk in castrated dogs. Mol Cell Endocrinol. 2002 Nov 29;197(1-2):251-5.

4 Bryan JN, Keeler MR, Henry CJ, Bryan ME, Hahn AW, Caldwell CW. A population study of neutering status as a risk factor for canine prostate cancer. Prostate. 2007 Aug 1;67(11):1174-81.

5 Villamil JA1, Henry CJ, Hahn AW, Bryan JN, Tyler JW, Caldwell CW. Hormonal and sex impact on the epidemiology of canine lymphoma. J Cancer Epidemiol. 2009;2009:591753. doi: 10.1155/2009/591753. Epub 2010 Mar 14.

Worms

Tapeworms
Tapeworms are flat, segmented worms that attach to an animal's intestine where they suck nutrients through the tissue. An adult tapeworm can be up to 20 inches (50 cm) long.

How a dog gets tapeworms: These are mainly transmitted via ingesting tapeworm larvae, fleas that contain tapeworm eggs, or wildlife such as mice or birds.

Signs: Tapeworms can lead to lack of growth (with puppies), anemia, intestinal blockage, and weight loss.

Signs of the worms: Dried segments of tapeworms about the size of a grain of rice around the anus, irritation on the anal opening (a dog may scoot his rear along the ground), and/or seeing segments of worms in a dog's stools.

Diagnosing: Stool sample testing.

Treatment: De-worming medication. Nutritional and vitamin supplements and/or other treatment will be given as needed.

Prevention: Regular testing for parasites. In addition, careful supervision to prevent ingestion of contaminated grass, feces, or small wildlife such as mice or birds, and regular flea protection. Note that most broad-based protection medications do not work for tapeworms.

Hookworms
This parasite hooks onto a dog's intestine with its sharp teeth, pokes a hole in a blood vessel, and feeds off of the blood. A dog with an infestation of 300 hookworms, can lose 5 to 10% of his blood supply each day due to both blood taken by the hookworm and internal bite marks that actively bleed afterward.

How a dog gets hookworms: A puppy may be born with them or contract them when nursing (if the dam is infected), or a dog of any age may ingest hookworm larva via contaminated feces, matter (grass, soil, etc.), or water.

Signs: Diarrhea (often black or bloody), vomiting, loss of appetite, pale lips, ear flaps, and/or nostrils, malnourishment (weakness, weight loss, etc.), and/or cough (if hookworms travel to the lungs).

Signs of the worms: These are not typically visible in a dog's stools.

Diagnosing: Stool sample testing.

Treatment: De-worming medication. Nutritional and vitamin supplements and/or other treatment will be given as needed. In cases of severe blood loss, a blood transfusion may be needed.

Prevention: Regular de-wormings for young puppies, regular prevention meds from that point on for dogs of all ages, and regular testing for parasites. In addition, In addition, careful supervision to prevent ingestion of contaminated grass, feces, or unclean outdoor water sources.

Roundworms
Roundworms are one of the most common parasites found in dogs. These white worms that resemble a strand of cooked spaghetti can reside inside a dog's intestine and live off of partially digested food. An adult roundworm can be up to 4 inches (10 cm) long.

How a dog gets roundworms: A puppy may be born with them or contract them when nursing (if the dam is infected), or a dog of any age may ingest roundworm eggs via contaminated feces, matter (grass, soil, etc.), or wildlife such as mice or birds.

Signs: Pot-bellied appearance, mild to severe vomiting and/or diarrhea, malnourishment (weakness, weight loss, etc.), and/or coughing (if they travel to the lungs).

Signs of the worms: Live worms in stools (or rarely in vomit) that resemble cooked pieces of spaghetti.

Diagnosing: Stool sample testing.

Treatment: De-worming medication. Nutritional and vitamin supplements and/or other treatment will be given as needed.

Prevention: Regular de-wormings for young puppies, regular prevention meds from that point on for dogs of all ages, and regular testing for parasites. In addition, careful supervision to prevent ingestion of contaminated grass, feces, or small wildlife such as mice or birds.

Whipworms
Whipworms can reside in a dog's small and large intestines, feeding on secretions. An adult roundworm can be up to 3 inches (7.6 cm) long.

How a dog gets whipworms: A dog of any age may ingest whipworms eggs via contaminated feces, water, matter (grass, soil, etc.), or wildlife such as mice or birds.

Signs: Pot-bellied appearance, diarrhea (sometimes bloody), malnourishment (weakness, weight loss, etc.), and/or dehydration.

Signs of the worms: Not seen in stools often; if so, will look like thin pieces of thread.

Diagnosing: Stool sample testing.

Treatment: De-worming medication. Nutritional and vitamin supplements and/or other treatment will be given as needed.

Prevention: Regular de-wormings for young puppies, regular prevention meds from that point on for dogs of all ages, and regular testing for parasites. In addition, careful supervision to prevent ingestion of contaminated grass, feces, small wildlife such as mice or birds, and unclean outdoor water sources.

Heartworms
A case of heartworms is serious and often fatal. These worms live inside the right ventricle of a dog's heart and nearby blood vessels. Adult heartworms can be up to 14 inches (35.5 cm) long.

How a dog gets heartworms: This is transmitted via mosquitoes.

Signs: Many dogs do not show signs until later stages at which time it may be too late for treatment. If there are early signs, this may include trouble breathing, vomiting, weight loss, coughing, and/or weakness. Late stage signs include exercise intolerance and/or fainting.

Diagnosing: Blood test.

Treatment: Once a dog is badly infected, non-surgical treatment involves arsenic-based drugs, and this involves in-patient care, lasting at least several days. There can be complications including pulmonary embolism due to heartworms blocking blood vessels, and this can be fatal. In severe cases, surgery is performed to remove the worms. Both of these treatments are not always successful. In some cases, a dog needs to be euthanized.

Prevention: Regular heartworm prevention medication. See 'Prevention for Puppies and Adults' at the end of this section.

Ringworms
Contrary to its name, ringworm is not a worm, it's a fungus called dermatophytes (or dermatophytosis) that lives on the skin, feeding off of dead skin tissue and hairs. Dermatophytosis means 'skin plant'. There are 3 different types, with Microsporum canis being the most common to canines.

How a Dog Gets ringworms: This is very contagious. Transmission can happen via direct contact with an infected animal or a person. It can be passed from dogs to cats and vice versa, from pets to humans, from humans to pets, and from other animals such as cats, cows, goats, pigs, and horses.

It can also be transmitted by coming into contact with spores that may be in the environment including grooming equipment, bedding, carpeting, and so forth. In rare cases, ringworm can be spread by contact with infected soil. Some dogs are more susceptible to ringworm than others; healthy adults typically have good resistance to them. Dogs may be carriers but show no symptoms.

Signs: A round hairless lesion, typically on the face, ears, tail, or paws, but may appear anywhere. Dissimilar to how it is with humans, there may *not* be a circle within a circle. The lesion may expand in size, either remaining circular or becoming irregular. It may scale over and/or become red or inflamed, and there may be itching.

Diagnosing: Examining a fur or skin sample under a microscope, wood's lamp test, and/or culture grown in a lab.

Treatment: In some cases, ringworm will resolve itself within 2 to 5 months. In other cases, anti-fungal medication and/or lime-sulfur dips may be prescribed. With any soil suspected of containing ringworm spores, a solution of bleach and water can kill these.

De-worming Schedule
Typically, de-worming for young puppies is at 2, 4, 6, and 8 weeks of age, then again at 3 months old and then 4 months old. While some owners choose to do this at home, we recommend having this done by the veterinarian, since proper dosing is important. You will be at the vet's at any rate, for inoculations and weight checks.

Prevention for Puppies and Adults
Once a puppy has received his 'new puppy' de-wormings, from this point on, through adulthood, and for the rest of a dog's life, regular protection must be given. Most heartworm prevention products will also cover most parasitic worms, and some also work for fleas and/or some forms of mange. For example, Advantage Multi (which is one that toy breeds seem to tolerate well) works for heartworms, roundworms, hookworms, whipworms, fleas, and sarcoptic mange. In addition, wellness checks (yearly for adults and twice-per-year for seniors) will involve stool testing to check for parasites.

Female Issues

Heat

Heat (estrus cycle, 'coming into season') is a female dog's cycle of menstruation. During part of the cycle, she is able to conceive and become pregnant.

Age: The age of the first cycle is generally between 6 and 8 months. However, it can happen as early as 4 months and as late as 15 months. If your female has not been spayed, is over 12-months-old, and you have not noticed the first heat, she should be examined by the veterinarian.

The 4 Stages of a Female's Cycle:

1) **Proestrus.** Estrogen levels rise for an average of 9 days. A female is not able to conceive and will not be receptive to a male's advances.
2) **Estrus *.** This is the stage of 'heat'. Estrogen levels drop while progesterone levels rise. Typically, signs of heat will be obvious. This lasts from 14 to 21 days; though, there is a smaller window of time within these 2 to 3 weeks that a female will be receptive to a male. That 'window' typically ranges from 7 to 10 days.
3) **Diestrus.** Progesterone levels are still elevated for roughly 2 months; however, a female will not be receptive to a male.
4) **Anestrus.** This is the 'resting' stage once hormone levels are completely back to normal and it lasts until the first stage, proestrus, starts again.

Signs:

- **Swollen vulva.** It's a good idea for first-time owners to take note their female dog's vulva so that this sign can be noticed.
- **Discharge.** May vary from light pink to red and may change throughout the cycle.
- **Interest from intact male dogs.** Males that have not been neutered can detect scents deposited by a female when she urinates; in some cases from up to 3 miles away. Males within sight of her will attempt to make contact if they are physically able to do so. If receptive, a female will 'flag' the male, by lifting her tail and presenting herself.
- **Possible changes in behavior.** Some dogs may become clingy, others may retreat.

How Long Heat Lasts For: The heat cycle lasts for 2 to 3 weeks.

How Often the Heat Cycle Occurs: Heat occurs approximately 2 times per year, spaced approximately 4 to 6 months apart. Heat cycles may continue up into the senior years; though may be spaced further apart and/or with less discharge.

Confusing Heat Discharge with Anal Gland Secretion: There can be some confusion between bloody discharge due to the heat cycle and scent oil discharge due to burst anal glands. Bloody discharge has very little odor and ranges from pink to red. Scent oil from burst anal glands has a strong foul-smelling odor and can range in color (clear, yellow, yellow-brown, reddish-brown). See also 'Health & Care - Body Part Specific: Anal Glands'.

Pain and Behavioral Changes During Heat: While no one can say for sure, studies suggest that a female may feel some cramping or discomfort. A female may 'nest', wanting to rest in a comfortable area, sometimes wishing to be alone, and arranging toys and other soft items around her. Some females will become moody, distancing themselves, having less tolerance for others, or appearing restless. Others may become clingier.

Split Heats: Once in a while a dog can have a 'split heat'. The cycle will begin, stop for days (or a few weeks in some cases), and then begin again. This is not two heat cycles; it is technically one that is disrupted. It is thought that this occurs due to changing hormone levels.

Silent Heats: A silent heat refers to when a dog does indeed go through the estrus cycle but does not show any of the typical signs. Do note that this is a different event than a skipped heat.

Skipped Heats: There are some health conditions that can cause a dog to skip a heat cycle. This includes but is not limited to malnourishment, canine diabetes, hypothyroidism, and Cushing's disease. If your female misses a heat, this warrants a veterinary visit.

Spaying: Spaying will bring an end to heat cycles, as the uterus and ovaries are removed. While there are some risks, most veterinarians agree that spaying gives females a better chance for a healthy life. See also: 'Health – Other: Spaying and Neutering'.

Care During a Heat Cycle: One aspect will be hygiene. While it is generally light, discharge will accumulate and soak into bedding, blankets, pillows, furniture, and more. Therefore, it's best to place a doggie diaper on your female during the heat cycle. There are both disposable and washable diapers. Some owners cover this up with a canine 'panty' simply for the cuteness factor.

Another element is safety. Intact males from up to 3 miles away will be able to pick up on lingering scents left in her urine puddles out in the yard. And if able to reach her, intact males that see her will try to mount her. Do not bring her out to public places where there may be other dogs, and always supervise when bringing her outside for bathroom needs. Be sure to scan for any stray dogs.

Finally, you may be wondering if you should be doing anything for possible cramps. Many dogs are fine without any extra care in this regard. However, if you suspect some discomfort, you can place a warm (not hot) water bottle against her tummy. Be sure to allow your female to rest and/or retreat as she wishes.

Breeding

The American Kennel Club offers a wealth of knowledge (both text and video) if you are thinking about breeding. This is under the 'Responsible Breeding' section of their website. The URL address is http://www.akc.org/dog-breeders/responsible-breeding; however, you can typically find it by searching for 'AKC breeding'. They cover everything including how to prepare, choosing mates, studying genetics, contracts, health checks, whelping, registering litters, weaning, and more. The AKC did a fantastic job with all of their breeding information, so please make use of it; You will find that it covers a lot!

Breeding Elements to Keep in Mind: Deciding to breed is an enormous responsibility and much time should be spent deciding if you are prepared for everything that is involved. Breeding is a lot more complicated than just allowing two dogs to mate. Rushing into this without understanding the responsibilities can lead to feeling overwhelmed and risking your dog's health and the health of future litters.

Before you decide to breed, keep the following elements in mind:

1) **It is important to study the genetics and backgrounds of the dogs in question.** You will want to feel confident that it will be a sound breeding. Dam and sire should meet AKC standards so that the pairing lends toward the betterment of the breed, and defects and flaws will not continue down the bloodline. The AKC requires pre-breeding screening of a cardiac exam, ophthalmologist evaluation, and patella evaluation.

2) **Appropriate size of the dam.** The dam should be larger than the sire and have proper pelvic breadth.

3) **Appropriate age.** The AKC states that a dam must not be younger than 8 months and the sire not less than 7 months. You may wish to consider a breeding age of at least 2-years-old for the dam; she will be physically mature yet still have enough youthful flexibility. A male's sperm will be viable at 7-months-old (it typically is by 4-months); however, you may wish to wait until the 1-year-mark to ensure strong sperm. Additionally, a female should be retired from breeding at 7-years-old, if health status does not warrant this done sooner.

4) **Have your breeding goal clearly defined.** What sort of registration will you provide? AKC? CKC? Will you focus on certain colors? Will you keep show-quality dogs? How will you handle the sale and follow-up?

5) **Never over-breed.** While each dog should be individually evaluated, in general, a dam is bred twice in a row and then allowed a rest, or bred every other heat cycle. The most important element is that the female is evaluated after each litter to see if she is even able to handle having a future litter. When a dam must have a cesarean section, in many cases she should not have any more litters.

6) **Be very aware of the costs that are involved.** Breeding is a huge undertaking and is expensive. It often involves taking time out of work and finances for veterinarian checkups for all dogs and all future puppies, shots, de-wormings, high-quality puppy and adult dog food, beds, pens, toys, dishes, gates, cleaning supplies, bathing supplies, grooming tools, and possible emergency cesarean sections.

7) **You will have to be emotionally prepared for loss.** Even the most careful breeder may experience the loss of a newborn pup.

8) **Ethical breeding requires dedication to shaping the pups' personalities.** Interaction between a breeder and a pup is essential and plays a role in shaping a pup's personality. This includes handling and having one-on-one interaction for proper socialization and desensitization. Without this, puppies will not have the needed skills to transition well into their new homes.

9) **This is a long-term commitment.** You will need to commit to keeping puppies that are not able to be sold for any reason, including health issues. And you will need to commit to keeping adults that are not able to be re-homed once retired. Finally, most breeders offer a contract that states a puppy can be returned for any reason (as opposed to being surrendered at a shelter), and you will be expected to honor this.

Pregnancy

Important Facts to Know:

1) **A female can become pregnant during the first heat cycle, even if there is hardly any discharge**. For the Chihuahua, this is typically between 6 and 8-months-old, but can be as young as 4-months.

2) **It is during the estrus phase of the cycle that a female can become pregnant.** This stage lasts between 2 and 3 weeks. Within this time, there is a smaller window lasting 7 to 10 days, usually starting somewhere between Day 10 to Day 15 (beginning a count from Day 1 that discharge begins) that eggs will drop and the female can become pregnant.

3) **Pregnancy can occur even if a tie does not appear successful.** Even if you stopped a mount, it may be too late.

4) **A female can become pregnant by more than one dog at the same time.** This is known as a multi-sired or dual-sired litter. Ova (the eggs produced by the ovaries) can remain available for several days. So, for example, a female may be mounted on Day 1 (with an egg being fertilized) and then if mounted on Day 3 by a different male, another egg may become fertilized. [*Photo courtesy of ChiChiBabies Chihuahuas]*

5) **Impregnation by a much larger dog can be dangerous** since this can result in pups too large for toy breeds to safely carry and whelp.

6) **A dog can have a false pregnancy.** This is also referred to as pseudopregnancy and is thought to occur due to hormonal imbalances of progesterone and prolactin. There can be an enlarged abdomen, swollen mammary glands, and in rare cases, milk production. The veterinarian may suggest warm or cold packs to be placed on mammary tissue to reduce uncomfortable swelling. This normally ebbs away within 3 weeks. If it persists, this may need to be treated with hormone supplements.

7) **Litter size** generally ranges from 1 to 3 puppies; though, 5 or even 6 is not unheard of.

How to Know if Your Female is Pregnant: When you wish to have the veterinarian confirm a pregnancy, the earliest this can be done is Day 22. Let's take a look at the options (this is counting out from the day of mating):

- A blood test can confirm pregnancy as early as Day 22
- An ultrasound can confirm pregnancy as early as Day 28
- Palpation can also confirm pregnancy as early as Day 28
- An x-ray can confirm pregnancy as early as Day 42; however, it is suggested to wait until Day 55 for an accurate reading of how many puppies to expect.

Why It's Important to See the Veterinarian: With a planned breeding, both male and female dogs have testing *before* a pairing, to ensure their health and to rule out the possibility of passing on any hereditary conditions to a potential litter. In addition, the female's pelvic width is checked to see if she can naturally whelp puppies. With unplanned pregnancies, it is very important to bring the female to the vet right away, as both of these elements are of great concern.

Signs of Pregnancy:

Week 1. At this early stage, there will usually be no signs. Towards the end of Week 1, there may be some slight nausea that causes decreased appetite.

Weeks 2 and 3. Signs will begin to emerge, though minimal. This may include some lethargy, a *slightly* swollen abdomen, possible increase in self-cleaning, and/or slightly enlarged nipples. During Week 2 there may still be slight nausea. This is typically brief, as a heartier appetite emerges as she moves into Week 3.

Week 4. Signs are now very clear. The abdomen will be swollen to the point that there is no doubt she is carrying a litter, nipples will be enlarged, darkened, and some that were previously flush may be popped out, and mammary glands (breast tissue) will be swollen. She may also have nesting tendencies and her appetite should be strong.

Weeks 5 and 6. As a dam approaches the end of the gestation period, she may tire much more easily, may prefer to remain at home resting in a quiet spot, and will usually be less social.

Pregnancy lasts for 63 Days, on average: This is a general figure. It can vary from Day 58 to Day 65 and be considered normal.

Morning Sickness: This type of nausea can happen at any time of the day or night. If there is vomiting, change to a very bland diet for 2 to 3 days. This should be one protein (typically plain white chicken or lean beef) and one starch (typically sweet potato or white rice). If vomiting persists speak to your veterinarian about the possibility of providing anti-nausea medication. This may also require steps to rehydrate and replace lost electrolytes, and should be done with veterinary supervision.

Feeding Overview: A dam does not need an increase in food for the first few weeks; calorie requirements increase as she moves into Week 3. Many vets suggest a change to puppy food. If possible, stay with the same brand, choosing the 'puppy' formula. Do NOT give any calcium-rich foods or any sort of supplement that contains calcium. By the end of Week 3, calories should be approximately 25% more than normal. She may do best with more frequent meals as opposed to larger portions. Just before delivery, a dog may refuse food; this is a sign that labor will soon begin.

Expected Weight Gain: Weight gain is comprised of not just the pups but also fluids (water, amniotic fluids, colostrum) and tissue (amniotic sacs that surround each fetus, umbilical cords). During the entire course of pregnancy, a female will gain *about* 20% of her normal body weight. For example, a 6-lb. Chihuahua will gain approximately 1.2 lbs., ending at 7.2 lbs. Check with the veterinarian if you suspect too little or too much weight gain.

Supplements: In most cases, a pregnant dog should not be given any extra vitamins or supplements without explicit veterinarian instruction. Doing so can be detrimental to both dam and litter. This is particularly true of calcium; the amount that is in the dam's regular food is all that is needed. Do NOT give any extra; it is linked to eclampsia (which can be fatal), difficult deliveries, and soft tissue calcium deposits and joint abnormalities in developing fetuses. However, the veterinarian may recommend that you give extra calcium *right as labor is beginning* (to help with contractions) and during nursing (for proper lactation).

Care Overview:

• **Activity** – Unless there are any exercise restrictions set in place by the veterinarian, continue to offer twice daily walks, at a good pace, albeit perhaps a bit slower. This will keep a dog fit and healthy for labor. Do not allow any jumping that would cause a jarring (this should be the rule for all Chihuahuas due to being prone to patella luxation). During the final 2 weeks, depending on how many pups a dam is carrying, there may be some trouble with maneuvering around and walks can be put on pause at this time.

• **Comfort** – Nesting instincts will be strong. If it is not already set up, offer a bed within a playpen or gated area. She should not be isolated; have this in a quiet corner of a room that the family uses.

• **Other Dogs** – A pregnant female may become nervous by the presence of other dogs in the house (male or female); If so, surround her resting spot with portable baby gates. If the sire is in the house, separate the two dogs starting at the beginning of Week 6. He can re-join her, with supervision, when the pups are 4 weeks old. He can have full access once the puppies are fully weaned.

Pregnancy Week by Week Care:

Day One of the tie:
• On a calendar, count ahead 56 days from the tie and mark that day. This is the day you should be 100% prepared for her to give birth.
• If the tie is successful, plan to take a break from work beginning on Day 56 and ideally for at least 2 weeks. After Day 56, the dam should not be left alone if at all possible; you will not want her to give birth while you are not home.
• Immediately restrict calcium-rich foods and do not give any sort of supplement that contains calcium.
• If you have not done so already, fully 'puppy-proof' the house and continue to do this daily.

Pregnancy Week 1 through 3 (Days 1 to 21): Mild nausea and slight moodiness are normal. There
may be a light pink discharge. During these 3 weeks, the fertilized egg divides. As it travels between the ovary and uterine horn, it keeps splitting; it will be a 4, 8, 16, 32, and then a 64-celled embryo. By the end of Week 3, primitive body parts are starting to form. *Care during this time:*
• Continue to restrict calcium-rich foods and do not give any sort of supplement that contains calcium.
• Keep up with regular daily walks.
• Do not give any medications or supplements or use flea treatment without vet approval.
• The dam cannot be given any live vaccinations.

Pregnancy Week 4 (Days 22 to 28): The dam is clearly pregnant, with a swollen abdomen, swollen
mammary tissue, and extended nipples. By now, pregnancy should have been confirmed by the veterinarian. There may be a clear, odorless vaginal discharge; this is normal. At the end of this week, the body of the fetus is taking form, retinas in the eyes are developing, eyes are open during this time. *Care during this time:*
• Continue to restrict calcium-rich foods and do not give any sort of supplement that contains calcium.
• Limit long walks, but continue short daily walks.
• Per vet instruction, switch to puppy food.
• Feed 25% extra (1/8 cup added to each normally given 1/2 cup) to comply with increased appetite.

Pregnancy Week 5 (Days 29 to 35): The dam may be tiring easily now and may wish to spend more
time resting. Appetite should still be strong. The fetus's facial features are becoming defined, eyelids are now closed and will remain so until about 10 days after being born. *Care during this time:*
• Continue to restrict calcium-rich foods and do not give any sort of supplement that contains calcium.
• Remain limiting long walks, but continue short daily walks.
• Keep feeding increased food to meet appetite.

Pregnancy Week 6 (Days 36 to 42): The dam's nesting instincts are strong. She may prefer to spend some time alone. The abdomen is very extended. The fetus's bones are forming and skin pigmentation is present. ***Care during this time:***
- Continue to restrict calcium-rich foods and do not give any sort of supplement that contains calcium.
- It is time to prepare the whelping box in a quiet area. Encourage (but not force) her to sleep there.
- As always, never let your dam outdoors without full supervision. Sometimes, pregnant dogs have an urge to run away to give birth.
- If the sire is in the house, separate the two dogs.

Pregnancy Week 7 (Days 43 to 49): The dam may start shedding some stomach hair. The production of breast milk (colostrum) may begin as early as day 45. A fetus's movement may be seen and can often be felt by touching the dam's abdomen. ***Care during this time:***
- Continue to restrict calcium-rich foods and do not give any sort of supplement that contains calcium.
- Stop any rough playing and all jumping.

Pregnancy Week 8 (Days 50 to 57): The production of breast milk (colostrum) is well underway. Now is the time to be prepared in case the puppies come early. ***Care during this time:***
- Continue to restrict calcium-rich foods and do not give any sort of supplement that contains calcium.
- Call your veterinarian to schedule x-rays to determine the size and number of pups. Days 55 or 56 are the best days to do this.
- Have your whelping area and all supplies ready. Have a plan in place if an emergency trip to the clinic is needed.
- It will be normal for a dam to be fussy with food this week.

Pregnancy Week 9 (Days 58 to 65): The litter will be born during this time, between Day 58 and 65, with 63 days being the average. ***Care during this time:***
- Appetite may decrease.
- The mucus plug will shed. This develops in the cervix during pregnancy. As the dam approaches full term, this may begin to shed into dry pieces or may loosen and be expelled as a whitish-yellow discharge. This happens hours to days before labor begins.
- Start taking her temperature as follows:
  On **Day 57:** 3 times a day, **Day 58:** 4 times a day, **Day 59:** 5 times a day, and once in the middle of the night, **Day 60+:** Every 2 hours during the day and every 4 hours at night. Make sure that the thermometer is inserted at least 1.5 to 2 inches (3.81 to 5 cm) into the rectum, using petroleum jelly as a lubricant.
- When the dam's temperature drops by 1 degree, *per vet recommendation*, you may offer her cottage cheese, whole white yogurt, or another safe food that contains calcium.

Preparing the Birthing Area/ Whelping Box: While you can find impressive construction plans for all types of elaborate whelping boxes, there are two easy methods:

1) Use a sturdy cardboard box. These work well since aside from being free of cost, they are portable, easy to discard of, and can be cut to create a doorway. The box should be lined with an abundance of clean cloths and/or newspaper. During the birthing process, as the paper becomes soaked with fluids, you can slip out the top layer to expose a clean dry layer underneath, quickly throwing away the wet newspaper/cloths into a leak-proof trash bag.

2) A Perla dog bed. These are plastic dog beds and can be prepared in the same way.

Place the whelping box in a quiet room where there will be no disturbances or commotion. A heating pad will be needed after the puppies are born, so be sure to choose a spot where the cord will easily reach.

Whelping

Items You Will Need to Prepare for Labor and Whelping:

1) Infant's nasal aspirator (bulb syringe) **2)** Towels **3)** Dental floss **4)** Sterilized scissors **5)** Iodine **6)** Sterilized cups

The Sign that Labor is Starting:

When a dam's temperature drops from its normal 101 to 102.5°F (38.3 to 39.2°C) to below 100° F (37.7 C), labor will typically begin within 24 hours. As noted under 'Pregnancy Week 9: Care during this time', you'll be taking her temperature quite regularly.

Call the vet ASAP if:
- The dam has been pregnant for more than 65 days.
- It has been 24 hours since her temperature dropped, but she has not delivered the litter.
- One puppy came out, but it has been more than 2 hours without any more coming out (and you know there are more)
- If her temperature has risen
- If discharge fluids have a foul smell

Whelping: Stage 1 of Labor: Make sure the dam is in her whelping box. If the sire or other males are in the house, block access.

During the first stage of labor, the cervix will dilate, and contractions begin. This can be extremely painful. The dam may be uncomfortable, restless, quite possibly pacing, shivering, panting, and may whine. She may not want to eat and she may even vomit. This is the longest stage of labor, typically lasting 6 to 18 hours.

Stage 2 of Labor: Each puppy is born in his/her own individual amniotic sac. This may break right before the puppy is pushed out, simultaneously, or the dam may immediately tear it open with her teeth.

Puppies will usually be pushed out every 10 to 30 minutes of forceful straining. Pups can be born head first or tail first. If you see the rear legs of a puppy but he appears to be stuck, you can gently pull the puppy out in a downward and rearward arcing motion.

As the pups emerge, the dam will lick them clean and bite off the umbilical cord. It is important to let her do this. The rough licking stimulates the puppies to breathe, and it gets their circulation going. It is normal for the dam to ingest the afterbirth tissues, including the amniotic sacs.

If the dam does not bite the umbilical cord, you will need to tie and cut it.

1. Tie two pieces of dental floss around the umbilical cord. A first piece should be about 1 inch (2.5 cm) away from the puppy's belly. A second piece should be tied 0.25 inch (0.64 cm) away from the first piece, toward the placenta.
2. Using sterilized scissors, cut the umbilical cord between the two pieces of floss.

3. Pour iodine into a sterilized cup and dip the end of the cord into this. The umbilical cord will then usually fall off within a few days to a week.

Stage 3 of Labor: Once all the puppies have been born, a dam enters this third stage during which time the uterus contracts fully, expelling any remaining placenta, blood, and fluid.

Bleeding and Other Complications: A female will have some bleeding and discharge for up to 10 days after giving birth. This is normal if the bleeding/discharge lessens each day and if there are no signs of a health issue. By Day 12, all bleeding and/or discharge should have stopped. Take your dog to the vet ASAP if bleeding is excessive, bleeding increases, there is a foul odor from the blood or discharge, the dam is lethargic, will not eat, or has a fever, and/or if there are any other signs of ill health.

After Whelping: Newspapers should be taken away and soft, clean blankets placed down. Clean the surrounding area with soap and bleach, but do not allow the dam or pups to inhale any fumes. In the whelping box, *under* the blankets, place a heating pad. With a Perla bed, the heating pad can go under a blanket or under the Perla bed. There should be areas in the box/bed that are a warm 80 to 85°F (26.6 to 29.4°C).

Clean the dam with a warm, soapy sponge, patting her dry afterward.

If the coloring of the puppies is very similar, you may find it helpful to mark the pups. Some people use white-out liquid eraser or food coloring to place a tiny dot on each pup in a different area. There are also 'puppy whelping ID bands' that can be obtained. These go around the neck as a collar would; take care to check these often, since newborns literally grow each day.

Keep a very close eye on all puppies. Some will need to be gently moved over to nurse. Use a kitchen scale to weigh the puppies each day, looking for a *daily* weight increase.

Tips:

• The newborn pups should be gaining weight EACH DAY. If not, contact the veterinarian ASAP.
• By Week 4, the dam will begin to need a bit of time away from the puppies. You may wish to add another box to the whelping box, connecting the two with cut-away sections. The puppies may begin to roam from the dam to the second 'room' to play and begin to learn about toys, etc.

Is There Something Wrong with the Dam? If you even *suspect* that something is wrong, call the veterinarian ASAP. This is not the time to write emails or post questions online. By doing so, you are taking away precious time that your dog could have been receiving treatment.

If she is displaying any behavioral changes or any physical changes that make you question things or be concerned about her, do not delay seeking help. Aside from the aforementioned bleeding that can occur as the uterus is being cleaned out, there are **no** health issues that are 'normal'. It is not normal for her to be vomiting, be in pain, have discharging pus, be aggressive, be limping, have sunken-in eyes, have dizziness, refuse to eat, or any other red flag issues.

Eclampsia

Eclampsia ('milk fever' or 'puerperal tetany') is an acute, life-threatening disease that happens most often with nursing dogs within 1 to 3 weeks of being birth, but may occur with pregnant dogs as well. During this time, there is a strong demand for calcium for the dam's milk supply. As it is being diverted there, a dam's own body can become severely depleted.

Symptoms: Signs include restlessness or nervousness, a stiff gait, trouble walking, and/or disorientation. If untreated, this will progress to inability to walk, rigid limbs, high fever over 105°F (40.5°C), and/or heavy breathing. Without treatment, death can occur at this point.

Treatment: If you suspect your pregnant or post-pregnant female has eclampsia, stop the puppies from nursing (they can be bottle-fed a milk replacer) and immediately bring your dam to the veterinarian's office or the closest animal hospital.

The veterinarian can confirm eclampsia via blood testing. This is treated with IV calcium supplementations. Oral calcium supplements may be given once she is discharged. If she responds exceptionally well, she may be able to resume nursing the puppies; however, this must be with the veterinarian's approval.

Prevention: Too much calcium during pregnancy can increase the odds of developing eclampsia. This can be via supplements or calcium-rich foods. Calcium is regulated by the parathyroid hormone. Extra calcium causes parathyroid levels to decrease. Then, when calcium is needed for milk production, those low levels of parathyroid make this near impossible. Blood calcium levels drop and eclampsia can develop.

Once a dog has had eclampsia, there is a higher chance that she will also have it with future litters.

Mastitis

Mastitis is a bacterial infection of the milk glands. It occurs with nursing dogs, but can also occur with those that have just had a false pregnancy (pseudopregnancy). It can be a serious condition, able to develop and worsen quickly, in as little as 12 hours.

Symptoms:
- Milk glands feel hot to the touch, hard, and/or cause discomfort when touched
- Milk may be off-colored
- Decreased appetite or refusal to eat
- Increased thirst
- Temperature may rise to as high as 105°F (40.5°C)

- Possible pus-like discharge
- Possible vomiting
- Possible aggression toward the puppies
- Puppies could show signs of malnutrition (they will not be gaining weight each day)

Treatment: Treatment varies greatly, depending on the severity of the infection, ranging from at-home care to a multiple-day stay at the clinic. This may include simple treatments such as applying warm compresses to the area and expressing the milk glands or may involve IV intervention to treat electrolyte imbalances or even surgery to remove the glands, if there are abscesses or if tissue has been severely damaged.

Pyometra

Pyometra is a very serious infection of the uterus. It can develop and worsen exceedingly fast and can be fatal if not treated. It is reported that this affects 23% of intact female canines. There is also a rare condition, stump pyometra, that can occur with females that were spayed, but the remaining stump of the uterus was not removed.

Pyometra happens more often to older females, but can develop at any age, regardless of whether a dog has been bred or not. The most dangerous 'window' of risk is 2 to 8 weeks after the end of a heat cycle. During the heat cycle, the cervix is open. This allows discharge to be released and exit from the body. Normally, as the heat cycle ends, the cervix gradually closes. During this time, if bacteria finds its way in, there can be an infection.

If the cervix is still open, the infected tissue has a way to leave the body, so this may be easier to treat. This is known as open pyometra.

If the cervix is fully closed, this is gravely serious. The uterus can rupture, pus can escape into the abdomen, and death can occur quickly. This is known as closed pyometra.

Symptoms: With *open pyometra*, there is often is a pus-like discharge seen most commonly within 2 to 8 weeks after a heat cycle ends, sometimes along with excessive licking of the vulva. There *may* be fever, lethargy, depression, and/or refusal to eat.

With *closed pyometra*, signs include vomiting, lethargy, depression, refusal to eat, possible increased thirst, increased urination, and/or fever (seen in less than 1/3 of cases). This can quickly progress to septic shock, which is a life-threatening emergency.

Diagnosis: If you suspect pyometra, immediately bring your female to the veterinarian's office or the closest animal hospital. Testing may include blood tests, x-rays, and/or ultrasound.

Treatment: There will be an emergency spay to remove the infected uterus. This eliminates the infection, prevents recurrence in most cases (except for the very rare 'stump pyometra', only in cases that the uterine stump is not removed during the spaying procedure), and can save the dog's life.

Alternative Treatments: For open pyometra only, there is another treatment option if the owner wishes to breed their female; however, this comes with risk and not all veterinarians will agree to this. It involves giving medications normally given to induce labor as a means of flushing out the uterus, along with long-term antibiotics. Success may be less than 30%. Once bred, the dog should then be spayed because the chances of another pyometra infection are quite high, up to 70%.

Newborn Care

Weaning

Weaning is the interim stage of transitioning a puppy from a liquid diet (the dam's milk) to solid food. This usually starts at about the 4-week mark. The dam is not producing as much milk and the pup may be heading to a new home soon. So, as a pup's food source is dwindling and he must be prepared to live away from the dam, his body and gastrointestinal tract must be slowly acclimated to solid food.

A pup that is weaned too early and does not have a smooth transition from dam's milk to solid food can develop food allergies and/or intestinal distress.

How to Wean: The goal will be to offer gradual steps to solid food. This is done by using a blender to mix a canine liquid milk replacer with the puppy formula of the same brand of food that the dam was eating (so that limited new ingredients are added that could cause any stomach upset), and if needed (especially in the beginning), hot water. ***Note:*** Do not use cow's milk or goat's milk. Canines are lactose intolerant and cannot properly digest these dairy products.

Begin this at the beginning of Week 4 with a mixture that is a *very* soupy substance. This can be placed in a shallow dish, or in a shallow container such as a baking sheet. You may need to pick up the puppies, bring them to this, and encourage them to lap at it. Over the course of two weeks, incrementally transition to a thicker 'stew' via less water, then no water at all and less milk replacer. By week 6 and generally no later than week 7, the puppies should be fully on solid food and be eating at least 4 times per day.

Tips:

1) Pay attention to when the puppies go to the dam to nurse. You will want to politely interrupt this to offer the food that you have prepared. Once they are done eating, you can allow them to go back to the dam for a bit of nursing.

2) Another aspect to weaning is that it creates separation from the dam, which is needed for a pup to gain independence and to get adjusted to your presence.

3) It is not normal for pups to maintain or lose weight during weaning; appetite should be robust and weight gains rather steady. If a pup struggles, this warrants immediate veterinary care.

Newborn Tips & Milestones

Basic reflexes: Newborns have developing nervous systems, yet have basic reflexes: **1)** Burrowing; this allows a pup to seek warmth by snuggling close to dam and littermates **2)** Suckling; this allows a pup to nurse **3)** Perineal reflex; this is in regard to urination and bowel movements; the dam often triggers this by licking the pup's belly and under the tail. **4)** Carrying reflex; this allows the pup to automatically tense and stiffen if the dam grabs him by the scuff to move him.

Weight gain: Newborns should be gaining weight every day; anywhere from 2 to 20 grams on the first day and some degree for all additional days. Using a digital kitchen scale is the easiest method to do daily weigh-ins. By Day 7 to 10, weight should be doubled from Day 1.

Newborn care tips: For the first 3 weeks, the dam will be the sole caretaker for the puppies, feeding and cleaning them. They should all be together in an area (playpen, fresh whelping box, etc.) lined with newspaper or pee pads and with a warm resting and sleeping area (large flat canine mattress or a soft, warm blanket).

If a puppy is having a trouble reaching the dam for milk or is regularly pushed away by littermates, you can remove the other pups for a little while to a warm area close by or to another section within the same box, to allow that puppy to be alone to nurse. Expect newborns to sleep the majority of the time, only waking for nursing needs.

2-weeks-old: Eyelids are *beginning* to open. Hearing is *starting* to come in. Milk teeth may be just starting to erupt. Tails are wagging. The 2-week-old is crawling but may make some wobbly short-lived attempts at walking. The first de-worming is done at this age.

3-weeks-old: Puppies can hear and eyes are now fully open. Pups are becoming more active and able to walk around, having mastered the skill in 3 days or less. The door from the whelping box should now lead into another box where the puppies can walk around and play; this should be lined with newspaper or pee pads Do not allow the newborns to leave the boxes and roam the house. Vocalization may begin; this will sound like 'peeps' and 'squeaks'.

4-weeks-old: If you have not already done so, the entire house should be puppy-proofed. Please refer to 'Puppy Care: Puppy Proofing Your Home'. Once complete, the puppies can begin to venture out of the whelping box to begin exploring while supervised. Play between littermates can be quite animated; a pup that is significantly smaller than the rest may need to be kept separate during playtime to prevent injury.

Newborn vocalizations will continue, and a pup may start to better find his voice. Milk teeth are erupting and weaning should begin. As the pups start to spend time away from the dam, begin taking over some of the cleaning responsibilities by wiping down pups with hypoallergenic grooming wipes or soft baby-sized washcloths.

5-weeks-old: The puppy is now doing well with weaning; he is almost on a completely solid diet. If you have an outside area in which NO other animals (pets - excluding those that are fully up-to-date on vaccinations, and any wildlife) have access to, the pups can follow the dam outside for bathroom needs. Pups should all be held and handled each day to become accustomed to human touch.

6-weeks-old: Weaning should be complete at this age. The puppy has fully developed its sight and hearing. The puppy is, however, a bit too young to respond to his name. A pup of this age will be very curious and want to explore his 'world'; encourage this as he investigates new sights, sounds, and smells within the house. You should still be cleaning the pup with a hypoallergenic grooming wipe or soft baby-sized washcloth; though baths will be starting soon. The first round of vaccinations is given at this age and another de-worming is done.

8-weeks-old: In many states, a puppy is now old enough to go to his new home, to begin a life-long adventure filled with love and family fun.

Age

The idea that a dog ages 7 years for every human year is a generalization. This was something put out there quite a while ago, based on the human lifespan being about 70 years, and a dog's lifespan being about 10. In actuality, canines will age at varying rates, with their breed size being the determining factor. Toy dogs mature much faster than larger dogs and have longer lifespans.

The rate at which a dog matures is not equal at all stages of his life. For toy breeds, there is rapid maturity growth during the first year of a 15-year equivalent, then a 9-year equivalent jump for year two, and then things even out, in increments of 4-year jumps.

Age of Chihuahua	Human Age Equivalent
1	15
2	24
3	28
4	32
5	36
6	40
7	44
8	48
9	52
10	56
11	60
12	64
13	68
14	72
15	76
16	80
17	84
18	88

Aging Milestones:

1 month. The beginning of a pup's 'socialization phase' in which acceptance or fears are formed. The pup should be handled often and allowed to safely explore. Growth is rapid at this time.

2 months. Most puppies are ready to transition to their new homes. While this is a huge adjustment, it's an exciting time as well. A puppy of this age can become easily startled by something, but fears are still not set into place. Part of your job as owner of a new puppy is to take advantage of a young pup's natural curiosity and gradually introduce a wide range of elements. If so, the pup often learns to tolerate (or even enjoy) them. This includes touching the teeth (for future dental cleanings), brushing the coat, exposure to all sorts of household noises, and introducing toys (will come in handy when the pup starts to teethe).

The pup is being free-fed this month. A de-worming is done at 8-weeks, and a combination vaccine will be given at the 8 or 9-week mark. Housebreaking begins. The pup is sleeping a lot, 18 hours on average, with both nighttime sleep and naps. Growth is rapid at this time.

3 months. This is the beginning of the 'ranking phase' in which a puppy learns his place within the hierarchy of the home. To canines, the order of hierarchy is very clear: Within the den (house) lives the pack (all humans and animals), and that pack has a leader (the Alpha). Everyone under the leader is a follower (Beta) since they follow the leader's commands.

Some understanding of hierarchy will be learned just by a pup observing you and being handled and cared for. However, now is the time to make your leadership clear; if not, training of any type can be difficult and behavioral issues can arise, including territorial marking. You may wish to refer to 'Training: Teaching Proper Hierarchy'.

The pup is now eating 3 meals per day, plus 4 or 5 small dry snacks. Moist treats are given for reward. Puppy shots are complete or near complete, at which time you can start taking the puppy for twice-per-day walks and offer playtime outside in the yard (which must be supervised). House training is still underway but there should be progress. The pup is staying awake more now during the day and is doing better with nighttime sleep. Growth is still rapid at this time and the 3-month-old pup is exceedingly hyper.

4 months. The 'ranking phase' is still underway, and lessons are being learned. The puppy is now much more aware of his surroundings. Some fears may have set in. At this age, the pup may protest being left alone more so than when he was younger. Separation anxiety issues may develop or become stronger. House training is near complete. Teething begins just about now, chewing urges will be strong. Un-neutered males have viable sperm. Growth is still rapid at this time, and energy levels are high.

6 months. This is the beginning of the adolescent stage and puberty is underway for both males and females. If not spayed, females have their first heat right around this time. Teething may be winding down somewhat while hyper puppy-behavior is decreasing; this often brings about a level of calm to the house, after things may have seemed a bit chaotic earlier. If training started at 2-months, a puppy should now be fully housebroken. Growth is slowing down.

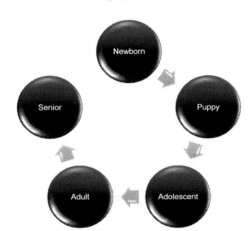

9 months. Most Chihuahua puppies will stop growing by the age of 9 or 10 months. For others, just a bit of weight will be gained from now until 12 months or so. Teething is complete or nearly complete.

1 Year. A Chihuahua is deemed an adult. The 1-year-old young adult is alert, active, and wants to be kept engaged. There is, however, less hyper behavior.

1.5 Years to 9 Years. The Chihuahua is in his or her prime.

10+ Years. There is no exact age that a dog is declared to be a senior. Because toy breeds live relatively long lives, they become seniors later than larger breeds. The declaration that any certain dog is a senior is done by the veterinarian who is familiar with the dog's health history. Many vets will classify a Chihuahua be a senior by age 10.

Senior Care

It's never easy to accept the fact that our dogs age so much quicker than we do. In general, the Chihuahua has a relatively long life span of 14 to 18 years, with 15.5 years being the average, which is the human equivalent of 78-years-old.

There is not an official age that a dog becomes a senior; it is the veterinarian who will make the call. However, in general, it is at the 10-year mark. Declaring a dog to be a senior is an important element, since once-per-year wellness checks will transition to twice-per-year geriatric checks. This is because a dog's risk for many health problems increases with age. Seniors will be screened every 6 months for earlier diagnosis which is vital for effective treatment and good prognosis.

As your dog grows older, keep an eye out for any changes that require adjustments in care.

Changes to Expect

Stamina, mobility, and activity level: Several elements combine to cause a general

'slowing down' of senior dogs. The body's ability to turn protein into muscle decreases, this causes muscles to lose strength and flexibility. The body produces less glucosamine and chondroitin which can lead to stiff joints and other issues including osteoarthritis (80% of seniors have some level of osteoarthritis). In

addition, all major organs gradually lose function, including the heart, which can cause a senior to reach his exercise limit faster than his younger counterparts.

ChaCha, beautiful as ever at 15 years old; Photo courtesy of YankeeBelle Chihuahuas.

What you can do to help:

1) Keep up with daily walks; the 'use it or lose it' expression applies here very fittingly. Do, however, adjust pace according to ability, and take more frequent breaks for rest and rehydration.

2) Try to avoid 'full day outings'; if you take your senior to someone's home for a full-day visit, bring along his bed or cot and set up an area for rests and naps.

3) Speak to the veterinarian regarding diagnosis and treatment of osteoarthritis, which can include massage, NSAIDs, arthritis drugs like Adequan® injections, and/or steroidal anti-inflammatories. See also 'Health – Other: Arthritis'.

4) Starting at age 8, give a daily glucosamine and chondroitin supplement to help prevent osteoarthritis. At the 10-year mark, it may be a good idea to transition glucosamine, chondroitin, MSM, and CoQ10, which is a powerful combination to help relieve issues associated with osteoarthritis. See 'Feeding and Nutrition: Supplements'.

5) Offer an omega-3 EPA and DHA supplement, which can help with discomfort and inflammation. A liquid omega-3 derived from wild fish is recommended. See 'Feeding and Nutrition: Supplements'.

6) Set up pet steps or ramps for your senior to access furniture.

7) Apply paw wax once per week to help with traction both indoors on slippery floors and outside.

Sleep: Seniors tend to have disrupted sleep at night, leading to more daytime naps. There's also an

increase in total hours of sleep needed, which will incrementally rise each year. This is due in part to the body producing less melatonin, which helps regulate the sleep cycle. Discomfort from stiff joints plays a role as well.

What you can do to help:

1) For any joint-related discomfort, refer to the advice as mentioned earlier regarding speaking to the veterinarian and offering supplements.

2) Provide a quality orthopedic memory foam canine bed and encourage your senior to use it.

3) Reassess your senior's resting and sleeping spots. What was once an appropriate area may now be a bit too noisy or busy. Preferences may change as well (window view vs. non-window view, closer to a heating source, further away from the TV, etc.). Though a senior should never feel isolated, a quiet corner is usually appreciated.

Appetite: As dogs age, the metabolism slows down; a senior does not require as many calories as his adult counterpart. This, in turn, can cause a dog to self-regulate and eat less. If so, weight will be maintained. However, many health issues can cause a decreased appetite and dental problems led to trouble eating, so if your senior is losing weight, this warrants a vet visit.

What you can do to help:

1) One of the main reasons for 'senior formula' dog foods is to address the need for fewer calories to prevent obesity in older dogs. With toy breeds, obesity is rarely a problem. Another reason is increased demand for fiber since a senior can have a sluggish digestive system. Therefore, if your senior is doing just fine with weight, you do not necessarily need to switch to a senior formula. If needed, there are ways to add fiber to the diet, such as offering apple slices (no core, no seeds, no peel) or pumpkin (real pumpkin, not the pumpkin pie filling) to meals.
2) If there are issues with chewing due to tooth loss, kibble can be drizzled with low-sodium chicken or beef broth and then warmed in the microwave. Alternatively, you can mix some wet food into the dry kibble; however, keep in mind that this can lead to loose stools. If you do this, try to stick with the same brand.

Skin and Coat: Just like with humans, skin thins as a dog ages. It's more prone to drying and irritations. The coat may lose some of its shine and hairs can become dry and brittle.

What you can do to help:

1) If you are not already, use high-quality shampoo, conditioner, and a really good leave-in coat spray. See 'Grooming: Shampoo and Coat Products'.
2) Dry paws and nose can be helped with an effective paw wax and a quality nose butter. See 'Grooming: Specifics of Grooming Tasks'.
3) An omega-3 EPA and DHA supplement, which you may already be giving for joint-issues, will help improve skin and coat health as well. See 'Feeding and Nutrition: Supplements'.
4) Continue to follow guidelines for summer and winter care. See 'Seasonal Care'.
5) Address dry skin issues as soon as they are noticed. Treatment may involve a restorative skin lotion. See 'Health – Other: Skin Problems – Quick Reference: Dry skin'.

Hazing of the Eyes: As a dog ages, the eyes may develop a hazy white, blue, or gray transparent clouding over the pupil.

In some cases, it will be an issue of lenticular sclerosis (also known as nuclear sclerosis), which is an age-related discoloration of the lens that does not affect vision. This can begin at the age of 6 to 8-years-old; however, is generally not noticed by owners until a few years later. However, hazing or clouding can also point to cataracts.

Some dogs can do fine with mild cataracts (under 30 % opacity). Cataracts that are due to diabetes or that are over 60% opacity need to be treated to prevent possible progression to blindness. So, it will be essential to have any clouding or hazing checked by the veterinarian to determine the cause. See also 'Health & Care – Body Part Specific: Eyes: Cataracts'.

Reduced hearing: Some seniors may have reduced hearing to some degree. This may occur in one ear or both. Some signs to look for include not responding when called and/or acting startled when you approach or wake him (due to not hearing your footsteps). A vet exam should be done first to rule out other health issues, such as an infection, excessive wax buildup, or foreign body in the ear. If there is age-related hearing loss, it cannot be reversed; however, there are steps that you can take to keep him safe and make him comfortable.

What you can do to help:

1) Flip on light switches before you enter a room
2) If you need to wake your senior, do so by first holding your hand in front of his nose, then gently touching his back
3) Give physical praise (petting)
4) Start to incorporate hand signals for common commands.

Reduced Vision: Some reduced vision is normal for senior dogs; however, seniors are also much more prone to glaucoma, cataracts, and other eye conditions linked to certain issues such as hypertension (high blood pressure). Signs of trouble with vision include general clumsiness (bumping into walls and furniture), startling easily, apprehensive behavior, inability to easily find toys, and/or reluctance to go out at night.

What you can do to help:

1) Never assume vision issues are a normal part of aging. The veterinarian should check for eye conditions including glaucoma, cataracts, and displaced retinas.
2) Do not make changes to the layout of furniture in the home.
3) Do not change walking routes.
4) Approach your senior from the side and at his level, as not to startle him.
5) Gate off any staircases that may present a falling hazard.

Caring for a senior with hearing loss
- Flip light switches before entering a room, as not to startle your senior
- Give physical praise (petting) if a senior cannot hear 'good dog'
- Start to incorporate hand signals with your commands

Caring for a senior with vision loss
- Do not make changes to the layout of the house
- Stick with the same walking routes
- Approach your senior from the side & at his level, as not to startle
- Gate off areas that may be dangerous (steps, etc.)

Incontinence: It's not uncommon for dogs late into their senior years to have incontinence issues due to a weakening of the bladder and/or bowel muscles. However, health conditions such as urinary tract infection, polyps, and even tumors can mimic age-related incontinence.

What you can do to help:

Never assume that urinating or eliminating in the house is due to old age. Have all possible health issues ruled out. If the veterinarian deems the issue to be senior incontinence, doggie diapers can be placed on either gender for bowel movements and females for urination, and belly bands can be placed on males for urination. While this is a big change that takes time for both dogs and humans to get used to, it is far better than the alternative of messes in the house.

Canine Cognitive Dysfunction

This is the canine equivalent of dementia, which can affect a senior's thought process, ability to learn, memory, awareness, and response to stimuli. A study done at by the University of California at Davis, and published in the Journal of the American Veterinary Medical Association[1], showed that 28% of dogs between the ages of 11 and 12 showed some impairment. This grew to 68% for dogs 15 to 16-years-old.

Signs of this include:

- Confusion, even in familiar places
- Becoming 'trapped' behind familiar furniture or in room corners
- Trouble navigating through doorways or down hallways
- Not responding to familiar commands or to his/her name being called
- Acting withdrawn, unwillingness to play, go for walks, or go outdoors
- Not recognizing family members
- Pacing or wandering aimlessly throughout the house
- Difficulty learning new tasks, commands, or routes
- Housebreaking accidents
- Sleeping more during the day but less at night
- Staring at walls or into space
- Appearing startled when lights or the television are turned on or off
- A decreasing need for your attention, becoming clingy
- Hesitant to eat or drink

Diagnosing: There is no test for this; therefore, health issues that can cause some of these signs will be ruled out. This includes hearing loss, vision loss, urinary tract infection (can cause confusion and similar signs with seniors), and kidney disease. This may involve blood tests, ultrasound, and/or x-rays. If no other issues are found to be a cause of the behavior, a diagnosis of CCD is often given.

Maisie, 11 years old, a 'Napping Professional'; Photo courtesy of YankeeBelle Chihuahuas

Treatment: There is no cure for CCD; however, some medications may help some dogs. As of the time of this writing, the only FDA approved drug to treat canine senility is selegiline. This is an MAO-B inhibitor that works by increasing the amount of dopamine in the brain, which is linked to nerve impulses and brain function. It has been shown to help up to 70% of canines after 1 month of treatment. There are some possible side effects, though not seen often, including vomiting, diarrhea, restlessness, and lethargy. The veterinarian may also prescribe certain supplements including antioxidants, beta-carotene, omega-3, vitamins E and C, and selenium, which may help improve cognitive function.

At home, you can help by:

1) Not changing the layout of furniture in the home
2) Declutter the house
3) Do not introduce a lot of new stimuli (new places, people, or events)
4) Have a regular schedule for meals, grooming tasks, and bedtime

1 Neilson, J.C., Hart, B.L., Cliff, K.D., & Ruehl, W.W. (2001). Prevalence of behavioral changes associated with age-related cognitive impairment in dogs. Journal of the American Veterinary Medical Association, 218(11), 1787-91. (DOI:10.2460/javma.2001.218.1787)

Life Expectancy of the Chihuahua

The life expectancy of the Chihuahua is between 14 to 18 years with a median age of 15.5 years. Female dogs live, on average, 1.5 years longer than males. This is considered a reasonably long lifespan and is moderately longer than the average lifespan of domesticated canines in general, which is 12.67 years in the US, 12.8 in Canada, and 11.08 years in the UK. The figure of 12.67 years in the US is death by natural causes. When death by trauma and other means are factored in the number goes down to 11.1 years.

Leading Causes of Death for the Chihuahua

A helpful study was conducted by the University of Georgia[1] that lasted over two decades to record and summarize the top causes of death of dogs by looking at veterinary records. They documented 82 breeds, along with mixed breeds. There were 74,556 dogs in all, including 573 Chihuahuas.

The findings give us a good understanding of the cause of death for this breed, and you may be surprised to learn that some are preventable. Results are divided into two groups: Puppies, which are dogs under the age of 1-year, and adults which are dogs 1-year and older.

Cause of Death for Puppies

For puppies (dogs under the age of 1-year), leading cause of death was the same for all breeds:

#1 Infection. This included parvovirus, distemper, and leptospirosis.

#2 Trauma. Death by trauma included fatal injury to the head, body, or both. Some completely avoidable fatal injuries include being stepped on, falling down a staircase, being dropped, being hit by a car, and being the victim of a car accident as a passenger.

Cause of Death for Adult Chihuahuas

#1 Cardiovascular disease. 18.5% of Chihuahuas died due to cardiovascular disease. The Chihuahua is predisposed to mitral valve disease, which is just one type of cardiovascular disease, often leading to congestive heart failure. Since the heart can only function for a set number of years, dogs that succumb to heart failure are often classified as dying of old age. Details regarding mitral valve disease are found under Health – Other: Heart Issues.

#2 Trauma. A dreadful 16.8% of adult Chihuahuas died due to trauma. This is a staggering number that all owners should consider very carefully. Many cases could have prevented. As mentioned under 'Cause of Death for Puppies', completely avoidable fatal injuries include being stepped on, falling down a staircase, being dropped, being hit by a car, and being the victim of a car accident as a passenger.

#3 Infection. 10.5 % of adult Chihuahuas died due to a fatal infection which is the 1st leading cause of death for puppies of all breeds. This includes the diseases as discussed previously with puppies but with adults there are more cases of fungal infections (such as blastomycosis and histoplasmosis) and protozoal disease (such as babesiosis and leishmaniasis). Additionally, this includes anaerobic bacterial infection, which can develop around a wound, such as bone fractures and breaks (which again, brings in the issue of trauma). Finally, this includes sepsis, which is a full body infection that can stem from, among other things, an untreated dental infection.

1 Fleming JM, Creevy KE, Promislow DE. (2011). Mortality in north american dogs from 1984 to 2004: an investigation into age-, size-, and breed-related causes of death. Journal of Veterinary Internal Medicine.

Extending the Lifespan of Your Dog

There are many things that you can do to help your canine family member live as long as possible. Care that you give from the day you bring home your puppy, through adulthood, and into the senior years will have a great impact on health, quality of life, and lifespan.

Most of the elements on this list are found within this book:

- ✓ Keep up with vaccinations and recommended booster shots
- ✓ Proof the house on a regular basis
- ✓ Never let your dog off leash when outside unless in a secure fenced-in area and you are there to supervise
- ✓ Never let your dog outside alone
- ✓ Do not allow your dog to ingest feces or grass
- ✓ If your dog tends to dash for the door when it's opened, take steps to prevent running and escaping
- ✓ Have everyone in the house on guard that this is an 'under-the-foot' dog
- ✓ Do not allow your puppy or dog to jump down from heights
- ✓ Children should be taught proper handling methods and youngsters should be only allowed to carry the dog if they can handle this important task
- ✓ Always have your puppy or dog in a canine car seat when driving him
- ✓ Feed a wholesome all-natural food, with no additives, fillers, or inferior ingredients
- ✓ Follow this rule for all snacks and training treats as well
- ✓ Never offer unfiltered tap water
- ✓ Do not feed table scraps, particularly high-fat or high-sodium foods
- ✓ Provide daily dental care and have professional dental exams and cleanings done as needed
- ✓ Do not miss yearly or twice-per-year vet wellness checks
- ✓ Be vigilant about daily exercise
- ✓ Do not delay vet visits if a health issue is suspected

Letting Go and Saying Goodbye

There may very well come a time when you must make a decision regarding letting your canine family  member pass on. This most often happens when an older, senior dog is diagnosed with a health issue that causes pain or distress that no medication or treatment can relieve.

In any case such as this, we highly recommend seeking a second opinion, no matter how long you may have had the same veterinarian or how much you admire or trust him or her. This will put your mind at ease that the diagnosis and prognosis are absolutely correct. And, there is always a chance that a different veterinarian or specialist may have an alternative diagnosis or proposed treatment plan.

The decision to euthanize a dog should be based on a dog's pain level. Our pets depend on us to care for them, and a huge part of that is not to allow suffering. Once you are at the point of needing to make a decision, we can only say that loving your canine family member means putting his or her needs ahead of your own. If your dog is in pain or distress the majority of the time, you may opt to take on the emotional pain of saying goodbye in order to give your best friend the gift of being free from physical pain. This is the most unselfish, loving thing that you can do.

If you have had to say goodbye to a canine family member, our hearts and prayers are with you and hugs are sent your way.

Safety and Happiness

Traveling

Whether you are traveling near or far, the main concerns are safety and comfort. After all, you want your puppy or dog to find traveling to be a fun (or at least tolerable) experience so that future adventures can be met without trepidation.

Car Travel

Motion sickness: This is very common with dogs, particularly toy and small-sized breeds. It caused by a disconnect between what the body is feeling (motion via vibrations, body swaying during turns, and speed changes) and what the eyes are seeing (interior of the car). This can make a dog feel terribly nauseous and/or overwhelmingly discombobulated. There can be whining, restlessness, drooling, panting, panicked behavior, and/or vomiting. A bad experience in the car can lead to a fear of being driven, and it's easy to understand why a dog would not want a repeat of such an ordeal.

Safety: While this was covered under 'Care Items – Chihuahuas of All Ages: Car Seats', it's worth repeating that car accident injury can be life-altering, and death can be violent. When a dog is not restrained, any notable accident will cause the dog to be thrown with a certain amount of 'crash force'. As examples, if a car is traveling 35 MPH, a 5-lb. dog will be thrown as if he is a 175-lb. object. If a car is traveling at 55 MPH, that same dog will be thrown as if he is a 275-lb. object. And, going 60 MPH, an adult Chihuahua of 7 lbs. will be thrown as if he is a 420-lb. object.

This, of course, is enough to injure a dog horribly, if not fatally. In addition, a 100+ lb. 'projectile' is a risk to both the driver and other passengers.

Do not be lulled into a false sense of security if you rarely get into accidents, only drive locally, or are an exceptional driver. People will have an average of 3 accidents during their life, most accidents happen within 15 miles of home, and you have zero control over the actions of other drivers.

Resolving both issues:

1) Have your dog in a raised car booster seat. Quite frankly, if you would buckle up a child, buckle up your puppy or dog. This can be life-saving and is an effective method to help prevent motion sickness, as it keeps the body secure to reduce swaying and lifts a dog up high enough to both see out of windows and feel air from an open window. Note that car seats have an inner buckle that must be snapped to a dog's harness, NOT a collar, as that could cause grave neck injury. The safest

place for a car seat is in the back seat due to front passenger airbags. If you do place your dog in the front, disable the airbags and slide your car's seat as far back as it can go.

2) Do not drive your dog right after a meal. Time things so that at least 1 hour has passed.

3) But, 15 or 20 minutes before leaving, offer a small, dry snack.

4) In addition, a little bit of sugar can help calm a queasy stomach; often 1 small jelly bean given 15 minutes prior to getting in the car does the trick.

5) Even when in a proper car seat, many dogs cannot put up with extended rides. There may be a tipping point at which confinement and motion are getting to be too much. Offer a break before it reaches this point. For long rides, take a break every 30 minutes. Pull over into a safe area, have your dog on leash, allow him to stretch his legs, go to the bathroom if needed, and have a drink and/or a small dry snack.

6) Keep a window open just enough that your dog can feel some fresh air rushing in.

If your dog has developed a fear of the car due to past experiences, start a desensitization program to reintroduce him to being driven with the aforementioned tips in place.

o **Step One:** Secure your dog into the car seat and sit behind the wheel. Turn the car on, but do not drive anywhere. The goal is to just sit in the driveway with the engine on. Start off with 5 minutes and work your way up to 15. Do this for 7 to 10 days, at least once per day, if you are able.

o **Step Two:** This will be slow movement back and forth in the driveway. Take care when applying the brakes, making the transition as easy as possible. If you have a very short drive, you can jump to the next step. It's best to do this for 1 week, with 5 to 10-minute sessions.

o **Step Three:** Short drives lasting 15 minutes in a thinly settled district where you can safely drive 35 mph or under.

o **Step Four:** Now, you are ready to take longer rides in the car, and make the destination be a fun one such as a visit with a doggie friend or a trip to the park. However, in any case, a reward treat when exiting should be given.

Taxis and Car Services
Make sure that your dog is very familiar with cars before trying to take him into a taxi or other car service. Not all will accept dogs; in most cities, this is the driver's discretion. What they fear most is a dog soiling the car or vomiting. If you are unable to bring along your dog's car seat, keep in mind that many drivers will accept a small dog as a passenger on the condition that he is in a carry bag or crate. These do nothing to protect a dog should there be an accident, so you will need to make a judgement call. If you do not have the car seat and have to hold your dog while being driven, be sure to buckle up. Have your dog wearing a harness and on leash. Hold him on your lap, facing forward, and grip the leash about two inches from where it connects to the harness.

Buses and Trains
There is not one blanket rule for these types of transportation. Each bus and train line has different guidelines. Some only allow dogs if they are checked as luggage, in a crate. Others will allow small dogs if they are in canine travel bags and yet others will allow a dog if on leash. As of the time of this writing, a good travel source is the Pet Travel Guide (www.pettravel.com/passports_pubtrans.cfm) that lists out rules by city and even covers traveling by ferry.

Airplane Travel

For this, a lot of preparation will need to be done. Not all airlines allow pets in the passenger cabin; some have dogs go into the cargo compartment with luggage and this can be risky. It can be overwhelmingly stressful, not to mention the extreme temperature changes. In the U.S. 30+ dogs die each year on airlines. And while this is a small number compared to how many dogs there are, even one is too many.

For safe and comfortable airplane travel, here is a list of things to know and do:

1. Check an airline's exact rules and regulations, then call to double-check the information. You'll want to choose a flight that allows your dog to travel with you as a passenger, in a travel carrier. Airlines will also have rules regarding weight limits for pets.

2. Choose the travel carrier wisely. For those airlines that do allow pets to travel with owners, this will be in a travel carrier crate, case, or bag. Luckily, this can be easily accomplished with toy breeds. However, rules on the size of the carrier are strict. Take measurements to be absolutely sure that it meets the regulations.

3. Allow your dog plenty of time to become used to the carrier. Even if he does well in a car seat, canine travel crates are much different. Keep this in a room with the door of it open. Place treats and toys inside and allow your dog to explore it. Do not, however, close the door quite yet. After 1 to 2 weeks of becoming accustomed to the carrier, you can softly close the door while peeking inside and speaking in an animated tone to keep your dog amused. Let him out a few minutes later, and if possible, work on extending the time.

4. Book a direct flight. Changing planes is stressful enough without having to exit and board again with your dog.

5. Have vet papers. Many airlines will require you to produce papers stating that your dog is in good health and up-to-date on shots. In most cases, this must be dated within 10 days of travel. Therefore, you'll want to plan ahead to obtain this from the veterinarian. If you will be traveling overseas, there may be much stricter regulations, so you'll want to inquire about this.

6. Plan for bathroom needs. Unless the flight is very short, your dog will need to go to the bathroom at some point. If allowed to do this in the crate, it can be uncomfortable for your dog, not to mention the noses of every other passenger. This is where doggie diapers can come in handy. While you'll have some cleaning up to do once you land (via quality canine body wipes), you'll be happy you chose this method.

7. Calming remedies. If you know that your dog doesn't do well with planes, you may want to consider a calming supplement. Some holistic ones work to varying degrees, but not for all dogs. Since canine calming supplements are not regulated by the FDA, there few real studies to show if these work.

Ingredients common to these include a colostrum complex (thought to have a calming effect on animals), L-theanine (found in many teas and said to provide a calming effect), and vitamin B (said to help manage stress). If you want to try this, at the time of this writing we recommend Pet Naturals of Vermont Calming for Small Dogs, which has both L-theanine and colostrum.

Benadryl can help to both calm and reduce motion sickness. Though this is considered to be safe for most dogs, it is recommended to ask the vet before giving this, because it can interfere with some medications, should not be given to dogs with certain health conditions, and it's important to give the right dose. This must be just diphenhydramine and not one that has any other ingredients (alcohol, decongestants, etc.). In regard to the tablet form, dosing is typically 1 mg for each 1 lb. (.45 kg) of body weight.

It is not recommended to use prescribed tranquilizers unless there is a strong, valid reason. Many are not tested to see how animals respond when at high altitude and if a dog were to have an allergic reaction, tens of thousands of feet in the sky is not where you want to be.

Arriving at Your Travel Destination

While you may have been looking forward to your vacation for quite a while, your dog may not share your excitement. The two biggest mistakes that owners make when traveling are not having a plan for their dog in regards to lots of walking and assuming that their dog will be fine staying at a new house or in a hotel.

Walking. If your destination will involve a lot of walking or sightseeing, take steps so that your little guy or gal does not tire out and is not overwhelmed walking among a bunch of people in a new setting. While it's just fine to let your dog explore a bit (safe on leash and harness), you may want to look into using a canine carry sling, body-carrier, or pet stroller that keeps this little breed up safely away from lots of foot traffic.

New environment. While you can't take everything with you when traveling, bringing along your dog's bed can help him settle into a new place. It can also help to bring along food and water bowls since there can be an attachment to these and a dog may be finicky about eating out of new dishes. And of course, bring along favorite toys.

First Aid
First Aid Kits

Not everyone has a first aid kit for themselves, let alone their pets. However, having a few things put together is the wise move; it can save you the stress of running around looking for what you need, allow you to offer immediate aid, and in some cases, it can even save your dog's life.

If you're traveling or heading out on an excursion with your dog, it's a good idea to bring the kit along with you.

Let's go over what you actually may need at some point:

- ✓ **Canine rectal thermometer.** It's important to be able to take your dog's temperature if there is a question of heat stroke or fever. Normal body temperature for puppies and dogs is between 101 and 102.5°F (38.3 to 39.2°C).
- ✓ **Petroleum jelly.** This to use in conjunction with the thermometer.
  Note: The most accurate way to take a dog's temperate is with an anal thermometer. Have your dog lie on his side. Lubricate the tip of the thermometer and insert it the same length as your dog's paws (i.e. 1" paw = 1" insertion). For a glass-bulb thermometer, wait 3 minutes. For a digital one, wait for the 'beep'.
- ✓ **Betadine Solution.** This is a fast-acting, broad-spectrum antiseptic to clean cuts or scrapes and reduce bacteria that can cause serious infection. Veterinarians do not recommend using soap, rubbing alcohol, or hydrogen peroxide. Soap is not effective for moderate cuts, alcohol can damage tissue, and hydrogen peroxide is best used if infection has already set in.
- ✓ **Gauze pads.** Sterile gauze pads are used to apply the betadine.
- ✓ **Plastic syringe.** Alternative method to apply betadine to avoid touching a wound.
- ✓ **Antibacterial ointment.** To dab onto cuts or scrapes after washing them, to help prevent infection.

✓ **Paw bandages.** For a nasty cut or injury to a paw, these are ideal for wrapping the area, if needed.

✓ **Hydrogen Peroxide.** In case of poisoning, you *may* be instructed to immediately induce vomiting. This is dependent on what a dog ingested (some toxins are more dangerous if vomited out). If you are instructed to induce vomiting, one of the most effective methods is to give a dog hydrogen peroxide. Check with your vet; however, the typical dose is 1 teaspoon for each 5 pounds of body weight with another dose given after 10 minutes if the dog does not vomit.

✓ **Activated charcoal tablets.** In case of poisoning, you *may* be instructed to give this to absorb to toxins. This is dependent on what a dog ingested. The veterinarian will instruct you in regard to dosing.

✓ **Medicine syringe.** If you need your dog to swallow hydrogen peroxide to induce vomiting, you'll want one of these. An effective method is to hook a finger to the side of the mouth to it back and create a small pocket, and deposit the liquid between the cheek and the teeth.

✓ **Thermal blanket.** If your dog is severely injured (hit by a car, etc.), this can be lifesaving. Wrapping a dog in a thermal blanket can stop a dog from going into shock while he is transported to the animal hospital.

✓ **Canine saline eye rinse.** This is to flush any contaminants or debris that has gotten into an eye. If you are alone with your dog, hold the bottle above your dog's head (where he cannot see it) and let the drops drip down into the eye. If you have a helper, one person can hold the bottom lid out a bit, and drops are put into the pocket of the bottom lid.

✓ **Artificial tears.** If you have to flush out the eyes, you may want to use an artificial tears product afterward to help soothe them.

✓ **Benadryl (diphenhydramine).** This must be used with caution; however, it may help in the event of certain insect stings (this does not work for all dogs). Though this is considered to be safe for most dogs, it is recommended to ask the vet before giving this, because it can interfere with some medications, should not be given to dogs with certain health conditions, and it's important to give the right dose. This must be just diphenhydramine and not one that has any other ingredients (alcohol, decongestants, etc.). In regard to the tablet form, dosing is typically 1 mg for each 1 lb. (.45 kg) of body weight.

✓ **Baking soda.** In the event of a bee or yellow jacket sting, a paste made of water and baking soda can be applied to the area for 15 minutes.

What you may not need: Some items suggested for pet first aid kits are not needed or advice to use the items is wrong and can make things worse.

This includes: **5 inch hemostat** (seen on lists as a tool to clamp blood vessels to stem bleeding; typical owners are not qualified to do this), **bandana and/or nylon stocking** (suggested by some to tie up a dog's muzzle to prevent biting in the case of injury; this is rare and can impede a dog's breathing), **dishwashing liquid** (seen on lists to flush wounds; this is not recommend), **ice pack** (suggested by some to treat heat stroke; it's best to use cold, wet towels), **Nexaban** (Do not use this. This is skin glue to close wounds. The veterinarian will determine how a cut should be closed and glue can trap infection under the closure.).

Giving First Aid

How to Treat a Cut

1. Apply pressure to stop the blood, using sterile gauze pads. Do this for about 10 minutes, then check. During those 10 minutes, if the blood soaks through the gauze, don't lift it off, just add more. If it's still bleeding when you check it, do another 10 minutes. If blood is still flowing after that, the cut most likely needs to be stitched by the vet.

2. Once the bleeding has stopped, use a plastic syringe to gently flush the cut with a mixture of betadine and water (add water until it has the color of iced tea). If you don't have a plastic syringe, you can dab it (not wipe) with gauze pads.

3. Apply a thin strip of antibacterial ointment.

4. If it oozes any pus, if the skin is raised or red, or if it is not showing any signs of healing after 3 days, you'll want the vet to take a look. It may need to be butterfly bandaged, be stitched, and/or medication for infection may be needed.

Bees, Wasps and Other Stinging Insects

Dogs, and especially toy breeds, are targets for stinging insects. Many of these offenders hover near the ground and are exceedingly fast.

❶ Only the honey bee dies after stinging; all other varieties can sting numerous times.
❷ A wasp rarely stings once, and pain can last a long time since the venom slows down blood flow that would otherwise dilute it.
❸ Yellow jackets can both sting (with stingers) and bite (with mandibles), and often do so completely unprovoked.
❹ Hornets can sting a dog repeatedly and can be more painful than wasps due to a high level of venom.

What to Do if Your Dog is Being Attacked by Bees or Other Stinging Insects: Whether a single stinging insect or a swarm is attacking your dog, you should react in the same way since you will not know how he will react to the venom (it can change over time) or how many times a single insect may inject his stinger.

1. The only viable action is pick up your puppy or dog securely so that he is not jostled and run as quickly as possible.
2. Your goal will be to seek a sheltered area (your house, a building, or even your car), while being prepared that some insects may follow you inside. Keep these tips in mind:
    o   Do not swat the insects or flail your arms; this can be interpreted as an aggressive action that triggers a stronger attack.
    o   If possible, tuck your dog under your shirt and then pull up the top of your shirt over your face while not obscuring your view. While you can both be stung through clothing, it offers somewhat of a barrier.
    o   Run in a straight line and if possible run into the wind as this can slow them down.
    o   Keep in mind that a bee can fly 12+ miles an hour, so you cannot run faster than them. However, most attacks are territorial and many bees, wasps, hornets, etc. will give up chase after about 50 yards. Very aggressive bees can give chase up to 100 yards and Africanized honey bees may not give up for a mile.
3. If any enter the house, you can dash to another room and close the door. In some cases, running into the bathroom and jumping into the shower can make them fly away. If you can run into a well-lit building, they can get temporarily confused and be attracted to the windows.

What to Do After Your Dog Has Been Stung: Carefully part the coat to look for stingers. Be sure to check all areas of the body including the tail and under the chin.

The most important element is to remove the stingers since many types will continue to release venom until they are taken out. However, if they are pulled out by fingers or even tweezers, this can release more venom into your dog's bloodstream. The best method is to grab a driver's license or credit card and use a scraping motion over the skin to pull them out.

At-home Care vs. Vet Care: In many cases, even if a dog feels fine, an immediate vet visit is recommended. This is why:

- Any puppy or dog can have an allergic reaction to any stinging insect.
- Not having an allergic response in the past does not mean it cannot happen the next time.
- Even if a dog has proven not to be allergic to one type of stinging insect, he may have a response to another.
- It can take up to 45 minutes for signs of an allergic reaction to appear. If so, you'll want your dog already at the vet clinic.
- A **huge** concern with toy breeds is a buildup of toxins, which is a separate problem from allergic reactions. For dogs, 5 stings per 2.2 lbs. (1 kg) of body weight can cause acute toxic overload and 10 stings per 2.2 lbs. of body weight can be fatal. For young puppies, it may be even fewer than this. With this, serious issues can occur *days after* an attack. Proteins in the venom break down and can damage cells in the body. The kidneys can then become clogged, causing kidney failure.

  Therefore, if you have any concerns, bring your dog to the veterinarian. He can be checked for stingers that you may have missed, be treated for pain and/or swelling, and be given either precautionary allergy medication, or should there be signs of anaphylactic shock, the reactionary treatment of epinephrine.

At-home Care: If the previous does not apply and you feel safe in treating your dog at home, there are some steps that can help with discomfort and swelling:

1. Be sure that all stingers have been properly removed by scraping them out.
2. Clean the injection site with warm water and your dog's shampoo to remove body oils that may impede further treatment.
3. If it was a wasp or hornet sting, a small piece of cloth soaked in vinegar should be applied to the site for 15 minutes. This will help neutralize the alkaline in the venom. If it was a bee or yellow jacket sting, a paste made of water and baking soda should be applied to the site for 15 minutes. If you are not sure what type of sting it was, use baking soda. Treatment may be repeated if discomfort persists or if the area remains red.
4. It can help to apply a small ice pack to help with the swelling.
5. Anything other than a very minor case of an allergic reaction MUST be treated at the veterinarians where a powerful drug such as epinephrine may need to be used (see next section). With this said, for minor cases, you may be able to give Benadryl (diphenhydramine). Note that not all dogs respond to this medication. Though this is considered to be safe for most dogs, it is recommended to ask the vet before giving this, because it can interfere with some medications, should not be given to dogs with certain health conditions, and it's important to give the right dose. This must be just diphenhydramine and not one that has any other ingredients (alcohol, decongestants, etc.). In regard to the tablet form, dosing is typically 1 mg for each 1 pound of body weight.
6. Keep a very close eye on your dog to look for any signs of an allergic reaction. This can come on quickly and it can take up to 45 minutes to develop.

Signs of an Allergic Reaction: While rare, stings can cause anaphylaxis, which is a life-threatening allergic reaction. Without treatment, it can lead to shock, cardiac arrest, and death. The most common signs include:

- Swelling of the face (includes one or both eyes, around the lips, or any other area)
- Severe swelling at the sting site
- Weakness
- Trouble breathing
- Rash (sometimes)
- Vomiting (sometimes)
- Pale gums
- Cold limbs
- Drooling

Anaphylaxis needs immediate treatment with epinephrine. In some cases, this will need to be administered literally within minutes, and for this reason, keep a close eye on your dog or bring him to the vet after being stung regardless of how he appears to be doing.

Poisoning and Chemical Exposure

Ingested Toxins: The list of things that are toxic to dogs includes the *hundreds* of elements that are also toxic to humans, any sort of human medication or supplement, and:

- Alcohol
- Caffeine (any food/drink with caffeine)
- Cherries
- Chocolate
- Currents
- Garlic (a bit of garlic powder is not toxic; pieces of garlic are)
- Grapes (extremely toxic and can be fatal)
- Grapefruit
- Mushrooms (not all types; but it is better to be safe than sorry)
- Onions
- Potatoes (when raw or green)
- Raisins (like grapes can be fatal if eaten)
- Rhubarb
- Seeds or core of any fruit
- Tomato leaves, stems, and any other part of the plant (but not tomatoes themselves)
- Xylitol (sweetener found in some gums and candies)

Signs of toxic poisoning via ingestion: While it varies by the toxin, signs can include vomiting, diarrhea, drooling, 'drunken' behavior, nosebleed, lethargy, ***and/or*** rapid heartbeat.

What to do: If you know your dog has ingested a harmful element, or your dog is showing signs of poisoning, call the vet ASAP. Do not delay. Depending on what has been ingested, you may be instructed to induce vomiting (by giving hydrogen peroxide; 1 teaspoon for each 5 pounds of body weight with another dose given after 10 minutes if the dog does not vomit), give activated charcoal, give milk **or** rush him to the clinic. If your dog has vomited, bring as large of a sample as possible with you to the clinic.

If you cannot reach the vet and want to call a helpline, note that as of the time of this writing, there is a substantial fee for these. This said, the phone number for the Animal Poison Control Center hotline is 1-888-426-4435 (available 365 days/year, 24 hours/day) and the number for the Pet Poison Helpline is 1-855-213-6680 (U.S. numbers).

Chemical Exposure: This includes any airborne chemical that is inhaled or any chemical that a dog has touched, including but not limited to cleaning products, poison for rodent control, pesticides, and anti-freeze.

If Skin is Exposed to a Chemical – Read the label and follow the instructions; in many cases, you will flush with water.

If a Chemical Has Been Inhaled – Bring your dog outside for fresh air. Then, call the veterinarian.

If a Dog is Choking

1. Stay calm. If you panic, it may be difficult to follow through with what you need to do.
2. If possible, have another person call the veterinarian while you help your dog.
3. You will need to open the airway. This is done by gently pulling the tongue out of the mouth until it is flat. If you are able, look to see if you can spot any foreign objects in the mouth or the back of the throat.
4. If you DO see an object, you can try to remove it with tweezers or thin pliers. Do not spend a lot of time doing this; 30 seconds at the most.
5. If you see an object but cannot remove it, place your dog in your lap, belly up. Place both hands on the sides of his ribcage. Apply quick, firm pressure 3 times in a row. If this does not work, lie your dog down belly-up, and using the palm of your hand, strike the rib cage firmly 3 times.
6. If you do not see an object OR if your dog is not breathing, perform rescue breathing. This is done by closing the dog's mouth with your hand and breathing directly into the nose. The chest should expand outward when you do this. Perform every 4 seconds (count out 'one Mississippi', 'two Mississippi', etc.) until you arrive at the clinic.

If a Dog is Swallows a Rock, a Chicken Bone, a Battery or a Coin

Rocks: What you do will depend on the size of the stone vs. the size of the dog. If you know that the pebble was approximately the size of a pill that your dog could hypothetically gulp down, there is a good chance that it will pass through. However, in some cases, rocks can become lodged as they travel through the intestines. **What to do:**

1. **Call the vet to report what happened and follow his/her instructions.**
2. **Watch for red flags.** Someone should remain home with the dog. You'll be looking for any signs of distress including vomiting, dry heaving, straining when going to the bathroom, a hunched over posture or odd positioning, breathing issues, weakness, and/or reluctance to eat. Any of these signs should be considered an emergency that warrants an immediate vet visit.
3. **If there are no signs of distress,** most vets will instruct owners to take a 'wait and see' approach for the rock to pass; instructions may be given to help prompt this along with a high fiber diet

(added green beans and/or pumpkin). It will be important for someone to be watching your dog for several days since obstruction can occur at any time as the rock moves through the digestive system.

Chicken bone:
Bones, and particularly cooked bones, should not be given to puppies or dogs due to their tendency to splinter. Chicken bones are the biggest cause for concern, although any small bone such as those from spare ribs, turkey, fish, and cuts of beef can be dangerous as well. **What to do:**

Crazy Things Dogs Have Swallowed, Confirmed by X-rays & Removed Via Surgery
6-inch corn dog stick
Rubber duck
Metal shish-kabob skewers
43 socks (by a Great Dane, all removed at once)
A15 series light bulb (by a Golden Retriever, it remained intact)
Fishing hook (done by many dogs, including a Shih Tzu that gobbled down a mackerel with the hook inside)
9 sewing needles (by a Chihuahua)
2-cups of gravel from a turtle tank
1 quarter & 104 pennies (by a Pug)
Pocket knife
Hacky sack ball
Matchbox car
Mini headphones
Arrowhead
Tube of antibiotic cream
Candy wrapper
Engagement ring
Metal fork
Phone charger
10-inch bread knife (by a Jack Russell Terrier)
Bra (by a 3-month-old Rat Terrier)

1. **Call your vet to report what happened and follow his/her instructions.**
2. **Inspect your dog's mouth for any signs of injury.** Look at the tongue, inner cheek tissue, and between all teeth. Small bone fragments are similar to needles and can pierce the skin quite deeply; the piece may be embedded.
3. **It is often not recommended to induce vomiting** since the bone can cause quite a bit of damage on the way up. If it made its way to the stomach, it's best to allow it to remain there and take the next step.
4. **Feeding certain foods** after a dog eats a chicken bone can help offer a cushion around it, and this can help it pass through the body. Some good choices are rice and bread. You'll want to make this as tempting to your dog as possible, so adding some warm chicken or beef broth over the food can entice an otherwise not-so-hungry dog to ingest a bit of the mixture.
5. **Keep a very close eye on your dog for at least 3 days.** Someone should remain home with the dog. You'll be looking for any signs of distress including vomiting, dry heaving, straining when going to the bathroom, a hunched over posture or odd positioning, breathing issues, weakness, and/or reluctance to eat. Any of these signs should be considered an emergency that warrants an immediate vet visit.

Batteries:
While it will generally be smaller watch batteries that a toy breed may swallow, any size can be chewed and cause serious issues; All cases of battery ingestion or chewing must be taken very seriously. AAA, AA, C, D and 9-volt batteries all have corrosive properties.

What can happen: If the battery case is punctured, burns to the mouth can occur immediately, though signs of this can take up to 12 hours to manifest. These can be very serious tissue burns that manifest as painful ulcers on the tongue, lips, and inside the mouth. And even if a small battery is swallowed whole, there are dangers since the casing may have been punctured by a sharp tooth before being swallowed. In addition, depending on the size of the battery, stomach or intestinal blockage is always a concern.

What to do:

1. **Call the veterinarian ASAP and be prepared to rush to the clinic or the closest animal hospital.** Even if your dog appears to be fine, internal burns can take hours to appear and it will be imperative to have x-rays taken to determine where the battery is located in the body. You may be instructed to take steps before you leave.
2. **Do not induce vomiting.** This can cause serious burns to the throat.

3. **You may be instructed to first rinse your dog's mouth with lukewarm water or small amounts of milk** for 10 to 15 minutes.

4. **At the clinic, the mouth and esophagus will be examined** to look for potential chemical burns and treated accordingly. Medications will be given in an attempt to protect the gastrointestinal tract. This may be given at the clinic, as well as at home afterward. X-rays will be taken to determine the location of the battery and if surgery will be required to remove it. If it is suspected that the battery is leaking fluid in the stomach, it will need to be removed ASAP.

The full extent of burns from a dog eating a battery can take up to 12 hours to appear. For this reason, a dog may be kept at the clinic or may be sent home where owners will need to keep an exceedingly close eye on things. Signs to look for include developing lesions in the mouth and/or lips, drooling, weakness, reluctance to eat, vomiting and/or any signs of pain or distress. Battery burns on dogs are often treated with strong pain medication and antibiotics to help prevent infection. Those with oral injury are often fed soft wet foods until the burns have healed.

Coins:

Penny: This can cause life-threatening toxicity. Pennies minted from 1982 on, are predominantly zinc (97.5 % zinc, 2.5% copper) which is considered to be highly toxic to canines. Pennies made from 1962 to 1982 contain smaller levels of zinc alloy (5%). The time that it takes for a dog's stomach acid to dissolve the penny enough to release the zinc into the bloodstream can range from minutes to hours.

Signs of zinc poisoning include weakness, lack of appetite, vomiting, diarrhea, a yellowing of the eyes, and/or dark urine. If your dog swallowed a penny or got into some coins and you are not sure if a penny was included, call the vet ASAP and prepare to rush your dog to the clinic. It will be important to have x-rays taken to determine the number and location of the pennies, which then can typically be removed via endoscopy.

Nickel or Dime: If you are *100% positive* that a penny was not swallowed, the vet may recommend take a 'wait and see' approach for nickels or dimes to pass; instructions may be given to help prompt this along with a high fiber diet (added green beans and/or pumpkin). Or, if more than one coin was swallowed, the vet may recommend x-rays to determine how many are present and if intervention is needed to prevent blockage.

How to Prevent Your Dog from Being

Attacked

Being Attacked by Dogs and Other Animals in the Yard

It's reasonable to assume that your own yard is a relatively safe place, particularly if it's enclosed. However, a fenced-in property does not prevent this danger; it only limits the number of aggressive dogs and other animals that can get into your yard. *Let's look at some examples of attacks that occurred right in an owner's own back or front yard.*

Attacks by other dogs. In Lakeside, CA, a 9-lb. Chihuahua named Pico was in his fenced-in front yard when two pit bulls attacked. His injuries were quite severe and emergency surgery including having his jaws wired was needed to save him. In Tallahassee, FL, a 9-year-old Chihuahua named Meha was killed in her own yard by a lab mix. In Texas, a Chihuahua named Chiquita was attacked by an Australian Cattle Dog in the backyard of a pet sitter. Thankfully, she survived after having emergency surgery.

Attacks by wild animals. Coyotes, which are found in every single state in the U.S. aside from Hawaii, should be taken as a serious danger. These animals have learned that small dogs and cats are easy prey. In Antioch, IL, a 12-year-old Chihuahua named Tucker was out in the yard. When his owner heard yelping, he ran out to find a coyote had Tucker by the leg. Fortunately, the owner was able to scare off the wild animal.

In Littleton, CO, a 4-year-old Chihuahua named Buster was let out into his yard to play after being taken for a walk. His owner heard a terrible scream, and ran outside to see Buster being carried away in the mouth of a coyote. Then, two pit bills that were being walked ran toward the coyote, which caused it to drop Buster and take off. The two hero dogs stood guard while the little Chi scurried under a bush. Thankfully, with emergency surgery, Buster survived.

In Wallingford, CT, two Chihuahuas named Cody and Khloe were let outside to play. After hearing a bark, the owner ran outside to find a coyote there. Khloe was found some distance away, severely injured and did not survive. Cody was never found.

And, there are other dangerous wild animals. In Sedona, AZ an 8-year-old Chihuahua mix named Irie was let outside. After hearing noises, the owner ran outside to see a bobcat running away and Irie making his way home. By a miracle, the only injuries were a laceration requiring 12 stitches. In Steveston, VA, a Chihuahua that was out alone in the yard was attacked by a raccoon. The owner beat the raccoon away with a broom and the Chi survived after receiving treatment and stitches.

There are also many instances of dogs of all sizes being attacked by alligators, porcupines, fox, groundhogs, and even skunks.

Attacks by hawks and other birds. It is not a myth that birds-of-prey fly away with small dogs; it happens. And, hawks are a danger to small dogs year-round; not all of them fly south for the winter. Older hawks and those with established territories often choose to remain in place all year.

In Apex, NC, a 15-year-old Chihuahua named Cocoa was outside in a fenced-in garden. Right as his owner opened the door to see her, a hawk grabbed the little dog in its claws. The owner yelled and the bird-of-prey let go, but the Chi did not survive.

In Traverse City, MI, a 5-lb. 2-year-old Chihuahua named Pippa was let out into the yard for bathroom needs early in the morning. After hearing a scream, the owner ran outside and quickly realized that the yelps were coming from the sky. The owner ran, following the sounds, finally finding the little Chi on a hill, 200 to 300 feet away, severely injured. Based on the puncture wounds and the time of the attack, it is believed that Pippa's attacker was an <u>owl</u>.

In Cape Girardeau, MO, a Chihuahua was let outside to play when a hawk swooped down and attacked her. The Chi was rushed to the veterinary clinic, but had to be euthanized.

How to Keep your Dog Safe from Attacks in the Yard

- The #1 rule is to never let your dog outside alone; always supervise. owls/hawks/other dogs
- Be visible (not sitting at an outdoor table under an umbrella, etc.)
- Before you exit with your dog, do a visual sweep of the area.
- If the sun is about to set or it's dark out, put on outdoor lights and bring along a flashlight.
- Keep a whistle on you; in an emergency, it may scare away a wild animal.
- Pick up your dog's poop; feces can attract wild animals, mainly coyotes, that are known to stalk their prey.
- A fence needs to be at least 6 feet high and not made of chain link to prevent coyotes.
- Remove any bird feeders; these attract small birds and small rodents which are prey for hawks and large wildlife.
- Hanging shiny objects in the yard may help deter hawks.
- Keep trash bins sealed tight so that these do not attract wild animals.

Being Attacked While Out on a Walk

Unfortunately, attacks by larger dogs can happen just about anywhere and is mostly seen when there is an encounter with a larger dog that's off-leash. In Edmonton, Alberta, Canada, two Chihuahuas named Lola and Presley were being taken for a walk when an unleashed pit bull attacked. The attacking dog pounced on Lola before her owner could grab her. The owner punched the pit bull, at which time it attacked the other Chi, Presley. Lola was fatally injured and Presley survived after emergency surgery.

In Marion County, FL, a 9-year-old 10-lb. Chihuahua was killed by a pit bull-type dog that allegedly was known for roaming the area. In Garson, Ontario, a Chihuahua named Nina was fatally attacked by a German Shepherd. In San Francisco, CA, two pit bulls attacked a 52-year-old woman while she was walking her Chihuahua-mix named Joey. The little dog did not survive.

In Abbotsford, British Columbia, Canada a 7-lb. Chihuahua named Maggie was being walked alongside a Miniature Pinscher name Harry when an un-leashed Rottweiler attacked. The owner hit the attacking dog on the head and Harry tried to help. Thankfully, Maggie survived after emergency surgery. And, the list goes on…

How to Keep your Dog Safe from Attacks While Walking

While this in no way should stop you from taking your dog for a walk (daily exercise is vitally important for good health), it's wise to be prepared:

- The #1 rule is to keep your Chihuahua on leash and harness. The leash ensures that your dog is always close by to you. The harness allows you to quickly reel your dog in, or even lift him right up by the leash, in an emergency.
- Remain aware of your surroundings.
- If you see another dog off leash, pick up your dog and walk away from the area. Do not stare at the other dog; but, know where he is.
- If a larger dog is barking and bearing his teeth, hold your dog close to your body and remain calm. Often, yelling at an aggressive dog only riles him up.
- Consider carrying a walking stick or even an umbrella. If an aggressive dog is getting close, it can help to give a firm and confident 'No!', stand tall, and use the object to claim your space and maintain distance.

- Consider carrying an air horn, pepper spray, or bear spray (depending on what is legal in your city or town).
- If a dog is attacking, put anything you can between it and you and your dog, for example, a jacket or bag.

The Importance of Veterinary Wellness Checks

Of course, a dog should be brought to the vet for injuries or illness. However, it's also vital to realize the importance of wellness checks. These yearly (for dogs age 1 and up) or twice-per-year (typically starting at age 8) visits are crucial for good health, prevention, and good prognosis should any issues be detected.

It's easy to dismiss the need. Your dog is doing well, nothing seems to be wrong; so, why pay for a visit when everything's okay? However, wellness checks screen for a host of possible issues common with canines in which symptoms may not be noticeable yet but damage is occurring.

This ranges from tooth decay to more serious conditions involving the organs. Even if you take care of your dog's teeth at home, dental issues can develop. Catch this early, and it will usually be easy to treat; catch this late and the consequences can be severe. Infection can travel into the bloodstream and to organs throughout the body. Diabetes, kidney disease, liver issues, thyroid disease, heart problems, vision and hearing issues... these are all things that may not have immediate symptoms. Even with parasite prevention, sometimes parasites slip through including heartworms (nicknamed a 'silent killer').

Bottom line, if you want your dog to live a long, healthy life, regular veterinary visits are a part of that. And, responsible pet ownership includes budgeting for this. Depending on the exact screening and testing that is done and if a booster shot is needed, the price for a wellness check can vary. It is something that can be worked into a budget by putting away $15 to $25 a month.

What Will Happen at the Vet's Office: Your dog will have a full physical examination to check for issues seen with canines in general and conditions that this breed is prone to. Vitals will be taken (temperature, pulse rate, respiratory rate) and your dog will be weighed. The head will be checked (eyes, ears, nose, mouth). The coat and the skin will be examined to look for any signs of concern that you may not have noticed.

The vet will look for proper posture, knees and hips will be examined, and reflexes will be checked. A stool sample will be tested for possible parasites and a blood test will be run to measure red and white blood cell counts (to evaluate overall health and flag any infections), organ function, and electrolyte and protein levels. Senior dogs may have more advanced testing, including x-rays.

Veterinarians also know how to assess a dog in other ways as well, such as how a dog is responding and his level of alertness. The vet will speak to you about prevention steps for issues common to the breed or for possible 'borderline' issues that may have been detected.

You will discuss your dog's diet and exercise routine. This is also your opportunity to ask any questions; you are not expected to just sit quietly; a good owner is an involved owner!

Your Relationship with Your Canine Family Member

Your Responsibilities and the Significance of This

As we discussed way back at the beginning of this book, canines have the intelligence level of at least a 2.5-year-old human and experience a range of emotions (distress, disgust, fear, anger, suspicion, shyness, contentment, excitement, joy, affection, and love). Will you acknowledge this level of intellect? Will you respect your dog's feelings?

As your dog's human, you are in complete control of how small or large your dog's world will be. His or her entire life will be played out within the boundaries that you set. Will this world be limited with restricted experiences? Or will it be virtually infinite with exploration, challenges, and discoveries?

It is your job to teach your dog everything from housebreaking to interacting with other dogs to chewing on approved toys. Your dog will stumble and make mistakes during these learning processes. Will you be a kind and forgiving teacher, offering patient guidance? Or will your dog fear the repercussions of slipups?

You have the power to shape your dog's personality. Learning commands, playing puzzle games, meeting people, experiencing varying events, and reaping the rewards of 'jobs well done' can greatly increase a dog's self-confidence level. Will your dog be insecure? Or poised?

Whether you're just starting out with a new puppy or have an older dog and perhaps some mistakes were made along the way, today is a fresh start. If you commit to taking care of your canine family member to the very best of your ability, you literally cannot do more. And, what else could a dog ask for?

Bonding with Your Dog

In any case at all - puppy or older dog, bought or adopted, established or new - there are steps you can take to strengthen the bond that you have with your canine family member. Just like any other relationship, it needs to be cultivated. Ways to increase bonding include:

1) **Establish yourself as the leader.** Should you be your dog's friend, mentor, family member, parental figure? You can be all of these things and more. But first, what you need to be is his or her leader. And, while your dog will certainly depend on you, once you set the tone for leadership as Alpha, you'll find that your Beta helps you out quite a bit as well.

As covered earlier in this book, canines see their world in terms of hierarchy, which is the status and ranking order of every member of the household, both humans and pets. To dogs, the order of hierarchy is very clear: Within the den (house) lives the pack (all humans and animals), and that pack has a leader (the Alpha). Everyone under the leader is a follower (Beta) since they follow the leader's commands. This is the canine way of seeing things, and there are no exceptions.

Not all dogs automatically see their human as the leader. And, if this is the case, there can be behavioral issues such as territorial marking, intolerance, or aggression, and certainly a lack of respect that spills over into just about every aspect of pet ownership. So, take the time to instill proper hierarchy; this will be the foundation for creating a stronger bond. You may wish to refer to 'Training: Teaching Proper Hierarchy'.

2) **Teach your dog an agility exercise.** Pole weaving and tunnel running are agility skills that any dog can learn and can be set up indoors or outdoors. While you can use just about any objects for weaving, both of you may have more fun if you use actual weaving poles which are colorful and appropriately sized.

3) **Teach your dog a new command or trick.** When a dog and an owner are working hard toward a goal, this itself is a great bonding experience, regardless of how long it takes. And, of course, a great added benefit is that your dog will be well-trained. Whether you aim for a simple 'Sit' or a more complicated 'Shake Hands', this is a fantastic method to achieve something together.

4) **Bring your dog with you as often as you can.** Don't worry that spending time together may increase any separation anxiety issues; it won't. Having a full and happy life outside of 'home alone' times can only increase a dog's overall happiness.

And, don't rush out to get things done as quickly as possible while leaving your dog home, rationalizing that you'll be back soon. This is a missed opportunity to bond. Whether you're dashing off to grab milk at the corner store or need to explore a hardware store for just the right item, your dog may appreciate going along with you.

5) **Take on a new challenge.** Whether this is getting your dog a life vest, dabbing sunscreen on his nose and taking him out on a canoe… waking up early to finally see the sunrise over the ocean… or choosing an 'easy' hiking trail that will lead you both to new sights and sounds… Choose something new to do. If so, your little guy or gal will live up to his/her designation as a companion dog!

Lifelong Care Checklist

You may wish to check off which important points in this book you are implementing; this can help to establish your objectives for optimal health, care, comfort, and happiness:

☐ Have a trusted veterinarian & always make an appointment when needed
☐ Ensure that all de-wormings and puppy vaccinations are given
☐ Consider spaying or neutering, if this hasn't been done already
☐ Start with socialization and desensitization at a young age
☐ Bring your adult for yearly wellness checks at the vet's and your senior for twice-per-year visits
☐ 'Puppy-proof' the house regularly, no matter your dog's age
☐ Create a safe and secure 'den', using a canine playpen or another method
☐ Supply the right toys, depending on your dog's needs
☐ Address separation anxiety issues
☐ Nix the idea of a collar while on leash; use a harness
☐ Always have your puppy or dog in a car seat when in the car
☐ Bathe and groom on a regular basis
☐ Use only quality skin and coat care products
☐ Give regular heartworm and parasite prevention
☐ Address any issues like dry skin, peeling noses or paws, or poor coat health right away
☐ Provide preventative at-home dental care; seek professional cleanings when needed
☐ Choose the absolute best food possible for main meals, snacks, and training treats
☐ Offer supplements as needed
☐ Never give unfiltered tap water
☐ Work to resolve allergies, if present
☐ Make changes in care according to the season
☐ Take your dog for 2 walks a day & have daily 'fetch' sessions
☐ Take care at parks and other places where dogs may be
☐ Never let your dog be outside alone, even if you have a fenced-in yard
☐ Correct behaviors such as destructive chewing, jumping, and running off
☐ Do not allow your puppy or dog to ingest grass or feces or lap water from outside sources
☐ Teach proper hierarchy and train for basic commands and heeling
☐ Make adjustments as your dog transitions into the senior years
☐ Know how to react to emergencies and first aid issues commonly seen with dogs
☐ Spend time with your dog, expanding his/her world

What are your thoughts?

We truly hope you found this book to be a helpful resource in caring for your Chihuahua. If so, we would love for you to take a moment to write a review on Amazon. It will help other owners learn about this book and if it may be right for them. You may leave a review by entering Amazon, searching under 'My Orders' or just for *PetChiDog's GIANT Book of Chihuahua Care*, and clicking/tapping on 'Leave a review'. ~ Thank you!

We have lots more for you!

Be sure to visit the PetChiDog website. We're always working to offer you helpful & interesting new articles regarding your Chihuahua's care and happiness.

If you are not yet a free PetChiDog Member, take a moment to sign up! (a button is at the top of all site pages)

When you're a Member, this allows you to receive a friendly notice regarding updates. And, you'll be able to submit photos of your adorable Chi.

All of recommended care products are on the Supplies page of PetChiDog.com which is updated as new products emerge.

Loves, Hugs & Chihuahua Kisses,

The PetChiDog Team

Printed in Great Britain
by Amazon